Lecture Notes in Artificial Intelligence   3487

Edited by J. G. Carbonell and J. Siekmann

Subseries of Lecture Notes in Computer Science

João Leite   Paolo Torroni (Eds.)

Computational Logic in Multi-Agent Systems

5th International Workshop, CLIMA V
Lisbon, Portugal, September 29-30, 2004
Revised Selected and Invited Papers

 Springer

Series Editors

Jaime G. Carbonell, Carnegie Mellon University, Pittsburgh, PA, USA
Jörg Siekmann, University of Saarland, Saarbrücken, Germany

Volume Editors

João Leite
Universidade Nova de Lisboa, Departamento de Informática
Faculdade de Ciências e Tecnologia
Quinta da Torre, 2829-516 Caparica, Portugal
E-mail: jleite@di.fct.unl.pt

Paolo Torroni
Università di Bologna
Dipartimento di Elettronica, Informatica e Sistemistica
Viale Risorgimento 2, 40136 Bologna, Italy
E-mail: paolo.torroni@unibo.it

Library of Congress Control Number: 2005929660

CR Subject Classification (1998): I.2.11, I.2, C.2.4, F.4

ISSN   0302-9743
ISBN-10   3-540-28060-X Springer Berlin Heidelberg New York
ISBN-13   978-3-540-28060-6 Springer Berlin Heidelberg New York

This work is subject to copyright. All rights are reserved, whether the whole or part of the material is
concerned, specifically the rights of translation, reprinting, re-use of illustrations, recitation, broadcasting,
reproduction on microfilms or in any other way, and storage in data banks. Duplication of this publication
or parts thereof is permitted only under the provisions of the German Copyright Law of September 9, 1965,
in its current version, and permission for use must always be obtained from Springer. Violations are liable
to prosecution under the German Copyright Law.

Springer is a part of Springer Science+Business Media

springeronline.com

© Springer-Verlag Berlin Heidelberg 2005
Printed in Germany

Typesetting: Camera-ready by author, data conversion by Scientific Publishing Services, Chennai, India
Printed on acid-free paper   SPIN: 11533092   06/3142   5 4 3 2 1 0

Preface

The notion of agency has recently increased its influence in the research and development of computational logic based systems, while at the same time significantly gaining from decades of research in computational logic. Computational logic provides a well-defined, general, and rigorous framework for studying syntax, semantics and procedures, for implementations, environments, tools, and standards, facilitating the ever important link between specification and verification of computational systems.

The purpose of the Computational Logic in Multi-agent Systems (CLIMA) international workshop series is to discuss techniques, based on computational logic, for representing, programming, and reasoning about multi-agent systems in a formal way. Former CLIMA editions were conducted in conjunction with other major computational logic and AI events such as CL in July 2000, ICLP in December 2001, FLoC in August 2002, and LPNMR and AI-Math in January 2004.

The fifth edition of CLIMA was held Lisbon, Portugal, in September 29–30, 2004. We, as organizers, and in agreement with the CLIMA Steering Committee, opted for co-location with the 9th European Conference on Logics in Artificial Intelligence (JELIA 2004), wishing to promote the CLIMA research topics in the broader community of logics in AI, a community whose growing interest in multi-agent issues has been demonstrated by the large number of agent-related papers submitted to recent editions of JELIA.

The workshop received 35 submissions – a sensible increase from the previous edition. The submitted papers showed that the logical foundations of multi-agent systems are felt by a large community to be a very important research topic, upon which classical AI and agent-related issues are to be addressed.

In line with the high standards of previous CLIMA editions, the review process was very selective, the final acceptance rate being below 50%. A Program Committee of 24 top-level researchers from 11 countries and 12 additional reviewers selected 16 papers for presentation, authored by 46 researchers worldwide. The workshop program featured an invited lecture by Alessio Lomuscio (University College London) on Specification and Verification of Multiagent Systems, as well as a panel discussion organized by Marina de Vos (University of Bath) on Logic-Based Multi-agent Systems and Industry. Around 50 delegates attended the two-day event.

This book contains a selection, based on a second round of reviewing, of extended CLIMA V papers, and it starts with an invited contribution by Bożena Woźna and Alessio Lomuscio. The papers are divided into four parts: (i) foundations, (ii) architectures, (iii) interaction, and (iv) planning and applications. There follows a brief overview of the book.

Foundations. In the first paper of this book, *A Logic for Knowledge, Correctness, and Real Time*, Woźna and Lomuscio present and exemplify TCTLKD, a logic for knowledge, correctness and real time interpreted on real-time deontic interpreted systems, and extension to continuous time of deontic interpreted systems.

In *Dynamic Logic for Plan Revision in Intelligent Agents*, van Riemsdijk et al. present, with a sound and complete axiomatization, a dynamic logic for a propositional version of the agent programming language 3APL, tailored to handle the revision of plans.

Grossi et al. present in their paper *Contextual Taxonomies* a characterization of the notion of a taxonomy with respect to specific contexts, addressing problems stemming from the domain of normative system specifications for modelling multi-agent systems.

From Logic Programs Updates to Action Description Updates is where Alferes et al. propose a macro language for the language EVOLP and provide translations from some fragments of known action description languages into the newly defined one.

In *Dynamic Logic Programming: Various Semantics Are Equal on Acyclic Programs*, Homola investigates multi-dimensional dynamic logic programming, establishing some classes of programs for which several known semantics coincide.

Architectures. *Declarative Agent Control*, by Kakas et al., extends the architecture of agents based upon fixed, one-size-fits-all cycles of operation by providing a framework for the declarative specification of agent control in terms of *cycle theories*, which define possible alternative behaviors of agents.

In *Metareasoning for Multi-agent Epistemic Logics*, Arkoudas and Bringsjord present an encoding of a sequent calculus for a multi-agent epistemic logic in Athena, an interactive theorem proving system for many-sorted first-order logic, to enable its use as a metalanguage in order to reason about the multi-agent logic as an object language.

In *Graded BDI Models for Agent Architectures*, Casali et al. propose a general model for a graded BDI agent, specifying an architecture able to deal with the environment uncertainty and with graded mental attitudes.

Interaction. Dastani et al., in their article *Inferring Trust*, extend Liau's logic of Belief, Inform and Trust in two directions: with questions, and with a formalization of topics used to infer trust in a proposition from trust in another proposition.

In *Coordination Between Logical Agents*, Sakama and Inoue investigate on the use of answer set programming for belief representation, namely by addressing the problem of finding logic programs that combine the knowledge from different agents, while preserving some properties, useful to achieve agent coordination.

In *A Computational Model for Conversation Policies for Agent Communication*, Bentahar et al. propose a formal specification of a flexible persuasion protocol between autonomous agents, using an approach based on social commitments and arguments, defined as a combination of a set of conversation policies.

The last paper of this section is *Verifying Protocol Conformance for Logic-Based Communicating Agents*, by Baldoni et al., which describes a method for automatically verifying a form of "structural" conformance by translating AUML sequence diagrams into regular grammars and, then, interpreting the problem of conformance as a problem of language inclusion.

Planning and Applications. In the preliminary report *An Application of Global Abduction to an Information Agent Which Modifies a Plan Upon Failure*, Satoh uses a form of abductive logic programming called global abduction to implement an information agent that deals with the problem of plan modification upon action failure.

In *Planning Partially for Situated Agents*, Mancarella et al. use an abductive variant of the event calculus to specify planning problems as the base of their proposal for a framework to design situated agents capable of computing partial plans.

Han and Barber, in *Desire-Space Analysis and Action Selection for Multiple Dynamic Goals*, use macro actions to transform the state space for the agent's decision problem into the desire space of the agent. Reasoning in the latter allows us to approximately weigh the costs and benefits of each of the agent's goals at an abstract level.

Hirsch et al. conclude this book with the article *Organising Software in Active Environments*, in which they show how logic-based multi-agent systems are appropriate to model active environments. They do so by illustrating how the structuring of the "agent space" can represent both the physical and virtual structures of an application.

We would like to conclude with a glance at the future of this workshop series. The sixth CLIMA edition is being organized by Francesca Toni and Paolo Torroni, and will take place at the City University of London, UK, in June 27–29, 2005, in conjunction with the EU-funded SOCS Project Dissemination Workshop. CLIMA VI will feature a tutorial program and a competition, besides the usual technical content based on the presentation of papers.

We can not miss this opportunity to thank the authors and delegates, who made of CLIMA a very interesting and fruitful event; our generous Program Committee members who did not skimp on time to help us put together a very rich volume after two rounds of reviewing, discussion, and selection; and our sponsoring institutions, Universidade Nova de Lisboa, Fundação para a Ciência e Tecnologia, FBA, and AgentLink III.

April 2005   João Leite
                                                                                    Paolo Torroni

Organization

Workshop Chairs

João Leite, New University of Lisbon, Portugal
Paolo Torroni, University of Bologna, Italy

Program Committee

José Alferes, New University of Lisbon, Portugal
Gerd Brewka, University of Leipzig, Germany
Jürgen Dix, Technical University of Clausthal, Germany
Klaus Fisher, DFKI, Germany
Michael Fisher, The University of Liverpool, UK
James Harland, Royal Melbourne Institute of Technology, Australia
Katsumi Inoue, National Institute of Informatics, Japan
Sverker Janson, Swedish Institute of Computer Science, Sweden
João Leite, New University of Lisbon, Portugal
Yves Lespérance, York University, Canada
John-Jules Ch. Meyer, Utrecht University, The Netherlands
Leora Morgenstern, IBM, USA
Wojciech Penczek, Polish Academy of Sciences, Poland
Jeremy Pitt, Imperial College London, UK
Enrico Pontelli, New Mexico State University, USA
Fariba Sadri, Imperial College London, UK
Ken Satoh, National Institute of Informatics, Japan
Renate Schmidt, The University of Manchester, UK
Tran Cao Son, New Mexico State University, USA
Francesca Toni, University of Pisa, Italy
Wiebe van der Hoek, The University of Liverpool, UK
Paolo Torroni, University of Bologna, Italy
Makoto Yokoo, Kyushu University, Japan
Cees Witteveen, Delft University of Technology, The Netherlands

Additional Reviewers

Federico Banti
Thomas Eiter

Ulle Endriss
Ullrich Hustadt

Magdalena Kacprzak
Olle Olsson

Inna Pivkina   Kostas Stathis   Gregory Wheeler
Chiaki Sakama   Maciej Szreter   Yingqiang Zhang

Secretariat

Filipa Mira Reis   Sílvia Marina Costa

Local Organization

António Albuquerque   Jamshid Ashtari   Miguel Morais
Duarte Alvim   Joana Lopes   Sérgio Lopes
Eduardo Barros   Miguel Maurício

Steering Committee

Jürgen Dix, Technical University of Clausthal, Germany
João Leite, New University of Lisbon, Portugal
Fariba Sadri, Imperial College London, UK
Ken Satoh, National Institute of Informatics, Japan
Francesca Toni, University of Pisa, Italy
Paolo Torroni, University of Bologna, Italy

Sponsoring Institutions

Table of Contents

Foundations

Architectures

Interaction

Planning and Applications

A Logic for Knowledge, Correctness, and Real Time[*]

Bożena Woźna and Alessio Lomuscio

Department of Computer Science,
University College London,
Gower Street, London WC1E 6BT,
United Kingdom
{B.Wozna, A.Lomuscio}@cs.ucl.ac.uk

Abstract. We present TCTLKD, a logic for knowledge, correctness and real time. TCTLKD is interpreted on real time deontic interpreted systems, and extension to continuous time of deontic interpreted systems. We exemplify the use of TCTLKD by discussing a variant of the "railroad crossing system".

1 Introduction

Logic has a long tradition in the area of formal theories for multi-agent systems (MAS). Its role is to provide a precise and unambiguous specification language to describe, reason about, and predict the behaviour of a system.

While in the early 80's existing logical formalisms from other areas such as philosophical logic, concurrency theory, etc., were imported with little of no modification to the area of MAS, from the late 80's onwards specific formalisms have been designed, studied, and tailored to the needs of MAS. Of particular note is the case of epistemic logic, or the logic of knowledge.

Focus on epistemic logics in MAS began with the use of the modal logic system $S5$ developed independently by Hintikka [1] and Aumann [2] in formal logic and economics respectively. This starting point formed the core basis of a number of studies that appeared in the past 20 years, including formalisations of group knowledge [3, 4, 5], combinations of epistemic logic with time [6, 7, 8], auto-epistemic logics [9, 10], epistemic updates [11, 12], broadcast systems and hypercubes [13, 14], etc. Epistemic logic is no longer a remarkable special case of a normal modal system, but has now become an area of study on its own with regular thematic workshops and conferences.

In particular, combinations of epistemic and temporal logics allow us to reason about the temporal evolution of epistemic states, knowledge of a changing world, etc. Traditionally, this is achieved by combining a temporal logic for discrete linear time [15, 16, 17] with the logic $S5$ for knowledge [18]. Various classes

---

[*] The authors acknowledge support from the EPSRC (grant GR/S49353), and the Nuffield Foundation (grant NAL/690/G).

J. Leite and P. Torroni (Eds.): CLIMA V, LNAI 3487, pp. 1–15, 2005.
© Springer-Verlag Berlin Heidelberg 2005

of MAS (synchronous, asynchronous, perfect recall, no learning, etc.) can be identified in this framework, and axiomatisations have been provided [19, 20]. More recently, combinations of branching time logic CTL [21, 22, 23] with the epistemic logic $S5$ have been studied, and axiomatisation provided [8].

All efforts above have focused on a discrete model of time, either in its linear or branching versions. While this is useful and adequate in most applications, certain classes of scenarios (notably robotics and networking) require a model of time as a continuous flows of events.

In the area of timed-systems the modal logic TCTL has been suggested as an adequate formalism to model real time. In this paper we propose a logic (which we call TCTLKD) combining the temporal aspects of TCTL with the notions defined by the epistemic logic $S5$, as well as the correctness notion defined in [24]. This combination allows us to reason about the real time evolution of epistemic states, the correct functioning of multi-agent systems with respect to real time, and any combination of these.

Traditionally, the semantics of temporal epistemic logic is defined on variants of interpreted systems to provide an interpretation to the epistemic modalities. These use the notion of *protocol* to provide a basis for the action selection mechanism of the agents. Since we are working on real time, here we shall use the finer grained semantics of timed automata to model the agents' evolution. We then synchronise networks of timed automata to provide a general model of a MAS.

The rest of the paper is organised as follows. In Section 2 we define the concept of interpreted systems on real time by taking the parallel composition of timed automata. In Section 3 we define the logic TCTLKD as an extension to real time of the logic for knowledge and correctness as defined in [24, 25]. In Section 4 we provide a case study analysis to demonstrate its use in applications. We conclude in Section 5 by discussing related and future work on this subject.

2   Interpreted Systems over Real Time

Interpreted systems are traditionally defined as a set of infinite runs on global states [18]. In this model each run is a discrete sentence representing events. At each global state, each agent selects an action according to a (possibly non-deterministic) protocol. In this section we extend (discrete) interpreted systems to real time interpreted systems in two aspects. First, we specify the agents' behaviour by a finer grained semantics: timed automata. Second, by means of parallel composition of timed automata, we define a class of interpreted systems operating on real time.

We begin by recalling the concept of timed automata, as introduced in [26]. Timed automata are extensions of finite state automata with constraints on timing behaviour. The underlying finite state automata are augmented with a set of real time variables.

2.1   Timed Automata

Let $\mathbb{R} = [0, \infty)$ be a set of non-negative real numbers, $\mathbb{R}_+ = (0, \infty)$ be a set of positive real numbers, $\mathbb{N} = \{0, 1, 2, \ldots\}$ a set of natural numbers, and $\mathcal{X}$ a finite set of real variables, called *clocks*. The set of *clock constraints* over $\mathcal{X}$ is defined by the following grammar:

$$\mathfrak{cc} := true \mid x \sim c \mid \mathfrak{cc} \wedge \mathfrak{cc},$$

where $x \in \mathcal{X}, c \in \mathbb{N}$, and $\sim \in \{\leq, <, =, >, \geq\}$. The set of all the clock constraints over $\mathcal{X}$ is denoted by $\mathcal{C}(\mathcal{X})$. A *clock valuation* on $\mathcal{X}$ is a tuple $v \in \mathbb{R}^{|\mathcal{X}|}$. The value of the clock x in v is denoted by $v(x)$. For a valuation v and $\delta \in \mathbb{R}$, $v + \delta$ denotes the valuation v' such that for all $x \in \mathcal{X}$, $v'(x) = v(x) + \delta$. Moreover, let $\mathcal{X}^*$ be the set $\mathcal{X} \cup \{x_0\}$, where x_0 is a clock whose value is always 0, that is, its value does not increase with time as the values of the other clocks. Then, an *assignment* $\mathfrak{as}$ is a function from $\mathcal{X}$ to $\mathcal{X}^*$, and the set of all the assignments over $\mathcal{X}$ is denoted by $\mathfrak{A}(\mathcal{X})$. By $v[\mathfrak{as}]$ we denote the valuation v' such that for all $x \in \mathcal{X}$, if $\mathfrak{as}(x) \in \mathcal{X}$, then $v'(x) = v(\mathfrak{as}(x))$, otherwise $v'(x) = 0$.

Let $v \in \mathbb{R}^{|\mathcal{X}|}$, the satisfaction relation $\models$ for a clock constraint $\mathfrak{cc} \in \mathcal{C}(\mathcal{X})$ is defined inductively as follows:

$$\begin{aligned}
&v \models true, \\
&v \models (x \sim c) \quad \text{iff} \quad v(x) \sim c, \\
&v \models (\mathfrak{cc} \wedge \mathfrak{cc}') \quad \text{iff} \quad v \models \mathfrak{cc} \text{ and } v \models \mathfrak{cc}'.
\end{aligned}$$

For a constraint $\mathfrak{cc} \in \mathcal{C}(\mathcal{X})$, by $[\![\mathfrak{cc}]\!]$ we denote the set of all the clock valuations satisfying $\mathfrak{cc}$, i.e., $[\![\mathfrak{cc}]\!] = \{v \in \mathbb{R}^{|\mathcal{X}|} \mid v \models \mathfrak{cc}\}$.

Definition 1 (Timed Automaton). *A timed automaton is a tuple* $\mathcal{TA} = (\mathfrak{Z}, L, l^0, \mathcal{X}, E, \mathfrak{I})$, *where*

- $\mathfrak{Z}$ *is a finite set of actions,*
- L *is a finite set of locations,*
- $l^0 \in L$ *is an initial location,*
- $\mathcal{X}$ *is a finite set of clocks,*
- $E \subseteq L \times \mathfrak{Z} \times \mathcal{C}(\mathcal{X}) \times \mathfrak{A}(\mathcal{X}) \times L$ *is a transition relation,*
- $\mathfrak{I} : L \to \mathcal{C}(\mathcal{X})$ *is a function, called a* location invariant, *which assigns to each location* $l \in L$ *a clock constraint defining the conditions under which* $\mathcal{TA}$ *can stay in* l.

Each element e *of* E *is denoted by* $l \overset{a, \mathfrak{cc}, \mathfrak{as}}{\longrightarrow} l'$, *where* l *is a source location,* l' *is a target location,* a *is an action,* $\mathfrak{cc}$ *is the enabling condition for* e, *and* $\mathfrak{as}$ *is the assignment for* e.

Note that we deal with "diagonal-free" automata. This is because ultimately we would like to verify MAS specified in this formalism, and the model checking methods for real time systems (based on the Difference Bound Matrices [27], variants of Boolean Decision Diagrams [28, 29], or SAT methods [30, 31, 32]) are problematic when the components of the systems are modelled by "diagonal automata".

In order to reason about systems represented by timed automata, for a set of propositional variables $\mathcal{PV}$, we define a valuation function $V_{\mathcal{TA}} : L \to 2^{\mathcal{PV}}$, which assigns propositions to the locations.

Definition 2 (Dense State Space). *The* dense state space *of a timed automaton* $\mathcal{TA} = (\mathfrak{Z}, L, l^0, \mathcal{X}, E, \mathfrak{I})$ *is a structure* $\mathrm{D}(\mathcal{TA}) = (Q, q^0, \to)$, *where*

- $Q = L \times \mathbb{R}^{|\mathcal{X}|}$ *is the set of all the instantaneous states,*
- $q^0 = (l^0, v^0)$ *with* $v^0(x) = 0$ *for all* $x \in \mathcal{X}$, *is the initial state,*
- $\to \subseteq Q \times (\mathfrak{Z} \cup \mathbb{R}) \times Q$ *is the transition relation, defined by action- and time-successors as follows:*
  - *for* $a \in \mathfrak{Z}$, $(l, v) \overset{a}{\to} (l', v')$ *iff* $(\exists \mathfrak{cc} \in \mathcal{C}(\mathcal{X}))(\exists \mathfrak{as} \in \mathfrak{A}(\mathcal{X}))$ *such that* $l \overset{a, \mathfrak{cc}, \mathfrak{as}}{\longrightarrow} l' \in E$, $v \in [\![\mathfrak{cc}]\!], v' = v[\mathfrak{as}]$ *and* $v' \in [\![\mathfrak{I}(l')]\!]$ *(action successor),*
  - *for* $\delta \in \mathbb{R}$, $(l, v) \overset{\delta}{\to} (l, v + \delta)$ *iff* $v + \delta \in [\![\mathfrak{I}(l)]\!]$ *(time successor).*

For $(l, v) \in Q$, let $(l, v) + \delta$ denote $(l, v + \delta)$. A *q-run* ρ of a $\mathcal{TA}$ is a sequence of instantaneous states: $q_0 \overset{\delta_0}{\to} q_0 + \delta_0 \overset{a_0}{\to} q_1 \overset{\delta_1}{\to} q_1 + \delta_1 \overset{a_1}{\to} q_2 \overset{\delta_2}{\to} \ldots$, where $q_0 = q \in Q$, $a_i \in \mathfrak{Z}$, and $\delta_i \in \mathbb{R}_+$ for each $i \in \mathbb{N}$. A run ρ is said to be *progressive* iff $\Sigma_{i \in \mathbb{N}} \delta_i$ is unbounded. A $\mathcal{TA}$ is *progressive* if all its runs are progressive. For simplicity of presentation, we consider only progressive timed automata. Note that progressiveness can be checked as in [33].

2.2   Parallel Composition of Timed Automata

In general, we will model a multi-agent system by taking several timed automata running in parallel and communicating with each other. These concurrent timed automata can be composed into a global timed automaton as follows: the transitions of the timed automata that do not correspond to a shared action are interleaved, whereas the transitions labelled with a shared action are synchronised.

There are many different definitions of parallel composition. We use a *multi-way synchronisation*, requiring that each component that contains a communication transition (labelled by a shared action) has to perform this action. Let $\mathcal{TA}_i = (\mathfrak{Z}_i, L_i, l_i^0, E_i, \mathcal{X}_i, \mathfrak{I}_i)$ be a timed automaton, for $i = 1, \ldots, m$. To define a parallel composition of m timed automata, we assume that $L_i \cap L_j = \emptyset$ for all $i, j \in \{1, \ldots, m\}$, and $i \neq j$. Moreover, by $\mathfrak{Z}(a) = \{1 \leq i \leq m \mid a \in \mathfrak{Z}_i\}$ we denote a set of numbers of the timed automata containing an action a.

Definition 3 (Parallel Composition). The parallel composition *of* m *timed automata* $\mathcal{TA}_i$ *is a timed automaton* $\mathcal{TA} = (\mathfrak{Z}, L, l^0, E, \mathrm{X}, \mathfrak{I})$, *where* $\mathfrak{Z} = \bigcup_{i=1}^m \mathfrak{Z}_i$, $L = \prod_{i=1}^m L_i$, $l^0 = (l_1^0, \ldots, l_m^0)$, $\mathcal{X} = \bigcup_{i=1}^m \mathcal{X}_i$, $\mathfrak{I}(l_1, \ldots, l_m) = \bigwedge_{i=1}^m \mathfrak{I}_i(l_i)$, *and a transition* $((l_1, \ldots, l_m), a, \mathfrak{cc}, \mathfrak{as}, (l_1', \ldots, l_m')) \in E$ *iff* $(\forall i \in \mathfrak{Z}(a)) (l_i, a, \mathfrak{cc}_i, \mathfrak{as}_i, l_i') \in E_i$, $\mathfrak{cc} = \bigwedge_{i \in \mathfrak{Z}(a)} \mathfrak{cc}_i$, $\mathfrak{as} = \bigcup_{i \in \mathfrak{Z}(a)} \mathfrak{as}_i$, *and* $(\forall j \in \{1, \ldots, m\} \setminus \mathfrak{Z}(a)) l_j' = l_j$.

Note that in the above any automaton is allowed to set a value of any clock, including the ones associated with other agents.

Let PV_i be a set of propositional variables containing the symbol **true**, $V_{\mathcal{TA}_i} : L_i \to 2^{PV_i}$ be a valuation function for the ith automaton, where $i \in \{1, \ldots, m\}$, and $\mathcal{PV} = \bigcup_{i=1}^{m} \mathcal{PV}_i$. Then, the valuation function $V_{\mathcal{TA}} : L \to 2^{\mathcal{PV}}$ for the parallel composition of m timed automata, is defined as follows $V_{\mathcal{TA}}((l_1, \ldots, l_m)) = \bigcup_{i=1}^{m} V_{\mathcal{TA}_i}(l_i)$.

2.3   Real Time Deontic Interpreted System

In line with much of the multi-agent systems literature, we use interpreted systems as a semantics for a temporal epistemic language. For this, we need to adapt them to work on real time: this is why we take timed automata as the underlying modelling concept (as opposed to the standard protocols of interpreted systems). To define *real time deontic interpreted systems*, we first partition the set of clock valuations as in [34].

Let $\mathcal{TA}$ be a timed automaton, $\mathcal{C}(\mathcal{TA}) \subseteq \mathcal{C}(\mathcal{X})$ be a non-empty set containing all the clock constrains occurring in any enabling condition used in the transition relation E or in a state invariant of $\mathcal{TA}$. Moreover, let c_{max} be the largest constant appearing in $\mathcal{C}(\mathcal{TA})$. For $\sigma \in \mathbb{R}$, $frac(\sigma)$ denotes the fractional part of σ, and $\lfloor \sigma \rfloor$ denotes its integral part.

Definition 4 (Equivalence of Clock Valuations). *For two clock valuations v and v' in $\mathbb{R}^{|\mathcal{X}|}$, we say that $v \simeq v'$ iff for all $x, y \in \mathcal{X}$ the following conditions are met:*

1. *$v(x) > c_{max}$ iff $v'(x) > c_{max}$*
2. *if $v(x) \leq c_{max}$ and $v(y) \leq c_{max}$ then*
   a.) $\lfloor v(x) \rfloor = \lfloor v'(x) \rfloor$,
   b.) $frac(v(x)) = 0$ iff $frac(v'(x)) = 0$, and
   c.) $frac(v(x)) \leq frac(v(y))$ iff $frac(v'(x)) \leq frac(v'(y))$.

The equivalence classes of the relation $\simeq$ are called *zones*, and denoted by Z, Z' and so on.

Now we are ready to define a *Real Time Deontic Interpreted System* that will be semantics for the logic presented in the next section.

Let $\mathcal{AG}$ be a set of m agents, where each agent is modelled by a timed automaton $\mathcal{TA}_i = (\mathfrak{Z}_i, L_i, l_i^0, E_i, \mathcal{X}_i, \mathfrak{I}_i)$, for $i \in \{1, \ldots, m\}$. Moreover, assume, in line with [24, 25], that for every agent, its set L_i of local locations is partitioned into "allowed" locations, denoted by $\mathcal{G}_i$, and "disallowed" locations, denoted by $\mathcal{R}_i$ and defined by $\mathcal{R}_i = L_i \setminus \mathcal{G}_i$. We shall call these locations *green* and *red* respectively. Further, assume that the parallel composition $\mathcal{TA} = (\mathfrak{Z}, L, l^0, E, \mathrm{X}, \mathfrak{I})$ of all the agents is given[1], and that $l_i : Q \to L_i$ is a function that returns the location of agent i from a global state. Then, a *real time deontic interpreted system* is defined as follows.

Definition 5 (Real Time Deontic Interpreted System). *A real time deontic interpreted system is a tuple $M_c = (Q, q^0, \to, \sim_1^K, \ldots, \sim_m^K, R_1^O, \ldots, R_m^O, \mathcal{V}_c)$, where:*

---

[1] Note that the set L, which defines all the possible *global locations*, is defined as the Cartesian product $L_1 \times \ldots \times L_m$, such that $L_1 \supseteq \mathcal{G}_1, \ldots, L_m \supseteq \mathcal{G}_m$.

– Q, q^0, and $\rightarrow$ are defined as in Definition 2,
– $\sim_i^K \subseteq Q \times Q$ is a relation defined by: $(l, v) \sim_i^K (l', v')$ iff $l_i((l, v)) = l_i((l', v'))$ and $v \simeq v'$, for each agent i. Obviously $\sim_i^K$ is an equivalence relation.
– $R_i^O \subseteq Q \times Q$ is a relation defined by: $(l, v) R_i^O (l', v')$ iff $l_i((l', v')) \in \mathcal{G}_i$, for each agent i.
– $V_c : Q \rightarrow 2^{\mathcal{PV}}$ is a valuation function that extends V_{TA} as follows $V_c((l, v)) = V_{TA}(l)$, i.e., V_c assigns the same propositions to the states with the same locations.

3   The Logic TCTLKD

In this section, we formally present the syntax and semantics of a *real time computation tree logic for knowledge and correctness* (TCTLKD), which extends the standard TCTL [34], the logic for real time, by means of modal operators for knowledge and correctness.

The language generalises classical propositional logic, and thus it contains the standard propositional connectives $\neg$ (not) and $\vee$ (or); the remaining connectives ($\wedge$ (and), $\rightarrow$ (implies), $\leftrightarrow$ (if, and only if) are assumed to be introduced as abbreviations in the usual way. With respect to real time temporal connectives, we take as primitives U_I (for "until within interval I"), and G_I (for "always within interval I"); the remaining operators, F_I (for "eventually within interval I") and R_I (for "release within interval I"), are assumed to be introduced as abbreviations in the usual way. The language also contains two path quantifiers: A (for "for all the runs") and E (for "there exists a run"). Further, we assume a set $\mathcal{AG} = \{1, \ldots, m\}$ of agents, and we use the indexed modalities K_i, $\mathcal{O}_i$, and $\hat{K}_i^j$ to represent the knowledge of agent i, the correct functioning circumstances of agent i, and the knowledge of agent i under assumption of correct functioning of agent j, respectively. Furthermore, we use the indexed modalities D_Γ, C_Γ to represent distributed and common knowledge in a group of agents $\Gamma \subseteq \mathcal{AG}$, and we use the operator E_Γ to represent the concept "everybody in Γ knows".

3.1   Syntax of TCTLKD

We assume a set $\mathcal{PV}$ of propositional variables, and a finite set $\mathcal{AG}$ of m agents. Furthermore, let I be an interval in $\mathbb{R}$ with integer bounds of the form $[n, n']$, $[n, n')$, $(n, n']$, (n, n'), (n, ∞), and $[n, \infty)$, for $n, n' \in \mathbb{N}$. The set of TCTLKD formulas is defined inductively as follows:

- every member p of $\mathcal{PV}$ is a formula,
- if α and β are formulas, then so are $\neg\alpha$, $\alpha \vee \beta$, $EG_I\alpha$, and $E(\alpha U_I \beta)$,
- if α is formula, then so are $K_i\alpha$, $\hat{K}_i^j\alpha$, and $\mathcal{O}_i\alpha$, for $i, j \in \mathcal{AG}$,
- if α is formula, then so are $D_\Gamma\alpha$, $C_\Gamma\alpha$, and $E_\Gamma\alpha$, for $\Gamma \subseteq \mathcal{AG}$.

The other basic temporal, epistemic, and correctness modalities are defined as follows:

- $\mathrm{EF}_I\varphi \overset{def}{=} \mathrm{E}(\mathbf{true}\mathrm{U}_I\varphi)$, $\mathrm{AF}_I\varphi \overset{def}{=} \neg\mathrm{EG}_I(\neg\varphi)$, $\mathrm{AG}_I\varphi \overset{def}{=} \neg\mathrm{EF}_I(\neg\varphi)$,
- $\mathrm{A}(\alpha\mathrm{U}_I\beta) \overset{def}{=} \neg\mathrm{E}(\neg\beta\mathrm{U}_I(\neg\beta \wedge \neg\alpha)) \wedge \neg\mathrm{EG}_I(\neg\beta)$,
- $\mathrm{A}(\alpha\mathrm{R}_I\beta) \overset{def}{=} \neg\mathrm{E}(\neg\alpha\mathrm{U}_I\neg\beta)$, $\mathrm{E}(\alpha\mathrm{R}_I\beta) \overset{def}{=} \neg\mathrm{A}(\neg\alpha\mathrm{U}_I\neg\beta)$,
- $\overline{\mathrm{K}}_i\alpha \overset{def}{=} \neg\mathrm{K}_i\neg\alpha$, $\overline{\mathcal{O}}_i\alpha \overset{def}{=} \neg\mathcal{O}_i\neg\alpha$, $\overline{\hat{\mathrm{K}}}_i^j\alpha \overset{def}{=} \neg\hat{\mathrm{K}}_i^j\neg\alpha$,
- $\overline{\mathrm{D}}_\Gamma\alpha \overset{def}{=} \neg\mathrm{D}_\Gamma\neg\alpha$, $\overline{\mathrm{C}}_\Gamma\alpha \overset{def}{=} \neg\mathrm{C}_\Gamma\neg\alpha$, $\overline{\mathrm{E}}_\Gamma\alpha \overset{def}{=} \neg\mathrm{E}_\Gamma\neg\alpha$.

3.2   Semantics of TCTLKD

Let $\mathcal{AG}$ be a set of m agents, where each agent is modelled by a timed automaton $\mathcal{TA}_i = (\mathfrak{Z}_i, L_i, l_i^0, E_i, \mathcal{X}_i, \mathfrak{I}_i)$, for $i = \{1, \ldots, m\}$, $\mathcal{TA} = (\mathfrak{Z}, L, l^0, E, \mathrm{X}, \mathfrak{I})$ be their parallel composition, and $M_c = (Q, q^0, \rightarrow, \sim_1^K, \ldots, \sim_m^K, R_1^O, \ldots, R_m^O, \mathcal{V}_c)$ be a *real time deontic interpreted system*. Moreover, let $\rho = q_0 \overset{\delta_0}{\rightarrow} q_0 + \delta_0 \overset{a_0}{\rightarrow} q_1 \overset{\delta_1}{\rightarrow} q_1 + \delta_1 \overset{a_1}{\rightarrow} q_2 \overset{\delta_2}{\rightarrow} \ldots$ be a run of $\mathcal{TA}$ such that $\delta_i \in \mathrm{I\!R}_+$ for $i \in \mathrm{I\!N}$, and let $f_{\mathcal{TA}}(q)$ denote the set of all such q-runs of $\mathcal{TA}$. In order to give a semantics to TCTLKD, we introduce the notation of a *dense path* π_ρ corresponding to run ρ. A dense path π_ρ corresponding to ρ is a mapping from $\mathrm{I\!R}$ to a set of states[2] such that $\pi_\rho(r) = s_i + \delta$ for $r = \Sigma_{j=0}^i \delta_j + \delta$ with $i \geq 0$ and $0 \leq \delta < \delta_i$. Moreover, as usual, we define the following epistemic relations: $\sim_\Gamma^E = \bigcup_{i \in \Gamma} \sim_i$, $\sim_\Gamma^C = (\sim_\Gamma^E)^+$ (the transitive closure of $\sim_\Gamma^E$), and $\sim_\Gamma^D = \bigcap_{i \in \Gamma} \sim_i$, where $\Gamma \subseteq \mathcal{AG}$.

Definition 6 (Satisfaction of TCTLKD**).** *Let* $M_c, q \models \alpha$ *denote that* α *is true at state s in the model* M_c. M_c *is omitted, if it is implicitly understood. The relation* $\models$ *is defined inductively as follows:*

$$
\begin{array}{lll}
q_0 \models p & \text{iff } p \in \mathcal{V}_c(q_0), \\
q_0 \models \neg\varphi & \text{iff } q_0 \not\models \varphi, \\
q_0 \models \varphi \vee \psi & \text{iff } q_0 \models \varphi \text{ or } q_0 \models \psi, \\
q_0 \models \varphi \wedge \psi & \text{iff } q_0 \models \varphi \text{ and } q_0 \models \psi, \\
q_0 \models \mathrm{E}(\varphi\mathrm{U}_I\psi) & \text{iff } (\exists\, \rho \in f_{\mathcal{TA}}(q_0))(\exists\, r \in I)\big[\pi_\rho(r) \models \psi \text{ and } (\forall r' < r)\, \pi_\rho(r') \models \varphi\big], \\
q_0 \models \mathrm{EG}_I\varphi) & \text{iff } (\exists\, \rho \in f_{\mathcal{TA}}(q_0))(\forall r \in I)\, \pi_\rho(r) \models \varphi, \\
q_0 \models \mathrm{K}_i\alpha & \text{iff } (\forall q' \in Q)((q_0 \sim_i^K q') \text{ implies } q' \models \alpha), \\
q_0 \models \mathcal{O}_i\alpha & \text{iff } (\forall q' \in Q)(q_0 R_i^O q') \text{ implies } q' \models \alpha), \\
q_0 \models \hat{\mathrm{K}}_i^j\alpha & \text{iff } (\forall q' \in Q)((q_0 \sim_i^K q' \text{ and } q_0 R_j^O q') \text{ implies } q' \models \alpha), \\
q_0 \models \mathrm{D}_\Gamma\alpha & \text{iff } (\forall q' \in Q)((q_0 \sim_\Gamma^D q') \text{ implies } q' \models \alpha), \\
q_0 \models \mathrm{E}_\Gamma\alpha & \text{iff } (\forall q' \in Q)((q_0 \sim_\Gamma^E q') \text{ implies } q' \models \alpha), \\
q_0 \models \mathrm{C}_\Gamma\alpha & \text{iff } (\forall q' \in Q)((q_0 \sim_\Gamma^C q') \text{ implies } q' \models \alpha).
\end{array}
$$

Intuitively, the formula $\mathrm{E}(\alpha\mathrm{U}_I\beta)$ holds at a state q_0 in a real time deontic interpreted system M_c if there exists a run starting at q_0 such that β holds in some state in time interval I, and until then α always holds. The formula $\mathrm{EG}_I\alpha$ holds at a state q_0 in a real time deontic interpreted system M_c if there exists a

---

[2] This can be done because of the assumption that $\delta_i > 0$, i.e., $\delta_i \in \mathrm{I\!R}_+$.

run starting at q_0 such that α holds in all the states on the run in time interval I. The formula $K_i\alpha$ holds at state q_0 in a real time deontic interpreted system M_c if α holds at all the states that are indistinguishable for agent i from q_0. The formula $\mathcal{O}_i\alpha$ holds at state q_0 in a real time deontic interpreted system M_c if α holds at all the states where agent i is functioning correctly. The formula $\hat{K}_i^j\alpha$ holds at state q_0 in a real time deontic interpreted system M_c if α holds at all the states that agent i is unable to distinguish from the actual state q_0, and in which agent j is functioning correctly. The formula $E_\Gamma\alpha$ holds at state q_0 in a real time deontic interpreted system M_c if α is true in all the states that the group Γ of agents is unable to distinguish from the actual state q_0. Note that $E_\Gamma\alpha$ can be defined by $\bigwedge_{i\in\Gamma} K_i\alpha$. The formula $C_\Gamma\alpha$ is equivalent to the infinite conjunction of the formulas $E_\Gamma^k\alpha$ for $k \geq 1$. So, $C_\Gamma\alpha$ holds at state q_0 in a real time deontic interpreted system M_c if everyone knows α holds at q_0, everyone knows that everyone knows α holds at q_0, etc. The formula $D_\Gamma\alpha$ holds at state q_0 in a real time deontic interpreted system M_c if the "combined" knowledge of all the agents in Γ implies α. We refer to [34, 18, 24] for more details on the operators above.

A TCTLKD formula φ is *satisfiable* if there exists a real time deontic interpreted system $M_c = (Q, q^0, \to, \sim_1^K, \ldots, \sim_m^K, R_1^O, \ldots, R_m^O, \mathcal{V}_c)$ and a state q of M_c, such that $M_c, q \models \varphi$. A TCTLKD formula φ is *valid in M_c* (denoted $M_c \models \varphi$) if $M_c, q^0 \models \varphi$, i.e., φ is true at the initial state of the model M_c.

Note that the "full" logic of real time (TCTL) is undecidable [34]. Since real time deontic interpreted systems can be shown to be as expressive as the TCTL-structure of a time graph [34], and the fusion [35] between TCTL, $S5$ for knowledge [18], and $KD45^{i-j}$ for the deontic dimension [24] is a proper extension of TCTL, it follows that problem of satisfiability for the TCTLKD logic will be also undecidable. Still, it is easy to observe that given a TCTLKD formula φ and a real time deontic interpreted system M_c, the problem of deciding whether $M_c \models \varphi$ is decidable. This result is our motivation for introducing TCTLKD. We are not interested in using the whole class of real time deontic interpreted systems, but only to study particular examples by means of this logic. We exemplify this in the next section.

4   Applications

One of the motivations for developing the formalism presented in this paper is that we would like to be able to analyse what epistemic and temporal properties hold, when agents follow or violate their specifications while operating on real time.

As an example of this we discuss the *Railroad Crossing System* (RCS) [36], a well-known example in the literature of real-time verification. Here we analyse the scenario not only by means of temporal operators but also by means of epistemic and correctness modalities. The system consists of three agents: Train, Gate, and Controller running in parallel and synchronising through the events: *"approach"*, *"exit"*, *"lower"*, and *"raise"*.

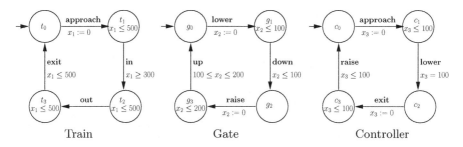

Fig. 1. Agents Train, Gate, and Controller for the correct RCS system

Let us start by considering what we call the *correct RCS*, as modelled by timed automata (Figure 1). The correct RCS operates as follows. When Train approaches the crossing, it sends an *approach* signal to Controller, and enters the crossing between 300 and 500 seconds from this event. When Train leaves the crossing, it sends an *exit* signal to Controller. Controller sends a signal *lower* to Gate exactly 100 seconds after the *approach* signal is received, and sends a *raise* signal within 100 seconds after *exit*. Gate performs the transition *down* within 100 seconds of receiving the request *lower*, and responds to *raise* by moving *up* between 100 and 200 seconds.

Assume the following set of propositional variables: $\mathcal{PV} = \{\mathfrak{p}, \mathfrak{q}, \mathfrak{r}, \mathfrak{s}\}$ with $\mathcal{PV}_{Train} = \{\mathfrak{p}, \mathfrak{q}\}$, $\mathcal{PV}_{Gate} = \{\mathfrak{r}\}$, and $\mathcal{PV}_{Cont} = \{\mathfrak{s}\}$. The proposition $\mathfrak{p}$ represents the fact that an approach signal was sent by Train, $\mathfrak{q}$ that Train is on the cross, $\mathfrak{r}$ that Gate is down, and $\mathfrak{s}$ that Controller sent the signal *lower* to Gate. A real time deontic interpreted system M_{RCS} can be associated with the correct RCS as follows. For the sets $L_1 = \{t_0, t_1, t_2, t_3\}$, $L_2 = \{g_0, g_1, g_2, g_3\}$, and $L_3 = \{c_0, c_1, c_2, c_3\}$ of locations for Train, Gate, and Controller respectively, the set of "green" locations and the dense state space for RCS are defined by $G_1 = L_1, G_2 = L_2, G_3 = L_3$, and $Q = L_1 \times L_2 \times L_3 \times \mathbb{R}^3$, respectively. The valuation functions for Train ($V_{Train} : L_1 \to 2^{\mathcal{PV}_{Train}}$), Gate ($V_{Gate} : L_2 \to 2^{\mathcal{PV}_{Gate}}$), and Controller ($V_{Cont} : L_3 \to 2^{\mathcal{PV}_{Cont}}$) are defined as follows:

- $V_{Train}(t_1) = \{\mathfrak{p}\}$, $V_{Train}(t_2) = \{\mathfrak{q}\}$, and $V_{Train}(t_0) = V_{Train}(t_3) = \emptyset$.
- $V_{Gate}(g_2) = \{\mathfrak{r}\}$, and $V_{Gate}(g_0) = V_{Gate}(g_1) = V_{Gate}(g_3) = \emptyset$.
- $V_{Cont}(c_2) = \{\mathfrak{s}\}$, and $V_{Cont}(c_0) = V_{Cont}(c_1) = V_{Cont}(c_3) = \emptyset$.

The valuation function $V_{RCS} : L_1 \times L_2 \times L_3 \to 2^{\mathcal{PV}}$, for the RCS system, is built as follows: $V_{RCS}(l) = V_{Train}(l_1) \cup V_{Gate}(l_2) \cup V_{Cont}(l_3)$, for all $l = (l_1, l_2, l_3) \in L_1 \times L_2 \times L_3$. Thus, according to the definition of the real time deontic interpreted system, the valuation function $V_{M_{RCS}} : L_1 \times L_2 \times L_3 \times \mathbb{R}^3 \to 2^{\mathcal{PV}}$ of M_{RCS} is defined by $V_{M_{RCS}}(l, v) = V_{RCS}(l)$.

Using the TCTLKD logic, we can specify properties of the correct RCS system that cannot be specified by standard propositional temporal epistemic logic. For example, we consider the following:

$$AG_{[0,\infty]}(\mathfrak{p} \to K_{Controller}(AF_{[300,\infty]}\mathfrak{q})) \tag{1}$$

$$AG_{[0,\infty]}K_{Train}(\mathfrak{p} \to AF_{[0,200]}\mathfrak{r}) \tag{2}$$

$$K_{Controller}(\mathfrak{s} \to AF_{[0,100]}\mathfrak{r}) \tag{3}$$

Formula (1) states that forever in the future if an approach signal is sent by agent Train, then agent Controller knows that in some point after 300 seconds later Train will enter the cross. Formula (2) states that forever in the future agent Train knows that, if it sends an approach signal, then agent Gate will send the signal down within 200 seconds. Formula (3) states that agent Controller knows that if it sends an lower signal, then agent Gate will send the signal down within 100 seconds.

All the formulas above can be shown to hold on M_{RCS} on the initial state. We can also check that the following properties do not hold on M_{RCS}.

$$AG_{[0,\infty]}(\mathfrak{p} \to K_{Controller}(AF_{[0,300]}\mathfrak{q})) \tag{4}$$

$$K_{Train}(AG_{[0,\infty]}EF_{[10,90]}\mathfrak{s}) \tag{5}$$

$$K_{Controller}(\mathfrak{s} \to AF_{[0,50]}\mathfrak{r}) \tag{6}$$

Formula (4) states that forever in the future if an approach signal is sent by agent Train, then agent Controller knows that at some point in the future within 300 seconds Train will enter the crossing. Formula (5) states that agent Train knows that always in the future it is possible that within interval $[10, 90]$ the gate will be down. Formula (6) states that agent Controller knows that if it sends the lower signal, then agent Gate will send the signal down within 50 seconds.

Let us now consider a variant of the RCS system described above, and let us assume that agent Controller is faulty. Let us assume that because of a fault the signal *lower* may not be sent in the specified interval, and the transition to the faulty state $\overline{c_2}$ may be triggered. We are allowing for Controller to recover from the fault once in $\overline{c_2}$ by means of the action *lower* (see Figure 2).

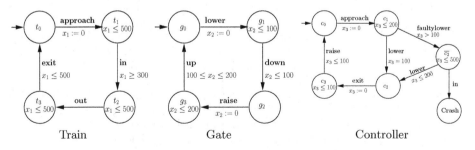

Fig. 2. Agents Train, Gate, and Controller for the faulty RCS system

We examine the scenario by considering the following set of propositional variables: $\mathcal{PV} = \{\mathfrak{p}, \mathfrak{q}, \mathfrak{r}, \mathfrak{s}, \mathfrak{crash}\}$ with $\mathcal{PV}_{Train} = \{\mathfrak{p}, \mathfrak{q}\}$, $\mathcal{PV}_{Gate} = \{\mathfrak{r}\}$, and $\mathcal{PV}_{Cont} = \{\mathfrak{s}, \mathfrak{crash}\}$. The propositions $\mathfrak{p}, \mathfrak{q}, \mathfrak{r}$, and, $\mathfrak{s}$ have the same meaning as in the case of the correct RCS system; the proposition $\mathfrak{crash}$ represents the fact that Train is on the cross and Gate is still open. A real time deontic interpreted system M_{RCS} can be associated with the faulty RCS system as follows[3].

For the sets $L_1 = \{t_0, t_1, t_2, t_3\}$, $L_2 = \{g_0, g_1, g_2, g_3\}$, and $L_3 = \{c_0, c_1, c_2, c_3, \overline{c_2}, crash\}$ of locations for Train, Gate, and Controller, the set of "green" locations are defined by $G_1 = L_1$, $G_2 = L_2$, $G_3 = \{c_0, c_1, c_2, c_3\}$, respectively. The dense state space for RCS is defined by $Q = L_1 \times L_2 \times L_3 \times \mathbb{R}^3$. The valuation functions for Train (V_{Train}), Gate (V_{Gate}), and Controller (V_{Cont}) are defined as follows:

- $V_{Train} : L_1 \rightarrow 2^{\mathcal{PV}_{Train}}$, and $V_{Train}(t_1) = \{\mathfrak{p}\}$, $V_{Train}(t_2) = \{\mathfrak{q}\}$, and $V_{Train}(t_0) = V_{Train}(t_3) = \emptyset$.
- $V_{Gate} : L_2 \rightarrow 2^{\mathcal{PV}_{Gate}}$, and $V_{Gate}(g_0) = V_{Gate}(g_1) = V_{Gate}(g_3) = \emptyset$, and $V_{Gate}(g_2) = \{\mathfrak{r}\}$.
- $V_{Cont} : L_3 \rightarrow 2^{\mathcal{PV}_{Cont}}$, and $V_{Cont}(c_0) = V_{Cont}(c_1) = V_{Cont}(c_3) = V_{Cont}(\overline{c_2}) = \emptyset$, $V_{Cont}(c_2) = \{\mathfrak{s}\}$, and $V_{Cont}(crash) = \{\mathfrak{crash}\}$.

The valuation functions $V_{RCS} : L_1 \times L_2 \times L_3 \rightarrow 2^{\mathcal{PV}}$, and $V_{M_{RCS}} : L_1 \times L_2 \times L_3 \times \mathbb{R}^3 \rightarrow 2^{\mathcal{PV}}$ are defined in the same way as in the correct version of the RCS system.

Using TCTLKD, we can specify the following properties of the faulty RCS system. These can be checked to hold on the real time deontic interpreted system for the faulty RCS.

$$AG_{[0,\infty]}K_{Train}\mathcal{O}_{Controller}(\mathfrak{p} \rightarrow AF_{[0,200]}\mathfrak{r}) \tag{7}$$

$$K_{Train}\mathcal{O}_{Controller}(\mathfrak{p} \rightarrow AF_{[0,200]}\mathfrak{r}) \tag{8}$$

$$\hat{K}_{Train}^{Controller}(\mathfrak{p} \rightarrow AF_{[0,200]}\mathfrak{r}) \tag{9}$$

$$AG_{[0,\infty]}K_{Train}\mathcal{O}_{Controller}(\neg\mathfrak{crash}) \tag{10}$$

$$AG_{[0,\infty]}\hat{K}_{Train}^{Controller}(\neg\mathfrak{crash}) \tag{11}$$

$$AG_{[0,\infty]}\hat{K}_{Train}^{Controller}(\mathfrak{p} \rightarrow AF_{[0,100]}\mathfrak{s}) \tag{12}$$

Formula (7) states that forever in the future agent Train knows that whenever agent Controller is functioning correctly, if Train sends the *approach* signal, then agent Gate will send the signal down within 200 seconds. Formula (8) states that agent Train knows that whenever agent Controller is functioning correctly, if the *approach* signal was sent by Train, then at some point in the future, within 200 second, Gate will be down. Formula (9) states that agent Train knows that under the assumption of agent Controller functioning correctly, if the *approach* signal was sent by Train, then at some point in the future, within 200 second, Gate will be down. Formula (10) states that always in the future agent Train knows that whenever agent Controller is functioning correctly under no circumstances

---

[3] Note that the names of the mathematical objects we use to represent the faulty RCS are the same as the ones employed previously for the correct RCS. Given that these appear in different contexts we trust no confusion arises.

there will be a situation in which Train is on the crossing and Gate is open. Formula (11) states that always in the future agent Train knows that under the assumption of agent Controller functioning correctly, under no circumstances there will be a situation in which Train is on the crossing and Gate is open. Formula (12) states that always in the future agent Train knows that under the assumption of agent Controller functioning correctly, if the *approach* signal was sent by Train, then at some point in the future, within 100 second, the signal *lower* will be sent by Controller.

The following formulas can be checked not to hold on the faulty RCS.

$$K_{Train}(\mathfrak{p} \to AF_{[0,200]}\mathfrak{r}) \tag{13}$$

$$AG_{[0,\infty]}K_{Train}(\neg\mathfrak{crash}) \tag{14}$$

$$AG_{[0,\infty]}K_{Train}(\mathfrak{p} \to AF_{[0,100]}\mathfrak{s}) \tag{15}$$

Formula (13) states that agent Train knows that, if it sends the *approach* signal, then at some point in the future, within 200 second, Gate will be down. Formula (14) states that always in the future agent Train knows that under no circumstances there will be a situation where Train is on the cross and Gate is open. Formula (15) states that always in the future agent Train knows that, if it sends the *approach* signal, then at some point in the future, within 100 second, the signal *lower* will be sent by Controller.

5   Conclusions

In the paper we have proposed TCTLKD, a real time logic for knowledge and correctness. TCTLKD is a fusion of three well known logics: TCTL for real time [34], S5 for knowledge [18], and KD45^{i-j} for the correctness dimension [24].

Previous attempts of combinations of real time and knowledge have included [37, 38, 39]. In [37] a technique for determining the temporal validity of shared data in real-time distributed systems is proposed. The approach is based on a language consisting of Boolean, epistemic, dynamic, and real-time temporal operators, but the semantics for these is not defined. In [38] a fusion of the branching time temporal logic (CTL) and the standard epistemic logic is presented. The semantics of the logic is given over an interpreted system defined like in [18] with the difference of using runs defined from real numbers. This language is used to establish sound and complete termination conditions for motion planning of robots, given initial and goal states. [39] presents a framework for knowledge-based analysis of clocks synchronisation in systems with real-time constraints. In that work a relation of timed precedence as a generalisation of previous work by Lamport is defined, and it is shown how (inherent) knowledge about timed precedences can be applied to synchronise clocks optimally. Like in [38], the semantics consists of runs that are functions over real time. The epistemic relations defined in this work assume that agents have perfect recall.

Our paper differs from the approaches above by considering quantitative temporal operators such as $EF_{[0,10]}$ (meaning "possibly within 10 time units"), rather than qualitative operators EF (meaning "possibly in the future", but with no bound), and by not forcing the agents to have perfect recall. In addition, the logic TCTLKD also incorporates a notion of correctness of execution with respect to specifications, a concept not tackled in previous works, and associates a set of clocks to every agent not just to the system as a whole. While the satisfiability problem for TCTLKD is undecidable, the TCTLKD model checking problem, i.e., the problem of validity in a given model, is decidable. Given this, it seems worthwhile to develop model checking methods for TCTLKD in the same fashion to what has been pursued for the same modalities but on discrete time [42]. In fact, a preliminary version of the TCTLK[4] bounded model checking method is presented in [40, 41].

References

1. Hintikka, J.: Knowledge and Belief, An Introduction to the Logic of the Two Notions. Cornell University Press, Ithaca (NY) and London (1962)
2. Aumann, R.J.: Agreeing to disagree. Annals of Statistics **4** (1976) 1236–1239
3. Fagin, R., Vardi, M.Y.: Knowledge and implicit knowledge in a distributed environment: Preliminary report. In Halpern, J.Y., ed.: TARK: Theoretical Aspects of Reasoning about Knowledge, San Francisco (CA), Morgan Kaufmann (1986) 187–206
4. Halpern, J., Moses, Y.: A guide to completeness and complexity for modal logics of knowledge and belief. Artificial Intelligence **54** (1992) 319–379
5. van der Hoek, W.: Sytems for knowledge and belief. Journal of Logic and Computation **3** (1993) 173–195
6. Halpern, J.Y., Vardi, M.Y.: The complexity of reasoning about knowledge and time. In: ACM Symposium on Theory of Computing (STOC '86), Baltimore, USA, ACM Press (1986) 304–315
7. Halpern, J.Y., Vardi, M.Y.: The complexity of reasoning about knowledge and time 1: lower bounds. Journal of Computer and System Sciences **38** (1989) 195–237
8. van der Meyden, R., Wong, K.: Complete axiomatizations for reasoning about knowledge and branching time. Studia Logica **75** (2003) 93–123
9. Marek, W., Truszczyński, M.: Autoepistemic logic. Journal of the ACM **38** (1991) 587–618
10. Moore, R.: Possible-world semantics autoepistemic logic. In: Proceedings of Workshop on Non-Monotonic Reasoning, The AAAI Press (1984) 344–354
11. Baltag, A., Moss, L.S., Solecki, S.: The logic of public announcement, common knowledge, and private suspicions. In Gilboa, I., ed.: Proceedings of the 7th Conference on Theoretical Aspects of Rationality and Knowledge (TARK-98), San Francisco, Morgan Kaufmann (1998) 125–132
12. Lomuscio, A., Ryan, M.: An algorithmic approach to knowledge evolution. Artificial Intelligence for Engineering Design, Analysis and Manufacturing (AIEDAM) **13** (1999)
13. Fagin, R., Halpern, J.Y., Moses, Y., Vardi, M.Y.: Knowledge-based programs. Distributed Computing **10** (1997) 199–225

---

[4] The TCTLK logic is like TCTLKD but it does not contain the correct functioning operator, i.e, the operator $\mathcal{O}_i$ for $i \in \mathcal{AG}$.

14. Lomuscio, A., van der Meyden, R., Ryan, M.: Knowledge in multi-agent systems: Initial configurations and broadcast. ACM Transactions of Computational Logic **1** (2000)

15. Manna, Z., Pnueli, A.: The Temporal Logic of Reactive and Concurrent Systems: Specification. Springer-Verlag (1991)

16. Manna, Z., Pnueli, A.: Temporal Verification of Reactive Systems: Safety. Springer-Verlag (1995)

17. Manna, Z., Pnueli, A.: Completing the temporal picture. In: Selected papers of the 16th international colloquium on Automata, languages, and programming, Elsevier Science (1991) 97–130

18. Fagin, R., Halpern, J.Y., Moses, Y., Vardi, M.Y.: Reasoning about Knowledge. MIT Press, Cambridge (1995)

19. Halpern, J., Meyden, R., Vardi, M.Y.: Complete axiomatisations for reasoning about knowledge and time. SIAM Journal on Computing **33** (2003) 674–703

20. van der Meyden, R.: Axioms for knowledge and time in distributed systems with perfect recall. In: Proceedings, Ninth Annual IEEE Symposium on Logic in Computer Science, Paris, France, IEEE Computer Society Press (1994) 448–457

21. Ben-Ari, M., Pnueli, A., Manna, Z.: The temporal logic of branching time. Acta Informatica **20** (1983) 207–226

22. Emerson, E.A.: Temporal and modal logic. In van Leeuwen, J., ed.: Handbook of Theoretical Computer Science, Elsevier Science Publishers (1990) 996–1071

23. Emerson, E.A., Halpern, J.Y.: Decision procedures and expressiveness in the temporal logic of branching time. Journal of Computer and System Sciences **30** (1985) 1–24

24. Lomuscio, A., Sergot, M.: Deontic interpreted systems. Studia Logica **75** (2003) 63–92

25. Lomuscio, A., Sergot, M.: Violation, error recovery, and enforcement in the bit transmission problem. Journal of Applied Logic **1**(2): 93–116, 2004

26. Alur, R., Dill, D.: Automata for modelling real-time systems. In: Proceedings of the International Colloquium on Automata, Languages and Programming (ICALP'90). Volume 443 of Lecture Notes in Computer Science., Springer-Verlag (1990) 322–335

27. Dill, D.: Timing assumptions and verification of finite state concurrent systems. In: Automatic Verification Methods for Finite-State Systems. Volume 407 of Lecture Notes in Computer Science., Springer-Verlag (1989) 197–212

28. Behrmann, G., Larsen, K., Pearson, J., Weise, C., Yi, W.: Efficient timed reachability analysis using clock difference diagrams. In: Proceedings of the 11th International Conference on Computer Aided Verification (CAV'99). Volume 1633 of Lecture Notes in Computer Science., Springer-Verlag (1999) 341–353

29. Wang, F.: Efficient data structure of fully symbolic verification of real-time software systems. In: Proceedings of the 6th International Conference on Tools and Algorithms for Construction and Analysis of Systems (TACAS'00). Volume 1785 of Lecture Notes in Computer Science., Springer-Verlag (2000) 157–171

30. Penczek, W., Woźna, B., Zbrzezny, A.: SAT-based bounded model checking for the universal fragment of TCTL. Technical Report 947, ICS PAS, Ordona 21, 01-237 Warsaw (2002)

31. Penczek, W., Woźna, B., Zbrzezny, A.: Towards bounded model checking for the universal fragment of TCTL. In: Proceedings of the 7th International Symposium on Formal Techniques in Real-Time and Fault Tolerant Systems (FTRTFT'02). Volume 2469 of Lecture Notes in Computer Science., Springer-Verlag (2002) 265–288

32. Seshia, S., Bryant, R.: Unbounded, fully symbolic model checking of timed automata using boolean methods. In: Proceedings of the 15th International Conference on Computer Aided Verification (CAV'03). Volume 2725 of Lecture Notes in Computer Science., Springer-Verlag (2003) 154–166
33. Tripakis, S., Yovine, S.: Analysis of timed systems using time-abstracting bisimulations. Formal Methods in System Design **18** (2001) 25–68
34. Alur, R., Courcoubetis, C., Dill, D.: Model checking in dense real-time. Information and Computation **104** (1993) 2–34
35. Blackburn, P., de Rijke, M., Venema, Y.: Modal Logic. Volume 53 of Cambridge Tracts in Theoretical Computer Science. Cambridge University Press (2001)
36. Kang, I., Lee, I.: An efficient state space generation for the analysis of real-time systems. In: Proceedings of International Symposium on Software Testing and Analysis. (1996)
37. Anderson, S., Kuster-Filipe, J.: Guaranteeing temporal validity with a real-time logic of knowledge. In: Proceedings of the 1st International Workshop on Data Distribution for Real-Time Systems (DDRTS'03), ICDCS 2003 Workshop, Providence, Rhode Island, USA (2003) 178–183
38. Brafman, R.I., Latombe, J.C., Moses, Y., , Shoham, Y.: Application of a logic of knowledge to motion planning under uncertainty. Journal of the ACM **44** (1997) 633–668
39. Moses, Y., Bloom, B.: Knowledge, timed precedence and clocks. In: Proceedings of the 13th ACM symposium on Principles of Distributed Computing, ACM Press (1994) 274–303
40. Woźna, B., Lomuscio, A., Penczek, W.: Verification of deontic and epistemic properties of multiagent systems and its application to the bit transmission problem with faults. In: Proceedings of the 2nd Workshop on Logic and Communication in Multi-Agent Systems (LCMAS'04). (2004)
41. Lomuscio, A., Woźna, B., Penczek, W.: Bounded model checking for knowledge over real time. In: Proceedings of the International Workshop on Concurrency, Specification and Programming (CS&P'04). Volume 170 of Informatik-Berichte. (2004) 398–414
42. Raimondi, F., Lomuscio, A.: Automatic verification of deontic interpreted systems by model checking via OBDD's. In: Proceedings of the Sixteenth European Conference on Artificial Intelligence (ECAI04). (2004)

Dynamic Logic for Plan Revision in Intelligent Agents

M. Birna van Riemsdijk[1], Frank S. de Boer[1,2,3], and John-Jules Ch. Meyer[1]

[1] ICS, Utrecht University, The Netherlands
[2] CWI, Amsterdam, The Netherlands
[3] LIACS, Leiden University, The Netherlands

Abstract. In this paper, we present a dynamic logic for a propositional version of the agent programming language 3APL. A 3APL agent has beliefs and a plan. The execution of a plan changes an agent's beliefs. Plans can be revised during execution. Due to these plan revision capabilities of 3APL agents, plans cannot be analyzed by structural induction as in for example standard propositional dynamic logic. We propose a dynamic logic that is tailored to handle the plan revision aspect of 3APL. For this logic, we give a sound and complete axiomatization.

1   Introduction

An agent is commonly seen as an encapsulated computer system that is situated in some environment and that is capable of flexible, autonomous action in that environment in order to meet its design objectives [1]. Programming these flexible computing entities is not a trivial task. An important line of research in this area, is research on *cognitive* agents. These are agents endowed with high-level mental attitudes such as beliefs, desires, goals, plans, intentions, norms and obligations. Intelligent cognitive agents should be able to reason with these mental attitudes in order to exhibit the desired flexible problem solving behavior.

The very concept of (cognitive) agents is thus a complex one. It is imperative that programmed agents be amenable to precise and formal specification and verification, at least for some critical applications. This is recognized by (potential) appliers of agent technology such as NASA, which organizes specialized workshops on the subject of formal specification and verification of agents [2, 3].

In this paper, we are concerned with the verification of agents programmed in (a simplified version of) the cognitive agent programming language *3APL*[1] [4, 5, 6]. This language is based on theoretical research on cognitive notions [7, 8, 9, 10]. In the latest version [6], a 3APL agent has a set of beliefs, a plan and a set of goals. The idea is, that an agent tries to fulfill its goals by selecting appropriate plans, depending on its beliefs about the world. Beliefs should thus represent the world or environment of the agent; the goals represent the state of

---

[1] 3APL is to be pronounced as "triple-a-p-l".

J. Leite and P. Torroni (Eds.): CLIMA V, LNAI 3487, pp. 16–32, 2005.
© Springer-Verlag Berlin Heidelberg 2005

the world the agent wants to realize and plans are the means to achieve these goals.

As explained, cognitive agent programming languages are designed to program flexible behavior using high-level mental attitudes. In the various languages, these attitudes are handled in different ways. An important aspect of 3APL is the way in which plans are dealt with. A plan in 3APL can be executed, resulting in a change of the beliefs of the agent[2]. Now, in order to increase the possible flexibility of agents, 3APL [4] was endowed with a mechanism with which the programmer can program agents that can *revise* their plans during execution of the agent. This is a distinguishing feature of 3APL compared to other agent programming languages and architectures [11, 12, 13, 14]. The idea is, that an agent should not blindly execute an adopted plan, but it should be able to revise it under certain conditions. As this paper focusses on the plan revision aspect of 3APL, we consider a version of the language with only beliefs and plans, i.e., without goals. We will use a propositional and otherwise slightly simplified variant of the original 3APL language as defined in [4].

In 3APL, the plan revision capabilities can be programmed through plan revision rules. These rules consist of a head and a body, both representing a plan. A plan is basically a sequence of so-called basic actions. These actions can be executed. The idea is, informally, that an agent can apply a rule if it has a plan corresponding to the head of this rule, resulting in the replacement of this plan by the plan in the body of the rule. The introduction of these capabilities now gives rise to interesting issues concerning the characteristics of plan execution, as will become clear in the sequel. This has implications for reasoning about the result of plan execution and therefore for the formal verification of 3APL agents, which we are concerned with in this paper.

To be more specific, after defining (a simplified version of) 3APL and its semantics (section 2), we propose a dynamic logic for proving properties of 3APL plans in the context of plan revision rules (section 3). For this logic, we provide a sound and complete axiomatization (section 4).

As for related work, verification of agents programmed in an agent programming language has for example been addressed in [15]. This paper addresses model checking of the agent programming language AgentSpeak. A sketch of a dynamic logic to reason about 3APL agents has been given in [5]. This logic however is designed to reason about a 3APL interpreter or deliberation language, whereas in this paper we take a different viewpoint and reason about plans. In [16], a programming logic (without axiomatization) was given for a fragment of 3APL without plan revision rules. Further, the operational semantics of plan revision rules is similar to that of procedures in procedural programming. In fact, plan revision rules can be viewed as an extension of procedures. Logics and semantics for procedural languages are for example studied in De Bakker [17]. Although the operational semantics of procedures and plan revision rules are similar, techniques for reasoning about procedures cannot be used for plan

---

[2] A change in the environment is a possible "side effect" of the execution of a plan.

revision rules. This is due to the fact that the introduction of these rules results in the semantics of the sequential composition operator no longer being compositional (see section 3). This issue has also been considered from a semantic perspective in [18, 19]. In [20], a framework for planning in dynamic environments is presented in a logic programming setting. The approach is based on hierarchical task network planning. The motivation for that work is similar to the motivation for the introduction of plan revision rules.

To the best of our knowledge, this is the first attempt to design a logic and deductive system for plan revision rules or similar language constructs. Considering the semantic difficulties that arise with the introduction of this type of construct, it is not a priori obvious that it would be possible at all to design a deductive system to reason about these constructs. The main aim of this work was thus to investigate whether it is possible to define such a system and in this way also to get a better theoretical understanding of the construct of plan revision rules. Whether the system presented in this paper is also practically useful to verify 3APL agents, remains to be seen and will be subject to further research.

2   3APL

2.1   Syntax

Below, we define belief bases and plans. A belief base is a set of propositional formulas. A plan is a sequence of basic actions and abstract plans. Basic actions can be executed, resulting in a change to the beliefs of the agent. An abstract plan can, in contrast with basic actions, not be executed directly in the sense that it updates the belief base of an agent. Abstract plans serve as an abstraction mechanism like procedures in procedural programming. If a plan consists of an abstract plan, this abstract plan could be transformed into basic actions through the application of plan revision rules, which will be introduced below[3].

In the sequel, a language defined by inclusion shall be the smallest language containing the specified elements.

Definition 1. *(belief bases)* Assume a propositional language $\mathcal{L}$ with typical formula q and the connectives $\wedge$ and $\neg$ with the usual meaning. Then the set of belief bases Σ with typical element σ is defined to be $\wp(\mathcal{L})$.[4]

Definition 2. *(plans)* Assume that a set BasicAction with typical element a is given, together with a set AbstractPlan with typical element p. Then the set of plans Π with typical element π is defined as follows:

- BasicAction $\cup$ AbstractPlan $\subseteq \Pi$,
- if $c \in$ (BasicAction $\cup$ AbstractPlan) and $\pi \in \Pi$ then $c\,;\pi \in \Pi$.

---

[3] Abstract plans could also be modelled as non-executable basic actions.
[4] $\wp(\mathcal{L})$ denotes the powerset of $\mathcal{L}$.

Basic actions and abstract plans are called atomic plans and are typically de-noted by c. For technical convenience, plans are defined to have a list structure, which means strictly speaking, that we can only use the sequential composition operator to concatenate an atomic plan and a plan, rather than concatenating two arbitrary plans. In the following, we will however also use the sequential composition operator to concatenate arbitrary plans π_1 and π_2 yielding $\pi_1; \pi_2$. The operator should in this case be read as a function taking two plans that have a list structure and yielding a new plan that also has this structure. The plan π_1 will thus be the prefix of the resulting plan.

We use ϵ to denote the empty plan, which is an empty list. The concatenation of a plan π and the empty list is equal to π, i.e., $\epsilon; \pi$ and $\pi; \epsilon$ are identified with π.

A plan and a belief base can together constitute a so-called configuration. During computation or execution of the agent, the elements in a configuration can change.

Definition 3. *(configuration)* Let Σ be the set of belief bases and let Π be the set of plans. Then $\Pi \times \Sigma$ is the set of configurations of a 3APL agent.

Plan revision rules consist of a head π_h and a body π_b. Informally, an agent that has a plan π_h, can replace this plan by π_b when applying a plan revision rule of this form.

Definition 4. *(plan revision (PR) rules)* The set of PR rules $\mathcal{R}$ is defined as follows: $\mathcal{R} = \{\pi_h \leadsto \pi_b \mid \pi_h, \pi_b \in \Pi, \pi_h \neq \epsilon\}$.[5]

Take for example a plan $a; b$ where a and b are basic actions, and a PR rule $a; b \leadsto c$. The agent can then either execute the actions a and b one after the other, or it can apply the PR rule yielding a new plan c, which can in turn be executed. A plan p consisting of an abstract plan cannot be executed, but can only be transformed using a procedure-like PR rule such as $p \leadsto a$.

Below, we provide the definition of a 3APL agent. The function $\mathcal{T}$, taking a basic action and a belief base and yielding a new belief base, is used to define how belief bases are updated when a basic action is executed.

Definition 5. *(3APL agent)* A 3APL agent $\mathcal{A}$ is a tuple $\langle \text{Rule}, \mathcal{T} \rangle$ where $\text{Rule} \subseteq \mathcal{R}$ is a finite set of PR rules and $\mathcal{T} : (\text{BasicAction} \times \sigma) \to \sigma$ is a partial function, expressing how belief bases are updated through basic action execution.

2.2   Semantics

The semantics of a programming language can be defined as a function taking a statement and a state, and yielding the set of states resulting from executing the

---

[5] In [4], PR rules were defined to have a guard, i.e., rules were of the form $\pi_h \mid \phi \leadsto \pi_b$. For a rule to be applicable, the guard should then hold. For technical convenience and because we want to focus on the plan revision aspect of these rules, we however leave out the guard in this paper. The results could be extended for rules with a guard.

initial statement in the initial state. In this way, a statement can be viewed as a transformation function on states. In 3APL, plans can be seen as statements and belief bases as states on which these plans operate. There are various ways of defining a semantic function and in this paper we are concerned with the so-called *operational* semantics (see for example De Bakker [17] for details on this subject).

The operational semantics of a language is usually defined using transition systems [21]. A transition system for a programming language consists of a set of axioms and derivation rules for deriving transitions for this language. A transition is a transformation of one configuration into another and it corresponds to a single computation step. Let $\mathcal{A} = \langle \text{Rule}, \mathcal{T} \rangle$ be a 3APL agent and let BasicAction be a set of basic actions. Below, we give the transition system $\text{Trans}_{\mathcal{A}}$ for our simplified 3APL language, which is based on the system given in [4]. This transition system is specific to agent $\mathcal{A}$.

There are two kinds of transitions, i.e., transitions describing the execution of basic actions and those describing the application of a plan revision rule. The transitions are labelled to denote the kind of transition. A basic action at the head of a plan can be executed in a configuration if the function $\mathcal{T}$ is defined for this action and the belief base in the configuration. The execution results in a change of belief base as specified through $\mathcal{T}$ and the action is removed from the plan.

Definition 6. *(action execution)* Let $a \in \text{BasicAction}$.

$$\frac{\mathcal{T}(a, \sigma) = \sigma'}{\langle a; \pi, \sigma \rangle \rightarrow_{exec} \langle \pi, \sigma' \rangle}$$

A plan revision rule can be applied in a configuration if the head of the rule is equal to a prefix of the plan in the configuration. The application of the rule results in the revision of the plan, such that the prefix equal to the head of the rule is replaced by the plan in the body of the rule. A rule $a; b \rightsquigarrow c$ can for example be applied to the plan $a; b; c$, yielding the plan $c; c$. The belief base is not changed through plan revision.

Definition 7. *(rule application)* Let $\rho : \pi_h \rightsquigarrow \pi_b \in \text{Rule}$.

$$\langle \pi_h; \pi, \sigma \rangle \rightarrow_{app} \langle \pi_b; \pi, \sigma \rangle$$

In the sequel, it will be useful to have a function taking a PR rule and a plan, and yielding the plan resulting from the application of the rule to this given plan. Based on this function, we also define a function taking a set of PR rules and a plan and yielding the set of rules applicable to this plan.

Definition 8. *(rule application)* Let $\mathcal{R}$ be the set of PR rules and let Π be the set of plans. Let $\rho : \pi_h \rightsquigarrow \pi_b \in \mathcal{R}$ and $\pi, \pi' \in \Pi$. The partial function $apply : (\mathcal{R} \times \Pi) \rightarrow \Pi$ is then defined as follows.

$$apply(\rho)(\pi) = \begin{cases} \pi_b; \pi' & \text{if } \pi = \pi_h; \pi', \\ \text{undefined} & \text{otherwise.} \end{cases}$$

The function $applicable : (\wp(\mathcal{R}) \times \Pi) \rightarrow \wp(\mathcal{R})$ yielding the set of rules applicable to a certain plan, is then as follows: $applicable(\mathsf{Rule}, \pi) = \{\rho \in \mathsf{Rule} \mid apply(\rho)(\pi)$ is defined$\}$.

Using the transition system, individual transitions can be derived for a 3APL agent. These transitions can be put in sequel, yielding transition sequences. From a transition sequence, one can obtain a *computation sequence* by removing the plan component of all configurations occurring in the transition sequence. In the following definitions, we formally define computation sequences and we specify the function yielding these sequences, given an initial configuration.

Definition 9. *(computation sequences)* The set Σ^+ of finite computation sequences is defined as $\{\sigma_1, \dots, \sigma_i, \dots, \sigma_n \mid \sigma_i \in \Sigma, 1 \leq i \leq n, n \in \mathbb{N}\}$.

Definition 10. *(function for calculating computation sequences)* Let $x_i \in \{exec, app\}$ for $1 \leq i \leq m$. The function $\mathcal{C}^{\mathcal{A}} : (\Pi \times \Sigma) \rightarrow \wp(\Sigma^+)$ is then as defined below.

$$\mathcal{C}^{\mathcal{A}}(\pi, \sigma) = \{\sigma, \dots, \sigma_m \in \Sigma^+ \mid \theta = \langle \pi, \sigma \rangle \rightarrow_{x_1} \dots \rightarrow_{x_m} \langle \epsilon, \sigma_m \rangle$$

is a finite sequence of transitions in $\mathsf{Trans}_{\mathcal{A}}\}$.

Note that we only take into account successfully terminating transition sequences, i.e., those sequences ending in a configuration with an empty plan. Using the function defined above, we can now define the operational semantics of 3APL.

Definition 11. *(operational semantics)* Let $\kappa : \wp(\Sigma^+) \rightarrow \wp(\Sigma)$ be a function yielding the last elements of a set of finite computation sequences, which is defined as follows: $\kappa(\Delta) = \{\sigma_n \mid \sigma_1, \dots, \sigma_n \in \Delta\}$. The operational semantic function $\mathcal{O}^{\mathcal{A}} : \Pi \rightarrow (\Sigma \rightarrow \wp(\Sigma))$ is defined as follows:

$$\mathcal{O}^{\mathcal{A}}(\pi)(\sigma) = \kappa(\mathcal{C}^{\mathcal{A}}(\pi, \sigma)).$$

We will sometimes omit the superscript $\mathcal{A}$ from functions as defined above, for reasons of presentation. The example below is used to explain the definition of the operational semantics.

Example 1. Let $\mathcal{A}$ be an agent with PR rules $\{p; a \rightsquigarrow b, p \rightsquigarrow c\}$, where p is an abstract plan and a, b, c are basic actions. Let σ_a be the belief base resulting from the execution of a in σ, i.e., $\mathcal{T}(a, \sigma) = \sigma_a$, let be σ_{ab} the belief resulting from executing first a and then b in σ, etc.

   Then $\mathcal{C}^{\mathcal{A}}(p; a)(\sigma) = \{(\sigma, \sigma, \sigma_b), (\sigma, \sigma, \sigma_c, \sigma_{ca})\}$, which is based on the transition sequences $\langle p; a, \sigma \rangle \rightarrow_{app} \{b, \sigma\} \rightarrow_{exec} \langle \epsilon, \sigma_b \rangle$ and $\langle p; a, \sigma \rangle \rightarrow_{app} \langle c; a, \sigma \rangle \rightarrow_{exec} \langle a, \sigma_c \rangle \rightarrow_{exec} \langle \epsilon, \sigma_{ca} \rangle$. We thus have that $\mathcal{O}^{\mathcal{A}}(p; a)(\sigma) = \{\sigma_b, \sigma_{ca}\}$.

3   Dynamic Logic

In programming language research, an important area is the specification and verification of programs. Program logics are designed to facilitate this process. One such logic is dynamic logic [22, 23], with which we are concerned in this paper. In dynamic logic, programs are explicit syntactic constructs in the logic. To be able to discuss the effect of the execution of a program π on the truth of a formula ϕ, the modal construct $[\pi]\phi$ is used. This construct intuitively states that in all states in which π halts, the formula ϕ holds.

Programs in general are constructed from atomic programs and composition operators. An example of a composition operator is the sequential composition operator $(;)$, where the program $\pi_1; \pi_2$ intuitively means that π_1 is executed first, followed by the execution of π_2. The semantics of such a compound program can in general be determined by the semantics of the parts of which it is composed. This compositionality property allows analysis by structural induction (see also [24]), i.e., analysis of a compound statement by analysis of its parts. Analysis of the sequential composition operator by structural induction can in dynamic logic be expressed by the following formula, which is usually a validity: $[\pi_1; \pi_2]\phi \leftrightarrow [\pi_1][\pi_2]\phi$. For 3APL plans on the contrary, this formula does not always hold. This is due to the presence of PR rules.

We will informally explain this using the 3APL agent of example 1. As explained, the operational semantics of this agent, given initial plan $p; a$ and initial state σ, is as follows: $\mathcal{O}(p; a)(\sigma) = \{\sigma_b, \sigma_{ca}\}$. Now compare the result of first "executing"[6] p in σ and then executing a in the resulting belief base, i.e., compare the set $\mathcal{O}(a)(\mathcal{O}(p)(\sigma))$. In this case, there is only one successfully terminating transition sequence and it ends in σ_{ca}, i.e., $\mathcal{O}(a)(\mathcal{O}(p)(\sigma)) = \{\sigma_{ca}\}$. Now, if it would be the case that $\sigma_{ca} \models \phi$ but $\sigma_b \not\models \phi$, the formula $[p; a]\phi \leftrightarrow [p][a]\phi$ would not hold[7].

Analysis of plans by structural induction in this way thus does not work for 3APL. In order to be able to prove correctness properties of 3APL programs however, one can perhaps imagine that it is important to have *some* kind of induction. As we will show in the sequel, the kind of induction that can be used to reason about 3APL programs, is induction on the *number of PR rule applications in a transition sequence*. We will introduce a dynamic logic for 3APL based on this idea.

3.1   Syntax

In order to be able to do induction on the number of PR rule applications in a transition sequence, we introduce so-called *restricted plans*. These are plans,

---

[6] We will use the word "execution" in two ways. Firstly, as in this context, we will use it to denote the execution of an arbitrary plan in the sense of going through several transition of type *exec* or *app*, starting in a configuration with this plan and resulting in some final configurations. Secondly, we will use it to refer to the execution of a basic action in the sense of going through a transition of type *exec*.

[7] In particular, the implication would not hold from right to left.

annotated with a natural number[8]. Informally, if the restriction parameter of a plan is n, the number of rule applications during execution of this plan cannot exceed n.

Definition 12. *(restricted plans)* Let Π be the language of plans and let $\mathbb{N}^- = \mathbb{N} \cup \{-1\}$. Then, the language Π_r of restricted plans is defined as $\{\pi\lceil_n \mid \pi \in \Pi, n \in \mathbb{N}^-\}$.

Below, we define the language of dynamic logic in which properties of 3APL agents can be expressed. In the logic, one can express properties of restricted plans. As will become clear in the sequel, one can prove properties of the plan of a 3APL agent by proving properties of restricted plans.

Definition 13. *(plan revision dynamic logic (PRDL))* Let $\pi\lceil_n \in \Pi_r$ be a restricted plan. Then the language of dynamic logic $\mathcal{L}_{\mathsf{PRDL}}$ with typical element ϕ is defined as follows:

- $\mathcal{L} \subseteq \mathcal{L}_{\mathsf{PRDL}}$,
- if $\phi \in \mathcal{L}_{\mathsf{PRDL}}$, then $[\pi\lceil_n]\phi \in \mathcal{L}_{\mathsf{PRDL}}$,
- if $\phi, \phi' \in \mathcal{L}_{\mathsf{PRDL}}$, then $\neg\phi \in \mathcal{L}_{\mathsf{PRDL}}$ and $\phi \wedge \phi' \in \mathcal{L}_{\mathsf{PRDL}}$.

3.2 Semantics

In order to define the semantics of PRDL, we first define the semantics of restricted plans. As for ordinary plans, we also define an operational semantics for restricted plans. We do this by defining a function for calculating computation sequences, given an initial restricted plan and a belief base.

Definition 14. *(function for calculating computation sequences)* Let $x_i \in \{exec, app\}$ for $1 \leq i \leq m$. Let $N_{app}(\theta)$ be a function yielding the number of transitions of the form $s_i \to_{app} s_{i+1}$ in the sequence of transitions θ. The function $\mathcal{C}_r^{\mathcal{A}} : (\Pi_r \times \Sigma) \to \wp(\Sigma^+)$ is then as defined below.

$$\mathcal{C}_r^{\mathcal{A}}(\pi\lceil_n, \sigma) = \{\sigma, \ldots, \sigma_m \in \Sigma^+ \mid \theta = \langle \pi, \sigma \rangle \to_{x_1} \ldots \to_{x_m} \langle \epsilon, \sigma_m \rangle$$
$$\text{is a finite sequence of transitions in } \mathsf{Trans}_{\mathcal{A}} \text{ where } 0 \leq N_{app}(\theta) \leq n\}$$

As one can see in the definition above, the computation sequences $\mathcal{C}_r^{\mathcal{A}}(\pi\lceil_n, \sigma)$ are based on transition sequences starting in configuration $\langle \pi, \sigma \rangle$. The number of rule applications in these transition sequences should be between 0 and n, in contrast with the function $\mathcal{C}^{\mathcal{A}}$ of definition 10, in which there is no restriction on this number.

  Based on the function $\mathcal{C}_r^{\mathcal{A}}$, we define the operational semantics of restricted plans by taking the last elements of the computation sequences yielded by $\mathcal{C}_r^{\mathcal{A}}$. The set of belief bases is empty if the restriction parameter is equal to -1.

---

[8] Or with the number -1. The number -1 is introduced for technical convenience and it will become clear in the sequel why we need this.

Definition 15. *(operational semantics)* Let κ be as in definition 11. The operational semantic function $\mathcal{O}_r^{\mathcal{A}} : \Pi_r \rightarrow (\Sigma \rightarrow \wp(\Sigma))$ is defined as follows:

$$\mathcal{O}_r^{\mathcal{A}}(\pi\lceil_n)(\sigma) = \begin{cases} \kappa(\mathcal{C}_r^{\mathcal{A}}(\pi\lceil_n, \sigma)) & \text{if } n \geq 0, \\ \emptyset & \text{if } n = -1. \end{cases}$$

In the following proposition, we relate the operational semantics of plans and the operational semantics of restricted plans.

Proposition 1.

$$\bigcup_{n \in \mathbb{N}} \mathcal{O}_r(\pi\lceil_n)(\sigma) = \mathcal{O}(\pi)(\sigma)$$

Proof. Immediate from definitions 15, 14, 11 and 10.

Using the operational semantics of restricted plans, we can now define the semantics of the dynamic logic.

Definition 16. *(semantics of* PRDL*)* Let $q \in \mathcal{L}$ be a propositional formula, let $\phi, \phi' \in \mathcal{L}_{\mathsf{PRDL}}$ and let $\models_{\mathcal{L}}$ be the entailment relation defined for $\mathcal{L}$ as usual. The semantics $\models_{\mathcal{A}}$ of $\mathcal{L}_{\mathsf{PRDL}}$ is then as defined below.

$$\begin{aligned} \sigma \models_{\mathcal{A}} q & \Leftrightarrow \sigma \models_{\mathcal{L}} q \\ \sigma \models_{\mathcal{A}} [\pi\lceil_n]\phi & \Leftrightarrow \forall \sigma' \in \mathcal{O}_r^{\mathcal{A}}(\pi\lceil_n)(\sigma) : \sigma' \models_{\mathcal{A}} \phi \\ \sigma \models_{\mathcal{A}} \neg\phi & \Leftrightarrow \sigma \not\models_{\mathcal{A}} \phi \\ \sigma \models_{\mathcal{A}} \phi \wedge \phi' & \Leftrightarrow \sigma \models_{\mathcal{A}} \phi \text{ and } \sigma \models_{\mathcal{A}} \phi' \end{aligned}$$

As $\mathcal{O}_r^{\mathcal{A}}$ is defined in terms of agent $\mathcal{A}$, so is the semantics of $\mathcal{L}_{\mathsf{PRDL}}$. We use the subscript $\mathcal{A}$ to indicate this. Let Rule $\subseteq \mathcal{R}$ be a finite set of PR rules. If $\forall \mathcal{T}, \sigma : \sigma \models_{\langle \mathsf{Rule}, \mathcal{T} \rangle} \phi$, we write $\models_{\mathsf{Rule}} \phi$.

In the dynamic logic PRDL, one can express properties of restricted plans, rather than of ordinary 3APL plans. The operational semantics of ordinary plans $\mathcal{O}$ and of restricted plans $\mathcal{O}_r$ are however related (proposition 1). As the semantics of the construct $[\pi\lceil_n]\sigma$ is defined in terms of $\mathcal{O}_r$, we can use this construct to specify properties of 3APL plans, as shown by the following corollary.

Corollary 1.

$$\forall n \in \mathbb{N} : \sigma \models_{\mathcal{A}} [\pi\lceil_n]\phi \Leftrightarrow \forall \sigma' \in \mathcal{O}^{\mathcal{A}}(\pi)(\sigma) : \sigma' \models_{\mathcal{A}} \phi$$

Proof. Immediate from proposition 1 and definition 16.

4   The Axiom System

In order to prove properties of restricted plans, we propose a deductive system for PRDL in this section. Rather than proving properties of restricted plans, the aim is however to prove properties of 3APL plans. We thus want to prove properties of the form $\forall n \in \mathbb{N} : [\pi\lceil_n]\phi$, as these are directly related to 3APL by corollary 1. The idea now is, that these properties can be proven by induction on n. We will explain this in more detail after introducing the axiom system for restricted plans.

Definition 17. *(axiom system (AS$_{Rule}$))* Let BasicAction be a set of basic actions, AbstractPlan be a set of abstract plans and Rule $\subseteq \mathcal{R}$ be a finite set of PR rules. Let $a \in$ BasicAction, let $p \in$ AbstractPlan, let $c \in$ (BasicAction $\cup$ AbstractPlan) and let ρ range over $applicable(\text{Rule}, c; \pi)$. The following are then the axioms of the system AS$_{Rule}$.

(PRDL1) $[\pi\lceil_{-1}]\phi$
(PRDL2) $[p\lceil_0]\phi$
(PRDL3) $[\epsilon\lceil_n]\phi \leftrightarrow \phi$ if $0 \leq n$
(PRDL4) $[c; \pi\lceil_n]\phi \leftrightarrow [c\lceil_0][\pi\lceil_n]\phi \wedge \bigwedge_\rho [apply(\rho, c; \pi)\lceil_{n-1}]\phi$ if $0 \leq n$

(PL)   axioms for propositional logic
(PDL) $[\pi\lceil_n](\phi \to \phi') \to ([\pi\lceil_n]\phi \to [\pi\lceil_n]\phi')$

The following are the rules of the system AS$_{Rule}$.

(GEN)

$$\frac{\phi}{[\pi\lceil_n]\phi}$$

(MP)

$$\frac{\phi_1, \ \phi_1 \to \phi_2}{\phi_2}$$

As the axiom system is relative to a given set of PR rules Rule, we will use the notation $\vdash_{Rule} \phi$ to specify that ϕ is derivable in the system AS$_{Rule}$ above.

The idea is that properties of the form $\forall n \in \mathbb{N} : \vdash_{Rule} [\pi\lceil_n]\phi$ can be proven by induction on n as follows. If we can prove $[\pi\lceil_0]\phi$ and $\forall n \in \mathbb{N} : ([\pi\lceil_n]\phi \vdash_{Rule} [\pi\lceil_{n+1}]\phi)$, we can conclude the desired property. These premises should be proven using the axiom system above. Consider for example an agent with a PR rule $a \rightsquigarrow a; a$ and assume that $\mathcal{T}$ is defined such that $[a\lceil_0]\phi$. One can then prove $\forall n : [a\lceil_n]\phi$ by proving $[a\lceil_n]\phi \vdash_{Rule} [a\lceil_{n+1}]\phi$, for arbitrary n.

We will now explain the PRDL axioms of the system. The other axioms and the rules are standard for propositional dynamic logic (PDL) [22]. We start by explaining the most interesting axiom: (PRDL4). We first observe that there are two types of transitions that can be derived for a 3APL agent: action execution and rule application (see definitions 6 and 7). Consider a configuration $\langle a; \pi, \sigma \rangle$ where a is a basic action. Then during computation, possible next configurations are $\langle \pi, \sigma' \rangle$[9] (action execution) and $\langle apply(\rho, a; \pi), \sigma \rangle$ (rule application) where ρ ranges over the applicable rules, i.e., $applicable(\text{Rule}, a; \pi)$[10]. We can thus analyze the plan $a; \pi$ by analyzing π after the execution of a, and the plans resulting from applying a rule, i.e., $apply(\rho, a; \pi)$[11]. The execution of an action can be

---

[9] Assuming that $\mathcal{T}(a, \sigma) = \sigma'$.
[10] See definition 8 for the definitions of the functions *apply* and *applicable*.
[11] Note that one could say we analyze a plan $a; \pi$ partly by structural induction, as it is partly analyzed in terms of a and π.

represented by the number 0 as restriction parameter, yielding the first term of the right-hand side of (PRDL4): $[a|_0][\pi|_n]\phi^{12}$. The second term is a conjunction of $[apply(\rho, c; \pi)|_{n-1}]\phi$ over all applicable rules ρ. The restriction parameter is $n-1$ as we have "used" one of our n permitted rule applications. The first three axioms represent basic properties of restricted plans. (PRDL1) can be used to eliminate the second term on the right-hand side of axiom (PRDL4), if the left-hand side is $[c; \pi|_0]\phi$. (PRDL2) can be used to eliminate the first term on the right-hand side of (PRDL4), if c is an abstract plan. As abstract plans can only be transformed through rule application, there will be no resulting states if the restriction parameter of the abstract plan is 0, i.e., if no rule applications are allowed. (PRDL3) states that if ϕ is to hold after execution of the empty plan, it should hold "now". It can be used to derive properties of an atomic plan c, by using axiom (PRDL4) with the plan $c; \epsilon$.

Example 2. Let $\mathcal{A}$ be an agent with one PR rule, i.e., Rule $= \{a; b \leadsto c\}$ and let $\mathcal{T}$ be such that $[a|_0]\phi$, $[b|_0]\phi$ and $[c|_0]\phi$. We now want to prove that $\forall n : [a; b|_n]\phi$. We have $[a; b|_0]\phi$ by using that this is equivalent to $[a|_0][b|_0]\phi$ by proposition 3 (section 4.1). The latter formula can be derived by applying (GEN) to $[b|_0]\phi$. We prove $\forall n \in \mathbb{N} : ([a; b|_n]\phi \vdash_{\mathsf{Rule}} [a; b|_{n+1}]\phi)$ by taking an arbitrary n and proving that $[a; b|_n]\phi \vdash_{\mathsf{Rule}} [a; b|_{n+1}]\phi$. Using (PRDL4) and (PRDL3), we have the following equivalences. In order to apply (PRDL4) to the conjunct $[c|_{n-1}]\phi$, n has to be greater than 0. This is however not a problem, as the result was proven separately for $n = 0$.

$$
\begin{aligned}
[a; b|_n]\phi &\leftrightarrow [a|_0][b|_n]\phi &&\wedge [c|_{n-1}]\phi \\
&\leftrightarrow [a|_0][b|_0][\epsilon|_n]\phi \wedge [c|_0][\epsilon|_{n-1}]\phi \\
&\leftrightarrow [a|_0][b|_0]\phi &&\wedge [c|_0]\phi
\end{aligned}
$$

Similarly, we have the following equivalences for $[a; b|_{n+1}]\phi$, yielding the desired result.

$$
\begin{aligned}
[a; b|_{n+1}]\phi &\leftrightarrow [a|_0][b|_{n+1}]\phi &&\wedge [c|_n]\phi \\
&\leftrightarrow [a|_0][b|_0][\epsilon|_{n+1}]\phi \wedge [c|_0][\epsilon|_n]\phi \\
&\leftrightarrow [a|_0][b|_0]\phi &&\wedge [c|_0]\phi
\end{aligned}
$$

4.1   Soundness and Completeness

The axiom system of definition 17 is sound.

Theorem 1. *(soundness)* Let $\phi \in \mathcal{L}_{\mathsf{PRDL}}$. Let Rule $\subseteq \mathcal{R}$ be an arbitrary finite set of PR rules. Then the axiom system $\mathsf{AS}_{\mathsf{Rule}}$ is sound, i.e.:

$$\vdash_{\mathsf{Rule}} \phi \implies \models_{\mathsf{Rule}} \phi.$$

Proof. We prove soundness of the PRDL axioms of the system $\mathsf{AS}_{\mathsf{Rule}}$.
(PRDL1) The proof is through observing that $\mathcal{O}_r(\pi|_{-1})(\sigma) = \emptyset$ by definition 15.

---

[12] In our explanation, we consider the case where c is a basic action, but the axiom holds also for abstract plans.

(PRDL2) The proof is analogous to the proof of axiom (PRDL1), with p for π and 0 for -1 and using definition 6 to derive that $\mathcal{O}_r^{\mathcal{A}}(p\!\restriction_0)(\sigma) = \emptyset$.

(PRDL3) The proof is through observing that $\kappa(\mathcal{C}_r(\epsilon\!\restriction_n, \sigma)) = \{\sigma\}$ by definition 14.

(PRDL4) Let $\pi \in \Pi$ be an arbitrary plan and $\phi \in \mathcal{L}_{\mathsf{PRDL}}$ be an arbitrary PRDL formula.

To prove: $\forall \mathcal{T}, \sigma : \sigma \models_{\langle \mathsf{Rule}, \mathcal{T} \rangle} [c; \pi\!\restriction_n]\phi \leftrightarrow [c\!\restriction_0][\pi\!\restriction_n]\phi \wedge \bigwedge_\rho [apply(\rho, c; \pi)\!\restriction_{n-1}]\phi$, i.e.:

$$\forall \mathcal{T}, \sigma : \sigma \models_{\langle \mathsf{Rule}, \mathcal{T} \rangle} [c; \pi\!\restriction_n]\phi \Leftrightarrow \forall \mathcal{T}, \sigma : \sigma \models_{\langle \mathsf{Rule}, \mathcal{T} \rangle} [c\!\restriction_0][\pi\!\restriction_n]\phi \text{ and}$$

$$\forall \mathcal{T}, \sigma : \sigma \models_{\langle \mathsf{Rule}, \mathcal{T} \rangle} \bigwedge_\rho [apply(\rho, c; \pi)\!\restriction_{n-1}]\phi.$$

Let $\sigma \in \Sigma$ be an arbitrary belief base and let $\mathcal{T}$ be an arbitrary belief update function. Assume $c \in \mathsf{BasicAction}$ and furthermore assume that $\langle c; \pi, \sigma \rangle \rightarrow_{execute} \langle \pi, \sigma_1 \rangle$ is a transition in $\mathsf{Trans}_{\mathcal{A}}$, i.e., $\kappa(\mathcal{C}_r^{\mathcal{A}}(c\!\restriction_0, \sigma)) = \{\sigma_1\}$ by definition 14. Let ρ range over $applicable(\mathsf{Rule}, c; \pi)$. Now, observe the following by definition 14:

$$\kappa(\mathcal{C}_r^{\mathcal{A}}(c; \pi\!\restriction_n, \sigma)) = \kappa(\mathcal{C}_r^{\mathcal{A}}(\pi\!\restriction_n, \sigma_1)) \cup \bigcup_\rho \kappa(\mathcal{C}_r^{\mathcal{A}}(apply(\rho, c; \pi)\!\restriction_{n-1}, \sigma)). \quad (1)$$

If $c \in \mathsf{AbstractPlan}$ or if a transition of the form $\langle c; \pi, \sigma \rangle \rightarrow_{execute} \langle \pi, \sigma_1 \rangle$ is not derivable, the first term of the right-hand side of (1) is empty.

$(\Rightarrow)$ Assume $\sigma \models_{\mathsf{Rule}} [c; \pi\!\restriction_n]\phi$, i.e., by definition 16 $\forall \sigma' \in \mathcal{O}_r^{\mathcal{A}}(c; \pi\!\restriction_n, \sigma) : \sigma' \models_{\mathsf{Rule}} \phi$, i.e., by definition 15:

$$\forall \sigma' \in \kappa(\mathcal{C}_r^{\mathcal{A}}(c; \pi\!\restriction_n, \sigma)) : \sigma' \models_{\mathsf{Rule}} \phi. \quad (2)$$

To prove: (A) $\sigma \models_{\mathsf{Rule}} [c\!\restriction_0][\pi\!\restriction_n]\phi$ and (B) $\sigma \models_{\mathsf{Rule}} \bigwedge_\rho [apply(\rho, c; \pi)\!\restriction_{n-1}]\phi$.

(A) If $c \in \mathsf{AbstractPlan}$ or if a transition of the form $\langle c; \pi, \sigma \rangle \rightarrow_{execute} \langle \pi, \sigma_1 \rangle$ is not derivable, the desired result follows immediately from axiom (PRDL2) or an analogous proposition for non executable basic actions. If $c \in \mathsf{BasicAction}$, we have the following from definitions 16 and 15.

$$\begin{aligned} \sigma \models_{\mathsf{Rule}} [c\!\restriction_0][\pi\!\restriction_n]\phi &\Leftrightarrow \forall \sigma' \in \mathcal{O}_r^{\mathcal{A}}(c\!\restriction_0, \sigma) : \sigma' \models_{\mathsf{Rule}} [\pi\!\restriction_n]\phi \\ &\Leftrightarrow \forall \sigma' \in \mathcal{O}_r^{\mathcal{A}}(c\!\restriction_0, \sigma) : \forall \sigma'' \in \mathcal{O}_r^{\mathcal{A}}(\pi\!\restriction_n, \sigma') : \sigma'' \models_{\mathsf{Rule}} \phi \\ &\Leftrightarrow \forall \sigma' \in \kappa(\mathcal{C}_r^{\mathcal{A}}(c\!\restriction_0, \sigma)) : \forall \sigma'' \in \kappa(\mathcal{C}_r^{\mathcal{A}}(\pi\!\restriction_n, \sigma')) : \sigma'' \models_{\mathsf{Rule}} \phi \\ &\Leftrightarrow \forall \sigma'' \in \kappa(\mathcal{C}_r^{\mathcal{A}}(\pi\!\restriction_n, \sigma_1)) : \sigma'' \models_{\mathsf{Rule}} \phi \end{aligned}$$
$$(3)$$

From 1, we have that $\kappa(\mathcal{C}_r^{\mathcal{A}}(\pi\!\restriction_n, \sigma_1)) \subseteq \kappa(\mathcal{C}_r^{\mathcal{A}}(c; \pi\!\restriction_n, \sigma))$. From this and assumption (2), we can now conclude the desired result (3).

(B) Let $c \in (\mathsf{BasicAction} \cup \mathsf{AbstractPlan})$ and let $\rho \in applicable(\mathsf{Rule}, c; \pi)$. Then we want to prove $\sigma \models_{\mathsf{Rule}} [apply(\rho, c; \pi)\!\restriction_{n-1}]\phi$. From definitions 16 and 15, we have the following.

$$\begin{aligned} \sigma \models_{\mathsf{Rule}} [apply(\rho, c; \pi)\!\restriction_{n-1}]\phi &\Leftrightarrow \forall \sigma' \in \mathcal{O}_r^{\mathcal{A}}(apply(\rho, c; \pi)\!\restriction_{n-1}, \sigma) : \sigma' \models_{\mathsf{Rule}} \phi \\ &\Leftrightarrow \forall \sigma' \in \kappa(\mathcal{C}_r^{\mathcal{A}}(apply(\rho, c; \pi)\!\restriction_{n-1}, \sigma)) : \sigma' \models_{\mathsf{Rule}} \phi \end{aligned}$$
$$(4)$$

From 1, we have that $\kappa(\mathcal{C}_r^{\mathcal{A}}(apply(\rho, c; \pi) \restriction_{n-1}, \sigma)) \subseteq \kappa(\mathcal{C}_r^{\mathcal{A}}(c; \pi \restriction_n, \sigma))$. From this and assumption (2), we can now conclude the desired result (4).

($\Leftarrow$) Assume $\sigma \models_{\mathsf{Rule}} [c\restriction_0][\pi\restriction_n]\phi$ and $\sigma \models_{\mathsf{Rule}} \bigwedge_\rho [apply(\rho, c; \pi)\restriction_{n-1}]\phi$, i.e., $\forall \sigma' \in \kappa(\mathcal{C}_r^{\mathcal{A}}(\pi\restriction_n, \sigma_1)) : \sigma' \models_{\mathsf{Rule}} \phi$ (3) and $\forall \sigma' \in \kappa(\mathcal{C}_r^{\mathcal{A}}(apply(\rho, c; \pi)\restriction_{n-1}, \sigma)) : \sigma' \models_{\mathsf{Rule}} \phi$ (4).

To prove: $\sigma \models_{\mathsf{Rule}} [c; \pi \restriction_n]\phi$, i.e., $\forall \sigma' \in \kappa(\mathcal{C}_r^{\mathcal{A}}(c; \pi \restriction_n, \sigma)) : \sigma' \models_{\mathsf{Rule}} \phi$ (2). If $c \in \mathsf{AbstractPlan}$ or if a transition of the form $\langle c; \pi, \sigma \rangle \rightarrow_{execute} \langle \pi, \sigma_1 \rangle$ is not derivable, we have that $\kappa(\mathcal{C}_r^{\mathcal{A}}(c; \pi \restriction_n, \sigma)) = \bigcup_\rho \kappa(\mathcal{C}_r^{\mathcal{A}}(apply(\rho, c; \pi)\restriction_{n-1}, \sigma))$ (1). From this and the assumption, we have the desired result.

If $c \in \mathsf{BasicAction}$ and a transition of the form $\langle c; \pi, \sigma \rangle \rightarrow_{execute} \langle \pi, \sigma_1 \rangle$ is derivable, we have (1). From this and the assumption, we again have the desired result.

In order to prove completeness of the axiom system, we first prove proposition 2, which says that any formula from $\mathcal{L}_{\mathsf{PRDL}}$ can be rewritten into an equivalent formula where all restriction parameters are 0. This proposition is proven by induction on the size of formulas. The size of a formula is defined by means of the function $size : \mathcal{L}_{\mathsf{PRDL}} \to \mathbb{N}^3$. This function takes a formula from $\mathcal{L}_{\mathsf{PRDL}}$ and yields a triple $\langle x, y, z \rangle$, where x roughly corresponds to the sum of the restriction parameters occurring in the formula, y roughly corresponds to the sum of the length of plans in the formula and z is the length of the formula.

Definition 18. *(size)* Let the following be a lexicographic ordering on tuples $\langle x, y, z \rangle \in \mathbb{N}^3$:

$$\langle x_1, y_1, z_1 \rangle < \langle x_2, y_2, z_2 \rangle \text{ iff } x_1 < x_2 \text{ or}$$
$$(x_1 = x_2 \text{ and } y_1 < y_2) \text{ or } (x_1 = x_2 \text{ and } y_1 = y_2 \text{ and } z_1 < z_2).$$

Let max be a function yielding the maximum of two tuples from $\mathbb{N}^3$ and let f and s respectively be functions yielding the first and second element of a tuple. Let l be a function yielding the number of symbols of a syntactic entity and let $q \in \mathcal{L}$. The function $size : \mathcal{L}_{\mathsf{PRDL}} \to \mathbb{N}^3$ is then as defined below.

$$
\begin{aligned}
size(q) &= \langle 0, 0, l(q) \rangle \\
size([\pi\restriction_n]\phi) &= \begin{cases} \langle n + f(size(\phi)), l(\pi) + s(size(\phi)), l([\pi\restriction_n]\phi) \rangle & \text{if } n > 0 \\ \langle f(size(\phi)), s(size(\phi)), l([\pi\restriction_n]\phi) \rangle & \text{otherwise} \end{cases} \\
size(\neg\phi) &= \langle f(size(\phi)), s(size(\phi)), l(\neg\phi) \rangle \\
size(\phi \wedge \phi') &= \langle f(max(size(\phi), size(\phi'))), s(max(size(\phi), size(\phi'))), l(\phi \wedge \phi') \rangle
\end{aligned}
$$

In the proof of proposition 2, we use the following lemma. The first clause specifies that the right-hand side of axiom (PRDL4) is smaller than the left-hand side. This axiom will usually be used by applying it from left to right to prove a formula such as $[\pi\restriction_n]\phi$. Intuitively, the fact that the formula will get "smaller" as specified through the function $size$, suggests convergence of the deduction process.

Lemma 1. Let $\phi \in \mathcal{L}_{\mathsf{PRDL}}$, let $c \in (\mathsf{BasicAction} \cup \mathsf{AbstractPlan})$, let ρ range over $applicable(\mathsf{Rule}, c; \pi)$ and let $n > 0$. The following then holds:

1. $size([c\lceil_0][\pi\lceil_n]\phi \wedge \bigwedge_\rho[apply(\rho, c; \pi)\lceil_{n-1}]\phi) < size([c; \pi\lceil_n]\phi)$,
2. $size(\phi) < size(\phi \wedge \phi')$ and $size(\phi') < size(\phi \wedge \phi')$.

Proof. The proof is simply by applying definition 18.

Proposition 2. Any formula $\phi \in \mathcal{L}_{\mathsf{PRDL}}$ can be rewritten into an equivalent formula ϕ_{PDL} where all restriction parameters are 0, i.e.:

$$\forall \phi \in \mathcal{L}_{\mathsf{PRDL}} : \exists \phi_{\mathsf{PDL}} \in \mathcal{L}_{\mathsf{PRDL}} : size(\phi_{\mathsf{PDL}}) = \langle 0, 0, l(\phi_{\mathsf{PDL}})\rangle \text{ and } \vdash_{\mathsf{Rule}} \phi \leftrightarrow \phi_{\mathsf{PDL}}.$$

Proof. The fact that a formula ϕ has the property that it can be rewritten as specified in the proposition, will be denoted by $\mathsf{PDL}(\phi)$ for reasons that will become clear in the sequel. The proof is by induction on $size(\phi)$.

- $\phi \equiv q$
  $size(q) = \langle 0, 0, l(q)\rangle$ and let $q_{\mathsf{PDL}} = q$, then $\mathsf{PDL}(q)$.
- $\phi \equiv [\pi\lceil_n]\phi'$
  If $n = -1$, we have that $[\pi\lceil_n]\phi'$ is equivalent with $\top$ (PRDL1). As $\mathsf{PDL}(\top)$, we also have $\mathsf{PDL}([\pi\lceil_n]\phi')$ in this case.

  Let $n = 0$. We then have that $size([\pi\lceil_n]\phi') = \langle f(size(\phi')), s(size(\phi')), l([\pi\lceil_n]\phi')\rangle$ is greater than $size(\phi') = \langle f(size(\phi')), s(size(\phi')), l(\phi')\rangle$. By induction, we then have $\mathsf{PDL}(\phi')$, i.e., ϕ' can be rewritten into an equivalent formula ϕ'_{PDL}, such that $size(\phi'_{\mathsf{PDL}}) = \langle 0, 0, l(\phi'_{\mathsf{PDL}})\rangle$. As $size([\pi\lceil_n]\phi'_{\mathsf{PDL}}) = \langle 0, 0, l([\pi\lceil_n]\phi'_{\mathsf{PDL}})\rangle$, we have $\mathsf{PDL}([\pi\lceil_n]\phi'_{\mathsf{PDL}})$ and therefore $\mathsf{PDL}([\pi\lceil_n]\phi')$.

  Let $n > 0$. Let $\pi \equiv \epsilon$. By lemma 1, we have $size(\phi') < size([\epsilon\lceil_n]\phi')$. Therefore, by induction, $\mathsf{PDL}(\phi')$. As $[\epsilon\lceil_n]\phi'$ is equivalent with ϕ' by axiom (PRDL3), we also have $\mathsf{PDL}([\epsilon\lceil_n]\phi')$. Now let $\pi \equiv c; \pi'$ and let $L = [c; \pi'\lceil_n]\phi'$ and $R = [c\lceil_0][\pi'\lceil_n]\phi' \wedge \bigwedge_\rho[apply(\rho, c; \pi')\lceil_{n-1}]\phi'$. By lemma 1, we have that $size(R) < size(L)$. Therefore, by induction, we have $\mathsf{PDL}(R)$. As R and L are equivalent by axiom (PRDL4), we also have $\mathsf{PDL}(L)$, yielding the desired result.
- $\phi \equiv \neg\phi'$
  We have that $size(\neg\phi') = \langle f(size(\phi')), s(size(\phi')), l(\neg\phi')\rangle$, which is greater than $size(\phi')$. By induction, we thus have $\mathsf{PDL}(\phi')$ and $size(\phi'_{\mathsf{PDL}}) = \langle 0, 0, l(\phi'_{\mathsf{PDL}})\rangle$. Then, $size(\neg\phi'_{\mathsf{PDL}}) = \langle 0, 0, l(\neg\phi'_{\mathsf{PDL}})\rangle$ and thus $\mathsf{PDL}(\neg\phi'_{\mathsf{PDL}})$ and therefore $\mathsf{PDL}(\neg\phi')$.
- $\phi \equiv \phi' \wedge \phi''$
  By lemma 1, we have $size(\phi') < size(\phi' \wedge \phi'')$ and $size(\phi'') < size(\phi' \wedge \phi'')$. Therefore, by induction, $\mathsf{PDL}(\phi')$ and $\mathsf{PDL}(\phi'')$ and therefore $size(\phi'_{\mathsf{PDL}}) = \langle 0, 0, l(\phi'_{\mathsf{PDL}})\rangle$ and $size(\phi''_{\mathsf{PDL}}) = \langle 0, 0, l(\phi''_{\mathsf{PDL}})\rangle$. Then, $size(\phi'_{\mathsf{PDL}} \wedge \phi''_{\mathsf{PDL}}) = \langle 0, 0, l(\phi'_{\mathsf{PDL}} \wedge \phi''_{\mathsf{PDL}})\rangle$ and therefore $size((\phi' \wedge \phi'')_{\mathsf{PDL}}) = \langle 0, 0, l((\phi' \wedge \phi'')_{\mathsf{PDL}})\rangle$ and we can conclude $\mathsf{PDL}((\phi' \wedge \phi'')_{\mathsf{PDL}})$ and thus $\mathsf{PDL}(\phi' \wedge \phi'')$.

Although structural induction is not possible for plans in general, it *is* possible if we only consider action execution, i.e., if the restriction parameter is 0. This is specified in the following proposition, from which we can conclude that a formula ϕ with $size(\phi) = \langle 0, 0, l(\phi)\rangle$ satisfies all standard PDL properties.

Proposition 3. *(sequential composition)* Let Rule $\subseteq \mathcal{R}$ be a finite set of PR rules. The following is then derivable in the axiom system AS$_{\text{Rule}}$.

$$\vdash_{\text{Rule}} [\pi_1; \pi_2 \lceil_0] \phi \leftrightarrow [\pi_1 \lceil_0][\pi_2 \lceil_0] \phi$$

Proof. The proof is through repeated application of axiom (PRDL4), first from left to right and then from right to left (also using axiom (PRDL1) to eliminate the rule application part of the axiom).

Theorem 2. *(completeness)* Let $\phi \in \mathcal{L}_{\text{PRDL}}$ and let Rule $\subseteq \mathcal{R}$ be a finite set of PR rules. Then the axiom system AS$_{\text{Rule}}$ is complete, i.e.:

$$\models_{\text{Rule}} \phi \Rightarrow \vdash_{\text{Rule}} \phi.$$

Proof. Let $\phi \in \mathcal{L}_{\text{PRDL}}$. By proposition 2 we have that a formula ϕ_{PDL} exists such that $\vdash_{\text{Rule}} \phi \leftrightarrow \phi_{\text{PDL}}$ and $size(\phi_{\text{PDL}}) = \langle 0, 0, l(\phi_{\text{PDL}}) \rangle$ and therefore by soundness of AS$_{\text{Rule}}$ also $\models_{\text{Rule}} \phi \leftrightarrow \phi_{\text{PDL}}$. Let ϕ_{PDL} be a formula with these properties.

$$
\begin{array}{ll}
\models_{\text{Rule}} \phi \Leftrightarrow \models_{\text{Rule}} \phi_{\text{PDL}} & (\models_{\text{Rule}} \phi \leftrightarrow \phi_{\text{PDL}}) \\
\Rightarrow \vdash_{\text{Rule}} \phi_{\text{PDL}} & (\text{completeness of PDL}) \\
\Leftrightarrow \vdash_{\text{Rule}} \phi & (\vdash_{\text{Rule}} \phi \leftrightarrow \phi_{\text{PDL}})
\end{array}
$$

The second step in this proof needs some justification. The general idea is, that all PDL axioms and rules are applicable to a formula ϕ_{PDL} and moreover, these axioms and rules are contained in our axiom system AS$_{\text{Rule}}$. As PDL is complete, we have $\models_{\text{Rule}} \phi_{\text{PDL}} \Rightarrow \vdash_{\text{Rule}} \phi_{\text{PDL}}$. There are however some subtleties to be considered, as our action language is not exactly the same as the action language of PDL, nor is it a subset (at first sight).

In particular, the action language of PDL does not contain abstract plans or the empty action ϵ. These are axiomatized in the system AS$_{\text{Rule}}$ and the question is, how these axioms relate to the axiom system for PDL. It turns out, that the semantics of $p\lceil_0$ and $\epsilon\lceil_0$ (or $\epsilon\lceil_n$, for that matter) correspond respectively to the special PDL actions `fail` (no resulting states if executed) and `skip` (the identity relation). These actions are respectively defined as $\mathbf{0}$? and $\mathbf{1}$?. Filling in these actions in the axiom for test ($[\psi?]\phi \leftrightarrow (\psi \to \phi)$), we get the following, corresponding exactly with the axioms (PRDL2) and (PRDL3).

$$
\begin{array}{llll}
[\mathbf{0}?]\phi \leftrightarrow (\mathbf{0} \to \phi) & \Leftrightarrow & [\mathbf{0}?]\phi & \Leftrightarrow [\mathbf{fail}]\phi \\
[\mathbf{1}?]\phi \leftrightarrow (\mathbf{1} \to \phi) & \Leftrightarrow & [\mathbf{1}?]\phi \leftrightarrow \phi & \Leftrightarrow [\mathbf{skip}]\phi \leftrightarrow \phi
\end{array}
$$

Our axiom system is complete for formulas ϕ_{PDL}, because it contains the PDL axioms and rules that are applicable to these formulas, that is, the axiom for sequential composition, the axioms for `fail` and `skip` as stated above, the axiom for distribution of box over implication and the rules (MP) and (GEN). The axiom for sequential composition is not explicitly contained in AS$_{\text{Rule}}$, but is derivable for formulas ϕ_{PDL} by proposition 3. Axiom (PRDL3), i.e., the more general version of $[\epsilon\lceil_0]\phi \leftrightarrow \phi$, is needed in the proof of proposition 2, which is used elsewhere in this completeness proof.

5   Conclusion and Future Research

In this paper, we presented a dynamic logic for reasoning about 3APL agents, tailored to handle the plan revision aspect of the language. As we argued, 3APL plans cannot be analyzed by structural induction. Instead, we proposed a logic of restricted plans, which should be used to prove properties of 3APL plans by doing induction on the restriction parameter.

Being able to do structural induction is usually considered an essential property of programs in order to reason about them. As 3APL plans lack this property, it is not at all obvious that it should be possible to reason about them, especially using a clean logic with sound and complete axiomatization. The fact that we succeeded in providing such a logic, thus at least demonstrates this possibility.

We did some preliminary experiments in actually using the logic to prove properties of certain 3APL agents. More research is however needed to establish the practical usefulness of the logic to prove properties of 3APL agents and the possibility to do for example automated theorem proving. In this light, incorporation of interaction with an environment in the semantics is also an important issue for future research.

References

1. Wooldridge, M.: Agent-based software engineering. IEEE Proceedings Software Engineering **144** (1997) 26–37
2. Rash, J., Rouff, C., Truszkowski, W., Gordon, D., Hinchey, M., eds.: Formal Approaches to Agent-Based Systems (Proceedings of FAABS'01). Volume 1871 of LNAI., Berlin, Springer (2001)
3. Hinchey, M., Rash, J., Truszkowski, W., Rouff, C., Gordon-Spears, D., eds.: Formal Approaches to Agent-Based Systems (Proceedings of FAABS'02). Volume 2699 of LNAI., Berlin, Springer (2003)
4. Hindriks, K.V., de Boer, F.S., van der Hoek, W., Meyer, J.J.Ch.: Agent programming in 3APL. Int. J. of Autonomous Agents and Multi-Agent Systems **2** (1999) 357–401
5. van Riemsdijk, M.B., van der Hoek, W., Meyer, J.J.Ch.: Agent programming in Dribble: from beliefs to goals using plans. In: Proceedings of the Second International Joint Conference on Autonomous Agents and Multiagent Systems (AAMAS'03), Melbourne (2003) 393–400
6. Dastani, M., van Riemsdijk, M.B., Dignum, F., Meyer, J.J.Ch.: A programming language for cognitive agents: goal directed 3APL. In: Programming multiagent systems, First International Workshop (ProMAS'03). Volume 3067 of LNAI. Springer, Berlin (2004) 111–130
7. Bratman, M.E.: Intention, plans, and practical reason. Harvard University Press, Massachusetts (1987)
8. Cohen, P.R., Levesque, H.J.: Intention is choice with commitment. Artificial Intelligence **42** (1990) 213–261

9. Rao, A.S., Georgeff, M.P.: Modeling rational agents within a BDI-architecture. In Allen, J., Fikes, R., Sandewall, E., eds.: Proceedings of the Second International Conference on Principles of Knowledge Representation and Reasoning (KR'91), Morgan Kaufmann (1991) 473–484

10. van der Hoek, W., van Linder, B., Meyer, J.J.Ch.: An integrated modal approach to rational agents. In Wooldridge, M., Rao, A.S., eds.: Foundations of Rational Agency. Applied Logic Series 14. Kluwer, Dordrecht (1998) 133–168

11. Rao, A.S.: AgentSpeak(L): BDI Agents Speak Out in a Logical Computable Language. In van der Velde, W., Perram, J., eds.: Agents Breaking Away (LNAI 1038), Springer-Verlag (1996) 42–55

12. Shoham, Y.: Agent-oriented programming. Artificial Intelligence **60** (1993) 51–92

13. Giacomo, G.d., Lespérance, Y., Levesque, H.: *ConGolog*, a Concurrent Programming Language Based on the Situation Calculus. Artificial Intelligence **121** (2000) 109–169

14. Evertsz, R., Fletcher, M., Jones, R., Jarvis, J., Brusey, J., Dance, S.: Implementing Industrial Multi-Agent Systems Using JACK™. In: Proceedings of the first international workshop on programming multiagent systems (ProMAS'03). Volume 3067 of LNAI. Springer, Berlin (2004) 18–49

15. Bordini, R.H., Fisher, M., Pardavila, C., Wooldridge, M.: Model checking AgentSpeak. In: Proceedings of the Second International Joint Conference on Autonomous Agents and Multiagent Systems (AAMAS'03), Melbourne (2003) 409–416

16. Hindriks, K.V., de Boer, F.S., van der Hoek, W., Meyer, J.J.Ch.: A programming logic for part of the agent language 3APL. In: Proceedings of the First Goddard Workshop on Formal Approaches to Agent-Based Systems (FAABS'00). (2000)

17. de Bakker, J.: Mathematical Theory of Program Correctness. Series in Computer Science. Prentice-Hall International, London (1980)

18. van Riemsdijk, M.B., Meyer, J.J.Ch., de Boer, F.S.: Semantics of plan revision in intelligent agents. In Rattray, C., Maharaj, S., Shankland, C., eds.: Proceedings of the 10th International Conference on Algebraic Methodology And Software Technology (AMAST04). Volume 3116 of LNCS, Springer-Verlag (2004) 426–442

19. van Riemsdijk, M.B., Meyer, J.J.Ch., de Boer, F.S.: Semantics of plan revision in intelligent agents. Technical report, Utrecht University, Institute of Information and Computing Sciences (2003) UU-CS-2004-002.

20. Hayashi, H., Cho, K., Ohsuga, A.: A new HTN planning framework for agents in dynamic environments. In: Proceedings of the Fourth International Workshop on Computational Logic in Multi-Agent Systems (CLIMA-IV). (2003) 108–133

21. Plotkin, G.D.: A Structural Approach to Operational Semantics. Technical Report DAIMI FN-19, University of Aarhus (1981)

22. Harel, D.: First-Order Dynamic Logic. Lectures Notes in Computer Science 68. Springer, Berlin (1979)

23. Harel, D., Kozen, D., Tiuryn, J.: Dynamic Logic. The MIT Press, Cambridge, Massachusetts and London, England (2000)

24. van Emde Boas, P.: The connection between modal logic and algorithmic logics. In: Mathematical foundations of computer science 1978. Volume 64 of LNCS. Springer, Berlin (1978) 1–15

Contextual Taxonomies

Davide Grossi, Frank Dignum, and John-Jules Ch. Meyer

Utrecht University,
The Netherlands
{davide, dignum, jj}@cs.uu.nl

Abstract. We provide a formal characterization of a notion of contextual taxonomy, that is to say, a taxonomy holding only with respect to a specific context. To this aim, a new proposal for dealing with "contexts as abstract mathematical entities" is set forth, which is geared toward solving some problems arising in the area of normative system specifications for modeling multi-agent systems. Contexts are interpreted as sets of description logic models for different languages, and a number of operations on contexts are defined. Using this framework, a simple scenario taken from the legal domain is modeled, and a formal account of the so called open-texture of legal terms is provided characterizing the notions of "core" and "penumbra" of the meaning of a concept.

1 Introduction

The motivation of this work lies in problems stemming from the domain of normative system specifications for modeling multi-agent systems ([1, 2]). In [3, 4, 5] contexts have been advocated to play a central role in the specification of complex normative systems. The notion of context has obtained attention in AI researches since the seminal work [6], and much work has been carried out with regard to the logical analysis of this notion (see [7, 8] for an overview). With this work, we intend to pursue this research line providing a logical framework for dealing with a conception of context specifically derived from the aforementioned application domain. We nevertheless deem that the formal analysis we are going to present may give valuable insights for understanding contexts in general, also outside our specific domain of interest.

In general, the purpose of the present work is to propose a framework for grounding a new formal semantics of expressions such as: "*A* counts as *B* ([9]) in institution *c*", or "*B* supervenes *A* in institution *c*" ([10]), or "*A* conventionally generates *B* in institution *c*" ([11]), or "*A* translates (means) *B* in institution *c*" ([5]). These expressions, known in legal theory as *constitutive rules*, will be interpreted essentially as contextualized subsumption relations establishing taxonomies which hold only with respect to a specific (institutional) context. We came to a notion of *contextual taxonomy* through the analysis of some well known problems of underspecification, or more technically open-texture ([12]), typical of legal terminologies. These vagueness-related issues constitute, more concretely,

J. Leite and P. Torroni (Eds.): CLIMA V, LNAI 3487, pp. 33–51, 2005.
© Springer-Verlag Berlin Heidelberg 2005

the direct target of the work. We quote here an excerpt from [13] neatly exposing this type of problems.

> [Suppose a] legal rule forbids you to take a vehicle into the public park. Plainly this forbids an automobile, but what about bicycles, roller skates, toy automobiles? What about airplanes? Are these, as we say, to be called "vehicles" for the purpose of the rule or not? If we are to communicate with each other at all, and if, as in the most elementary form of law, we are to express our intentions that a certain type of behavior be regulated by rules, then the general words we use like "vehicle" in the case I consider must have some standard instance in which no doubts are felt about its application. There must be a *core* of settled meaning, but there will be, as well, a *penumbra* of debatable cases in which words are neither obviously applicable nor obviously ruled out. [...] We may call the problems which arise outside the hard core of standard instances or settled meaning "problems of the penumbra"; they are always with us whether in relation to such trivial things as the regulation of the use of the public park or in relation to the multidimensional generalities of a constitution.

Given a general (regional) rule not allowing vehicles within public parks, there might be a municipality allowing bicycles in its parks, and instead another one not allowing them in. What counts as a vehicle according to the first municipality, and what counts as a vehicle according to the second one then? This type of problems has been extensively approached especially from the perspective of the formalization of defeasible reasoning: the regional rule "all vehicles are banned from public parks" is defeated by the regulation of the first municipality stating that "all vehicles that are bicycles are allowed in the park" and establishing thus an *exception* to the general directive. The formalization of norms via non-monotonic techniques (see [14] for an overview) emphasizes the existence of exceptions to norms while understanding abstract terms in the standard way (all instances of bicycles are always vehicles). It has also been proposed to view the inclusion rules themselves as defaults: "normally, if something is a bicycle, then it is a vehicle" (for example [15,5]). We deem these approaches, despite being effective in capturing the reasoning patterns involved in these scenarios, to be not adequate for analyzing problems related with the *meaning* of the terms that trigger those reasoning patterns. Those reasoning patterns are defeasible because the meaning of the terms involved is not definite, it is vague, it is -and this is the thesis we hold here- context dependent[1]. We propose therefore to analyze these *"problems of the penumbra"* in terms of the notion of context: according to (in the context of) the public parks regulation of the first municipality bicycles are not vehicles, according to (in the context of) the public parks regulation of the second one bicycles are vehicles. This reading will be interpreted as follows: "the subsumption of the concept `bicycle` under the concept `vehicle` holds in the context of the first municipality, but not in the context of the second one".

---

[1] The issue of the relationship between contextuality and defeasibility has been raised also in [7].

A defeasible reasoning analysis leads to a quite different reading, which flattens the meaning of concepts and handles its variations by means of the notion of exception: "every exceptional instance of `bicycle` is not an instance of `vehicle`". Bringing contexts into play will instead allow for a neat characterization of the notions of "core" and "penumbra" of the meaning of a concept, a characterization which is not obtainable via the use of a notion of exception.

The remainder of this paper is structured in accordance with the following outline. In Section 2 we will introduce the notion of *contextual taxonomy* making use of a concrete scenario; in Section 3 we will provide a formal framework based on a very simple type of description logic which accounts for this concept; in Section 4 we will provide a formalization of the scenario introduced, and we will formally characterize the notions of conceptual "core" and "penumbra"; in Section 5 we will discuss relations with other work; finally, in Section 6, some conclusive remarks are made.

2   Contextualizing Taxonomies

Let us now depict a simple scenario in order to state in clear terms the example used in the introduction.

Example 1. (**The public park scenario**) In the regulation governing access to public parks in region R it is stated that: "vehicles are not allowed within public parks". In this regulation no mention is made of (possible) subconcepts of the concept vehicle, e.g., cars, bicycles, which may help in identifying an instance of vehicle. In municipal regulations subordinated to this regional one, specific subconcepts are instead handled. In municipality M1, the following rule holds: "bicycles are allowed to access public parks". In M2 instead, it holds that: "bicycles are not allowed to access public parks". In both M1 and M2 it holds that: "cars are not allowed in public parks".

In this scenario the concept of `vehicle` is clearly open-textured. Instances of `car` (w.r.t. the taxonomies presupposed by M1 and M2) are "core" instances of `vehicle`, while instances of `bicycle` lay in the "penumbra" of `vehicle`. We will constantly refer back to this example in the remaining of the work. In fact, our first aim will be to provide a formal framework able to account for scenarios formally analogous to the aforementioned one[2].

Since the statement about the need for addressing "contexts as abstract mathematical entities" in [6], many formalizations of the notion have been proposed (see [7] or [8] for an overview). Our proposal pursues the line of developing a semantic approach to the notion of context according to what was originally presented in [16]. In that work contexts are formalized as sets of first order logic models. They are then connected via a relation called *compatibility relation*,

---

[2] Note that this scenario hides a typical form of contextual reasoning called "categorization" ([8]), or "perspective" ([7]).

which requires the sets of models constituting the different contexts to satisfy sets of domain specific inter-contextual inference rules (*bridge rules*). This theory has been variously used in work on specification of agent architectures ([17, 18]) where the stress lies in how contexts influence each other at a proof-theoretical level rather than at a semantical one (what can can be inferred in this context, given that something holds in some other context?). We follow the basic intuition of understanding contexts as sets of models. Nevertheless, since we are mainly interested in taxonomies, much simpler models will be used here[3]. Moreover, we will partly depart from the proposal in [16] trying to characterize also a set of operations meaningfully definable on contexts. In fact, what we are interested in is also an articulate characterization of the interplay between contexts: how can contexts be joined, abstracted, etc. Instead of focusing on bridge rules, which have to be introduced outside and separately from the contexts, we will define some operations on contexts such that all possible compatibility relations will be generated by the semantics of the contexts alone. This will provide intrinsic boundaries within which other bridge rules may later be defined.

To summarize, we will expose an approach to contexts which is driven by intuitions stemming from the analysis of normative terminologies, and which is based on description logic semantics.

3   A Formal Framework

The main requirements of the formal framework that we will develop are the following ones.

1. It should enable the possibility of expressing lexical differences. A much ac-knowledged characteristic of contextual reasoning is, indeed, that contexts should be specified on different languages ([19, 20, 21, 22]). The context of the national regulation about access to public parks should obviously be specified on a vocabulary that radically differs from the vocabulary used to specify the context of regulations about, for instance, immigration law: public park regulations do not talk about immigrants. Moreover, in Exam-ple 1, we observed that more concrete contexts make actually use of richer vocabularies: talking about vehicles comes down to talk about cars, bicycles, etc. In a nutshell, different contexts mean different ontologies and therefore different languages.
2. It should provide a formal semantics (as general as possible) for contextual-ized subsumption expressions, that is to say, for contextual taxonomies.
3. It should enable the possibility of describing operations between contexts.

Following these essential guidelines, a language and a semantics are introduced in what follows. The language will make use of part of description logic syntax, as regards the concept constructs, and will make use of a set of operators aimed at capturing the interplay of contexts. In particular, we will introduce:

---

[3] Basically models for description logic languages without roles. See Section 3.

- A *contextual conjunction* operator. Intuitively, it will yield a composition of contexts: the contexts "dinosaurs" and "contemporary reptiles" can be intersected on a language talking about crocodiles generating a common less general context like "crocodiles".
- A *contextual disjunction* operator. Intuitively, it will yield a union of contexts: the contexts "viruses" and "bacterias" can be unified on a language talking about microorganisms generating a more general context like "viral or bacterial microorganisms".
- A *contextual negation* operator. Intuitively, it will yield the context obtained via subtraction of the context negated: the negation of the context "viruses" on the language talking about microorganisms generates a context like "non viral microorganisms".
- A *contextual abstraction* operator. Intuitively, it will yield the context consisting of some information extracted from the context to which the abstraction is applied: the context "crocodiles", for instance, can be obtained via abstraction of the context "reptiles" on the language talking only about crocodiles. In other words, the operator prunes the information contained in the context "reptiles" keeping only what is expressible in the language which talks about crocodiles and abstracting from the rest.

Finally, also *maximum* and *minimum* contexts will be introduced: these will represent the most general, and respectively the less general, contexts on a language. As it appears from this list of examples, operators will need to be indexed with the language where the operation they denote takes place. The point is that contexts always belong to a language, and so do operations on them[4].

These intuitions about the semantics of context operators will be clarified and made more rigorous in Section 3.2 where the semantics of the framework will be presented, and in Section 4.1 where an example will be formalized.

3.1   Language

The language we are interested in defining is nothing but a formal metalanguage for talking about sets of subsumption relations, i.e., what in description logic are called terminological boxes (TBoxes). In fact, we consider only TBoxes specified on very simple languages containing just atomic concepts and boolean operators[5]. We decided to keep the syntax of these languages poor mainly for two reasons: firstly, because the use of boolean concept descriptions alone is enough

---

[4] Note that indexes might be avoided considering operators interpreted on operations taking place on one selected language, like the largest common language of the languages of the two contexts. However, this would result in a lack of expressivity that we prefer to avoid for the moment.

[5] In fact, we are going to extend the language of propositional logic. Nevertheless, the semantics we are going to use in Section 3.2 is not the semantics of propositional logic, and it is instead of a description logic kind. For this reason we deem instructive to refer to these simple languages also as description logic languages of the type $\mathcal{ALC}$ ([23]) but with an empty set of roles.

to model the scenario depicted in Example 1; secondly, because this is still a preliminary proposal with which we aim to show how contextual reasoning and reasoning about vague notions are amenable to being handled on the basis of computationally appealing logics. On this basis it will be natural, in future, to consider also richer languages.

The alphabet of the language $\mathcal{L}^{CT}$ (*language for contextual taxonomies*) contains therefore the alphabets of a family of languages $\{\mathcal{L}_i\}_{0 \leq i \leq n}$. This family is built on the alphabet of a given "global" language $\mathcal{L}$ which contains all the terms occurring in the elements of the family. Moreover, we take $\{\mathcal{L}_i\}_{0 \leq i \leq n}$ to be such that, for each non-empty subset of terms of the language $\mathcal{L}$, there exist a $\mathcal{L}_i$ which is built on that set and belongs to the family. Each $\mathcal{L}_i$ contains a non-empty finite set $\mathbf{A}_i$ of atomic concepts (A), the zeroary operators $\bot$ (bottom concept) and $\top$ (top concept), the unary operator $\neg$, and the binary operators $\sqcap$ and $\sqcup$[6].

Besides, the alphabet of $\mathcal{L}^{CT}$ contains a finite set of context identifiers $\mathbf{c}$, two families of zeroary operators $\{\bot_i\}_{0 \leq i \leq n}$ (minimum contexts) and $\{\top_i\}_{0 \leq i \leq n}$ (maximum contexts), two families of unary operators $\{abs_i\}_{0 \leq i \leq n}$ (context abstraction operators) and $\{\neg_i\}_{0 \leq i \leq n}$ (context negation operators), two families of binary operators $\{\lambda_i\}_{0 \leq i \leq n}$ (context conjunction operators) and $\{\curlyvee_i\}_{0 \leq i \leq n}$ (context disjunction operators), one context relation symbol $\preccurlyeq$ (context c_1 "is at most as general as" context c_2) and a contextual subsumption relation symbol " $. : . \sqsubseteq .$" (within context c, concept A_1 is a subconcept of concept A_2), finally, the sentential connectives $\sim$ (negation) and $\wedge$ (conjunction)[7]. Thus, the set $\varXi$ of context constructs (ξ) is defined through the following BNF:

$$\xi ::= c \mid \bot_i \mid \top_i \mid \neg_i \xi \mid abs_i \xi \mid \xi_1 \lambda_i \xi_2 \mid \xi_1 \curlyvee_i \xi_2.$$

Concepts and concept constructors are then defined in the usual way. The set $\varGamma$ of concept descriptions (γ) is defined through the following BNF:

$$\gamma ::= A \mid \bot \mid \top \mid \neg\gamma \mid \gamma_1 \sqcap \gamma_2 \mid \gamma_1 \sqcup \gamma_2.$$

The set $\mathcal{A}$ of assertions (α) is then defined through the following BNF:

$$\alpha ::= \xi : \gamma_1 \sqsubseteq \gamma_2 \mid \xi_1 \preccurlyeq \xi_2 \mid \sim \alpha \mid \alpha_1 \wedge \alpha_2.$$

Technically, a *contextual taxonomy* in $\mathcal{L}^{CT}$ is a set of subsumption relation expressions which are contextualized with respect to the same context, e.g.: $\{\xi : \gamma_1 \sqsubseteq \gamma_2, \xi : \gamma_2 \sqsubseteq \gamma_3\}$. This kind of sets of expressions are what we are interested in. Assertions of the form $\xi_1 \preccurlyeq \xi_2$ provide a formalization of the notion

---

[6] It is worth stressing again that, in fact, a language $\mathcal{L}_i$, as defined here, is just a sub-language of languages of the type $\mathcal{ALC}$. As we will see later in this section, to represent contextual TBoxes the subsumption symbol is replaced by a set of contextualized subsumption symbols.

[7] It might be worth remarking that language $\mathcal{L}^{CT}$ is, then, an expansion of each $\mathcal{L}_i$ language.

of *generality* often touched upon in context theory (see for example [6, 24]). In Section 4.1 the following symbol will be also used " $. : . \sqsubset .$ " (within context c, concept A_1 is a proper subconcept of concept A_2). It can be defined as follows:

$$\xi : \gamma_1 \sqsubset \gamma_2 \ =_{def} \ \xi : \gamma_1 \sqsubseteq \gamma_2 \wedge \ \sim \xi : \gamma_2 \sqsubseteq \gamma_1.$$

A last category of expressions is also of interest, namely expressions representing what a concept means in a given context: for instance, recalling Example 1, "the concept `vehicle` in context M1". These expressions, as it will be shown in Section 3.2, are particularly interesting from a semantic point of view. Let us call them *contextual concept descriptions* and let us define their set $\mathcal{D}$ through the following BNF:

$$\delta ::= \xi : \gamma.$$

As we will see in Section 3.2, contextual concept descriptions $\mathcal{D}$ play an important role in the semantics of contextual subsumption relations.

3.2   Semantics

In order to provide a semantics for $\mathcal{L}^{CT}$ languages, we will proceed as follows. First we will define a class of structures which can be used to provide a formal meaning to those languages. We will then characterize the class of operations and relations on contexts that will constitute the semantic counterpart of the operators and relation symbols introduced in Section 3.1. Definitions of the formal meaning of our expressions will then follow.

Before pursuing this line, it is necessary to recollect the basic definition of a description logic model for a language $\mathcal{L}_i$ ([23]).

Definition 1. (Models for $\mathcal{L}_i$'s)
A model m for a language $\mathcal{L}_i$ is defined as follows:

$$m = \langle \Delta_m, \mathcal{I}_m \rangle$$

where:

- Δ_m *is the (non empty) domain of the model;*
- $\mathcal{I}_m$ *is a function $\mathcal{I}_m : \mathbf{A}_i \longrightarrow \mathcal{P}(\Delta_m)$, that is, an interpretation of (atomic concepts expressions of) $\mathcal{L}_i$ on Δ_m. This interpretation is extended to complex concept constructs via the following inductive definition:*

$$\begin{aligned}
\mathcal{I}_m(\top) &= \Delta_m \\
\mathcal{I}_m(\bot) &= \emptyset \\
\mathcal{I}_m(\neg A) &= \Delta_m \setminus \mathcal{I}_m(A) \\
\mathcal{I}_m(A \sqcap B) &= \mathcal{I}_m(A) \cap \mathcal{I}_m(B) \\
\mathcal{I}_m(A \sqcup B) &= \mathcal{I}_m(A) \cup \mathcal{I}_m(B).
\end{aligned}$$

Out of technicalities, what a model m for a language $\mathcal{L}_i$ does, is to assign a denotation to each atomic concept (for instance the set of elements of Δ_m that instantiate the concept `bicycle`) and, accordingly, to each complex concept (for instance the set of elements of Δ_m that instantiate the concept `vehicle` $\sqcap \neg$ `bicycle`).

3.3   Models for $\mathcal{L}^{CT}$

We can now define a notion of *contextual taxonomy model* (ct-model) for languages $\mathcal{L}^{CT}$.

Definition 2. (ct-models)
A ct-model $\mathbb{M}$ is a structure:

$$\mathbb{M} = \langle \{\mathbf{M}_i\}_{0 \leq i \leq n}, \mathbb{I} \rangle$$

where:

- $\{\mathbf{M}_i\}_{0 \leq i \leq n}$ *is the family of the sets of models $\mathbf{M}_i$ of each language $\mathcal{L}_i$. That is, $\forall m \in \mathbf{M}_i$, m is a model for $\mathcal{L}_i$.*
- $\mathbb{I}$ *is a function $\mathbb{I} : \mathbf{c} \longrightarrow \mathcal{P}(\mathbf{M}_0) \cup \ldots \cup \mathcal{P}(\mathbf{M}_n)$. In other words, this function associates to each atomic context identifier in $\mathbf{c}$ a subset of the set of all models in some language $\mathcal{L}_i$: $\mathbb{I}(c) = M$ with $M \subseteq \mathbf{M}_i$ for some i s.t. $0 \leq i \leq n$. Function $\mathbb{I}$ can be seen as labeling sets of models on some language i via atomic context identifiers. Notice that $\mathbb{I}$ fixes, for each atomic context identifier, the language on which the context denoted by the identifier is specified. We could say that it is $\mathbb{I}$ itself which fixes a specific index for each atomic context identifier c.*
- $\forall m', m'' \in \bigcup_{0 \leq i \leq n} \mathbf{M}_i$, $\Delta_{m'} = \Delta_{m''}$. *That is, the domain of all models m is unique. We assume this constraint simply because we are interested in modeling different (taxonomical) conceptualizations of a same set of individuals.*

This can be clarified by means of a simple example. Suppose the alphabet of $\mathcal{L}^{CT}$ to be the set of atomic concepts {`allowed`, `vehicle`, `car`, `bicycle`} and the set of atomic context identifiers $\{c_{M1}, c_{M2}, c_R\}$. The number of possible languages $\mathcal{L}_i$ given the four aforementioned concepts is obviously $2^4 - 1$. A ct-model for this $\mathcal{L}^{CT}$ language would have as domain the set of the sets of all models for each of the $2^4 - 1$ $\mathcal{L}_i$ languages, and as interpretation a function $\mathbb{I}$ which assigns to each c_{M1}, c_{M2} and c_R a subset of an element of that set, i.e., a set of models for one of the $\mathcal{L}_i$ languages. We will come back to this specific language in Section 4.1, where we discuss the formalization of the public park scenario.

The key feature of this semantics is that contexts are characterized as sets of models for the same language. This perspective allows for straightforward model theoretical definitions of operations on contexts.

3.4   Operations on Contexts

Before getting to this, let us first recall a notion of *domain restriction* ($\restriction$) of a function f w.r.t. a subset C of the domain of f. Intuitively, a domain restriction of a function f is nothing but the function $C \restriction f$ having C as domain and s.t. for each element of C, f and $C \restriction f$ return the same image. The exact definition is the following one: $C \restriction f = \{\langle x, f(x) \rangle \mid x \in C\}$.

Definition 3. (Operations on contexts)
Let M' and M'' be sets of models:

$$\rceil_i M' = \{m \mid m = \langle \Delta_{m'}, \mathbf{A}_i \rceil \mathcal{I}_{m'} \rangle \ \& \ m' \in M'\} \tag{1}$$

$$M' \sqcap_i M'' = \rceil_i M' \cap \rceil_i M'' \tag{2}$$

$$M' \uplus_i M'' = \rceil_i M' \cup \rceil_i M'' \tag{3}$$

$$-_i M' = \mathbf{M}_i \setminus \rceil_i M'. \tag{4}$$

Intuitively, the operations have the following meaning: operation 1 allows for abstracting the relevant content of a context with respect to a specific language; operations 2 and 3 express basic set-theoretical composition of contexts; finally, operation 4 returns, given a context, the most general of all the remaining contexts. Let us now provide some technical observations. First of all notice that operation $\rceil_i$ yields the empty context when it is applied to a context M' the language of which is not an elementary expansion of $\mathcal{L}_i$. This is indeed very intuitive: the context obtained via abstraction of the context "dinosaurs" on the language of, say, "botanics" should be empty. Empty contexts can be also obtained through the $\sqcap_i$ operation. In that case the language is shared, but the two contexts simply do not have any interpretation in common. This happens, for example, when the members of two different football teams talk about their opponents: as a matter of fact, no interpretation of the concept **opponent** can be shared without jeopardizing the fairness of the match. The following propositions can be proved with respect to the operations on contexts.

Proposition 1. (Structure of contexts on a given language)
The structure of contexts $\langle \mathcal{P}(\mathbf{M}_i), \uplus_i, \sqcap_i, -_i, \mathbf{M}_i, \emptyset \rangle$ on a language $\mathcal{L}_i$ is a Boolean Algebra.

Proof. The proof follows straightforwardly from Definition 3. ∎

Proposition 2. (Abstraction operation on contexts)
Operation $\rceil_i$ is surjective and idempotent.

Proof. That $\rceil_i$ is surjective can be proved per absurdum. First notice that this operation is a function of the following type: $\rceil_i : \mathcal{P}(\mathbf{M}_0) \cup \ldots \cup \mathcal{P}(\mathbf{M}_n) \longrightarrow \mathcal{P}(\mathbf{M}_i)$ with $1 \leq i \leq n$. If it is not surjective then $\exists M'' \subseteq \mathbf{M}_i$ s.t. $\forall M'$ in the domain of $\rceil_i$, $\rceil_i M' \neq M''$. This means that $\forall M'$ in the domain of $\rceil_i$, $\{m \mid m = \langle \Delta_{m'}, \mathbf{A}_i \rceil \mathcal{I}_{m'} \rangle \ \& \ m' \in M'\} \neq M''$, which is impossible because we have at least that $\rceil_i M'' = M''$. The proof of the equation for idempotency $\rceil_i(\rceil_i M) = \rceil_i M$ is straightforward. ∎

These propositions clarify the type of conception of context we hold here: contexts are sets of models on different taxonomical languages; on each language the set of possible contexts is structured in a boolean algebra; the operation of abstraction allows for shifting from richer to simpler languages and it is, as we would intuitively expect, idempotent (abstracting from an abstraction yields the same first abstraction) and surjective (every context, even the empty one, can be seen as an abstraction of a different richer context, in the most trivial case, an abstraction of itself).

3.5   Formal Meaning of Ξ, $\mathcal{D}$, and $\mathcal{A}$

In Definition 2 atomic contexts are interpreted as sets of models on some language $\mathcal{L}_i$ for $0 \leq i \leq n$: $\mathbb{I}(c) = M \in \mathcal{P}(\mathbf{M}_0) \cup \ldots \cup \mathcal{P}(\mathbf{M}_n)$. The semantics of contexts constructs Ξ can be defined via inductive extension of that definition.

Definition 4. (Semantics of contexts constructs)
The semantics of context constructors is defined as follows:

$$\mathbb{I}(\perp_i) = \emptyset$$
$$\mathbb{I}(\top_i) = \mathbf{M}_i$$
$$\mathbb{I}(\xi_1 \curlywedge_i \xi_2) = \mathbb{I}(\xi_1) \sqcap_i \mathbb{I}(\xi_2)$$
$$\mathbb{I}(\xi_1 \curlyvee_i \xi_2) = \mathbb{I}(\xi_1) \sqcup_i \mathbb{I}(\xi_2)$$
$$\mathbb{I}(\neg_i \xi) = -_i \mathbb{I}(\xi)$$
$$\mathbb{I}(abs_i \xi) = \rceil_i \mathbb{I}(\xi).$$

The $\perp_i$ context is interpreted as the empty context (the same on each language); the $\top_i$ context is interpreted as the greatest, or most general, context on $\mathcal{L}_i$; the binary $\curlywedge_i$-composition of contexts is interpreted as the greatest lower bound of the restriction of the interpretations of the two contexts on $\mathcal{L}_i$; the binary $\curlyvee_i$-composition of contexts is interpreted as the lowest upper bound of the restriction of the interpretations of the two contexts on $\mathcal{L}_i$; context negation is interpreted as the complement with respect to the most general context on that language; finally, the unary abs_i operator is interpreted just as the restriction of the interpretation of its argument to language $\mathcal{L}_i$.

Semantics for the contextual concept description $\mathcal{D}$ and for the assertions $\mathcal{A}$ in $\mathcal{L}^{CT}$ is based on the function $\mathbb{I}$.

Definition 5. (Semantics of contextual concept descriptions: $\| \cdot \|_M$)
The semantics of contextual concept descriptions is defined as follows:

$$\|\xi : \gamma\|_M = \{D \mid \langle \gamma, D \rangle \in \mathcal{I}_m \ \& \ m \in \mathbb{I}(\xi)\}.$$

The meaning of a concept γ in a context ξ is the set of denotations D attributed to that concept by the models constituting that context.

It is worth noticing that if concept γ is not expressible in the language of context ξ, then $\|\xi : \gamma\|_M = \emptyset$, that is, concept γ gets no denotation at all in context ξ. This happens simply because concept γ does not belong to the domain of functions $\mathcal{I}_m$, and there therefore exists no interpretation for that concept in the models constituting ξ. This shows also how Definition 5 allows to capture the intuitive distinction between concepts which lack denotation ($\|\xi : \gamma\|_M = \emptyset$), and concepts which have a denotation which is empty ($\|\xi : \gamma\|_M = \{\emptyset\}$): a concept that lacks denotation is for example the concept **immigrant** in the context of public park access regulation; in the same context, a concept with empty denotation is for example the concept **car⊓¬car**.

In what follows we will often use the notation $\mathbb{I}(\xi : \gamma)$ instead of the heavier $\|\xi : \gamma\|_\mathbb{M}$.

Definition 6. (Semantics of assertions: $\models$)
The semantics of assertions is defined as follows:

$$\mathbb{M} \models \xi : \gamma_1 \sqsubseteq \gamma_2 \;\; \textit{iff} \;\; \mathbb{I}(\xi : \gamma_1), \mathbb{I}(\xi : \gamma_2) \neq \emptyset \text{ and } \forall m \in \mathbb{I}(\xi), \; \mathcal{I}_m(\gamma_1) \subseteq \mathcal{I}_m(\gamma_2)$$

$$\mathbb{M} \models \xi_1 \preccurlyeq \xi_2 \;\; \textit{iff} \;\; \mathbb{I}(\xi_1) \subseteq \mathbb{I}(\xi_2)$$

$$\mathbb{M} \models \sim \alpha \;\; \textit{iff} \;\; \text{not } \mathbb{M} \models \alpha$$

$$\mathbb{M} \models \alpha_1 \wedge \alpha_2 \;\; \textit{iff} \;\; \mathbb{M} \models \alpha_1 \text{ and } \mathbb{M} \models \alpha_2.$$

A contextual subsumption relation between γ_1 and γ_2 holds iff $\mathbb{I}(\xi)$ makes the meaning of γ_1 and γ_2 not empty and all models m of $\mathbb{I}(\xi)$ interpret γ_1 as a subconcept of γ_2. Note that this is precisely the clause for the validity of a subsumption relation in standard description logics, but together with the fact that the concepts involved are actually meaningful in that context. The $\preccurlyeq$ relation between context constructs is interpreted as a standard subset relation: $\xi_1 \preccurlyeq \xi_2$ means that context denoted by ξ_1 contains at most all the models that ξ_2 contains, that is to say, ξ_1 is *at most as general as* ξ_2. Note that this relation, being interpreted on the $\subseteq$ relation, is reflexive, antisymmetric and transitive. In [5] a generality ordering with similar properties was imposed on the set of context identifiers, and analogous properties for a similar relation have been singled out also in [11]. The interesting thing is that such an ordering is here emergent from the semantics. Note also that this relation holds only between contexts specified on the same language. Clauses for boolean connectives are the obvious ones.

The satisfaction clause of contextual subsumption relations deserves some more remarks. We observed that the satisfaction is conditioned to the meaningfulness of the terms involved with respect to the context. This condition is necessary because our contexts have different languages. Another way to deal with this would be to impose syntactic constraints on the formation of $\xi : \gamma_1 \sqsubseteq \gamma_2$ expressions, in order to distinguish the well-formed ones from the ill-formed ones. However, this would determine a dependence of the definition of well-formed expressions of $\mathcal{L}^{CT}$ on the models $\mathbb{M}$ of the language itself. Alternatively, the satisfaction relation itself might be restricted to consider only those subsumptions between concepts that, given the interpretation of the context, are interpreted as meaningful. Nevertheless, this option too determines a weird dependence, namely between the definition of the satisfaction relation and the models: the scope of the satisfaction would vary according to the models[8]. We chose for yet another solution, exploiting the possibility that our semantics enables of distinguishing meaningless concepts from concepts with empty extension (see Definition 5). By means of this feature it is possible to constrain the satisfaction of $\xi : \gamma_1 \sqsubseteq \gamma_2$ formulas, in such a way that, for them to be true, concepts γ_1 and γ_2 have

---

[8] Though in a completely different formal setting, this way is pursued in [21, 22].

to be meaningful in context ξ. Intuitively, we interpret contextual subsumption relations as inherently presupposing the meaningfulness of their terms.

4   Contextual Taxonomies, "Core" and "Penumbra"

4.1   Formalizing an Example

We are now able to provide a formalization of the simple scenario introduced in Example 1 based on the formal semantic machinery just exposed.

Example 2. (**The public park scenario formalized**) To formalize the public park scenario within our setting a language $\mathcal{L}^{CT}$ is needed, which contains the following atomic concepts: allowed, vehicle, car, bicycle. Three atomic contexts are at issue here: the context of the main regulation R, let us call it c_R; the contexts of the municipal regulations M1 and M2, let us call them c_{M1} and c_{M2} respectively. These contexts should be interpreted on two relevant languages. A language $\mathcal{L}_0$ for c_R s.t. $\mathbf{A}_0 = \{\text{allowed}, \text{vehicle}\}$; and a language $\mathcal{L}_1$ for c_{M1} and c_{M2} s.t. $\mathbf{A}_1 = \mathbf{A}_0 \cup \{\text{car}, \text{bicycle}\}$ (an abstract language concerning only vehicles and objects allowed to get into the park, and a more concrete one concerning, besides this, also cars and bicycles). A formalization of the scenario by means of $\mathcal{L}^{CT}$ formulas is the following one:

$$abs_0(c_{M1}) \curlyvee_0 abs_0(c_{M2}) \preccurlyeq c_R \tag{5}$$

$$c_R : \text{vehicle} \sqsubseteq \neg\text{allowed} \tag{6}$$

$$c_{M1} \curlyvee_1 c_{M2} : \text{car} \sqsubset \text{vehicle} \tag{7}$$

$$c_{M1} : \text{bicycle} \sqsubset \text{vehicle} \tag{8}$$

$$c_{M2} : \text{bicycle} \sqsubseteq \neg\text{vehicle} \tag{9}$$

$$c_{M1} \curlyvee_1 c_{M2} : \text{bicycle} \sqsubset \text{vehicle} \sqcup \text{allowed}. \tag{10}$$

Formula (5) plays a key role, stating that the two contexts c_{M1}, c_{M2} are concrete variants of context c_R. It tells this by saying that the context obtained by joining the two concrete contexts on language $\mathcal{L}_0$ (the language of c_R) is at most as general as context c_R. As we will see in discussing the logical consequences of this set of formulas, formula (5) makes c_{M1}, c_{M2} inherit what holds in c_R. Formula (6) formalizes the abstract rule to the effect that vehicles belong to the category of objects not allowed to access public parks. Formula (7) states that in both contexts cars count as vehicles. Formulas (8) and (9) state the two different conceptualizations of the concept of bicycle holding in the two concrete contexts at issue. These formulas show where the two contextual taxonomies diverge. Formula (10), finally, tells that bicycles either are vehicles or should be allowed in the park. Indeed, it might be seen as a clause avoiding "cheating" classifications such as: "bicycles counts as cars".

It is worth listing and discussing some straightforward logical consequences of the formalization.

$$(5), (6) \vDash c_{M1} : \texttt{vehicle} \sqsubseteq \neg\texttt{allowed}$$
$$(5), (6), (7) \vDash c_{M1} : \texttt{car} \sqsubset \neg\texttt{allowed}$$
$$(5), (6), (8) \vDash c_{M1} : \texttt{bicycle} \sqsubset \neg\texttt{allowed}$$

$$(5), (6) \vDash c_{M2} : \texttt{vehicle} \sqsubseteq \neg\texttt{allowed}$$
$$(5), (6), (7) \vDash c_{M2} : \texttt{car} \sqsubset \neg\texttt{allowed}$$
$$(5), (6), (9), (10) \vDash c_{M2} : \texttt{bicycle} \sqsubseteq \texttt{allowed}$$

These are indeed the formulas that we would intuitively expect to hold in our scenario. The list displays two sets of formulas grouped on the basis of the context to which they pertain. They formalize the two contextual taxonomies at hands in our scenario. Let us have a closer look. The first consequence of each group results from the generality relation expressed in (5), by means of which the content of (6) is shown to hold also in the two concrete contexts: in simple words, contexts c_{M1} and c_{M2} inherit the general rule stating that vehicles are not allowed to access public parks. Via this inherited rule, and via (7), it is shown that, in all concrete contexts, cars are also not allowed to access the park. As to cars then, all contexts agree. Where differences arise is in relation with how the concept of bicycle is handled. In context c_{M1}, since bicycles count as vehicles (8), bicycles are also not allowed. In context c_{M2}, instead, bicycles constitute an allowed class because they are not considered to be vehicles (9) and there is no bicycle which does not count as a vehicle and which does not belong to that class of allowed objects (10). In the following section we show in some more detail how a model for the formalization just exposed looks like.

4.2   A Model of the Formalization

Formulas (5)-(10) constrain ct-models in the following way:

$$\rceil_0 \mathbb{I}(c_{M1}) \cup \rceil_0 \mathbb{I}(c_{M2}) \subseteq \mathbb{I}(c_R)$$
$$\forall m \in \mathbb{I}(c_R), \ \mathcal{I}_m(\texttt{vehicle}) \subseteq \Delta_1 \setminus \mathcal{I}_m(\texttt{allowed})$$
$$\mathbb{I}(c_R : \texttt{vehicle}), \mathbb{I}(c_R : \texttt{allowed}) \neq \emptyset$$
$$\forall m \in \mathbb{I}(c_{M1}) \cup \mathbb{I}(c_{M2}), \ \mathcal{I}_m(\texttt{car}) \subset \mathcal{I}_m(\texttt{vehicle})$$
$$\mathbb{I}(c_{M1} \curlyvee_1 c_{M2} : \texttt{car}), \mathbb{I}(c_{M1} \curlyvee_1 c_{M2} : \texttt{vehicle}) \neq \emptyset$$
$$\forall m \in \mathbb{I}(c_{M1}), \ \mathcal{I}_m(\texttt{bicycle}) \subset \mathcal{I}_m(\texttt{vehicle})$$
$$\mathbb{I}(c_{M1} : \texttt{bicycle}), \mathbb{I}(c_{M1} : \texttt{vehicle}) \neq \emptyset$$
$$\forall m \in \mathbb{I}(c_{M2}), \ \mathcal{I}_m(\texttt{bicycle}) \subseteq \Delta_1 \setminus \mathcal{I}_m(\texttt{vehicle})$$
$$\mathbb{I}(c_{M2} : \texttt{bicycle}), \mathbb{I}(c_{M2} : \texttt{vehicle}) \neq \emptyset$$
$$\forall m \in \mathbb{I}(c_{M1}) \cup \mathbb{I}(c_{M2}), \ \mathcal{I}_m(\texttt{bicycle}) \subseteq \mathcal{I}_m(\texttt{vehicle}) \cup \mathcal{I}_m(\texttt{allowed})$$
$$\mathbb{I}(c_{M1} \curlyvee_1 c_{M2} : \texttt{bicycle}), \mathbb{I}(c_{M1} \curlyvee_1 c_{M2} : \texttt{allowed}) \neq \emptyset.$$

Besides the ones above, a model of the scenario can be thought of requiring two more constraints. Although the formal language as it is defined in 3.1 cannot express them, we show that they can be perfectly captured at a semantic level and therefore that new appropriate symbols might be accordingly added to the syntax.

- $\mathbb{I}(c_{M1} : \mathtt{bicycle}) = \mathbb{I}(c_{M2} : \mathtt{bicycle}) = \{\{a, b\}\}^9$ (c_{M1} and c_{M2} agree on the interpretation of $\mathtt{bicycle}$, say, the set of objects $\{a, b\}$);
- $\mathbb{I}(c_{M1} : \mathtt{car}) = \mathbb{I}(c_{M2} : \mathtt{car}) = \{\{c\}\}^{10}$ (c_{M1} and c_{M2} agree on the interpretation of $\mathtt{car}$, say, the singleton $\{c\}$).

Let us stipulate that the models m that will constitute our interpretation of contexts identifiers consist of a domain $\Delta_m = \{a, b, c, d\}$ and let us call the sets of all models for $\mathcal{L}_0$ and $\mathcal{L}_1$ on this domain respectively $\mathbf{M}_0$ and $\mathbf{M}_1$. Given the restrictions, a ct-model of the scenario can consist then of the domain $\mathbf{M}_0 \cup \mathbf{M}_1$ and of the function $\mathbb{I}$ s.t.:

- $\mathbb{I}(c_{M1}) = \{m_1, m_2\} \subseteq \mathbf{M}_1$ s.t. $\mathcal{I}_{m_1}(\mathtt{allowed}) = \{d\}$, $\mathcal{I}_{m_1}(\mathtt{vehicle}) = \{a, b, c\}$, $\mathcal{I}_{m_1}(\mathtt{bicycle}) = \{a, b\}$, $\mathcal{I}_{m_1}(\mathtt{car}) = \{c\}$ and $\mathcal{I}_{m_2}(\mathtt{allowed}) = \emptyset$, $\mathcal{I}_{m_2}(\mathtt{vehicle}) = \{a, b, c, d\}$, $\mathcal{I}_{m_2}(\mathtt{bicycle}) = \{a, b\}$, $\mathcal{I}_{m_2}(\mathtt{car}) = \{c\}$.
  In c_{M1} concepts $\mathtt{allowed}$ and $\mathtt{vehicle}$ are interpreted in two possible ways; notice that model m_2 makes no object allowed to access the park;
- $\mathbb{I}(c_{M2}) = \{m_3\} \subseteq \mathbf{M}_1$ s.t. $\mathcal{I}_{m_3}(\mathtt{allowed}) = \{a, b\}$, $\mathcal{I}_{m_3}(\mathtt{vehicle}) = \{c, d\}$, $\mathcal{I}_{m_3}(\mathtt{car}) = \{c\}$, $\mathcal{I}_{m_3}(\mathtt{bicycle}) = \{a, b\}$.
  In c_{M2}, which is constituted by a single model, the concept $\mathtt{vehicle}$ strictly contains $\mathtt{car}$, and excludes $\mathtt{bicycle}$. Notice also that $\mathtt{bicycle}$ coincide with $\mathtt{allowed}$.
- $\mathbb{I}(c_R) = \{m \mid \mathcal{I}_m(\mathtt{vehicle}) \subseteq \Delta_1 \setminus \mathcal{I}_m(\mathtt{allowed})\}$.
  In c_R, concepts $\mathtt{vehicle}$ and $\mathtt{allowed}$ get all possible interpretations that keep them disjoint.

We can now get to the main formal characterizations at which we have been aiming in this work.

4.3   Representing Conceptual "Core" and "Penumbra"

What is the part of a denotation of a concept which remains context independent? What is the part which varies instead? "Core" and "penumbral" meaning are formalized in the two following definitions.

Definition 7. $(\mathfrak{Core}(\gamma, \xi_1, \xi_2))$
The "core meaning" of concept γ w.r.t. contexts ξ_1, ξ_2 on language $\mathcal{L}_i$ is defined as:

$$\mathfrak{Core}(\gamma, \xi_1, \xi_2) =_{def} \bigcap (\mathbb{I}(\xi_1 : \gamma) \cup \mathbb{I}(\xi_2 : \gamma)).$$

---

[9] It might be worth recalling that the meaning of a concept in a context is a set of denotations, which we assume to be here, for the sake of simplicity (and in accordance with our intuitions about the scenario), a singleton.

[10] See previous footnote.

Intuitively, the definition takes just the conjunction of the union of the interpretations of γ in the two contexts. Referring back to Example 2, we have that $\mathfrak{Core}(\texttt{vehicle}, c_{M1}, c_{M2}) = \{c\}$, that is, the core of the concept $\texttt{vehicle}$ coincides, in those contexts, with the denotation of the concept $\texttt{car}$. The notion of "penumbra" is now easily definable.

Definition 8. ($\mathfrak{Penumbra}(\gamma, \xi_1, \xi_2)$)
The "penumbra" of concept γ w.r.t. contexts ξ_1, ξ_2 on language $\mathcal{L}_i$ is defined as:

$$\mathfrak{Penumbra}(\gamma, \xi_1, \xi_2) =_{def} \bigcup ((\mathbb{I}(\xi_1 : \gamma) \cup \mathbb{I}(\xi_2 : \gamma)) \setminus \mathfrak{Core}(\gamma, \xi_1, \xi_2)).$$

A "penumbral meaning" is then nothing else but the set of individuals on which the contextual interpretation of the concept varies. Referring back again to Example 2: $\mathfrak{Penumbra}(\texttt{vehicle}, c_{M1}, c_{M2}) = \{a, b, d\}$, that is to say, the penumbra of the concept $\texttt{vehicle}$ ranges over those individuals that are not instances of the core of $\texttt{vehicle}$, i.e., the concept $\texttt{car}$. Notice that the definitions are straightforwardly generalizable to formulations with more than two contexts.

5   Related Work

We already showed, in Section 2, how the present proposal relates to work developed in the area of logical modeling of the notion of context. Contexts have been used here in order to propose a different approach to vagueness (especially as it appears in the normative domain). In this section some words will be spent in order to put the present proposal in perspective with respect to some more standard approaches to vagueness, namely approaches making use of fuzzy sets ([25]) or rough sets ([26]).

The most characteristic feature of our approach, with respect to fuzzy or rough set theories, consists in considering vagueness as an inherently semantic phenomenon. Vagueness arises from the referring of a language to structures modeling reality, and not from those structures themselves. That is to say, the truth denotation of a predicate is, in our approach, always definite and crisp, even if multiple. Consequently, no degree of membership is considered, as in fuzzy logic, and no representation of sets in terms of approximations is used, as in rough set theory. Let us use a simple example in order to make this distinction evident. Consider the vague monadic predicate or, to use a description logic terminology, the concept $\texttt{tall\_person}$. Fuzzy approaches would determine the denotation of this predicate as a fuzzy set, i.e., as the set of elements with membership degree contained in the interval $]0, 1]$. Standard rough set theory approaches would characterize this denotation not directly, but on the basis of a given partition of the universe (the set of all individuals) and a lower and upper approximation provided in terms of that partition. For instance, a trivial partition might be the one consisting of the following three concepts: $\texttt{tall>2m}$, $\texttt{1.60m} \leq \texttt{tall} \leq \texttt{2m}$, $\texttt{tall<1.60m}$. Concept $\texttt{tall\_person}$ would then be approximated by means of the lower approximation $\texttt{tall>2m}$ (the elements of a set that are definitely also members of the to be approximated set), and the upper approximation 1.60m≤tall≤2m ⊔ tall>2m (the elements of a set that may be also members of the to be approximated set). In this rough set representation, set 1.60m≤tall≤2m constitutes the so called *boundary* of tall_person. Within our approach instead, the set tall_person can be represented crisply and without approximations. The key feature is that tall_person obtains multiple crisp interpretations, at least one for each context: in the context of dutch standards, concept tall_person does not subsume concept 1.60m≤tall≤2m, whereas it does in the context of pygmy standards. According to our approach, vagueness resides then in the contextual nature of interpretation rather than in the concepts themselves[11].

It is nevertheless easy to spot some similarities, in particular with respect to rough set theory. The notions of "core" and "penumbra" have much in common with the notions of, respectively, *lower approximation* and *boundary* developed in rough set theory: each of these pairs of notions denotes what is always, and respectively, in some cases, an instance of a given concept. But the characterization of the last pair is based on a partition of the universe denoting the equivalence classes imposed by a set of given known properties. The notions of "core" and "penumbra", instead, are yielded by the consideration of many contextual interpretations of the concept itself. With respect to fuzzy approaches, notice that sets 𝕮𝖔𝖗𝖊 can be viewed exactly as the sets of instances having a membership degree equal to one, while sets 𝔓𝖊𝖓𝖚𝖒𝖇𝖗𝖆 can be viewed as the sets of instances with degree of membership between zero and one. Besides, sets 𝔓𝖊𝖓𝖚𝖒𝖇𝖗𝖆 could be partitioned in sets X_n each containing instances that occur in a fixed number n of models constituting the "penumbra", thus determining a total and, notice,

---

[11] A clear position for our thesis can also be found within those analyses of vagueness, developed in the area of philosophical logic, which distinguish between *de re* and *de dicto* views of vagueness ([27]), the first holding that referents themselves are vague and therefore that vagueness constitutes something objective, whereas the second holding that it is the way referents are established that determines vagueness. Fuzzy set approaches lie within a *de re* conception of vagueness, while our approach is grounded on the alternative *de dicto* view (rough sets approaches have instead more to do with insufficient information issues). In philosophical logic, a formal theory has been developed which formalizes this *de dicto* approach to vagueness, the so called *superevaluationism* ([28]). On this view, when interpreting vague terms, we consider the many possible ways in which those terms can be interpreted:

"Whatever it is that we do to determine the 'intended' interpretation of our language determines not one interpretation but a range of interpretations. (The range depends on context [...])" ([29]).

As it is evident from Section 3.2, this intuition backs also our semantics. What our approach adds to formal accounts of *superevaluationism* such as [28, 30] consists in the explicit use of contexts as specific formal objects clustering the possible ways terms can be interpreted: contexts are precisely the range of admissible interpretations of the concepts at issue.

discrete ordering on membership: instances occurring in only one model in the "penumbra" will belong to the denotation of the concept at the minimum degree of membership, while instances occurring in the "core" at the maximum one.

Another relevant feature of our proposal, which we deem worth stressing, consists in the use of a fragment of predicate logic. This allows, first of all, the intra-contextual reasoning to be classical. Furthermore, the use of description logic, even if not yet fully elaborate in this work, allows for its well known interesting computability properties to be enabled at the intra-contextual reasoning level, thus making the framework appealing also in this respect.

6   Conclusions

Our aim was to account for a notion of contextual taxonomy, and by means of that, to rigorously characterize the notions of "core" and "penumbra" of a concept, that is to say, to define what is invariant and what is instead context dependent in the meaning of a concept. We did this contextualizing of a standard description logic notion of taxonomy by means of a formal semantics approach to contexts which provides also an account of a variety of forms of contexts interactions.

There are a number of issues which would be worth investigating in future work. First of all, it would be of definite interest to provide formal rigorous comparisons of our framework with:

- Related work in the area of context logics, like especially the *local model semantics* proposed in [16] to which we referred in Section 2.
- Related work in the area of fuzzy or rough sets treatment of conceptual ambiguities ([26, 25]), which have been informally touched upon in Section 5.
- Related work in the area of logic for normative systems specification, and in particular [31] where a modal logic semantics is used to account for expressions such as "A counts as B in context (institution) s". To this aim, we plan to apply the notion of contextual subsumption relation to modal logic semantics in order to contextualize accessibility relations. For example, it would be interesting to investigate applications to dynamic logic semantics in order to provide a formal account of the contextual meaning of actions: raising a hand in the context of a bidding means something different than raising a hand in the context of a scientific workshop. Some results on this issue have been presented in [32].

Secondly, we would like to enrich the expressivity of our framework considering richer description logic languages admitting also attributes (or roles) constructs. This would allow for a formal characterization of "*contextual terminologies*" in general, enabling the full expressive power description logics are able to provide. A first step along this line has been proposed in [33].

Acknowledgments

We would like to thank the anonymous reviewers of CLIMA V. Thanks to their comments, this work has been considerably improved.

References

1. Dignum, F.: Agents, markets, institutions, and protocols. In: Agent Mediated Electronic Commerce, The European AgentLink Perspective., Springer-Verlag (2001) 98–114
2. Vázquez-Salceda, J., Dignum, F.: Modelling electronic organizations. In V. Marik, J.M., Pechoucek, M., eds.: Proceedings CEEMAS'03. LNAI 2691, Berlin, Springer-Verlag (2003) 584–593
3. Dignum, F.: Abstract norms and electronic institutions. In: Proceedings of the International Workshop on Regulated Agent-Based Social Systems: Theories and Applications (RASTA '02), Bologna. (2002) 93–104
4. Vázquez-Salceda, J.: The role of Norms and Electronic Institutions in Multi-Agent Systems. Birkhuser Verlag AG (2004)
5. Grossi, D., Dignum, F.: From abstract to concrete norms in agent institutions. In Hinchey, M.G., Rash, J.L., Truszkowski, W.F., et al., eds.: Formal Approaches to Agent-Based Systems: Third International Workshop, FAABS 2004. Lecture Notes in Computer Science, Springer-Verlag (2004) 12–29
6. McCarthy, J.: Notes on formalizing contexts. In Kehler, T., Rosenschein, S., eds.: Proceedings of the Fifth National Conference on Artificial Intelligence, Los Altos, California, Morgan Kaufmann (1986) 555–560
7. Akman, V., Surav., M.: Steps toward formalizing context. AI Magazine **17** (1996) 55–72
8. Benerecetti, M., Bouquet, P., Ghidini, C.: Contextual reasoning distilled. Journal of Experimental and Theoretical Artificial Intelligence (JETAI) **12** (2000) 279–305
9. Searle, J.: The Construction of Social Reality. Free Press (1995)
10. Hage, J., Verheij, B.: The law as a dynamic interconnected system of states of affairs. IJHCS: International Journal of Human-Computer Studies **51** (1999) 1043–1077
11. Goldman, A.I.: A Theory of Human Action. Princeton University Press, Princeton (1976)
12. Hart, H.L.A.: The Concept of Law. Clarendon Press, Oxford (1961)
13. Hart, H.L.A.: Positivism and the separation of law and morality. Harvard Law Review **71** (1958) 593–629
14. Prakken, H.: Logical Tools for Modelling Legal Arguments. Kluwer (1997)
15. Royakkers, L., Dignum, F.: Defeasible reasoning with legal rules. In Nute, D., ed.: Defeasible Deontic Logic, Dordrecht, Kluwer (1997) 263–286
16. Ghidini, C., Giunchiglia, F.: Local models semantics, or contextual reasoning = locality + compatibility. Artificial Intelligence **127** (2001) 221–259
17. Parsons, S., Jennings, N.J., Sabater, J., Sierra, C.: Agent specification using multi-context systems. Foundations and Applications of Multi-Agent Systems (2002)
18. Casali, A., Godo, L., Sierra, C.: Graded bdi models for agent architectures. In this volume.
19. Giunchiglia, F., Serafini, L.: Multilanguage hierarchical logics or: How we can do without modal logics. Artificial Intelligence **65** (1994) 29–70

20. Giunchiglia, F.: Contextual reasoning. Epistemologia, special issue on I Linguaggi e le Macchine **16** (1993) 345–364
21. Buvač, S.V., Mason, I.A.: Propositional logic of context. Proceedings AAAI'93 (1993) 412–419
22. Buvač, S., Buvač, S.V., Mason, I.A.: The semantics of propositional contexts. Proceedings of the eight ISMIS. LNAI-869 (1994) 468–477
23. Baader, F., Calvanese, D., McGuinness, D., Nardi, D., Patel-Schneider, P.: The Description Logic Handbook. Cambridge University Press, Cambridge (2002)
24. McCarthy, J.: Generality in artificial intelligence. Communications of the ACM **30** (1987) 1030–1035
25. Wygralak, M.: Vaguely Defined Objects. Kluwer Academic Publishers (1996)
26. Lin, T.Y., Cercone, N.: Rough Sets and Data Mining. Analysis of Imprecise Data. Kluwer Academic Publishers (1997)
27. Varzi, A.: Vague names for sharp objects. In Obrst, L., Mani, I., eds.: Proceedings of the Workshop on Semantic Approximation, Granularity, and Vagueness, AAAI Press (2000) 73–78
28. van Fraassen, B.C.: Singular terms, truth-value gaps, and free logic. Journal of Philosophy **63** (1966) 481–495
29. Lewis, D.: Many, but almost one. In: Papers in Metaphysics and Epistemology, Cambridge University Press (1999) 164–182
30. Fine, K.: Vagueness, truth and logic. Synthese **30** (1975) 265–300
31. Jones, A.J.I., Sergot, M.: A formal characterization of institutionalised power. Journal of the IGPL **3** (1996) 429–445
32. Grossi, D., Meyer, J-J. Ch., Dignum, F.: Modal logic investigations in the semantics of counts-as. (Submitted)
33. Grossi, D., Aldewereld, H., Vázquez-Salceda, J., Dignum, F.: Ontological aspects of the implementation of norms in agent-based electronic institutions. To be presented at NorMAS (2005)

From Logic Programs Updates to Action Description Updates*

José Júlio Alferes[1], Federico Banti[1], and Antonio Brogi[2]

[1] CENTRIA, Universidade Nova de Lisboa, Portugal
{jja, banti}@di.fct.unl.pt
[2] Dipartimento di Informatica, Università di Pisa, Italy
brogi@di.unipi.it

Abstract. An important branch of investigation in the field of agents has been the definition of high level languages for representing effects of actions, the programs written in such languages being usually called action programs. Logic programming is an important area in the field of knowledge representation and some languages for specifying updates of Logic Programs had been defined. Starting from the update language Evolp, in this work we propose a new paradigm for reasoning about actions called Evolp action programs.

We provide translations of some of the most known action description languages into Evolp action programs, and underline some peculiar features of this newly defined paradigm. One such feature is that Evolp action programs can easily express changes in the rules of the domains, including rules describing changes.

1 Introduction

In the last years the concept of agent has become central in the field of Artificial Intelligence. *"An agent is just something that acts"* [26]. Given the importance of the concept, ways of representing actions and their effects on the environment have been studied. A branch of investigation in this topic has been the definition of high level languages for representing effects of actions [7, 12, 14, 15], the programs written in such languages being usually called *action programs*. Action programs specify which facts (or fluents) change in the environment after the execution of a set of actions. Several works exist on the relation between these action languages and Logic Programming (LP) (e.g. [5, 12, 21]). However, despite the fact that LP has been successfully used as a language for declaratively representing knowledge, the mentioned works basically use LP for providing an operational semantics, and implementation, for action programs. This is so because normal logic programs, and most of their extensions, have no in-built

* This work was partially supported by project FLUX (POSI/40958/SRI/2001), and by the European Commission within the 6th Framework Programme project REWERSE number 506779 (cf. http://rewerse.net).

J. Leite and P. Torroni (Eds.): CLIMA V, LNAI 3487, pp. 52–77, 2005.
© Springer-Verlag Berlin Heidelberg 2005

means for dealing with changes, something that is quite fundamental for action languages.

In recent years some effort was devoted to explore and study the problem of how to update logic programs with new rules [3, 8, 10, 19, 20, 17]. Here, knowledge is conveyed by sequences of programs, where each program in a sequence is an update to the previous ones. For determining the meaning of sequences of logic programs, rules from previous programs are assumed to hold by inertia after the updates (given by subsequent programs) unless rejected by some later rule. LP update languages [2, 4, 9, 19], besides giving meaning to sequences of logic programs, also provide in-built mechanisms for constructing such sequences. In other words, LP update languages extend LP by providing means to specify and reason about rule updates.

In [5] the authors show, by examples, a possible use the LP update language LUPS [4] for representing effects of actions providing a hint for the possibility of using LP updates languages as an action description paradigm. However, the work done does not provide a clear view on how to use LP updates for representing actions, nor does it establishes an exact relationship between this new possibility and existing action languages. Thus, the eventual advantages of the LP update languages approach to actions are still not clear.

The present work tries to clarify these points. This is done by establishing a formal relationship between one LP update language, namely the Evolp language [2], and existing action languages, and by clarifying how to use this language for representing actions in general.

Our investigation starts by, on top of Evolp, defining a new action description language, called Evolp Action Programs (EAPs), as a macro language for Evolp. Before developing a complete framework for action description based on LP updates, in this work we focus on the basic problem in the field, i.e. the prediction of the possible future states of the world given a complete knowledge of the current state and the action performed. Our purpose is to check, already at this stage, the potentiality of an action description language based on the Evolp paradigm.

We then illustrate the usage of EAPs by an example involving a variant of the classical Yale Shooting Problem. An important point to clarify is the comparison of the expressive capabilities of the newly defined language with that of the existing paradigms. We consider the action languages $\mathcal{A}$ [12], $\mathcal{B}$ [13] (which is a subset of the language proposed in [14]), and (the definite fragment of) $\mathcal{C}$ [15]. We provides simple translations of such languages into EAPs, hence proving that EAPs are *at least as expressive* as the cited action languages.

Coming to this point, the next natural question is what are the possible advantages of EAPs. The underlying idea of action frameworks is to describe dynamic environments. This is usually done by describing rules that specify, given a set of external actions, how the environment evolves. In a dynamic environment, however, not only the facts but also the "rules of the game" can change, in particular *the rules describing the changes*. The capability of describing such kind of *meta level changes* is, in our opinion, an important feature of an action description language. This capability can be seen as an instance of *elaboration tolerance* i.e. *"the ability to accept changes to a person's or a computer's representation of facts about a subject without having to start all over"* [25]. In [15] this capability is seen as a central point in the action descriptions field and the problem is addressed in the context of the $\mathcal{C}$ language. The final words of [15] are *"Finding ways to further increase the degree of elaboration tolerance of languages for describing actions is a topic of future work"*. We address this topic in the context of EAPs and show EAPs seem, in this sense, more flexible than other paradigms. Evolp provides specific commands that allow for the specification of updates to the initial program, but also provides the possibility to specify updates of these updates commands. We show, by successive elaborations of the Yale shooting problem, how to use this feature to describe updates of the problem that come along with the evolution of the environment.

The rest of the paper is structured as follows. In section 2 we review some background and notation. In section 3 we define the syntax and semantics of Evolp action programs, and we illustrate the usage of EAPs by an example involving a variant of the classical Yale Shooting Problem. In section 4 we establish the relationship between EAPs and the languages $\mathcal{A}$, $\mathcal{B}$ and $\mathcal{C}$. In section 5 we discuss the possibility of updating the EAPs, and provide an example of such feature. Finally, in section 6, we conclude and trace a route for future developments. To facilitate the reading, and given that some of the results have proofs of some length, instead of presenting proofs along with the text, we expose them all in appendix A.

2   Background and Notation

In this section we briefly recall syntax and semantics of *Dynamic Logic Programs* [1], and the syntax and semantics for Evolp [2]. We also recall some basic notions and notation for action description languages. For a more detailed background on action languages see e.g. [12].

2.1   Dynamic Logic Programs and Evolp

The main idea of logic programs updates is to update a logic program by another logic program or by a *sequence* of logic programs, also called *Dynamic Logic Programs* (DLPs). The initial program of a DLP corresponds to the initial knowledge of a given (dynamic) domain, and the subsequent ones to successive updates of the domain. To represent negative information in logic programs and their updates, following [3] we allow for default negation *not A* not only in the premises of rules but also in their heads i.e., we use generalized logic programs (GLPs) [22].

A language $\mathcal{L}$ is any set of propositional atoms. A literal in $\mathcal{L}$ is either an atom of $\mathcal{L}$ or the negation of an atom. In general, given any set of atoms $\mathcal{F}$, *we denote by $\mathcal{F}_L$ the set of literals over $\mathcal{F}$*. Given a literal F, if $F = Q$, where Q is an atom, by *not F* we denote the negative literal *not Q*. Viceversa, if $F = not\ Q$, by *not F* we denote the atom Q. A GLP defined over a propositional language $\mathcal{L}$ is a set of rules of the form $F \leftarrow Body$, where F is a literal in $\mathcal{L}$, and *Body* is a *set* of literals in $\mathcal{L}$.[1] An *interpretation* I over a language $\mathcal{L}$ is any set of literals in $\mathcal{L}$ such that, for each atom A, either $A \in I$ or *not* $A \in I$. We say a set of literals *Body* is true in an interpretation I (or that I satisfies *Body*) iff $Body \subseteq I$. In this paper we will use programs containing variables. As usual when programming within the stable models semantics, a program with variables stands for the propositional program obtained as the set of all possible ground instantiations of the rules.

Two rules τ and η are *conflicting* (denoted by $\tau \bowtie \eta$) iff the head of τ is the atom A and the head of η is *not* A, or viceversa. A Dynamic Logic Program over a language $\mathcal{L}$ is a sequence $P_1 \oplus \ldots \oplus P_m$ (also denoted $\oplus P_i^m$) where the P_is are GLPs defined over $\mathcal{L}$. The *refined stable model semantics* of such a DLP, defined in [1], assigns to each sequence $P_1 \oplus \ldots \oplus P_n$ a set of stable models (that is proven there to coincide with the stable models semantics when the sequence is formed by a single normal [11] or generalized program [22]). The rationale for the definition of a stable model M of a DLP is made in accordance with the *causal rejection principle* [10, 19]: If the body of a rule in a given update is true in M, then that rule rejects all rules in previous updates that are conflicting with it. Such rejected rules are ignored in the computation of the stable model. In the refined semantics for DLPs a rule may also reject conflicting rules that belong to the same update. Formally, the set of rejected rules of a DLP $\oplus P_i^m$ given an interpretation M is:

$$Rej^S(\oplus P_i^m, M) = \{\tau \mid \tau \in P_i : \exists \eta \in P_j \; i \leq j, \; \tau \bowtie \eta \; \wedge \; Body(\eta) \subseteq M\}$$

Moreover, an atom A is assumed false by default if there is no rule, in none of the programs in the DLP, with head A and a true body in the interpretation M. Formally:

$$Default(\oplus P_i^m, M) = \{not \; A \mid \nexists \; A \leftarrow Body \in \bigcup P_i \; \wedge \; Body \subseteq M\}$$

If $\oplus P_i^m$ is clear from the context, we omit it as first argument of the above functions.

Definition 1. *Let $\oplus P_i^m$ be a DLP over language $\mathcal{L}$ and M an interpretation. M is a refined stable model of $\oplus P_i^m$ iff*

$$M = least\left(\left(\bigcup_i P_i \setminus Rej^S(M)\right) \cup Default(M)\right)$$

where $least(P)$ denotes the least Herbrand model of the definite program [23] obtained by considering each negative literal not A in P as a new atom.

---

[1] Note that, by defining rule bodies as sets, the order and number of occurrences of literals do not matter.

Having defined the meaning of sequences of programs, we are left with the problem of how to come up with those sequences. This is the subject of LP update languages [2, 4, 9, 19]. Among the existing languages, Evolp [2] uses a particulary simple syntax, which extends the usual syntax of GLPs by introducing the special predicate $assert/1$. Given any language $\mathcal{L}$, the language $\mathcal{L}_{assert}$ is recursively defined as follows: every atom in $\mathcal{L}$ is also in $\mathcal{L}_{assert}$; for any rule τ over $\mathcal{L}_{assert}$, the atom $assert(\tau)$ is in $\mathcal{L}_{assert}$; nothing else is in $\mathcal{L}_{assert}$. An *Evolp program* over $\mathcal{L}$ is any GLP over $\mathcal{L}_{assert}$. An *Evolp sequence* is a sequence (or DLP) of Evolp programs. The rules of an Evolp program are called *Evolp rules*.

Intuitively an expression $assert(\tau)$ stands for "update the program with the rule τ". Notice the possibility in the language to nest an assert expression in another. The intuition behind the Evolp semantics is quite simple. Starting from the initial Evolp sequence $\oplus P_i^m$ we compute the set, $\mathcal{SM}(\oplus P_i^m)$, of the stable models of $\oplus P_i^m$. Then, for any element M in $\mathcal{SM}(\oplus P_i^m)$, we update the initial sequence with the program P_{m+1} consisting of the set of rules τ such that the atom $assert(\tau)$ belongs to M. In this way we obtain the sequence $\oplus P_i^m \oplus P_{m+1}$. Since $\mathcal{SM}(\oplus P_i^m)$ contains, in general, several models we may have different lines of evolution. The process continues by obtaining the various $\mathcal{SM}(\oplus P_i^{m+1})$ and, with them, various $\oplus P_i^{m+2}$. Intuitively, the program starts at step 1 already containing the sequence $\oplus P_i^m$. Then it updates itself with the rules asserted at step 1, thus obtaining step 2. Then, again, it updates itself with the rules asserted at this step, and so on. The evolution of any Evolp sequence can also be influenced by external events. An external event is itself an Evolp program. If, at a given step n, the programs receives the external update E_n, the rules in E_n are added to the last self update for the purpose of computing the stable models determining the next evolution but, in the successive step $n + 1$ they are no longer considered (that's why they are called *events*). Formally:

Definition 2. *Let n and m be natural numbers. An* evolution interpretation *of length n, of an evolving logic program $\oplus P_i^m$ is any finite sequence $\mathcal{M} = M_1, \ldots, M_n$ of interpretations over $\mathcal{L}_{assert}$. The* evolution trace *associated with $\mathcal{M}$ and $\oplus P_i^m$ is the sequence $P_1 \oplus \ldots P_m \oplus P_{m+1} \ldots \oplus P_{m+n-1}$, where, for $1 \leq i < n$*

$$P_{m+i} = \{\tau \mid assert(\tau) \in M_{m+i-1}\}$$

Definition 3 (Evolving stable models). *Let $\oplus P_i^m$ and $\oplus E_i^n$ be any Evolp sequences, and $\mathcal{M} = M_1, \ldots, M_n$ be an evolving interpretation of length n. Let $P_1 \oplus \ldots \oplus P_{m+n-1}$ be the evolution trace associated with $\mathcal{M}$ and $\oplus P_i^m$. We say that $\mathcal{M}$ is an evolving stable model of $\oplus P_i^m$ with event sequence $\oplus E_i^n$ at step n iff M_k is a refined stable model of the program $P_1 \oplus \ldots \oplus (P_k \cup E_k)$ for any k, with $m \leq k \leq m + n - 1$.*

2.2   Action Languages

The purpose of an action language is to provide ways of describing how an environment evolves given a set of external actions. A specific environment that can be modified through external actions is called an *action domain*. To any action domain we associate a pair of sets of atoms $\mathcal{F}$ and $\mathcal{A}$. We call the elements of $\mathcal{F}$ *fluent atoms* or simply *fluents*, and the elements of $\mathcal{A}$ *action atoms* or simply *actions*. Basically, the fluents are the observables in the environment and the actions are, clearly, the external actions. A *fluent literal* (resp. *action literal*) is an element of $\mathcal{F}_L$ (resp. an element of $\mathcal{A}_L$). In the following, we will use the letter Q to denote a fluent atom, the letter F to denote a fluent literal, and the letter A to denote an action atom. A *state of the world* (or simply a *state*) is any interpretation over $\mathcal{F}$. We say a fluent literal F is true at a given state s iff F belongs to s. Given a set (or, by abuse of notation, a conjunction) of fluent literals $Cond$ we say s *satisfies* $Cond$, and write $s \models Cond$, iff $Cond \subseteq s$.

Each action language provides ways to describe action domains through sets of expression called *action programs*. Usually, the semantics of an action program is defined in terms of a *transition system*, i.e. a function whose argument is any pair (s, K), where s is a state of the world and K is a subset of $\mathcal{A}$, and whose value is any set of states of the world. Intuitively, given the current state of the world, a transition system specifies which are the possible resulting states after simultaneously performing all actions in K.

Two kinds of expressions that are common within action description languages are *static* and *dynamic rules*. The *static rules* basically describe the rules of the domain, while *dynamic rules* describe effects of actions. A dynamic rule has a set of *preconditions*, namely conditions that have to be satisfied in the present state in order to have a particular effect in the future state, and *postconditions* describing such an effect.

In the following we will consider three existing action languages, namely: $\mathcal{A}$, $\mathcal{B}$ and $\mathcal{C}$. The language $\mathcal{A}$ [13] is very simple. It only allows dynamic rules of the form

$$A \textbf{ causes } F \textbf{ if } Cond$$

where $Cond$ is a conjunction of fluent literals. Such a rule intuitively means: performing the action A causes F to be true in the next state if $Cond$ is true in the current state. The language $\mathcal{B}$ [13] is an extension of $\mathcal{A}$ which also considers static rules. In $\mathcal{B}$, static rules are expressions of the form

$$F \textbf{ if } Body$$

where $Body$ is a conjunction of fluent literals. Intuitively, such a rule means: if $Body$ is true in the current state, then F is also true in the current state. A fundamental notion, in both $\mathcal{A}$ and $\mathcal{B}$, is *fluent inertia* [13]. A fluent F is inertial if its truth value is preserved from a state to another, unless it is changed by the (direct or indirect) effect of an action. Hereafter a program written in the language $\mathcal{B}$ will be called a $\mathcal{B}$ program.

The semantics of $\mathcal{B}$ is defined in terms of a transition system, as sketched above. For introducing the particular transition function that, given a state s and a set of actions K, determines the possible resulting states according to $\mathcal{B}$, we first consider the set $D(s, K)$ of fluents literals that are true as a (direct) consequence of actions. Any literal F is a direct consequence of state s and actions K if it is in the head of a dynamic rule $A \textbf{ causes } F \textbf{ if } Cond$ such that

$A \in K$ and $Cond$ is true in s. Then a state s' is a possible resulting states from s iff any fluent literal in s is an element of $D(s, K)$ or is a true literal in s (that followed by inertia) or is a consequence of a static rule:

Definition 4. *Let P be any $\mathcal{B}$ program with set of fluents $\mathcal{F}$, let $\mathcal{R}$ be the set of all static rules in P, and let s be a state and K any set of actions. Moreover, let $D(s, K)$ be the following set of literals*

$$D(s, K) = \{F : \exists A \textbf{ causes } F \textbf{ if } Cond \in P \text{ s.t. } A \in K \wedge s \models Cond\}$$

and let $\mathcal{R}^{LP}$ be the logic program:

$$\mathcal{R}^{LP} = \{F \leftarrow Body : F \textbf{ if } Body \in \mathcal{R}\}$$

A state s' is a resulting state from s given P and the set of actions K iff

$$s' = least(s \cap s' \cup D(s, K) \cup \mathcal{R}^{LP})$$

where $least(P)$ is as in Definition 1

For a detailed explanation of $\mathcal{A}$ and $\mathcal{B}$ see e.g. [13].

Static and dynamic rules are also the ingredients of the action language $\mathcal{C}$ [15, 16]. Static rules in $\mathcal{C}$ are of the form

caused J if H

while dynamic rules are of the form

caused J if H after O

where J and H are formulae such that any literal in them is a fluent literal, and O is any formula such that any literal in it is a fluent or an action literal. The formula O is the precondition of the dynamic rule and the static rule **caused J if H** is its postcondition. The semantic of $\mathcal{C}$ is based on *causal theories*[15]. Causal theories are sets of rules of the form **caused J if H**, each such rule meaning: If H is true this is an explanation for J. A basic principle of causal theories is that something is true iff it is caused by something else. Given any action program P, a state s and a set of actions K, we consider the causal theory T given by the static rules of P and the postconditions of the dynamic rules whose preconditions are true in $s \cup K$. Then s' is a possible resulting state iff it is a causal model of T.

3   Evolp Action Programs

As we have seen, Evolp and action description languages share the idea of a system that evolves. In both, the evolution is influenced by external events (respectively, updates and actions). Evolp is actually a programming language devised for representing any kind of computational problem, while action description languages are devised for the specific purpose of describing actions. A natural idea is then to develop special kind of Evolp sequences for representing actions, and then compare such kind of programs with existing action description languages. We will develop one such kind of programs, and call them *Evolp Action Programs* (EAPs).

Following the underlying notions of Evolp, we use the basic construct *assert* for defining special-purpose macros. As it happens with other action description languages, EAPs are defined over a set of fluents $\mathcal{F}$ and a set of actions $\mathcal{A}$. In EAPs, a state of the world is any interpretation over $\mathcal{F}$. To describe action domains we use an initial Evolp sequence, $I \oplus D$. The Evolp program D contains the description of the environment, while I contains some initial declarations, as it will be clarified later. As in $\mathcal{B}$ and $\mathcal{C}$, EAPs contain static and dynamic rules.

A *static rule* over $(\mathcal{F}, \mathcal{A})$ is simply an Evolp rule of the form

$$F \leftarrow Body.$$

where F is a fluent literal and $Body$ is a set of fluent literals.

A *dynamic rule* over $(\mathcal{F}, \mathcal{A})$ is a (macro) expression

$$\mathbf{effect}(\tau) \leftarrow Cond.$$

where τ is any static rule $F \leftarrow Body$ and $Cond$ is any set of fluent or action literals. The intuitive meaning of such a rule is that the static rule τ has to be considered *only* in those states whose predecessor satisfies condition $Cond$. Since some of the conditions literals in $Cond$ may be action atoms, such a rule may describe the effect of a given set of actions under some conditions. Such an expression stands for the following set of Evolp rules:

$$F \leftarrow Body,\ event(F \leftarrow Body). \qquad (1)$$
$$assert(event(F \leftarrow Body)) \leftarrow Cond. \qquad (2)$$
$$assert(not\ event(F \leftarrow Body)) \leftarrow event(\tau), not\ assert(event(F \leftarrow Body))(3)$$

where $event(F \leftarrow Body)$ is a new literal. Let us see how the above set of rules fits with its intended intuitive meaning. Rule (1) is not applicable whenever $event(F \leftarrow Body)$ is false. If at some step n, the conditions $Cond$ are satisfied, then, by rule (2), $event(F \leftarrow Body)$ becomes true at step $n + 1$. Hence, at step $n + 1$, rule (1) will play the same role as static rule $F \leftarrow Body$. If at step $n + 1$ $Cond$ is no longer satisfied, then, by rule (3) the literal $event(F \leftarrow Body)$ will become false again, and then rule (1) will be again not effective.

Besides static and dynamic rules, we still need another ingredient to complete our construction. As we have seen in the description of the $\mathcal{B}$ language, a notable concept is fluent inertia. This idea is not explicit in Evolp where *the rules* (and not the fluents) are preserved by inertia. Nevertheless, we can show how to obtain fluent inertia by using macro programming in Evolp. An *inertial declaration* over $(\mathcal{F}, \mathcal{A})$ is a (macro) expression $\mathbf{inertial}(\mathcal{K})$, where $\mathcal{K} \subseteq \mathcal{F}$. The intended intuitive meaning of such an expression is that the fluents in $\mathcal{K}$ are inertial. Before defining what this expression stands for, we state that the above mentioned program I is always of the form **initialize**$(\mathcal{F})$, where **initialize**$(\mathcal{F})$ stands for the set of rules $Q \leftarrow prev(Q)$, where Q is any fluent in $\mathcal{F}$, and $prev(Q)$ are new atoms not in $\mathcal{F} \cup \mathcal{A}$. The *inertial declaration* **inertial**$(\mathcal{K})$ stands for the set (where Q ranges over $\mathcal{K}$):

$$assert(prev(Q)) \leftarrow Q. \qquad assert(not\ prev(Q)) \leftarrow not\ Q.$$

Let us consider the behaviour of this macro. If we do not declare Q as an inertial fluent, the rule $Q \leftarrow prev(Q)$ has no effect. If we declare Q as an inertial literal, $prev(Q)$ is true in the current state iff in the previous state Q was true. Hence, in this case, Q is true in the current state *unless* there is a static or dynamic rule that rejects such assumption. Viceversa, if Q was false in the previous state, then Q is true in the current one iff it is derived by a static or dynamic rule. We are now ready to formalize the syntax of Evolp action programs.

Definition 5. *Let $\mathcal{F}$ and $\mathcal{A}$ be two disjoint sets of propositional atoms. An Evolp action program (EAP) over $(\mathcal{F},\ \mathcal{A})$ is any Evolp sequence $I \oplus D$, where $I = Initialize(\mathcal{F})$, and D is any set with static and dynamic rules, and inertial declarations over $(\mathcal{F}, \mathcal{A})$*

Given an Evolp action program $I \oplus D$, the initial state of the world s (which, as stated above, is an interpretation over $\mathcal{F}$) is passed to the program together with the set K of the actions performed at s, as part of an external event. A resulting state is the last element of any evolving stable model of $I \oplus D$ given the event $s \cup K$ restricted to the set of fluent literals. I.e:

Definition 6. *Let $I \oplus D$ be any EAP over $(\mathcal{F}, \mathcal{A})$, and s a state of the world. Then s' is a resulting state from s given $I \oplus D$ and the set of actions K iff there exists an evolving stable model M_1, M_2 of $I \oplus D$ given the external events $s \cup K, \emptyset$ such that $s' \equiv_{\mathcal{F}} M_2$ (where by $s' \equiv_{\mathcal{F}} M_2$ we simply mean $s' \cap \mathcal{F}_{Lit} = M_2 \cap \mathcal{F}_{Lit}$).*

This definition can be easily generalized to sequences of set of actions.

Definition 7. *Let $I \oplus D$ be any EAP and s a state of the world. Then s' is a resulting state from s given $I \oplus D$ and the sequence of sets of actions $K_1 \dots, K_n$ iff there exists an evolving stable model $M_1, \dots, M_{n+1}$ of $I \oplus D$ given the external events $(s \cup K_1), \dots, K_n, \emptyset$ such that $s' \equiv_{\mathcal{F}} M_{n+1}$.*

Since EAPs are based on the Evolp semantics, which in turn is an extension of the stable model semantics for normal logic programs, we can easily prove that the complexity of the computation of the two semantics is the same.

Theorem 1. *Let $I \oplus D$ be any EAP over $(\mathcal{F}, \mathcal{A})$, s a state of the world and $K \subseteq \mathcal{A}$. To find a resulting state s' from s given $I \oplus D$ and the set of actions K is an NP-complete problem.*

It is important to notice that, if the initial state s does not satisfies the static rules of the EAP, the correspondent Evolp sequence has no stable model, and hence there will be no successor state. This is, in our opinion, a good result: The initial state is just a state as any other. It would be strange if such state would not satisfy the rules of the domain. If this situation occurs, most likely either the translation of the rules, or the one of the state, presents some errors. From now onwards we will assume that the initial state satisfies the static rules of the domain.

To illustrate EAPs, we now show an example of their usage by elaborating on probably the most famous example of reasoning about actions. The presented elaboration highlights some important features of EAPs, viz. the possibility of handling non-deterministic effects of actions, non-inertial fluents, non-executable actions, and effects of actions lasting for just one state.

Example 1 (An elaboration of the Yale shooting problem). In the original Yale shooting problem [27], there is a single-shot gun which is initially unloaded, and a turkey which is initially alive. One can load the gun and shoot the turkey. If one shoots, the gun becomes unloaded and the turkey dies. We consider a slightly more complex scenario where there are several turkeys, and where the shooting action refers to a specific turkey. Each time one shoots as specific turkey, one either hits and kills the bird, or misses it. Moreover, the gun becomes unloaded and there is a bang. It is not possible to shoot with an unloaded gun. We also add the property that any turkey moves iff it is not dead.

For expressing that an action is not executable under some conditions, we make use of a well known behaviour of the stable model semantics. Suppose a given EAP contains a dynamic rules of the form **effect**$(u \leftarrow not\ u) \leftarrow Cond$, where u is a literal which does not appear elsewhere (in the following, for representing such rules, we use the notation **effect**$(\bot) \leftarrow Cond$). With such a rule, if $Cond$ is true in the current state, then there is no resulting state. This happens because, as it is well known, programs containing $u \leftarrow not\ u$ and no other rules for u, have no stable models.

To represent the problem, we consider the fluents $dead(X)$, $moving(X)$, $hit(X)$, $missed(X)$, $loaded$, $bang$, plus the auxiliary fluent u, and the actions $shoot(X)$ and $load$ (where the Xs range over the various turkeys). The fluents $dead(X)$ and $loaded$ are inertial fluents, since their truth value should remain unchanged until modified by some action effect. The fluents $missed(X)$, $hit(X)$ and $bang$ are not inertial. The problem is encoded by the EAP $I \oplus D$, where

$$I = \textbf{initialize}(dead(X), moving(X), missed(X), hit(X),\ loaded,\ bang,\ u)$$

and D is the following set of expressions

effect$(\bot) \leftarrow shoot(X),\ not\ loaded$	**inertial**$(loaded)$
$moving(X) \leftarrow not\ dead(X)$	**inertial**$(dead(X))$
effect$(dead(X) \leftarrow hit(X)) \leftarrow shoot(X)$	**effect**$(loaded) \leftarrow load$
effect$(hit(X) \leftarrow not\ missed(X)) \leftarrow shoot(X)$	**effect**$(bang) \leftarrow shoot(X)$
effect$(missed(X) \leftarrow not\ hit(X)) \leftarrow shoot(X)$	**effect**$(not\ loaded) \leftarrow shoot(X)$

Let us analyze this EAP. The first rule encodes the impossibility to execute the action $shoot(X)$ when the gun is unloaded. The static rule $moving(X) \leftarrow$

not dead(*X*) implies that, for any turkey *X*, *moving*(*X*) is true if *dead*(*X*) is false. Since this is the only rule for *moving*(*X*), it further holds that *moving*(*X*) is true iff *dead*(*X*) is false. Notice that declaring *moving*(*tk*) as inertial, would result, in our description, in the possibility of having a moving dead turkey! This is why fluents *moving*(*X*) have not been declared as inertial. In fact, suppose we insert **inertial**(*moving*(*X*)) in the EAP above. Suppose further that *moving*(*tk*) is true at state *s*, that one shoots at *tk* and kills it. Since *moving*(*tk*) is an inertial fluent, in the resulting state *dead*(*tk*) is true, but *moving*(*tk*) remains true by inertia. Also notable is how effects that last only for one state, like the noise provoked by the shoot, are easily encoded. The last three dynamic rules on the left encode a non deterministic behaviour: each shoot action can either hit and kill a turkey, or miss it.

To see how this EAP encodes the desired behaviour of this domain, consider the following example of evolution. In this example, to lightening the notation, we omit the negative literals belonging to interpretations. Let us consider the initial state {} (which means that all fluents are false). The state will remain unchanged until some action is performed. If one load the gun, the program is updated with the external event {*load*}. In the unique successor state, the fluent *loaded* is true and nothing else changes. The truth value of *loaded* remains then unchanged (by inertia) until some other action is performed. The same applies to fluents *dead*(*X*). The fluents *bang*, *missed*(*X*), and *hit*(*X*) remain false by default. If one shoots at a specific turkey, say Smith, and the program is updated with the event *shoot*(*smith*), several things happen. First, *loaded* becomes false, and *bang* becomes true, as an effect of the action. Moreover, the rules:

$$hit(smith) \leftarrow not\ missed(smith).$$
$$missed(smith) \leftarrow not\ hit(smith).$$
$$dead(smith) \leftarrow hit(smith).$$

are considered as rules of the domain for one state. As a consequence, there are two possible resulting states. In the first one, *missed*(*smith*) is true, and all the others fluents are false. In the second one *hit*(*smith*) is true, *missed*(*smith*) is false and, by the rule *dead*(*smith*) ← *hit*(*smith*), the fluent *dead*(*smith*) becomes true. In both the resulting states, nothing happens to the truth value of the fluents *dead*(*X*), *hit*(*X*), and *dead*(*X*) for *X* ≠ *smith*.

4   Relationship to Existing Action Languages

In this section we show embeddings into EAPs of the action languages $\mathcal{B}$ and (the definite fragment of) $\mathcal{C}^2$. We will assume that the considered initial states are consistent wrt. the static rules of the program, i.e. if the body of a static rule is true in the considered state, the head is true as well.

---

[2] The embedding of language $\mathcal{A}$ is not explicitly exposed here since $\mathcal{A}$ is a (proper) subset of the $\mathcal{B}$ language.

Let us consider first the $\mathcal{B}$ language. The basic ideas of static and dynamic rules are very similar in $\mathcal{B}$ and in EAPs. The main difference between the two is that in $\mathcal{B}$ *all* the fluents are inertial, whilst in EAPs only those that are declared as such are inertial. The translation of $\mathcal{B}$ into EAPs is then straightforward: All fluents are declared as inertial and then the syntax of static and dynamic rules is adapted. In the following we use, with abuse of notation, *Body* and *Cond* both for conjunctions of literals and for sets of literals.

Definition 8. *Let P be any action program in $\mathcal{B}$ with set of fluents $\mathcal{F}$. The translation $B(P, \mathcal{F})$ is the pair $(I^B \oplus D^{BP}, \mathcal{F}^B)$ where: $\mathcal{F}^B \equiv \mathcal{F}$, $I^B = $* **initialize($\mathcal{F}$)** *and D^{BP} contains exactly the following rules:*

- **inertial(Q)** *for each fluent $Q \in \mathcal{F}$*
- *a rule $F \leftarrow Body$ for any static rule F **if** Body in P.*
- *a rule **effect(F)** $\leftarrow A$, Cond. for any dynamic rule A **causes** F **if** Cond in P.*

Theorem 2. *Let P be any $\mathcal{B}$ program with set of fluents $\mathcal{F}$, $(I^B \oplus D^{BP}, \mathcal{F})$ its translation, s a state and K any set of actions. Then s' is a resulting state from s given P and the set of actions K iff it is a resulting state from s given $I^B \oplus D^{BP}$ and the set of actions K.*

This theorem makes it clear that there is a close relationship between *EAPs* and the $\mathcal{B}$ language. In practice, *EAPs* generalize $\mathcal{B}$ by allowing both inertial and non inertial fluents and by admitting rules, rather then simply facts, as effects of actions.

Let us consider now the action language $\mathcal{C}$. Given a complete description of the current state of the world and performed actions, the problem of finding a resulting state is a problem of the satisfiability of a causal theory, which is known to be Σ_P^2-hard (cf. [15]). So, this language belongs to a category with higher complexity than EAPs whose satisfiability is NP-complete. However, only a fragment of $\mathcal{C}$ is implemented and the complexity of such fragment is NP. This fragment is known as the *definite fragment* of $\mathcal{C}$ [15]. In this fragment, static rules are expressions of the form **caused** F **if** *Body* where F is a fluent literal and *Body* is a conjunction of fluent literals, while dynamic rules are expressions of the form **caused** *not* F **if** *Body* **after** *Cond* where *Cond* is a conjunction of fluent or action literals[3] For this fragment it is possible to provide a translation into EAPs.

The main problem of the translation of $\mathcal{C}$ into EAPs lies in the simulation of causal reasoning with stable model semantics. The approach followed here to encode causal reasoning with stable models is in line with the one proposed in [21]. We need to introduce some auxiliary predicates and define a syntactic

---

[3] The definite fragment defined in [15] is (apparently) more general, allowing *Cond* and *Body* to be arbitrary formulae. However, it is easy to prove that such kind of expressions are equivalent to a set of expressions of the form described above.

transformation of rules. Let $\mathcal{F}$ be a set of fluents, and let $\mathcal{F}^C$ denote the set of fluents $\mathcal{F} \cup \{Q_N \mid Q \in \mathcal{F}\}$. We add, for each $Q \in \mathcal{F}$, the constraints:

$$\leftarrow not\ Q, not\ Q_N. \tag{4}$$
$$\leftarrow Q,\ Q_N. \tag{5}$$

Let Q be a fluent and $Body = F_1, \dots, F_n$ a conjunction of fluent literals. We will use the following notation: $\overline{Q} = not\ Q_N$, $\overline{not\ Q} = not\ Q$ and $\overline{Body} = \overline{F_1}, \dots, \overline{F_n}$

Definition 9. *Let P be any action program in the definite fragment of $\mathcal{C}$ with set of fluents $\mathcal{F}$. The translation $C(P, \mathcal{F})$ is the pair $(I^C \oplus D^{CP}, \mathcal{F}^C)$ where: $\mathcal{F}^C$ is defined as above, $I^C \equiv \mathbf{initialize(\mathcal{F}^C)}$ and D^{CP} consists exactly of the following rules:*

- *a rule $\mathbf{effect}(Q \leftarrow \overline{Body}) \leftarrow Cond$, for any dynamic rule in P of the form $\mathbf{caused}\ Q\ \mathbf{if}\ Body\ \mathbf{after}\ Cond$;*
- *a rule $\mathbf{effect}(Q_N \leftarrow \overline{Body}) \leftarrow Cond$, for any dynamic rule in P of the form $\mathbf{caused}\ not\ Q\ \mathbf{if}\ Body\ \mathbf{after}\ Cond$;*
- *a rule $Q \leftarrow \overline{Body}$, for any static rule in P of the form $\mathbf{caused}\ Q\ \mathbf{if}\ Body$;*
- *a rule $Q_N \leftarrow \overline{Body}$, for a static rule in P of the form $\mathbf{caused}\ not\ Q\ \mathbf{if}\ Body$;*
- *The rules (4) and (5), for each fluent $Q \in \mathcal{F}$.*

For this translation we obtain a result similar to the one obtained for the translations of the $\mathcal{B}$ language:

Theorem 3. *Let P be any action program in the definite fragment of $\mathcal{C}$ with set of fluents $\mathcal{F}$, $(I^C \oplus D^{CP}, \mathcal{F}^C)$ its translation, s a state, s^C the interpretation over $\mathcal{F}^C$ defined as follows: $s^C = s \cup \{Q_N \mid Q \in s\} \cup \{not\ Q_N \mid not\ Q \in s\}$ and K any set of actions. Then s^* is a resulting state from s^C given $I^C \oplus D^{CP}$ and the set of actions K iff there exists s' such that s' is a resulting state from s, given P and the set K and $s^* \equiv_{\mathcal{F}_L} s'$.*

By showing translations of the action languages $\mathcal{B}$ and the definite fragment of $\mathcal{C}$ into EAPs, we proved that EAPs are *at least as expressive* as such languages. Moreover, the translations above are quite simple: basically one EAP static or dynamic rule for each static or dynamic rule in the other languages. The next natural question is: Are they *more expressive*?

5   Updates of Action Domains

Action description languages describe the rules governing a domain where actions are performed, and the environment changes. In practical situations, it may happen that the very rules of the domain change with time too. When this happens, it would be desirable to have ways of specifying the necessary updates to the considered action program, rather than to have to write a new one. EAPs are just a particular kind of Evolp sequences. So, as in general Evolp sequences, they can be updated by external events.

When one wants to update the existing rules with a rule τ, all that has to be done is to add the fact $assert(\tau)$ as an external event. This way, the rule τ is asserted and the existing Evolp sequence is updated. Following this line, we extend EAPs by allowing the external events to contain facts of the form $assert(\tau)$, where τ is an Evolp rule, and we show how they can be used to express updates to EAPs. For simplicity, below we use the notation $assert(R)$, where R is a set of rules, for the set of expressions $assert(\tau)$ where $\tau \in R$.

To illustrate how to update an EAP, we come back to Example 1. Let $I \oplus D$ be the EAP defined in there. Let us now consider that after some shots, and dead turkeys, rubber bullets are acquired. One can now either load the gun with normal bullets or with a rubber bullets, but not with both. If one shoots with a rubber loaded gun, the turkey is not killed.

To describe this change in the domain, we introduce a new inertial fluent representing the gun being loaded with rubber bullets. We have to express that, if the gun is rubber-loaded, one can not kill the turkey. For this purpose we introduce the new macro:

$$not \; \mathbf{effect}(F \leftarrow Body) \leftarrow Cond.$$

where F, is a fluent literal, $Body$ is a set of fluents literals and $Cond$ is a set of fluent or action literals. We refer to such expressions as *effects inhibitions*. This macro simply stands for the rule

$$assert(not \; event(F \leftarrow Body)) \leftarrow Cond.$$

where $event(F \leftarrow Body)$ is as before. The intuitive meaning is that, if the condition $Cond$ is true in the current state, any dynamic rule whose effect is the rule $F \leftarrow Body$ is ignored.

To encode the changes described above, we update the EAP with the external event E_1 consisting of the facts $assert(I_1)$ where

$$I_1 = (\mathbf{initialize}(rubber\_loaded))$$

Then, in the subsequent state, we update the program with the external update $E_2 = assert(D_1)$ where D_1 is the set of rules[4]

$\quad\quad\quad \mathbf{inertial}(rubber\_loaded).$
$\quad\quad\quad \mathbf{effect}(rubber\_loaded) \leftarrow rubber\_load.$
$\quad\quad\quad \mathbf{effect}(not \; rubber\_loaded) \leftarrow shoot(X).$
$\quad\quad\quad \mathbf{effect}(\bot) \leftarrow rubber\_loaded, \; load.$
$\quad\quad\quad \mathbf{effect}(\bot) \leftarrow loaded, \; rubber\_load.$
$\quad\quad\quad not \; \mathbf{effect}(dead(X) \leftarrow hit(X)) \leftarrow rubber\_loaded.$

---

[4] In the remainder, we use $assert(U)$, where U is a set of macros (which are themselves sets of Evolp rules), to denote the set of all facts $assert(\tau)$ such that there exists a macro η in U with $\tau \in \eta$.

Let us analyze the proposed update. First, the fluent *rubber_loaded* is initialized. It is important to initialize any fluent before starting to use it. The newly introduced fluent is declared as inertial, and two dynamic rules are added specifying that load actions are not executable when the gun is already loaded in a different way. Finally we use the new command to specify that the effect $dead(X) \leftarrow hit(X)$ does not occurs if, in the previous state, the gun was loaded with rubber bullets. Since this update is more recent than the original rule **effect**$(dead(X) \leftarrow hit(X)) \leftarrow shoot(X)$, the dynamic rule is updated.

Basically updating the original EAP with the rule

$$not \ \textbf{effect}(dead(X) \leftarrow hit(X)) \leftarrow rubber\_loaded.$$

has the effect of adding *not rubber_loaded* to the preconditions of the dynamic rule

$$\textbf{effect}(dead(X) \leftarrow hit(X)) \leftarrow shoot(X).$$

So far we have shown how to update the preconditions of a dynamic rule. It is also possible to update static rules and the descriptions of effects of actions. Suppose the cylinder of the gun becomes dirty and, whenever one shoots, the gun may either work properly or fail. If the gun fails, the action *shoot* has no effect. We introduce two new fluents in the program with the event $assert(I_2)$ where $I_2 = \textbf{initialize}(fails, work)$. Then, we assert the event $E_2 = assert(D_2)$ where D_2 is the following EAP

$$\textbf{effect}(fails \leftarrow not \ work) \leftarrow shoot(X).$$
$$\textbf{effect}(work \leftarrow not \ fails) \leftarrow shoot(X).$$
$$not \ missed(X) \leftarrow fails.$$
$$not \ hit(X) \leftarrow fails.$$
$$not \ bang \leftarrow fails.$$
$$\textbf{effect}(loaded \leftarrow fails) \leftarrow loaded.$$
$$\textbf{effect}(rubber\_loaded \leftarrow fails) \leftarrow rubber\_loaded.$$

The first two dynamic rules simply introduce the possibility that a failure may occur every time we shoot. The three static rules describe changes in the behaviour of the environment when the gun fails, and amount to negate what was entailed by static and dynamic rules in D. The last two dynamic rules update two of the dynamic rules in D and D_1, respectively. These rules specify that, when a failure occurs, the gun remain loaded with the same kind of bullet. Since the new rules of D_2 are more recent than the rules in D and D_1, they update these latter ones.

This last example shows how to update static and dynamic rules with new static and dynamic rules. To illustrate how this is indeed achieved in this example, we now show a possible evolution of the updated system. Suppose currently the gun is not loaded. One loads the gun with a rubber bullet, and then shoots at the turkey named Trevor. The initial state is {}. The first set of actions is {*rubber_load*} The resulting state after this action is $s' \equiv \{rubber\_loaded\}$. Suppose one performs the action *load*. Since the EAP is updated with the dynamic rule $\mathbf{effect}(\bot) \leftarrow rubber\_loaded, load$. there is no resulting state. This happens because we have performed a non executable action. Suppose, instead, that the second set of actions is $\{shoot(trevor)\}$. In this case there are three possible resulting states. In one the gun fails and, in it, the resulting state is again s'. In the second, the gun works but the bullet misses Trevor. In this case, the resulting state is $s_1'' \equiv \{missed(trevor)\}$. Finally, in the third, the gun works and the bullet hits Trevor. Since the bullet is a rubber bullet, Trevor is still alive. In this case the resulting state is $s_2'' \equiv \{hit(trevor)\}$.

The events may introduce changes in the behaviour of the original EAP. This opens a new problem. In classical action languages we do not care about the previous *history* of the world: If the current state of the world is s, the computation of the resulting states is not affected by the states before s. In the case of EAPs the situation is different, since external updates can change the behaviour of the considered EAP. Fortunately, we do not have to care about the *whole* history of the world, but just about those events containing new initializations, inertial declarations, effects inhibitions, and static and dynamic rules.

It is possible to have a compact description of an EAP that is updated several times via external events. For that we need to further extend the original definition of EAPs.

Definition 10. *An* updated *Evolp action program over* $(\mathcal{F}, \mathcal{A})$ *is any sequence* $I \oplus D_1 \oplus \ldots \oplus D_n$ *where I is* **initialize(** $\mathcal{F}$ **)**, *and the various D_k are sets consisting of static rules, dynamic rules, inertial declarations and effects inhibitions such that any fluent appearing in D_k belongs to $\mathcal{F}$.*

Definition 11. *Let* $I \oplus D_1 \oplus \ldots \oplus D_n$ *be any* updated *EAP and s a state of the world. Then s' is a resulting state from s given $I \oplus D_1 \oplus \ldots \oplus D_n$ and the sequence of sets of actions $K_1 \ldots,\ K_n$ iff there exists an evolving stable model $M_1, \ldots, M_n$ of $I \oplus D_1 \oplus \ldots \oplus D_n$ given the external events $(s \cup K_1), \ldots,\ K_n, \emptyset$ such that $s' \equiv_{\mathcal{F}} M_n$.*

In general, if we updated an Evolp action program $I \oplus D$ with the subsequent events $assert(I_1)$, $assert(D_1)$, where $I_1 \oplus D_1$ is another EAP, we obtain the equivalent updated Evolp action program $(I \cup I_1) \oplus D \oplus D_1$ Formally:

Theorem 4. *Let* $I_0 \cup I \oplus D_0 \oplus D_1 \oplus \ldots \oplus D_k$ *be any update EAP over* $(\mathcal{F}, \mathcal{A})$. *Let* $\bigoplus E_i^n$ *be a sequence of events such that:* $E_1 = K_1 \cup s$, *where s is any state of the world and K_1 is any set of actions; and the others E_is are any set of actions K_α, or any set $assert(\mathbf{initialize(}\mathcal{F}_\beta\mathbf{)})$ where $\bigcup \mathcal{F}_\beta \equiv I$, or any $assert(D_i)$ with $1 \leq i \leq k$. Let $s_1, \ldots, s_n$ be a sequence of possible resulting states from s given the EAP $I_0 \oplus D_0$ and the sequence of events $\bigoplus E_i^n$ and K_{n+1} a set of actions. Then $s_1, \ldots, s_n, s'$ is a resulting state from s given $I_0 \oplus D_0$ and the sequence of events $\bigoplus E_i^n \oplus K_{n+1}$ iff s' is a resulting state from s_n given $I_0 \cup I \oplus D_0 \oplus D_1 \oplus \ldots \oplus D_k$ and the set of actions K_{n+1}.*

By applying this theorem we can, for instance, simplify the updates to the original EAP of the example in this section into the updated EAP $I_{sum} \oplus D \oplus D_1 \oplus D_2$, where $I_{sum} \equiv I \cup I_1 \cup I_2$, I and D are as in Example 1, and the I_is and D_is are as described above.

Yet one more possibility opened by updated Evolp action programs is to cater for successive elaborations of a program. Consider an initial problem described by an EAP $I \oplus D$. If we want to describe an elaboration of the program, instead of *rewriting* $I \oplus D$ we can simply *update* it with new rules. This gives a new answer to the problem of elaboration tolerance [25] and also open the new possibility of *automatically update* action programs by other action programs.

The possibility to elaborate on an action program is also discussed in [15] in the context of the $\mathcal{C}$ language. The solution proposed there, is to consider $\mathcal{C}$ programs whose rules have one extra fluent atom in their bodies, all these extra fluents being false by default. The elaboration of an action program P is the program $P \cup U$ where U is a new action program. The rules in U can defeat the rules in P by changing the truth value of the extra fluents. An advantage of EAP over that approach is that in EAPs the possibility of updating rules is a built-in feature rather then a programming technique involving manipulation of rules and introduction of new fluents. Moreover, in EAPs we can simply encode the new behaviours of the domain by new rules and then let these new rules update the previous ones.

6   Conclusions and Future Work

In this paper we have explored the possibility of using logic programs updates languages as action description languages. In particular, we have focused our attention on the Evolp language [2]. As a first point, we have defined a new action language paradigm, christened Evolp action programs, defined as a macro language over Evolp. We have provided an example of usage of this language, and compared Evolp action programs with action languages $\mathcal{A}$, $\mathcal{B}$ and the definite fragment of $\mathcal{C}$, by defining simple translations into Evolp of programs in these languages. Finally, we have also shown and argued about the capability of EAPs to handle changes in the domain during the execution of actions.

Though all the results in this paper refer to the update language Evolp, it is not our stance that these could not be obtained if other LP update languages were used instead. For recasting (some) of the results in other LP update languages, one would have to resort to established relationships between the various LP update languages, such as the ones found in [2, 19]. Also, the possibility of handling changes in the domain shown by EAPs, could in principle be obtained if, instead of Evolp, another update language with the capability of updating update rules were used instead. Another LP update language with this capability is the KABUL language defined in [19]. However, the study of which of the existing LP update languages could be used as action description languages, in a way similar to what is described here for Evolp, is outside the scope of this paper, and would, in our opinion, fit better in a paper with a focus on relationship among various LP update languages. Our goal in this paper was to show that (at least) one LP update language can be used for describing effects of actions, and can be formally compared with existing action description languages. This goal was achieved by showing exactly that for the language Evolp.

Several important topics are not touched here, and will be subject of future work. Important fields of research are how to deal, in the Evolp context, with the problem of planning prediction and postdiction [24], when dealing with incomplete knowledge of the state of the world. Yet another topic involves the possibility of concurrent execution of actions. Nevertheless, we have not fully explored this topic, and confronted the results with extant works [6, 18].

The development of implementations for Evolp and EAPs is another necessary step. Finally EAPs have to be tested in real and complex contexts.

References

1. J. J. Alferes, F. Banti, A. Brogi, and J. A. Leite. Semantics for dynamic logic programming: a principled based approach. In *7th Int. Conf. on Logic Programming and Nonmonotonic Reasoning (LPNMR-7)*, volume 1730 of *LNAI*. Springer, 2004.
2. J. J. Alferes, A. Brogi, J. A. Leite, and L. M. Pereira. Evolving logic programs. In S. Flesca, S. Greco, N. Leone, and G. Ianni, editors, *8th European Conf. on Logics in AI (JELIA'02)*, volume 2424 of *LNAI*, pages 50–61. Springer, 2002.
3. J. J. Alferes, J. A. Leite, L. M. Pereira, H. Przymusinska, and T. C. Przymusinski. Dynamic updates of non-monotonic knowledge bases. *The Journal of Logic Programming*, 45(1–3):43–70, September/October 2000.
4. J. J. Alferes, L. M. Pereira, H. Przymusinska, and T. Przymusinski. LUPS: A language for updating logic programs. *Artificial Intelligence*, 132(1 & 2), 2002.
5. J. J. Alferes, L. M. Pereira, T. Przymusinski, H. Przymusinska, and P. Quaresma. Preliminary exploration on actions as updates. In M. C. Meo and M. V. Ferro, editors, *Joint Conference on Declarative Programming (AGP-99)*, 1999.
6. C. Baral and M. Gelfond. Reasoning about effects of concurrent actions. *Journal of Logic Programming*, 31:85–118, 1997.
7. C. Baral, M. Gelfond, and Alessandro Provetti. Representing actions: Laws, observations and hypotheses. *Journal of Logic Programming*, 31, April–June 1997.
8. F. Buccafurri, W. Faber, and N. Leone. Disjunctive logic programs with inheritance. In D. De Schreye, editor, *Proceedings of the 1999 International Conference on Logic Programming (ICLP-99)*, Cambridge, November 1999. MIT Press.
9. T. Eiter, M. Fink, G. Sabbatini, and H. Tompits. A framework for declarative update specifications in logic programs. In Bernhard Nebel, editor, *Proceedings of the seventeenth International Conference on Artificial Intelligence (IJCAI-01)*, pages 649–654, San Francisco, CA, 2001. Morgan Kaufmann Publishers, Inc.
10. T. Eiter, M. Fink, G. Sabbatini, and H. Tompits. On properties of semantics based on causal rejection. *Theory and Practice of Logic Programming*, 2:711–767, November 2002.
11. M. Gelfond and V. Lifschitz. The stable model semantics for logic programming. In R. Kowalski and K. A. Bowen, editors, *5th International Conference on Logic Programming*, pages 1070–1080. MIT Press, 1988.
12. M. Gelfond and V. Lifschitz. Representing actions and change by logic programs. *Journal of Logic Programming*, 17:301–322, 1993.
13. M. Gelfond and V. Lifschitz. Action languages. *Electronic Transactions on AI*, 16, 1998.
14. E. Giunchiglia, J. Lee, V. Lifschitz, N. Mc Cain, and H. Turner. Representing actions in logic programs and default theories: a situation calculus approach. *Journal of Logic Programming*, 31:245–298, 1997.

15. E. Giunchiglia, J. Lee, V. Lifschitz, N. McCain, and H. Turner. Nonmonotonic causal theories. *Artificial Intelligence*, 153:49–104, 2004.
16. E. Giunchiglia and V. Lifschitz. An action language based on causal explanation: Preliminary report. In *AAAI'98*, pages 623–630, 1998.
17. M. Homola. Dynamic logic programming: Various semantics are equal on acyclic programs. In this volume.
18. J. Lee and V. Lifschitz. Describing additive fluents in action language C+. In William Nebel, Bernhard; Rich, Charles; Swartout, editor, *Proc. IJCAI-03*, pages 1079–1084, Cambridge, MA, 2003.
19. J. A. Leite. *Evolving Knowledge Bases*, volume 81 of *Frontiers in Artificial Intelligence and Applications*. IOS Press, 2003.
20. J. A. Leite and L. M. Pereira. Generalizing updates: from models to programs. In *LPKR'97: workshop on Logic Programming and Knowledge Representation*, 1997.
21. V. Lifschitz. *The Logic Programming Paradigm: a 25-Year Perspective*, chapter Action languages, answer sets and planning, pages 357–373. Springer Verlag, 1999.
22. V. Lifschitz and T. Woo. Answer sets in general non-monotonic reasoning (preliminary report). In B. Nebel, C. Rich, and W. Swartout, editors, *Proceedings of the 3th International Conference on Principles of Knowledge Representation and Reasoning (KR-92)*. Morgan-Kaufmann, 1992.
23. John Wylie Lloyd. *Foundations of Logic Programming*. Springer,, Berlin, Heidelberg, New York,, 1987.
24. J. McCarthy. Programs with commons sense. In *Proceedings of Teddington Conference on The Mechanization of Thought Process*, pages 75–91, 1959.
25. J. McCarthy. *Mathematical logic in artificial intelligence*, pages 297–311. Daedalus, 1988.
26. S. Russel and P. Norvig. *Artificial Intelligence A Modern Approach*. Artificial Intelligence. Prentice Hall, 1995.
27. D. McDermott S. Hanks. Nonmonotonic logic and temporal projection. *Artificial Intelligence*, 33:379–412, (1987).

A   Proofs

Before presenting the proofs of the results in this paper, we present an alternative definition of the transition function of EAPs, and prove its equivalence to the original definition (Definition 6). We do so because in some proofs it is more convenient to use this alternative definition.

In this alternative definition, and in its prove, we will use the notation $S|_{\mathcal{I}}$ to denote the restriction of the set S to the literals in the set $\mathcal{I}$ i.e., to denote $S \cap \mathcal{I}$.

Theorem 5. *Let $I \oplus D$ be any EAP, s a state of the world and K a set of actions. Let $\mathcal{R}$ be the set of static rules in D, $\mathcal{I}$ the following set of fluent literals*

$$\mathcal{I} = \{Q \in \mathcal{F} : \; \textbf{inertial}(Q) \in D\} \cup \{not \; Q : \; Q \in \mathcal{F} : \; \textbf{inertial}(Q) \in D\}$$

and $D(s, K)$ be the following set of rules:

$$D(s, K) = \{\tau : \textbf{effect}(\tau) \leftarrow Cond \; \in D \; \wedge \; K \cup s \models Cond\}$$

Then s' is a resulting state from s given $I \oplus D$ and the set of actions K iff

$$s' = least\left((s \cap s' \cap \mathcal{I}) \cup Default(s', \mathcal{R} \cup D(s, K))|_{(\mathcal{F}_L \setminus \mathcal{I})} \cup D(s, K) \cup \mathcal{R}\right)$$
$$(6)$$

Proof. By Definition 6, s' is a resulting state from s given $I \oplus D$ and the set of actions K iff there exists an evolving stable model M_1, s^* of $I \oplus D$ given the external events $s \cup K, \emptyset$ such that $s' \equiv_{\mathcal{F}} s^*$. An interpretation M_1 is an evolving stable model of $I \oplus D$ given the external events $s \cup K$ iff M_1 is a refined stable models of $I \oplus D \cup s \cup K$ i.e.,

$$M_1 = least\left((I \cup D \cup s \cup K) \setminus Rej^s(M_1, I \oplus D \cup K \cup s) \cup Default(M_1)\right)$$

All the atoms of the form $event(\tau)$ where τ is the effect of a dynamic rule are false by default in $I \oplus D \cup K \cup s$. Hence the rules of the form (1) and (3), which have those atoms in their bodies, play no role when calculating the least model. Also all the literals of the form $prev(Q)$, where Q is a fluent literal, are false by default, and so the rules of the form $Q \leftarrow prev(Q)$ play no role either. Since the initial (starting) state s is always assumed consistent wrt. the static rules, there is no conflict between the static rules in D. Thus, static rules do not reject any literal in s nor do they infer any fluent literal that does not belong to s. So, we can simplify the expression above in the following way:

$$M_1 = least\left((D^* \cup s \cup K) \cup Default(M_1)\right)$$

where D^* is the set of all rules the form

$$assert(event(\tau)) \leftarrow Cond.$$

for which there is a dynamic rule **effect**$(\tau) \leftarrow Cond$ in D, union with the set of all rules of the form

$$assert(prev(Q)) \leftarrow Q. \qquad assert(not\ prev(Q)) \leftarrow not\ Q.$$

for every Q such that **inertial**(Q) belongs to D.

Hereafter, for sake of simplicity, in interpretations we omit the negative literals of the form $not\ A$ whenever A is an auxiliary atom or an action literal. In other words, we omit $not\ A$ whenever $A \notin \mathcal{F}$. Moreover, by $Prev(s)$ we denote the set of literals which are either of the form $prev(F)$ where F is a fluent literal that is declared as inertial in D and is true in s, or of the form $not\ prev(F)$ where F is a fluent literal that is declared as inertial in D and is false in s. Finally, by $ED(s, K)$ we mean the set of literals $event(\tau)$ such that

$$assert(event(\tau)) \leftarrow Cond.$$

belongs to D and $s \cup K \models Cond$.

Given this, it is easy to see that the trace associated with any evolving interpretation M_1, s^* is the sequence $\mathcal{J} : I \oplus D \oplus Prev(s) \cup ED(s, K)$. So, M_1, s^*

is an evolving stable model of $I \oplus D$ given the sequence of events $K, \emptyset$ iff s^* is a refined stable model of $\mathcal{J}$.

Let s^* be any interpretation over the language of $I \oplus D$, and $s' = s^*|_{\mathcal{F}}$. To prove the theorem, we simply have to prove that s^* is a refined stable model of $\mathcal{J}$ iff s' satisfies the equivalence (6). By definition of refined stable model, s^* is a refined stable model of $\mathcal{J}$ iff

$$s^* = least\left(\left(I \cup D \cup Prev(s) \cup D(s, K)\right) \setminus Rej^S(s^*) \cup Default(s^*)\right)$$

$\Rightarrow$ Assume that s^* is a refined stable model of $\mathcal{J}$. To prove that s' satisfies the equivalence, we start by simplifying the expression above defining s^*.

Let $s' = s^*_{\mathcal{F}}$. Since s' only has fluent literals, the dynamic rules and the inertial declarations in D play no role in verifying the equivalence. Hence, the only rules we are interested in are the static rules in $\mathcal{R}$. Moreover, since s^* is two valued, there is no mutual rejection between the rules in $\mathcal{R}$: otherwise there would be a fluent literal Q such that all the rules with head Q or $not\ Q$ would be rejected, and such that $not\ Q$ would not be in the set $Default(s^*)$ as well. In such a case, neither Q nor $not\ Q$ would be in s^* which would contradict the two valuedness of s^*. Finally, by partially evaluating the facts in $ED(s, K)$, in the rules of the form

$$F \leftarrow Body,\ event(F \leftarrow Body).$$

we can delete the atoms $event(\tau)$ from the body of those rules whenever $event(\tau) \in ED(s, K)$, and delete one such rule when $event(\tau) \notin ED(s, K)$. With this, we can simplify the equivalence for s' into:

$$s' = least\left(I \setminus Rej^S(s^*) \cup Prev(s) \cup \mathcal{R} \cup D(s, K) \cup Default(s^*)\right)$$

We can split the set of default assumptions into two subsets: the one concerning the inertial fluent literals; and the one concerning the fluent literals that are not inertial. Taking this splitting in consideration, the equivalence for s' becomes:

$$s' = least\begin{pmatrix} I \setminus Rej^S(s^*) \cup Prev(s) \cup Default(s^*)|_{\mathcal{I}} \cup \\ \mathcal{R} \cup D(s, K) \cup Default(s^*)|_{(\mathcal{F}_L \setminus \mathcal{I})} \end{pmatrix}$$

where $Default(s^*)$ stands for $Default(s^*, I \oplus \mathcal{R} \cup D(s, K))|_{(\mathcal{F}_L \setminus \mathcal{I})}$. Notice that the expression $Default(s^*, I \oplus \mathcal{R} \cup D(s, K))|_{(\mathcal{F}_L \setminus \mathcal{I})}$ is equivalent to $Default(s', \mathcal{R} \cup D(s, K))|_{(\mathcal{F}_L \setminus \mathcal{I})}$. Moreover, the expression $Default(s^*)|_{\mathcal{I}}$ is equivalent to $Default(s', s \cup \mathcal{R} \cup D(s, K))|_{(\mathcal{I})}$. Let $Inherit(s)$ be the set of rules:

$$Inherit(s^*) = \{Q \in \mathcal{F} : Q \leftarrow prev(Q) \in I \setminus Rej^S(s^*) \wedge prev(Q) \in Prev(s)\}$$

What remains to show in order to prove that s' satisfies the equivalence (6) is that

$$Inherit(s^*) \cup Default(s^*)|_{\mathcal{I}} \equiv (s \cap s' \cap \mathcal{I})$$

For showing this, we consider separately the negative and the positive fluent literals. Let Q be a fluent literal that belongs to $(s \cap s' \cap \mathcal{I})$. We want to prove this is equivalent to say that $Q \leftarrow prev(Q)$ belongs to $I \setminus Rej^S(s^*)$ and that $Prev(Q) \in Prev(s)$ i.e., we want to prove that $Q \in Inherit(s^*)$.

The literal Q belongs to $(s \cap s' \cap \mathcal{I})$ iff $Q \in \mathcal{I}$, not $Q \notin s$ and not $Q \notin s'$. This implies that there exists no rule in $\mathcal{R} \cup D(s, K)$ whose head is not Q and whose body is true. So, the rule $Q \leftarrow prev(Q)$ belongs to $I \setminus Rej^S(s^*)$ and, by $Q \in s$ and by definition of $Prev(s)$, we conclude that $Prev(Q) \in Prev(s)$. Let assume now $Q \leftarrow prev(Q)$ belongs to $I \setminus Rej^S(s^*)$, then there exists no rule in $\mathcal{R} \cup D(s, K)$ whose head is not Q and whose body is true. If, furthermore, $Prev(Q) \in Prev(s)$, then not $Q \notin Default(s^*)$ and so not Q is not derived by any rule nor by default assumption. Thus, not $Q \notin s'$ and so $Q \in s$. Moreover, by definition if $prev(Q) \in Prev(s)$ then $Q \in s$ and $Q \in \mathcal{I}$. So, we have proved that

$$Q \in (s \cap s' \cap \mathcal{I}) \Leftrightarrow Q \leftarrow prev(Q) \in I \setminus Rej^S(s^*) \ \wedge \ prev(Q) \in Prev(s)$$

Let us now consider the negative fluent literals. In this case we want to prove that, for any inertial fluent, the following equivalence holds.

$$not \ Q \in (s \cap s') \Leftrightarrow not \ Q \in Default(s', s \cup \mathcal{R} \cup D(s, K))|\mathcal{F}$$

We know not $Q \in s'$ iff $Q \notin s'$, which, since s' is a model of $\mathcal{R} \cup D(s, K)$, implies that there exists no rule in $\mathcal{R} \cup D(s, K)$ whose head is Q and whose body is satisfied by s'. This, together with the fact that $Q \notin s$, by definition of $Default$ implies that not $Q \in Default(s', s \cup \mathcal{R} \cup D(s, K))$, as desired.

$\Leftarrow$ Let us now suppose that s' satisfies the equivalence (6). i.e.

$$s' = least \left((s \cap s' \cap \mathcal{I}) \cup Default(s', \mathcal{R} \cup D(s, K))|_{(\mathcal{F}_L \setminus \mathcal{I})} \cup D(s, k) \cup \mathcal{R}\right)$$

Let NED be the set of literals of the form $\neg event(\tau)$ such that $event(\tau) \in ED(s, K)$ and there is no dynamic rule of the form $\mathbf{effect}(\tau) \leftarrow Cond$ such that s' satisfies $Cond$. Let s' be the following evolving interpretation (again we omit in the interpretation, the negative literals which are not fluent literals).

$$s^* = s' \cup Prev(s) \cup ED(s, K) \cup NED \cup assert(ED(s', K)) \cup$$
$$\cup assert(Prev(s))'$$

We have to prove that s^* is a refined stable model of $\mathcal{J}$. We start this proof by showing that

$$Inherit(s^*) \cup Default(s^*)|_\mathcal{I} \equiv (s \cap s' \cap \mathcal{I})$$

We start by assuming that Q is a fluent literal in $(s \cap s' \cap \mathcal{I})$. Q is such a fluent iff $Prev(Q) \in Prev(s)$, and not $Q \notin s'$. Since s' is a model of $\mathcal{R} \cup D(s, K)$, we conclude that there exists no rule in $\mathcal{R} \cup D(s, K)$ with head not Q and true body in s'. Thus, the rule $Q \leftarrow prev(Q) \in I \setminus Rej^S(s^*)$, and hence $Q \in Inherit(s^*)$.

Let assume now $Q \in Inherit(s^*)$ (i.e. $Q \leftarrow prev(Q) \in I \setminus Rej^S(s^*)$ and $prev(Q) \in Prev(s)$) then $Q \in s$. This implies that $not\ Q \notin s$, $Q \in \mathcal{I}$, and there exists no rule in $\mathcal{R} \cup D(s,K)$ with head Q whose body is true in s'. Consequently, $not\ Q \notin s'$ (i.e. $Q \in s'$), and finally $Q \in (s \cap s' \cap \mathcal{I})$.

Let us now consider the negative fluent literals. We want to prove that, for any inertial fluent, the following equivalence holds.

$$not\ Q \in (s \cap s') \Leftrightarrow not\ Q \in Default(s', s \cup \mathcal{R} \cup D(s,K))|\mathcal{F}$$

The proof proceeds in the same way as above, in order to conclude that

$$Inherit(s^*) \cup Default(s^*)|_\mathcal{I} \equiv (s \cap s' \cap \mathcal{I})$$

We obtain then the following equivalence

$$s' = least \left(\begin{array}{l} Inherit(s^*) \cup Default(s^*)|_\mathcal{I}\ \cup \\ Default(s', \mathcal{R} \cup D(s,K))|_{(\mathcal{F}_L \setminus \mathcal{I})}\ \cup D(s,k)\ \cup \mathcal{R} \end{array} \right)$$

which is equivalent to

$$s' = least\left(\ Inherit(s^*) \cup Default(s^*)\ \cup D(s,k)\ \cup \mathcal{R}\right)|_{\mathcal{F}_L}$$

Since s' is consistent wrt. $D(s,K)$ and $\mathcal{R}$, these sets of rules do not contain any pair of rules with conflicting heads and whose bodies are both true in s'. So, by replacing $Inherit(s^*)$ with $Prev(s) \cup I \setminus Rej^S(s^*)$ we obtain

$$s' = least\left(\ (I \cup D(s,K) \cup m\mathcal{R}) \setminus Rej^S(s^*) \cup Default(s^*)\right)|_{\mathcal{F}_L}$$

and from this, and by considering the definition of s^*

$$s^* = least\left((I \cup D \cup Prev(s) \cup D(s,K)) \setminus Rej^S(s^*) \cup Default(s^*)\right)$$

This equation is, by definition, equivalent to say that M_1, s^* is an evolving stable model of $I \oplus D$ given the sequence of events $K, \emptyset$. In other words, s' is a resulting state from s given $I \oplus D$ and the set of actions K.

In the extreme cases where the set of inertial fluents coincides with the whole set of fluents and, when the set if inertial fluents is empty, we obtain two simplifications of the equivalence (6).

Corollary 1. *Let $I \oplus D$ be any EAP, s a state of the world and K a set of actions. Let $\mathcal{R}$, $D(s,K)$ be as in theorem 5. Moreover let every fluent be an inertial fluent. Then s' is a resulting state from s given $I \oplus D$ and the set of actions K iff*

$$s' = least\,(s \cap s')\ \cup D(s,k)\ \cup \mathcal{R})$$

Proof. Follows trivially as a special case of theorem 5.

Corollary 2. *Let $I \oplus D$ be any EAP, s a state of the world and K a set of actions. Let $\mathcal{R}$, $D(s, K)$ be as in theorem 5. Moreover let the set of inertial fluents be the empty set. Then s' is a resulting state from s given $I \oplus D$ and the set of actions K iff s' is a stable model of the logic program $D(s, k) \cup \mathcal{R}$*

Proof. It follows trivially as a special case of theorem 5 that

$$s' = least \left(Default(s', \mathcal{R} \cup D(s, K))|_{(\mathcal{F}_L \setminus \mathcal{I})} \cup D(s, k) \cup \mathcal{R} \right)$$

As proved in [19] this amount to say s' is a stable model of $D(s, k) \cup \mathcal{R}$.

Having shown this alternative to the definition of the transition function of EAPs, and proven its equivalence to the original Definition 6, we are now ready to prove all of the theorems (that we recall here, for the sake of readability) in this paper.

Theorem 1 (Complexity of EAPs). *Let $I \oplus D$ be any EAP over $(\mathcal{F}, \mathcal{A})$, s a state of the world and $K \subseteq \mathcal{A}$. To find a resulting state s' from s given $I \oplus D$ and the set of actions K is an NP-complete problem.*

Proof. By corollary 2, and given that the problem of finding a stable model of a program is NP-hard, we conclude that finding a resulting state s' from s given $I \oplus D$ and the set of actions K is an NP-hard problem.

As for membership, from theorem 5 and from the observation that the computation of $least(P)$, where P is a logic program, is polynomial wrt. the number of rules in P (since $least(P)$ is the least Herbrand model of P considering the negative literals in P as new atoms), it follows that checking whether a given state s' is resulting state is a polynomial problem wrt. the number of rules in $I \oplus D$ plus the number of elements in $\mathcal{F} \cup \mathcal{A}$. Hence, the problem of finding a resulting state s' from s given $I \oplus D$ and the set of actions K is NP.

Theorem 2 (Relation to $\mathcal{B}$). *Let P be any $\mathcal{B}$ program with set of fluents $\mathcal{F}$, $(I^B \oplus D^{BP}, \mathcal{F})$ its translation, s a state and K any set of actions. Then s' is a resulting state from s given P and the set of actions K iff it is a resulting state from s given $I^B \oplus D^{BP}$ and the set of actions K.*

Proof. It trivially follows from corollary 1.

Theorem 3 (Relation to $\mathcal{C}$). *Let P be any action program in the definite fragment of $\mathcal{C}$ with set of fluents $\mathcal{F}$, $(I^C \oplus D^{CP}, \mathcal{F}^C)$ its translation, s a state, s^C the interpretation over $\mathcal{F}^C$ defined as follows: $s^C = s \cup \{Q_N \mid Q \in s\} \cup \{not\ Q_N \mid not\ Q \in s\}$ and K any set of actions. Then s^* is a resulting state from s^C given $I^C \oplus D^{CP}$ and the set of actions K iff there exists s' such that s' is a resulting state from s, given P and the set K and $s^* \equiv_{\mathcal{F}_L} s'$.*

Proof. By corollary 2, s^* is a resulting state from s^C given $I^C \oplus D^{CP}$ and the set of actions K iff s' is a stable model of the program $\mathcal{R} \cup D(s, K)$ where $\mathcal{R}$ and $D(s^C, K)$ are defined as in theorem 5. From the translation of definite causal theories into logic programs presented in [15], it follows that this is equivalent to say that s' is a model of the causal theory obtained by all the static rules of P plus the rules of the form **caused** J **if** H for which a dynamic rule

$$\textbf{caused } J \textbf{ if } H \textbf{ after } O$$

belongs to P and Q is true in $s \cup K$. This, in turn, is equivalent to saying that s' is a resulting state from s given P and the set of actions K, as desired.

Theorem 4 (Simplification of updated EAPs). *Let $I_0 \cup I \oplus D_0 \oplus D_1 \oplus \ldots \oplus D_k$ be any update EAP over $(\mathcal{F}, \mathcal{A})$. Let $\bigoplus E_i^n$ be a sequence of events such that: $E_1 = K_1 \cup s$, where s is any state of the world and K_1 is any set of actions; and the others $E_i s$ are any set of actions K_α, or any set assert($\textbf{initialize}(\mathcal{F}_\beta)$) where $\bigcup \mathcal{F}_\beta \equiv I$, or any assert($D_i$) with $1 \le i \le k$. Let $s_1, \ldots, s_n$ be a sequence of possible resulting states from s given the EAP $I_0 \oplus D_0$ and the sequence of events $\bigoplus E_i^n$ and K_{n+1} a set of actions. Then $s_1, \ldots, s_n, s'$ is a resulting state from s given $I_0 \oplus D_0$ and the sequence of events $\bigoplus E_i^n \oplus K_{n+1}$ iff s' is a resulting state from s_n given $I_0 \cup I \oplus D_0 \oplus D_1 \oplus \ldots \oplus D_k$ and the set of actions K_{n+1}.*

Proof. The sequence $s_1, \ldots, s_n, s'$ is a sequence of possible resulting states iff there exists a sequence of evolving interpretations $M_0, M_1, \ldots M_n, s^*$ such that $M_0|_{\mathcal{F}} \equiv s$, $M_i|_{\mathcal{F}} \equiv s_i$ and $s^*|_{\mathcal{F}} \equiv s'$. The trace of $M_0, M_1, \ldots M_n, s^*$ is the DLP $I_0 \oplus D_0 \oplus T_1 \ldots \oplus T_n$ where each $T_i s$ is a set of literal of one of the following forms:

$$T_i = Aux_i$$
$$T_i = Aux_i \cup \textbf{initialize}(\mathcal{F}_\beta)$$
$$T_i = Aux_i \cup D_j] \text{ for some } 0 \le j \le k$$

and Aux_i is a set of auxiliary literals of the form $Prev(Q)$ or $not\ Prev(Q)$, where Q is an inertial literal or $event(\tau)$ or $not\ event(\tau)$, τ being the effect of some dynamic rule.

To compute s^*, the only relevant part of the trace is formed by the various **initialize**($\mathcal{F}_\beta s$), $D_k s$ and the last set of auxiliary literals Aux_n. Moreover, the semantics does not change if we put the various **initialize**($\mathcal{F}_\beta s$) in the first program of the sequence, since a fluent only appears in a D_j after being initialized. Hence we can simplify the trace of $M_0, M_1, \ldots M_n, s^*$ into:

$$I_0 \cup I \oplus D_0 \oplus D_1 \oplus \ldots \oplus D_k \cup Aux_n$$

The set Aux_n can be split in three separate sets

$$Aux_n = Prev(s_n) \cup ED(s_n, K) \cup Retract(s_n)$$

where $Prev(s_n)$ and $ED(s_n, K)$ are as defined in the proof of theorem 5 and $Retract(s_n)$ is the set of all literals of the form $not\ event(\tau)$ coming from dynamic rules whose preconditions are true in s_{n-1} and false in s_n. The negative literals in $Retract(s_n)$ simply rejects facts of the form $event(\tau)$ from Aux_{n-1}. Since we have already simplified the trace by erasing all the $Aux_i s$ with $i < n$, we can ignore the set $Retract(s_n)$. Thus, we obtain that $s_1, \ldots s'$ is a sequence of possible resulting states iff an interpretation s^*, with $s^*|_{\mathcal{F}_L} \equiv s'$, is a refined stable model of $I_0 \cup I \oplus D_0 \oplus D_1 \oplus \ldots \oplus D_k \oplus ED(s_n, K) \cup Prev(s_n)$. This is equivalent to saying that s' is a resulting state from s given $I_0 \cup I \oplus D_0 \oplus D_1 \oplus \ldots \oplus D_k$ and the set of actions K_{n+1}, as desired.

Dynamic Logic Programming: Various Semantics Are Equal on Acyclic Programs

M. Homola

Comenius University, Bratislava, Slovakia
homola@tbc.sk

Abstract. Multidimensional dynamic logic programs (MDLPs) are suitable to represent knowledge dynamic in time, or more generally, information coming from various sources, partially ordered by arbitrary relevancy relation, e.g., level of authority. They have been shown useful for modeling and reasoning about multi-agent systems. Various approaches to define semantics of MDLPs have been presented. Most of the approaches can be characterized as based on rejection of rules.

It is understood that on some restricted classes of MDLPs several of these semantics coincide. We focus on acyclic programs. We show that for a MDLP $\mathcal{P}$ and a candidate model M, if $\mathcal{P}$ is acyclic to some extent then several of the known semantics coincide on M. It follows as a direct consequence that on the class of acyclic programs all of these semantics coincide.

1 Introduction

Background. In *Multidimensional Dynamic Logic Programs (MDLPs)*, introduced in [1], knowledge is encoded into several logic programs, partially ordered by a relevance relation. MDLPs have been shown as well suited for representing knowledge change in time, and as well, to provide favourable representation for reasoning over information structured by some relevancy relation, such as authority hierarchies.

Already in [1], authors have shown that MDLPs are useful to model and reason about multi-agent systems. Particularly in logic based multi-agent systems where knowledge of an agent is naturally represented by rules. Thus, knowledge associated with an agent at a given state is encoded into a logic program. Assume that the agent's knowledge evolves with time. With each new time-state new knowledge appears to the agent, in form of rules, perceived trough sensors or communicated with other agents. This new knowledge may be in general contrary to the knowledge inherited from the previous time-states. We want the agent to be able to resolve such conflicts, assigning more relevance to the more recent knowledge.

MDLPs allow us to do this in a natural way. Agent's initial state and subsequent perceptions are modeled as a sequence of logic programs. More recent information is treated as more relevant. MDLPs assign semantics to the sequence,

J. Leite and P. Torroni (Eds.): CLIMA V, LNAI 3487, pp. 78–95, 2005.
© Springer-Verlag Berlin Heidelberg 2005

resolving conflicts between rules according to their relevancy. Moreover, they enable for determining semantics of the agent's knowledge at arbitrary state, thus allowing us to query the agent's knowledge history.

Besides time, MDLPs are capable of handling other relevancy relations, like specificity of the information or authority. This is particularly handy in multi-agent communities where an authoritative hierarchy among the agents is present. Assume that the knowledge of each agent is represented by a logic program. If an agent is authoritatively superior to the another one, we treat also the program of the former one as more relevant than the program of the latter one. Assuming that the agents obey the authority, we are able to query the global knowledge of the system but as well the knowledge of a subsystem rendered by an agent together with all the agents that are inferior to it.

Moreover, the framework allows us to combine several "relevancy dimensions" into a single MDLP. Thus, we are able to model, e.g., the knowledge distributed over an authority-enabled community of agents and as well the change of the whole system in time. Hence, we favor MDLPs as a powerful framework for modeling and reasoning about knowledge distributed over multi-agent systems, logic-based in particular. However, a multi-agent system does not have to be associated with a single MDLP, nor the view provided by the MDLP has to be global. For instance, each agent may use a MDLP to maintain its own view of the system, reflecting its own preference amongst the chunks of information obtained by communication with other agents. Thus, MDLPs may also provide a local knowledge repository for each agent of the system. For a more detailed analysis, we refer the reader to [3, 1, 11, 12]. We also refer the reader to [13], in order to see how extensions of MDLPs can benefit to multi-agent systems, and to [14] to see how the knowledge of multiple agents can be combined when there is no authoritative order among the agents.

Motivation. Various approaches have been presented in order to provide a semantics of MDLPs. Most of these semantics are based on similar notions (e.g., generalization of stable model semantics, employing rejection of rules) and are very close, one to another. Such semantics include $\mathcal{P}$-Justified Update semantics introduced in [2, 3], Dynamic Stable Model semantics from [4, 1], Update Answer Set semantics from [5, 3] and Refined Dynamic Stable Model semantics of [6, 7]. (The latest one is only known for linearly ordered MDLPs.) Usually, a new semantics has been introduced to cope with drawbacks of the older ones. Most important contributions are those of Leite [3, 8], Eiter et al. [5, 9] and Alferes et al. [4, 6].

Typically, semantics assigns a set of models to a program. Models are picked among the interpretations of the program. Authors point out that for some particular pairs of semantics, for a given MDLP, the model-set of one semantics is always a subset of the model-set of the other one. Thus, a sort of hierarchy of the model-sets assigned to a MDLP by different semantics is organized (cf. [3, 5, 6, 10]).

Studying the differences and similarities between these semantics, helps us to evaluate them w.r.t. our intuitions. Perhaps we do not need such a rich family of semantics, indeed if the difference between them shows to be very small. Particularly, within the field of multi-agent systems, it helps us to determine whether or not MDLPs are appropriate for a particular application, and if yes, which semantics to choose.

Also, it is a shared opinion, that on "plain" MDLPs, which are not obfuscated with cyclic dependencies (cyclic chains of rules), conflicting rules within a same logic program and other unconvenient constructs, all of these semantics coincide. Different behavior on some "abnormal" MDLPs is usually assigned to the inability of some of the semantics to deal with these abnormalities. Several restrictive conditions on MDLPs have been introduced in order to identify classes of programs on which two or more semantics coincide (cf. [3, 5, 6]). From this point of view, We find several results of [5, 3, 7], about restricted classes of MDLPs on which some of the semantics coincide, not tight, as many MDLPs on which the semantics also match are beyond the proposed classes.

We focus on a hypothesis that has been sketched already (cf. [5, 3, 7]), that perhaps on MDLPs that do not contain cycles several of the semantics may coincide. We see this hypothesis as valuable, since acyclic programs form a broad subclass and it is known that for some, simpler, applications they are sufficient. So, we suggest further evaluation of these semantics w.r.t. the class of acyclic programs and programs with limited occurrence of cyclic dependencies.

Contribution. As in [3, 15], we build MDLPs over a more general language of generalized extended logic programs that unifies the previous approaches under a common framework, allowing for more elegant comparisons, while keeping the previous approaches as special cases, so the results are propagated.

We introduce a new concept of sufficient acyclicity. Logic program is sufficiently acyclic if each of its literals is supported by at least one acyclic derivation. As the main result we establish a restrictive condition, using the notion of sufficient acyclicity, under which four (five) of the semantics coincide on the given interpretation of the given MDLP (linear MDLP). It trivially follows that on acyclic programs these semantics coincide entirely. This article presents the results of the author's Master's thesis [10] that can be viewed as its extended version.

2   Preliminaries

We first introduce basic concepts from logic programming. Logic programs are build from propositional *atoms*. The set of all atoms is denoted by $\mathcal{A}$. We employ two kinds of negation, *explicit negation* $\neg$ and *default negation* not. Let p be a proposition. By $\neg p$ we intuitively mean that (we know that) A is not true. Default negation is sometimes called negation as failure. We use it to express lack of objective evidence: by $not\ p$ we intuitively mean that we have no evidence confirming that p is true.

An *objective literal* is an atom or an atom preceded by explicit negation (e.g., $A \in \mathcal{A}$ and $\neg A$ are objective literals). A *default literal* is an objective literal preceded by default negation (e.g., *not A*, *not ¬ A* are default literals, $A \in \mathcal{A}$). Both objective literal and default literal are *literals*. We denote the set of all objective literals by $\mathcal{O}$, the set of all default literals by $\mathcal{D}$ and the set of all literals by $\mathcal{L}$.

A *rule* is a formula $L \leftarrow L_1, \ldots, L_n$, where $n \geq 0$ and $L, L_1, \ldots, L_n \in \mathcal{L}$. A rule of a form $L \leftarrow$ (i.e., $n = 0$) is called a *fact*. For each rule r of a form $L \leftarrow L_1, \ldots, L_n$ we call the literal L the *head* of r and denote it by $h(r)$ and we call the set $\{L_1, \ldots, L_n\}$ the *body* of r and denote it by $b(r)$.

A set of rules P is called a *generalized extended logic program* (*logic program*, *GELP*). GELPs are the most general logic programs that we use. We favor the approach outlined in [3, 15], where MDLPs are built over GELPs, unifying the previous approaches under a common framework, allowing for more elegant comparisons, while keeping the previously used languages as special cases, so the results are propagated. We also remark, that GELPs enable to properly manipulate three truth values, "something is true", "something is false", and "we do not know", allowing to adequately switch from one to another, what we mark as a desirable feature, once dealing with knowledge updates.

Several other flavours of logic programs do exist. We mention *extended logic programs*, a subclass of GELPs formed by programs that do not contain default literals in heads of rules. *Generalized logic programs* do not allow explicit negation at all, i.e., for each objective literal L, contained in the program, it holds that $L \in \mathcal{A}$, and for each default literal *not L*, contained in the program, it holds that $L \in \mathcal{A}$. A logic program is *definite* if it only contains atoms of $\mathcal{A}$ in the heads, as well as in the bodies of its rules, i.e., definite logic programs do not allow negation at all.

Let P be a GELP. The expanded version of P is the program $\dot{P} = P \cup \{not \neg h(r) \leftarrow b(r) \mid r \in P \wedge h(r) \in \mathcal{O}\}$. Two literals $L \in \mathcal{O}$ and *not L* are said to be *conflicting*. Two rules are conflicting if their heads are conflicting literals. We denote this by $L \bowtie L'$ and by $r \bowtie r'$ respectively. For any set of literals S, $S^+ = S \cap \mathcal{O}$ and $S^- = S \cap \mathcal{D}$.

A set of literals that does not contain a pair of conflicting literals is called an *interpretation*. An interpretation is *total* if for each $L \in \mathcal{O}$ it contains L or *not L*. A literal L is *satisfied* in an interpretation I if $L \in I$ and we denote it by $I \vDash L$. Also $I \vDash S$, a set of literals S, if $I \vDash L$ for each $L \in S$. A rule r is satisfied in an interpretation I (denoted by $I \vDash r$) if $I \vDash h(r)$ whenever $I \vDash b(r)$. Let P be a definite logic program. We denote by $least(P)$ the unique *least model* of P that exists, as showed by van Emden and Kowalski in [16].

Most of the semantic approaches in dynamic logic programming build on ideas of the stable model semantics of logic programs that has been introduced by Gelfond and Lifschitz in [17]. According to this semantics a total interpretation M is a stable model of a GELP P if it holds that $M = least(P \cup M^-)$[1].

---

[1] With an abuse of notation, we commonly treat (sets of) literals as (sets of) facts, and also GELPs as definite programs, considering each negated literal as a new atom.

3 MDLPs and Various Semantics Based on Rejection of Rules

Logic programs have been proven useful in the area of knowledge representation. As long as the information we deal with is rather static we face no problem to encode it in form of a logic program. But we reach the barrier very soon, when dealing with information change in time, or when integrating information from several sources with various levels of relevancy.

To deal with this problem, the framework of dynamic logic programming has been introduced in [4]. In this framework information is encoded into several programs that are linearly ordered into a sequence by their level of relevancy. Such sequences are called dynamic logic programs.

This framework has been further generalized in [1] by allowing logic programs ordered by arbitrary (i.e., also non-linear) partial ordering. Multidimensional dynamic logic programs were born. We formalize the latter approach in Definition 1.

Definition 1. *Let $G = (V, E)$ be a directed acyclic graph with finite set of vertices V. Let $\mathcal{P} = \{P_i \mid i \in V\}$ be a set of logic programs. The pair $(\mathcal{P}, G)$ is a multidimensional dynamic logic program or often just program or MDLP.*

We often use just $\mathcal{P}$ instead of $(\mathcal{P}, G)$ and assume the existence of the corresponding G. The multiset of all rules of the expanded versions $\dot{P}_i$ of the logic programs P_i, $i \in V$ of $\mathcal{P}$ is denoted by $\Cup_{\mathcal{P}}$. Let $i, j \in V$, we denote by $i \prec j$ (and also by $P_i \prec P_j$) if there is a directed path from i to j in G. We denote by $i \preceq j$ (and by $P_i \preceq P_j$) if $i \prec j$ or if $i = j$.

A *dynamic logic program* (*DLP, linear* MDLP) is such a MDLP $\mathcal{P}$ whose G is collapsed into a single directed path. So, DLPs form a subclass of MDLPs, they are precisely all linearly ordered MDLPs.

Most of the semantic approaches in dynamic logic programming are based on the ideas of stable model semantics of simple logic programs. A set of models is assigned to a program by each of these semantics. Models are picked among the interpretations of the program.

As a MDLP in general may contain conflicting rules, semantics try to resolve these conflicts, when it is possible, according to the relevancy level of the conflicting rules. A common approach is to assign a set of *rejected rules* to a given program $\mathcal{P}$ and a "candidate model" interpretation M. Rejected rules are then subtracted from the union of all rules of $\mathcal{P}$, gaining the residue of $\mathcal{P}$ w.r.t. M. Also the set of *default assumptions* (sometimes just *defaults*) is assigned to $\mathcal{P}$ and M. Defaults are picked among the default literals. A fix-point condition is verified, whether M coincides with the least model of the union of the residue and the default assumptions. If so, then M is a model of P w.r.t. the semantics. A semantics that can be characterized in this manner is said to be *based on rejection of rules* or *rule-rejecting*.

Once we deal with several rule-rejecting semantics, then any difference between them originates in the way how particularly rejection of rules and default assumptions are implemented in these semantics. Two different kinds of rejection have been used with MDLPs. The original rejection used in [4, 1] keeps each rule intact as long as there is no reason for rejecting it in form of a more relevant rule that is satisfied in the considered interpretation. Formally, the set of rejected rules of $\mathcal{P}$ w.r.t. M is

$$Rej(\mathcal{P}, M) = \{r \in \dot{P}_i \mid (\exists r' \in \dot{P}_j) \; i \prec j, M \vDash b(r'), r \bowtie r'\} \; .$$

In [5], an alternative notion of rejection has been introduced, allowing each rule to reject other rules only if it is not rejected already. Such a set of rejected rules of $\mathcal{P}$ w.r.t. M is formalized as

$$Rej^{\star}(\mathcal{P}, M) = \{r \in \dot{P}_i \mid (\exists r' \in \dot{P}_j) \; i \prec j, M \vDash b(r'), r \bowtie r', r' \notin Rej^{\star}(\mathcal{P}, M)\} \; .$$

Originally, in [2], default assumptions have been computed just exactly as in the stable model semantics of logic programs. Formally,

$$Def^{\star}(\mathcal{P}, M) = M^- \; .$$

Later on, in [4, 1], another approach has been introduced, as the original set of defaults showed to be too broad. We formalize defaults according to this approach as

$$Def(\mathcal{P}, M) = \{not\ L \mid L \in \mathcal{O}, (\nexists r \in \mathbb{U}_{\mathcal{P}}) \; h(r) = L, M \vDash b(r)\} \; .$$

Combining two implementations of rejection and two of default assumptions immediately leads to four semantics of MDLPs. We define each of them formally in the following.

Definition 2. *A rule-rejecting semantics that uses $Rej(\mathcal{P}, M)$ for rejection and $Def^{\star}(\mathcal{P}, M)$ for defaults is called the* dynamic justified update (DJU) *semantics. That is, a total interpretation M is a model of a MDLP $\mathcal{P}$ w.r.t. the DJU semantics whenever $M = least(Res(\mathcal{P}, M) \cup Def^{\star}(\mathcal{P}, M))$, where $Res(\mathcal{P}, M) = \mathbb{U}_{\mathcal{P}} \setminus Rej(\mathcal{P}, M)$ is the residue.*

The DJU semantics is the very first rule-rejecting semantics that has been used in dynamic logic programming. If we restrict to DLPs build from generalized logic programs, it is identical with the $\mathcal{P}$-justified updates semantics of [2]. Soon the original default assumptions showed to be too broad. In [4, 1], they have been replaced by $Def(\mathcal{P}, M)$. The semantics is formally defined as follows.

Definition 3. *A rule-rejecting semantics that uses $Rej(\mathcal{P}, M)$ for rejection and $Def(\mathcal{P}, M)$ for defaults is called the* dynamic stable model (DSM) *semantics. Or equivalently, a total interpretation M is a model of a MDLP $\mathcal{P}$ w.r.t. the DSM semantics whenever $M = least(Res(\mathcal{P}, M) \cup Def(\mathcal{P}, M))$, where the residue is as in Definition 2.*

In [5], the alternative notion of rejection, $Rej^{\star}(\mathcal{P}, M)$, has been combined with $Def^{\star}(\mathcal{P}, M)$ to produce semantics for DLPs build from extended logic programs. The semantics has been originally called the update answer set semantics. In our setting we formalize it in Definition 4.

Definition 4. *A rule-rejecting semantics that uses $Rej^\star(\mathcal{P}, M)$ for rejection and $Def^\star(\mathcal{P}, M)$ for defaults is called the* backward dynamic justified update (BDJU) *semantics. In other words, a total interpretation M is a model of a MDLP $\mathcal{P}$ w.r.t. the BDJU semantics whenever $M = least(Res^\star(\mathcal{P}, M) \cup Def^\star(\mathcal{P}, M))$, where $Res^\star(\mathcal{P}, M) = \mathbb{U}_\mathcal{P} \setminus Rej^\star(\mathcal{P}, M)$ is the residue.*

By the label "backward" we indicate use of $Rej^\star(\mathcal{P}, M)$ rejection, as the algorithm for its computation from [5] traverses $\mathcal{P}$ in backward direction compared to the one for $Rej(\mathcal{P}, M)$ found in [4, 1]. In [3], the three above mentioned semantics have been brought to a more general platform offered by GELPs. Also a backward variant of the DSM semantics has been introduced, that we formalize in Definition 5. In [3], this semantics is called the U-model semantics.

Definition 5. *A rule-rejecting semantics that uses $Rej^\star(\mathcal{P}, M)$ for rejection and $Def(\mathcal{P}, M)$ for defaults is called the* backward dynamic stable model (BDSM) *semantics. That is, a total interpretation M is a model of a MDLP $\mathcal{P}$ w.r.t. the BDSM semantics whenever $M = least(Res^\star(\mathcal{P}, M) \cup Def(\mathcal{P}, M))$, where the residue is as in Definition 4.*

The set of all models of a program $\mathcal{P}$ w.r.t. the DJU semantics is denoted by $DJU(\mathcal{P})$. Similarly, $DSM(\mathcal{P})$, $BDJU(\mathcal{P})$ and $BDSM(\mathcal{P})$ are the sets of all models according to the remaining three semantics.

We have presented four rule-rejecting semantics of MDLPs. The following two examples taken from [3] show that each of this semantics is different.

Example 1. Let $\mathcal{P} = \{P_1 \prec P_2\}$ where $P_1 = \{a \leftarrow \}$, $P_2 = \{not\ a \leftarrow not\ a\}$. It holds that $DSM(\mathcal{P}) = BDSM(\mathcal{P}) = \{\{a, not\ \neg a\}\}$. But, for the other two, $DJU(\mathcal{P}) = BDJU(\mathcal{P}) = \{\{a, not\ \neg a\}, \{not\ a, not\ \neg a\}\}$.

Example 2. Let $\mathcal{P} = \{P_1 \prec P_2 \prec P_3\}$ where $P_1 = \{a \leftarrow \}$, $P_2 = \{not\ a \leftarrow \}$ and $P_3 = \{a \leftarrow a\}$. It holds that $DJU(\mathcal{P}) = DSM(\mathcal{P}) = \{\{not\ a, not\ \neg a\}\}$. On the other hand, $BDJU(\mathcal{P}) = BDSM(\mathcal{P}) = \{\{a, not\ \neg a\}, \{not\ a, not\ \neg a\}\}$.

Moreover, as it has been shown in [3], the sets of models assigned to arbitrary program $\mathcal{P}$, one set by each of these semantics, form a kind of hierarchy w.r.t. the set inclusion relation. The DSM semantics is the most restrictive one, the set of models w.r.t. DSM is always a subset of the other model-sets. On the other hand, the set of models w.r.t. any semantics is always a subset of the one w.r.t. BDJU, which always provides the broadest set of models. We summarize these observations in Theorem 1 taken from [3].

Theorem 1. *For each MDLP $\mathcal{P}$ it holds that*

$$DSM(\mathcal{P}) \subseteq DJU(\mathcal{P}) \subseteq BDJU(\mathcal{P}) \ ,$$
$$DSM(\mathcal{P}) \subseteq BDSM(\mathcal{P}) \subseteq BDJU(\mathcal{P}) \ .$$

4   Equality on the Class of Acyclic Programs

We have shown in Examples 1 and 2 that the four rule-rejecting semantics are in general distinct. However, many MDLPs exist, such as the one from Example 3, on which these four semantics coincide.

Example 3. Let $\mathcal{P} = \{P_1, P_2, P_3 \mid P_1 \prec P_3, P_2 \prec P_3\}$. Let $P_1 = \{a \leftarrow \}$, $P_2 = \{not\ a \leftarrow \}$ and $P_3 = \{a \leftarrow \}$. This simple MDLP can be viewed as a model of a community of three agents, who take part in the hierarchy of authorities. The first two of them are of incomparable authority and moreover, they have conflicting knowledge. This conflict is resolved by the third one of them, who is represented by logic program P_3 and its authority level is superior to the former two. All of the four semantics agree with this intuition and assign $M = \{a, not\ \neg a\}$ to $\mathcal{P}$ as its single model.

Examples like this one lead us to a hypothesis that there probably are vast classes of programs on which several semantics coincide. It shows that several rule-rejecting semantics possibly behave equally on "plain" programs, that are not obfuscated with cyclic dependencies among literals or other obstacles. Different behavior on such programs is supposed to be caused by different ability of the semantics to deal with such obstacles.

To evaluate cyclic dependencies among literals in programs we adopt the graph-theoretic framework introduced in [5]. An *AND/OR-graph* (N, C) is a hypergraph, whose set of nodes $N = N_A \uplus N_O$ decomposes into the set of *AND-nodes* N_A and the set of *OR-nodes* N_O, and its set of connectors $C = N \times \bigcup_{i=0}^{|N|} N^i$ is a function, i.e., for each $I \in N$ there is exactly one tuple $\langle O_1, \ldots, O_k \rangle$ s.t. $\langle I, O_1, \ldots, O_k \rangle \in C$. For any connector $\langle I, O_1, \ldots, O_k \rangle$, I is its *input node* and $O_1, \ldots, O_k$ are its *output nodes*.

Let (N, C) be an AND/OR-graph, $I \in N$ and $\langle I, O_1, \ldots, O_k \rangle \in C$. A tree p is a *path* in (N, C) *rooted in* I if one of the following conditions holds:

(i) $k = 0 \wedge p = \langle I \rangle$,
(ii) $k > 0 \wedge I \in N_A \wedge p = \langle I, p_1, \ldots, p_k \rangle$,
(iii) $k > 0 \wedge I \in N_O \wedge (\exists i)\ 1 \leq i \leq k \wedge p = \langle I, p_i \rangle$,

where p_i is a path in (N, C) rooted in O_i, $1 \leq i \leq k$.

Let $p = \langle I, p_1, \ldots, p_k \rangle$ be a path in an AND/OR-graph. A path p' is a *subpath* of p if $p' = p$ or p' is a subpath of p_i for some i, $1 \leq i \leq k$. A path p in an AND/OR-graph is said to be *acyclic* if for every subpath p' (including p) rooted in the node R, no subpath p'' of p' is rooted in R.

Definition 6. *Let P be a logic program. An AND/OR-graph $G_P = (N, C)$ is associated with P if both of the following conditions hold:*

(i) $N_A = P \wedge N_O = \mathcal{L}$,
(ii) $C = \{\langle r, L_1, \ldots, L_k \rangle \mid r = L \leftarrow L_1, \ldots, L_k \in P\}$
$\cup \{\langle L, r_1, \ldots, r_n \rangle \mid \{r_1, \ldots, r_n\} = \{r \in P \mid h(r) = L\}\}$.

Armed with such a framework we instantly identify the class of acyclic programs in Definition 7. Clearly, this definition is equivalent to the original one, as introduced in [18].

Definition 7. *We say that logic program P is* strictly acyclic *(or just* acyclic*) if G_P does not contain a path that is cyclic. We say that a MDLP $\mathcal{P}$ is strictly acyclic if $\mathbb{U}_\mathcal{P}$ is strictly acyclic.*

In [5], further reduction of $G_\mathcal{P}$ is utilized, once an interpretation M and a given notion of rejection are available. The resulting reduced AND/OR-graph is stripped from dependencies corresponding to rules that are rejected or that are not applicable.

Definition 8. *Let $\mathcal{P}$ be a MDLP, M a total interpretation and $Rejected(\mathcal{P}, M)$ a set of rejected rules according to some rule-rejecting semantics. The* reduced AND/OR-graph *of $\mathcal{P}$ with respect to M, $G_\mathcal{P}^M$ is obtained from $G_\mathcal{P}$ by*

1. *removing all $r \in N_A$ and their connectors (as well as removing r from all connectors containing it as an output node) if either $r \in Rejected(\mathcal{P}, M)$ or $M \nvDash b(r)$, and*
2. *replacing, for every $L \in \mathcal{O}$, the connector of not L by the 0-connector $\langle not\, L \rangle$, if L is associated with 0-connector after step 1 and no $r \in Rejected(\mathcal{P}, M)$ exists s.t. $h(r) = L$.*

Possessing the outlined framework, authors of [5] have introduced the "root condition" and the "chain condition", that we adopt in Definition 9 and 10 respectively.

Definition 9. *Let $\mathcal{P}$ be a MDLP, M a total interpretation and $Rejected(\mathcal{P}, M)$ a set of rejected rules according to some rule-rejecting semantics. We say that $\mathcal{P}$, M and $Rejected(\mathcal{P}, M)$ obey the* root condition *if, for each not $L \in M^-$, one of the following conditions holds:*

(i) *$(\forall r \in \mathbb{U}_\mathcal{P})\ h(r) = L \implies M \nvDash b(r)$,*
(ii) *there exists an acyclic path p in $G_\mathcal{P}^M$ rooted in not L.*

Definition 10. *We say that a MDLP $\mathcal{P}$ and a total interpretation M obey the* chain condition *if, for each pair of rules $r \in P_i$, $r' \in P_j$ s.t. $i \prec j$, $r \bowtie r'$, $M \vDash b(r)$, $M \vDash b(r')$ and $r' \in Rej^\star(\mathcal{P}, M)$, there also exists $r'' \in P_s$ s.t. $j \prec s$, $r' \bowtie r''$ and $b(r'') \subseteq b(r)$.*

A theorem follows in [5], stating that if both, the root and the chain condition, are satisfied by a DLP $\mathcal{P}$, a total interpretation M and $Rej(\mathcal{P}, M)$ then $M \in DSM(\mathcal{P})$ if and only if M is a model of $\mathcal{P}$ (both transformed to extended logic programs) w.r.t. the BDJU semantics.

In [3] relations between all four of these semantics are further investigated, once all four are generalized to the platform of GELPs. It is shown there, that the root condition renders a proper subclass of DLPs, in order to compare two semantics that utilize $Def(\mathcal{P}, M)$ and $Def^\star(\mathcal{P}, M)$ for defaults respectively, and share the same implementation of rejection. We adopt this proposition from [3] and generalize it to the platform of MDLPs in Theorem 2. In [3] it is also shown that two pairs of semantics that differ in rejection but use the same defaults, pairwise, coincide on a DLP $\mathcal{P}$ and a total interpretation M if they obey the chain condition. We adopt this proposition in Theorem 3.[2]

Theorem 2. *Let $\mathcal{P}$ be a MDLP, M a total interpretation. Then it holds that:*

(i) $M \in DJU(\mathcal{P}) \equiv M \in DSM(\mathcal{P})$ if and only if $\mathcal{P}$, M and $Rej(\mathcal{P}, M)$ obey the root condition,

(ii) $M \in BDJU(\mathcal{P}) \equiv M \in BDSM(\mathcal{P})$ if and only if $\mathcal{P}$, M and $Rej^\star(\mathcal{P}, M)$ obey the root condition.

Theorem 3. *Let $\mathcal{P}$ be a MDLP, M a total interpretation. If $\mathcal{P}$ and M obey the chain condition then each of the following propositions holds:*

(i) $M \in DJU(\mathcal{P}) \equiv M \in BDJU(\mathcal{P})$,

(ii) $M \in DSM(\mathcal{P}) \equiv M \in BDSM(\mathcal{P})$.

It follows in [3], that if both of the conditions are obeyed by $\mathcal{P}$ and M, then all four of the semantics coincide on $\mathcal{P}$ and M. However, as we show in Example 4, many times the chain condition is not obeyed but the semantics do coincide. We argue that this restriction is not accurate.

Example 4. Let $\mathcal{P} = \{P_1 \prec P_2 \prec P_3\}$, $P_1 = \{a \leftarrow \}$, $P_2 = \{not\, a \leftarrow \}$ and $P_3 = \{a \leftarrow not\, b\}$. The chain condition is not obeyed by $\mathcal{P}$ and $M = \{a, not\, b, not \neg a, not \neg b\}$. Yet, $DSM(\mathcal{P}) = BDSM(\mathcal{P}) = \{M\}$ and $DJU(\mathcal{P}) = BDJU(\mathcal{P}) = \{M\}$.

We now return to considerations about programs with restricted occurrence of cycles. We focus on a hypothesis that different behavior of semantics is always accompanied by presence of cyclic dependencies among literals. Our aim is to restrict somehow the occurrence of cyclic dependencies in order to establish the coincidence of the semantics.

Programs with cycles are often considered odd. Self-dependence, connected with presence of cycles, is marked as unpleasant and undesirable feature, as strict, deductive reasoning – closely interconnected with mathematical logic – forbids it. Yet, in logic programming cycles are useful, for example to express equivalence. Moreover there are programs that contain cycles and still different semantics match regarding them. Both of these features are apparent from Example 5. Hence we introduce yet another, weaker, condition of acyclicity in the consecutive Definition 11. With this condition, we are able to identify programs, where cycles may be present, but each literal is supported by at least one acyclic derivation.

---

[2] We remark that this property does not depend on the particular choice of defaults. In fact, it holds for arbitrary set of default assumptions. See [10] for details.

Example 5. Let $\mathcal{P} = \{P_1 \prec P_2\}$, $P_1 = \{a \leftarrow b; b \leftarrow a\}$ and $P_2 = \{a \leftarrow \}$. All of the four semantics match on $\mathcal{P}$. $DJU(\mathcal{P}) = DSM(\mathcal{P}) = BDJU(\mathcal{P}) = BDSM(\mathcal{P}) = \{\{a, b, not \neg a, not \neg b\}\}$. Actually, the cyclic information of program P_1 is not redundant in any way. P_1 states that the truth value of a is equivalent with the truth value of b and vice versa. Later, when the more recent knowledge of P_2 appears telling that a is true we derive that also b is true.

Definition 11. *We say that logic program P is* sufficiently acyclic *if for every literal $L \in \mathcal{L}$ there exists an acyclic path in the hypergraph G_P associated with P that is rooted in L. A MDLP $\mathcal{P}$ is* sufficiently acyclic *whenever $\mathbb{U}_{\mathcal{P}}$ is sufficiently acyclic.*

The application of the condition of sufficient acyclicity on MDLPs in general is, however, useless – as when the residue is computed, several rules are retracted and the condition may not be satisfied any more. So we resort to the one-model relations of two semantics quite like in the case of the root condition. The relation is established for a program and a given model. Possessing a candidate-model, the residue is determined, and the condition is applied on the residue instead of the whole program.

To establish one-model equivalence of two semantics on a program, we repeatedly use a method, that is sketched in Remark 1.

Remark 1. Let $\mathcal{P}$ be a MDLP and let M be a total interpretation. Let S_1 and S_2 be two rule-rejecting semantics with shared implementation of defaults and different implementation of rejection. Let D be the set of defaults assigned to $\mathcal{P}$ and M by these semantics and let R_1 and R_2 be the residues assigned to $\mathcal{P}$ and M by S_1 and S_2 respectively. If

(i) $M \in S_2(\mathcal{P})$,
(ii) $R_1 \subseteq R_2$,

then $M \in S_1(\mathcal{P})$ if and only if there exists such $R \subseteq R_1$ that $M = least(R \cup D) -$ i.e., we are able to find R, a subset of R_1, s.t. R still contains enough of rules that are necessary to compute M. Therefore we concentrate on searching for such sets $R \subseteq R_1$ in order to establish equivalence of S_1 and S_2 regarding $\mathcal{P}$ and M.

The condition for one-model equality of that pairs of semantics that differ in the implementation of rejection and use same defaults is expressed in Theorem 4. The theorem uses the following lemma.

Lemma 1. *Let S be the BDSM or the BDJU semantics. Let $\mathcal{P}$ be a MDLP, $M \in S(\mathcal{P})$ and let $Defaults(\mathcal{P}, M)$ be the default assumptions assigned to $\mathcal{P}$ and M by S. If the set R defined as*

$$R = \{r \mid r \in Res(\mathcal{P}, M) \wedge M \vDash b(r)\}$$

is sufficiently acyclic then M can be computed as a model in the given semantics using only the rules of R. That is, $M = least(R \cup Defaults(\mathcal{P}, M))$.

Proof. Since R is sufficiently acyclic, there exists a rule $r \in R$ such that for each $L \in b(r)$ for no $r' \in R$ holds $h(r') = L$. And $r \in R$ so it holds that $M \vDash b(r)$. From Definitions 2 and 4 and from how R is defined it follows that for each rule $q \in Res^\star(\mathcal{P}, M)$, $M \vDash b(q)$ there is a $q' \in R$ s.t. $h(q) = h(q')$ and since $M \in S(\mathcal{P})$ then $b(r) \subseteq Defaults(\mathcal{P}, M)$. We now construct

$$M^0 = Defaults(\mathcal{P}, M) \ , \qquad M^1 = M^0 \cup h(r) \ ,$$
$$R^0 = R \ , \qquad\qquad R^1 = R^0 \setminus \{r'' \mid h(r'') = h(r)\} \ .$$

Assume that M^j and R^j are constructed by adding one literal $L \in \mathcal{L}$ to M^{j-1} and removing all r'' from R^{j-1} such that $h(r'') = L$, $0 < j \leq i$. Again, as R is sufficiently acyclic, there is $r \in R^i$ s.t. for each $L \in b(r)$ for no $r' \in R^i$ holds $h(r') = L$. From the construction of D^i, R^i it follows that

$$(\forall j \leq i) \ M^j \cup \{h(r) \mid r \in R^j\} = M \ .$$

Therefore $b(r) \subseteq M^i$, and so we are able to construct

$$M^{i+1} = M^i \cup h(r) \ , \qquad R^{i+1} = R^i \setminus \{r'' \in R^i \mid h(r'') = h(r)\} \ .$$

It is straightforward that $\bigcup_{i=1}^{\infty} M^i = M$. This way we have computed M as a model in S only from the rules of R. (Step by step, we have simulated the iterations of the $least(\cdot)$ operator.) In other words,

$$M = least(R \cup Defaults(\mathcal{P}, M)) \ .$$

$\square$

Theorem 4. *Let $\mathcal{P}$ be a MDLP and M be its total interpretation. If the set*

$$R = \{r \mid r \in Res(\mathcal{P}, M) \wedge M \vDash b(r)\}$$

is sufficiently acyclic then it holds that

(i) $M \in DSM(\mathcal{P}) \equiv M \in BDSM(\mathcal{P})$, and also
(ii) $M \in DJU(\mathcal{P}) \equiv M \in BDJU(\mathcal{P})$.

Proof. The only-if part of both (i) and (ii) follows from Theorem 1. The if part proves as follows. Let $\mathcal{P}$ be a MDLP. Let $M \in BDSM(\mathcal{P})$ ($BDJU(\mathcal{P})$ respectively). Let R be sufficiently acyclic. From Lemma 1 we get that M can be computed only using the rules of R. Since

$$R \subseteq Res(\mathcal{P}, M) \subseteq Res^\star(\mathcal{P}, M) \ ,$$

it follows from Remark 1 that $M \in DSM(\mathcal{P})$ ($M \in DJU(\mathcal{P})$). $\square$

In Theorem 4 we have presented a restrictive condition for one-model equality of those pairs of semantics that differ in rejection and use same defaults. We now show (in Lemma 2) that under this condition also the root condition is satisfied. It follows as a direct consequence of this lemma and Theorem 4 that under our condition all four semantics coincide (Corollary 1).

Lemma 2. *Let $\mathcal{P}$ be a MDLP and M its total interpretation. Let*

$$R = \{r \mid r \in Res(\mathcal{P}, M) \wedge M \vDash b(r)\} \ .$$

If R is sufficiently acyclic then both of the triples $\mathcal{P}$, M, $Rej(\mathcal{P}, M)$ and $\mathcal{P}$, M, $Rej^{\star}(\mathcal{P}, M)$ obey the root condition.

Proof. R is sufficiently acyclic, hence for every $L \in M^{-}$ either $L \in Def(\mathcal{P}, M)$ and then condition (i) of Definition 9 (root condition) is satisfied or there exists a rule $r \in Res(\mathcal{P}, M)$ s.t. $M \vDash b(r)$ and $h(r) = L$ and therefore also $r' \in R$ s.t. $h(r') = L$ and so there is a path p in G_R rooted in L that is acyclic. The subpath p' of p, terminated in every $not\ L' \in \mathcal{D}$ whose connector was replaced by $\langle not\ L' \rangle$ in step 2 of the construction of $G_{\mathcal{P}}^{M}$, is an acyclic path in $G_{\mathcal{P}}^{M}$ rooted in L. And so condition (ii) of Definition 9 is satisfied. Hence the root condition is obeyed by $\mathcal{P}$, M and $Rej(\mathcal{P}, M)$.

As for each $r \in Res(\mathcal{P}, M)$, $M \vDash b(r)$ there exists such $r' \in Res^{\star}(\mathcal{P}, M)$ that $h(r') = h(r)$ and $M \vDash b(r')$ and vice versa, we get that also $\mathcal{P}$, M and $Rej^{\star}(\mathcal{P}, M)$ obey the root condition.   □

Corollary 1. *Let $\mathcal{P}$ be a MDLP and M its total interpretation. If the set*

$$R = \{r \mid r \in Res(\mathcal{P}, M) \wedge M \vDash b(r)\}$$

is sufficiently acyclic then

$$M \in DSM(\mathcal{P}) \equiv M \in BDSM(\mathcal{P}) \equiv M \in DJU(\mathcal{P}) \equiv M \in BDJU(\mathcal{P}) \ .$$

Moreover, as for a strictly acyclic program each of its subsets is sufficiently acyclic, it trivially follows that all four semantics coincide on strictly acyclic programs as we state in the following corollary.

Corollary 2. *Let $\mathcal{P}$ be a strictly acyclic MDLP. Then*

$$DSM(\mathcal{P}) = BDSM(\mathcal{P}) = DJU(\mathcal{P}) = BDJU(\mathcal{P}) \ .$$

We have shown that the four rule-rejecting semantics coincide on strictly acyclic programs. In Corollary 1 we have also established a more accurate restriction that renders the one-model equivalence of the semantics. However, comparing entire model-sets assigned to a program by two semantics one by one is computationally as complex as computing and enumerating these two model-sets. So, this result is rather of theoretical value.

5   RDSM Semantics and DLPs

In [7], Alferes et al. have introduced a new semantics for linear DLPs. Motivation for this new semantics roots in the observation that even the most restrictive semantics, DSM, provides counterintuitive models for some programs (cf. Example 6).

Example 6. Let $\mathcal{P} = \{P_1 \prec P_2\}$ where $P_1 = \{a \leftarrow ; not\ a \leftarrow \}$ and $P_2 = \{a \leftarrow a\}$. It holds that $DSM(\{P_1\}) = \emptyset$, it is not surprising as P_1 is contradictory. If we inspect the single rule of P_2 we see that it actually brings no new factual information. We suppose that addition of such rule should not add new models to the program. However, $DSM(\mathcal{P}) = \{\{a, not\ \neg a\}\}$.

Such rules as the one of P_2 from Example 6, having head a subset of the body, are called *tautological*. Tautological rules are in fact just a special case of cycles that only span throughout one rule. In [7], authors have identified even broader class of extensions of DLPs that, according to their intuition, should not yield new models of the programs. Such extensions are called *refined extensions*. Then a principle has been formed, stating that, having a proper semantics, if a program $\mathcal{P}'$ is just a refined extension of $\mathcal{P}$ then it should not have a model that is not also a model of $\mathcal{P}$. This principle is called the *refined extension principle*. We refer the reader who is interested in precise definitions to [7].

In [7], also a modified DSM semantics has been introduced. The modification is slight, two conflicting rules of the same program are allowed to reject each other. Formally, the set of rejected rules of this semantics is

$$Rej^R(\mathcal{P}, M) = \{r \in \dot{P}_i \mid (\exists r' \in \dot{P}_j)\ i \preceq j, M \models b(r'), r \bowtie r'\}\ .$$

The semantics is formalized in Definition 12.

Definition 12. *A rule-rejecting semantics of DLPs that uses $Rej^R(\mathcal{P}, M)$ for rejection and $Def(\mathcal{P}, M)$ for defaults is called the* refined dynamic stable model *(RDSM) semantics. In other words, a total interpretation M is a model of a DLP $\mathcal{P}$ w.r.t. the RDSM semantics whenever $M = least(Res^R(\mathcal{P}, M) \cup Def(\mathcal{P}, M))$, where $Res^R(\mathcal{P}, M)$ is the residue.*

We agree with [7] that the RDSM semantics is very favourable. It has been shown in [7] that it satisfies the refined extension principle and, as we adopt in Theorem 5, it always yields such model-set that is a subset of the model-set w.r.t. the DSM semantics. Moreover, it has been precisely described and motivated in [7], why some models provided by DSM should be excluded.

Theorem 5. *For any DLP $\mathcal{P}$ it holds that $RDSM(\mathcal{P}) \subseteq DSM(\mathcal{P})$.*

In [7], it further has been shown that for a program $\mathcal{P}$ that does not contain a pair of conflicting rules in the very same $P_i \in \mathcal{P}$, the RDSM and the DSM semantics coincide. However, this result neither is tight as many programs exist s.t. DSM and RDSM coincide on them and the condition is not satisfied.

The RDSM semantics has been introduced only for linear DLPs and according to our deepest knowledge all attempts to generalize it for MDLPs have failed so far (cf. [19]). Hence, in this section, we restrict our considerations to linear DLPs. In the remaining we show that under a very similar restriction as the one of Corollary 1, for a given model, all five of the semantics coincide.

First of all, the following example demonstrates why the condition has to be altered.

Example 7. Recall again the program $\mathcal{P}$ from Example 6. Let $M = \{a, not \neg a\}$. Even if $R = \{a \leftarrow, a \leftarrow a\}$ is sufficiently acyclic, $M \in DSM(P)$ and $M \notin RDSM(P)$. Indeed, the fact that $R \nsubseteq Res^R(\mathcal{P}, M)$ causes the trouble. The sufficient acyclicity is broken in $Res^R(\mathcal{P}, M)$ and therefore a can not be derived in the refined semantics.

The further restrictive condition is introduced in Theorem 6, where we prove the one-model coincidence of RDSM and DSM and we also confirm that the propositions of Theorem 4 hold under this modified condition as well. The theorem uses the following lemma.

Lemma 3. *Let semantics S be one of DSM, DJU, BDSM and BDJU. Let $\mathcal{P}$ be a DLP. Let $M \in S(\mathcal{P})$. Let $Rejected(\mathcal{P}, M)$ be the rejected rules, $Residue(\mathcal{P}, M)$ be the residue and $Defaults(\mathcal{P}, M)$ be the defaults assigned to $\mathcal{P}$ and M by S. If*

$$R' = \{r \mid r \in Res^R(\mathcal{P}, M) \wedge M \vDash b(r)\}$$

is sufficiently acyclic then M can be computed as a model in the given semantics using only the rules of R'. That is, $M = least(R' \cup Defaults(\mathcal{P}, M))$.

Proof. From Definitions 2, 4 and 12 and from how R' is defined it follows that if $M \in S(\mathcal{P})$ then for each rule $q \in Residue(\mathcal{P}, M)$, $M \vDash b(q)$ there is a $q' \in R'$ s.t. $h(q) = h(q')$. Once we are aware of this fact this lemma is proved exactly as Lemma 1.   □

Theorem 6. *Let $\mathcal{P}$ be a DLP and M be its total interpretation. If*

$$R' = \{r \mid r \in Res^R(\mathcal{P}, M) \wedge M \vDash b(r)\}$$

is sufficiently acyclic then the following propositions hold:

(i) $M \in DSM(\mathcal{P}) \equiv M \in RDSM(\mathcal{P})$,
(ii) $M \in DSM(\mathcal{P}) \equiv M \in BDSM(\mathcal{P})$,
(iii) $M \in DJU(\mathcal{P}) \equiv M \in BDJU(\mathcal{P})$.

Proof. Propositions (ii) and (iii) are proved like in the above Theorem 4. The if part of (i) follows from Theorem 5. The only if part of (i) proves as follows.

Let $M \in DSM(\mathcal{P})$. Let R' be sufficiently acyclic. From Lemma 3 we know that M can be computed using only the rules of R'. Also

$$R' \subseteq Res^R(\mathcal{P}, M) \subseteq Res(\mathcal{P}, M) ,$$

so it follows from Remark 1 that $M \in RDSM(\mathcal{P})$.   □

In the following lemma we show that even if we have slightly modified the condition, its satisfaction still implies that the root condition is also satisfied. Hence if the modified condition is satisfied, all five of the semantics for DLPs coincide on a given model as we state in Corollary 3.

Lemma 4. *Let $\mathcal{P}$ be a MDLP and M its total interpretation. Let*

$$R' = \{r \mid r \in Res^R(\mathcal{P}, M) \wedge M \vDash b(r)\} \ .$$

If R' is sufficiently acyclic and $M \in DJU(\mathcal{P})$ ($M \in BDJU(\mathcal{P})$) then $\mathcal{P}$, M, $Rej(\mathcal{P}, M)$ ($\mathcal{P}$, M, $Rej^\star(\mathcal{P}, M)$) obey the root condition.

Proof. This lemma the same way as Lemma 2 if we realize that when $M \in DJU(\mathcal{P})$ ($M \in BDJU(\mathcal{P})$) then for each rule $r \in Res(\mathcal{P}, M)$ ($r \in Res^\star(\mathcal{P}, M)$) s.t. $M \vDash b(r)$ and $h(r) = L$ there also exists $r' \in R'$ s.t. $h(r') = L$. $\qquad\square$

Corollary 3. *Let $\mathcal{P}$ be a DLP and M its total interpretation. If the set*

$$R' = \{r \mid r \in Res^R(\mathcal{P}, M) \wedge M \vDash b(r)\}$$

is sufficiently acyclic then

$$M \in DSM(\mathcal{P}) \equiv M \in BDSM(\mathcal{P}) \equiv M \in RDSM(\mathcal{P}) \equiv$$
$$\equiv M \in DJU(\mathcal{P}) \equiv M \in BDJU(\mathcal{P}) \ .$$

As for Corollary 1, also for Corollary 3 it holds that if, using it, we want to compare entire model-sets assigned to a program by a pair of semantics, computational complexity is the same as enumerating and comparing these two model-sets. Anyway, it trivially follows from this corollary that all five of the semantics coincide on strictly acyclic programs, as follows in Corollary 4.

Corollary 4. *Let $\mathcal{P}$ be a strictly acyclic DLP. Then*

$$DSM(\mathcal{P}) = BDSM(\mathcal{P}) = RDSM(\mathcal{P}) = DJU(\mathcal{P}) = BDJU(\mathcal{P}) \ .$$

6   Conclusion

In accordance with [3, 15], we have built MDLPs over a more general language of GELPs, that allows for more elegant comparisons, since no transformations are necessary, as the previous approaches are obtained as its special cases. We have then compared four different rule-rejecting semantics of MDLPs and in addition one more when restricted to linear DLPs. We have introduced sufficient acyclicity. Using this notion, we have provided a restrictive condition on a MDLP (DLP) $\mathcal{P}$ and a given candidate model M s.t. if it is satisfied all four (five) semantics coincide on $\mathcal{P}$ and M. As a trivial consequence we have stated the main result, that on strictly acyclic programs all four (five) of the semantics coincide.

There are several open problems. As there are programs that contain cycles and several of the five semantics coincide on them, the search for a more proper characterization of the class of programs on which these semantics coincide is still open. In this line, we suggest investigation of other well known classes, as stratified and call-consistent programs. One of the most favourable semantics, RDSM, is only known for DLPs, generalizing RDSM to MDLPs is a challenging problem. Comparing semantics that are based on rejection of rules with other approaches (such as the one of [15] based on Kripke structures) might be interesting. To meet this goal, we propose that more abstract criteria for evaluating these semantics should be introduced, seeing some of the present ones, e.g., the refined extension principle of [6, 7], too attached to the rule-rejecting framework.

Acknowledgements

I would like to thank to anonymous referees for valuable comments and suggestions. I would like to thank to Ján Šefránek and João A. Leite for their advising and help and to Michaela Danišová and to Martin Baláž for language and typographical corrections.

References

1. Leite, J.A., Alferes, J.J., Pereira, L.M.: Multi-dimensional dynamic logic programming. In Sadri, F., Satoh, K., eds.: Proceedings of the CL-2000 Workshop on Computational Logic in Multi-Agent Systems (CLIMA'00). (2000) 17–26
2. Leite, J.A., Pereira, L.M.: Iterated logic program updates. In Jaffar, J., ed.: Proceedings of the 1998 Joint International Conference and Symposium on Logic Programming (JICSLP'98), MIT Press (1998) 265–278
3. Leite, J.A.: Evolving Knowledge Bases: Specification and Semantics. Volume 81 of Frontiers in Artificial Intelligence and Applications, Dissertations in Artificial Intelligence. IOS Press, Amsterdam (2003)
4. Alferes, J.J., Leite, J.A., Pereira, L.M., Przymusinska, H., Przymusinski, T.C.: Dynamic logic programming. In Cohn, A.G., Schubert, L.K., Shapiro, S.C., eds.: Proceedings of the Sixth International Conference on Principles of Knowledge Representation and Reasoning (KR'98), Morgan Kaufmann (1998) 98–109
5. Eiter, T., Sabbatini, G., Fink, M., Tompits, H.: On updates of logic programs: Semantics and properties. Technical Report 1843-00-08, Institute of Information Systems, Vienna University of Technology (2002)
6. Alferes, J.J., Banti, F., Brogi, A., Leite, J.A.: The refined extension principle for semantics of dynamic logic programming. Studia Logica **79(1)** (2005) 7–32
7. Alferes, J.J., Banti, F., Brogi, A., Leite, J.A.: Semantics for dynamic logic programming: A principle-based approach. In Lifschitz, V., Niemela, I., eds.: Proceedings of the Seventh International Conference on Logic Programming and Nonmonotonic Reasoning (LPNMR-7), Springer-Verlag (2004)
8. Leite, J.: On some differences between semantics of logic program updates. In Lemaitre, C., Reyes, C.A., Gonzalez, J.A., eds.: Advances in Artificial Intelligence: Proceedings of the 9th Ibero-American Conference on AI (IBERAMIA-04). LNAI, Springer (2004)
9. Eiter, T., Sabbatini, G., Fink, M., Tompits, H.: On properties of update sequences based on causal rejection. Theory and Practice of Logic Programming (2002) 711–767

10. Homola, M.: On relations of the various semantic approaches in multidimensional dynamic logic programming. Master's thesis, Comenius University, Faculty of Mathematics Physics and Informatics, Bratislava (2004)

11. Leite, J.A., Alferes, J.J., Pereira, L.M.: Multi-dimensional logic programming. Technical report, Departamento de Informática, Faculdade de Ciências e Tecnologia, Universidade Nova de Lisboa (2001)

12. Leite, J.A., Alferes, J.J., Pereira, L.M.: Multi-dimensional dynamic knowledge representation. In Eiter, T., Faber, W., Truszczynski, M., eds.: Proceedings of the Sixth International Conference on Logic Programming and Nonmonotonic Reasoning (LPNMR'01), Springer (2001) 365–378

13. Alferes, J.J., Banti, F., Brogi, A.: From logic program updates to action description updates. In this volume.

14. Sakama, C., Inoue, K.: Coordination between logical agents. In this volume.

15. Šefránek, J.: Semantic considerations on rejection. In: Proceedings of the International Workshop on Non-Monotonic Reasoning (NMR 2004), Foundations of Nonmonotonic Reasoning. (2004)

16. van Emden, M.H., Kowalski, R.A.: The semantics of predicate logic as a programming language. Journal of the ACM **23** (1976) 733–742

17. Gelfond, M., Lifschitz, V.: The stable model semantics for logic programming. In Kowalski, R.A., Bowen, K.A., eds.: Logic Programming, Proceedings of the Fifth International Conference and Symposium, MIT Press (1988) 1070–1080

18. Apt, K.R., Bezem, M.: Acyclic programs. New Generation Computing **9** (1991) 335–363

19. Šiška, J.: Refined extension principle for multi-dimensional dynamic logic programming. Master's thesis, Comenius University, Faculty of Mathematics Physics and Informatics, Bratislava (2004)

Declarative Agent Control

Antonis Kakas[1], Paolo Mancarella[2], Fariba Sadri[3],
Kostas Stathis[2,4], and Francesca Toni[2,3]

[1] Dept. of Computer Science, University of Cyprus
antonis@cs.ucy.ac.cy
[2] Dip. di Informatica, Università di Pisa
{paolo, stathis, toni}@di.unipi.it
[3] Dept. of Computing, Imperial College London
{fs, ft}@doc.ic.ac.uk
[4] School of Informatics, City University London
kostas@soi.city.ac.uk

Abstract. In this work, we extend the architecture of agents (and robots) based upon fixed, one-size-fits-all cycles of operation, by providing a framework of declarative specification of agent control. Control is given in terms of *cycle theories*, which define in a declarative way the possible alternative behaviours of agents, depending on the particular circumstances of the (perceived) external environment in which they are situated, on the internal state of the agents at the time of operation, and on the agents' behavioural profile. This form of control is adopted by the KGP model of agency and has been successfully implemented in the PROSOCS platform. We also show how, via cycle theories, we can formally verify properties of agents' behaviour, focusing on the concrete property of agents' *interruptibility*. Finally, we give some examples to show how different cycle theories give rise to different, heterogeneous agents' behaviours.

1   Introduction

To make theories of agency practical, normally a control component is proposed within concrete agent (robot) architectures. Most such architectures rely upon a fixed, one-size-fits-all cycle of control, which is forced upon the agents whatever the situation in which they operate. This kind of control has many drawbacks, and has been criticised by many (e.g. in robotics), as it does not allow us to take into account changes in the environment promptly and it does not take into account agent's preferences and "personality".

In this paper, we present an alternative approach, which models agents' control via declarative, logic-based *cycle theories*, which provide *flexible control* in that: (i) they allow the same agent to exhibit different behaviour in different circumstances (internal and external to the agent), thus extending in a non-trivial way conventional, fixed cycles of behaviour, (ii) they allow us to state and verify formal properties of agent behaviour (e.g. their interruptibility), and thus (iii) provide implementation guidelines to design suitable agents for suitable

J. Leite and P. Torroni (Eds.): CLIMA V, LNAI 3487, pp. 96–110, 2005.
© Springer-Verlag Berlin Heidelberg 2005

applications. Furthermore, cycle theories allow different agents to have different patterns of behaviour in the same circumstances, by varying few, well-identified components. Thus, by adopting different cycle theories we obtain behaviourally *heterogeneous* agents.

The notion of cycle theory and its use to determine the behaviour of agents can in principle be imported into any agent system, to replace conventional fixed cycles. However, in defining the cycle theory of an agent, we will assume that the agent is equipped with a pool of *state transitions* that modify its internal state. We will understand the operation of agents simply in terms of sequences of such transitions. Such sequences can be obtained from *fixed cycles* of operation of agents as in most of the literature. Alternatively, such sequences can be obtained via fixed cycles together with the possibility of selecting amongst such fixed cycles according to some criteria e.g. the type of external environment in which the agent will operate (see the recent work of [4]). Yet another possibility, that we pursue in this paper, is to specify the required operation via more versatile cycle theories that are able to generate dynamically several cycles of operations according to the current need of the agent. This approach has been adopted in the KGP model of agency [10, 2] and implemented in the PROSOCS platform [16].

We will define a cycle theory as a logic program with priorities over rules. The rules represent possible follow-ups of (already executed) transitions. The priorities express high-level preferences of the particular agent equipped with the cycle theory, that characterise the operational behaviour of the agent, e.g. a preference in testing the preconditions of an action before it tries to execute it. We will assume that the choice for the next transition depends only on the transition that has just been executed (and the resulting state of the agent), and not on the longer history of the previous transitions. We believe this not to be restrictive, in that the effects of any earlier transitions may in any case be recorded in the internal state of the agent and reasoned upon by it. Also, the approach can be extended to take into account longer histories of transitions when deciding the next one.

2   Background

Cycle theories will be written in the general framework of Logic Programming with Priorities (LPP). Our approach does not rely on any concrete such framework. One such concrete framework could be the Logic Programming without Negation as Failure (LPwNF) [5, 8] suitably extended to deal with dynamic preferences [9]. Other concrete frameworks that could be used for LPP are, for instance, those presented in [13, 12]. Note also that our approach does not depend crucially on the use of the framework of LPP: other frameworks for the declarative specification of preference policies, e.g. Default Logic with Priorities [3], could be used instead. Note, however, that the use of a logic-based framework where priorities are encoded within the logic itself is essential, since it allows reasoning even with potentially contradictory preferences. Also, note that the choice of one logic rather than another might affect the properties of agents specified via cycle theories.

For the purposes of this paper, we will assume that an *LPP-theory*, referred to as $\mathcal{T}$, consists of four parts:

(i) a low-level part P, consisting of a logic program; each rule in P is assigned a name, which is a term; e.g., one such rule could be

$$n(X) : p(X) \leftarrow q(X, Y), r(Y)$$

with name $n(X)$;

(ii) a high-level part H, specifying conditional, dynamic priorities amongst rules in P; e.g., one such priority could be

$$h(X) : n(X) \succ m(X) \leftarrow c(X)$$

to be read: if (some instance of) the condition $c(X)$ holds, then the rule in P with name (the corresponding instance of) $n(X)$ should be given higher priority than the rule in P with name (the corresponding instance of) $m(X)$. The rule is given a name, $h(X)$;

(iii) an auxiliary part A, defining predicates occurring in the conditions of rules in P and H and not in the conclusions of any rule in P;

(iv) a notion of incompatibility which, for the purposes of this paper, can be assumed to be given as a set of rules defining the predicate *incompatible*, e.g.

$$incompatible(p(X), p'(X))$$

to be read: any instance of the literal $p(X)$ is incompatible with the corresponding instance of the literal $p'(X)$. We assume that incompatibility is symmetric, and refer to the set of all incompatibility rules as I.

Any concrete LPP framework is equipped with a notion of entailment, that we denote by $\models_{pr}$. Intuitively, $\mathcal{T} \models_{pr} \alpha$ iff α is the "conclusion" of a sub-theory of $P \cup A$ which is "preferred" wrt $H \cup A$ in $\mathcal{T}$ over any other any other sub-theory of $P \cup A$ that derives "conclusion" incompatible with α (wrt I). Here, we are assuming that the underlying logic programming language is equipped with a notion of "entailment" that allows to draw "conclusions". In [13, 12, 9, 8, 5], $\models_{pr}$ is defined via argumentation.

3   Abstract Agent Model

We assume that our agents conform to the following abstract model, which can be seen as a high-level abstraction of most agent systems in the literature. Agents are equipped with

- some *internal state*, which changes over the life-time of the agent, and is formalised in some logic-based language or via some concrete data structure in some programming language;
- some pool of *(state) transitions*, that modify the state of the agent, and may take some inputs to be "computed" or selected by
- some *selection functions* on their states.

For example, the state may consist of beliefs, desires and intentions, represented in some modal logics, as in the BDI architecture [14] and its follow-ups, e.g. [1], or commitments and commitment rules, as in [15], or beliefs, goals and capabilities, represented in concurrent logic programming, as in [7], or knowledge, goals and plan, represented in (extensions of) logic programming, as in [11].

The transitions in the given pool can be any, but, if we abstract away from existing agent architectures and models in the literature, we can see that we need at least a transition responsible for observing the environment, thus rendering the agents situated. This transition might modify the internal state differently in concrete agent architectures, to record the observed events and properties of the environment. Here, we will call such a transition *Passive Observation Introduction* (POI). POI is "passive" in the sense that, via such a transition, the agent does not look for anything special to observe, but rather it opens its "reception channel" and records any inputs what its sensors perceive. Another transition that is present in most agent systems is that of *Action Execution* (AE), whereby actions may be "physical", communicative, or "sensing", depending on the concrete systems.

Other useful transitions besides POI and AE (see e.g. [10, 2]) may include Goal Introduction (GI), to introduce new goals into the state of the agent, taking into account changes to the state and to the external environment that somehow affect the preferences of the agent over which goals to adopt, Plan Introduction (PI), to plan for goals, Reactivity (RE), to react to perceived changes in the environment by means of condition-action/commitment-like rules, Sensing Introduction (SI), to set up sensing actions for sensing the preconditions of actions in the agent's plan, to make sure these actions are indeed executable, Active Observation Introduction (AOI), to actively seek information from the environment, State Revision (SR) to revise the state currently held by the agent, and Belief Revision (BR), e.g. by learning.

Whatever pool of transitions one might choose, and whatever their concrete specification might be, we will assume that they are represented as

$$T(S, X, S', \tau)$$

where S is the state of the agent before the transition is applied and S' the state after, X is the (possibly empty) input taken by the transition, and τ is the time of application of the transition. Note that we assume the existence of a *clock* (possibly external to the agent and shared by a number of agents), whose task is to mark the passing of time. The clock is responsible for labelling the transitions with the time at which they are applied. This time (and thus the clock) might play no role in some concrete agent architectures and models, where time is not reasoned upon explicitly. However, if the framework adopted to represent the state of the agent directly manipulates and reasons with time, the presence of a clock is required. Note also that the clock is useful (if not necessary) to label executed actions, and in particular communicative actions, to record their time of execution, as foreseen e.g. by FIPA standards for communication [6].

As far as the selection functions are concerned, we will assume that each transition T available to the agent is equipped with a selection function f_T, whose specification depends on the representation chosen for the state and on the specification of the transition itself. For example, AE is equipped with a selection function f_{AE} responsible for choosing actions to be executed. These actions may be amongst those actions in the plan (intention/commitment store) part of the state of the agent whose time has not run-out at the time of selection (and application of the transition) and belonging to a plan for some goal which has not already been achieved by other means.

In the next Section, we will see that, for fixed cycles, the role of the selection functions is exclusively to select the inputs for the appropriate transition when the turn of the transition comes up. Later, in Section 5, we will see that the role of selection functions when using cycle theories is to help decide which transition is preferred and should be applied next, as well as provide its input.

4   Fixed Cycles and Fixed Operational Trace

Both for fixed cycles and cycle theories, we will assume that the operation of an agent will start from some *initial state*. This can be seen as the state of the agent when it is created. The state then evolves via the transitions, as commended by the fixed cycle or cycle theory. For example, the initial state of the agent could have an empty set of goals and an empty set of plans, or some designer-given goals and an empty set of plans. In the sequel, we will indicate the given initial state as S_0.

A *fixed cycle* is a fixed sequence of transitions of the form

$$T_1, \ldots, T_n$$

where each T_i, $i = 1, \ldots, n$, is a transition chosen from the given pool, and $n \geq 2$.

A fixed cycle induces a *fixed operational trace* of the agent, namely a (typically infinite) sequence of applications of transitions, of the form

$$T_1(S_0, X_1, S_1, \tau_1), T_2(S_1, X_2, S_2, \tau_2), \ldots, T_n(S_{n-1}, X_n, S_n, \tau_n),$$
$$T_1(S_n, X_{n+1}, S_{n+1}, \tau_{n+1}), \ldots, T_n(S_{2n-1}, X_{2n}, S_{2n}, \tau_{2n}), \ldots$$

where, for each $i \geq 1$, $f_{T_i}(S_{i-1}, \tau_i) = X_i$, namely, at each stage, X_i is the (possibly empty) input for the transition T_i chosen by the corresponding selection function f_{T_i}.

Then, a classical "observe-think-act" cycle (e.g. see [11]) can be represented in our approach as the fixed cycle:

$$POI, RE, PI, AE, AOI.$$

As a further example, a purely reactive agent, e.g. with its knowledge consisting of condition-action rules, can execute the cycle

$$POI, RE, AE.$$

Note that POI is interpreted here as a transition which is under the control of the agent, namely the agent decides when it is time to open its "reception channel". Below, in Section 8, we will see a different interpretation of POI as an "interrupt".

Note that, although fixed cycles such as the above are quite restrictive, they may be sufficiently appropriate in some circumstances. For example, the cycle for a purely reactive agent may be fine in an environment which is highly dynamic. An agent may then be equipped with a catalogue of fixed cycles, and a number of conditions on the environment to decide when to apply which of the given cycles. This would provide for a (limited) form of intelligent control, in the spirit of [4], paving the way toward the more sophisticated and fully declarative control via cycle theories given in the next Section.

5   Cycle Theories and Cycle Operational Trace

The role of the cycle theory is to dynamically control the sequence of the internal transitions that the agent applies in its "life". It regulates these "narratives of transitions" according to certain requirements that the designer of the agent would like to impose on the operation of the agent, but still allowing the possibility that any (or a number of) sequences of transitions can actually apply in the "life" of an agent. Thus, whereas a fixed cycle can be seen as a restrictive and rather inflexible catalogue of allowed sequences of transitions (possibly under pre-defined conditions), a cycle theory identifies *preferred patterns* of sequences of transitions. In this way a cycle theory regulates in a flexible way the operational behaviour of the agent.

Formally, a cycle theory $\mathcal{T}_{cycle}$ consists of the following parts.

- An *initial* part $\mathcal{T}_{initial}$, that determines the possible transitions that the agent could perform when it starts to operate (*initial cycle step*). More concretely, $\mathcal{T}_{initial}$ consists of rules of the form
  $$*T(S_0, X) \leftarrow C(S_0, \tau, X), now(\tau)$$
  sanctioning that, if the conditions C are satisfied in the initial state S_0 at the current time τ, then the initial transition should be T, applied to state S_0 and input X, if required. Note that $C(S_0, \tau, X)$ may be absent, and $\mathcal{T}_{initial}$ might simply indicate a fixed initial transition T_1.
  The notation $*T(S, X)$ in the head of these rules, meaning that the transition T can be potentially chosen as the next transition, is used in order to avoid confusion with the notation $T(S, X, S', \tau)$ that we have introduced earlier to represent the actual application of the transition T.
- A *basic* part $\mathcal{T}_{basic}$ that determines the possible transitions (*cycle steps*) following other transitions, and consists of rules of the form
  $$*T'(S', X') \leftarrow T(S, X, S', \tau), EC(S', \tau', X'), now(\tau')$$
  which we refer to via the name $\mathcal{R}_{T|T'}(S', X')$. These rules sanction that, after the transition T has been executed, starting at time τ in the state S and ending at the current time τ' in the resulting state S', and the conditions EC evaluated in S' at τ' are satisfied, then transition T' could be the next transition to be applied in the state S' with the (possibly empty) input X', if required. The conditions EC are called *enabling conditions* as they determine when a cycle-step from the transition T to the transition T' can be applied.

In addition, they determine the input X' of the next transition T'. Such inputs are determined by calls to the appropriate selection functions.

- A *behaviour* part $T_{behaviour}$ that contains rules describing dynamic priorities amongst rules in T_{basic} and $T_{initial}$. Rules in $T_{behaviour}$ are of the form
  $$\mathcal{R}_{T|T'}(S, X') \succ \mathcal{R}_{T|T''}(S, X'') \leftarrow BC(S, X', X'', \tau), now(\tau)$$
  with $T' \neq T''$, which we will refer to via the name $\mathcal{P}^T_{T' \succ T''}$. Recall that $\mathcal{R}_{T|T'}(\cdot)$ and $\mathcal{R}_{T|T''}(\cdot)$ are (names of) rules in $T_{basic} \cup T_{initial}$. Note that, with an abuse of notation, T could be 0 in the case that one such rule is used to specify a priority over the *first* transition to take place, in other words, when the priority is over rules in $T_{initial}$. These rules in $T_{behaviour}$ sanction that, at the current time τ, after transition T, if the conditions BC hold, then we prefer the next transition to be T' over T'', namely doing T' has *higher priority* than doing T'', after T. The conditions BC are called *behaviour conditions* and give the behavioural profile of the agent. These conditions depend on the state of the agent after T and on the parameters chosen in the two cycle steps represented by $\mathcal{R}_{T|T'}(S, X')$ and $\mathcal{R}_{T|T''}(S, X'')$. Behaviour conditions are *heuristic* conditions, which may be defined in terms of the *heuristic selection functions*, where appropriate. For example, the heuristic action selection function may choose those actions in the agent's plan whose time is close to running out amongst those whose time has not run out.

- An *auxiliary part* including definitions for any predicates occurring in the enabling and behaviour conditions, and in particular for selection functions (including the heuristic ones, if needed).

- An *incompatibility part*, including rules stating that all different transitions are incompatible with each other and that different calls to the same transition but with different input items are incompatible with each other. These rules are facts of the form
  $$incompatible(*T(S, X), *T'(S, X')) \leftarrow$$
  for all T, T' such that $T \neq T'$, and of the form
  $$incompatible(*T(S, X), *T(S, X')) \leftarrow X \neq X'$$
  expressing the fact that only one transition can be chosen at a time.

Hence, T_{cycle} is an LPP-theory (see Section 2) where:
(i) $P = T_{initial} \cup T_{basic}$, and (ii) $H = T_{behaviour}$.

In the sequel, we will indicate with T^0_{cycle} the sub-cycle theory $T_{cycle} \setminus T_{basic}$ and with T^s_{cycle} the sub-cycle theory $T_{cycle} \setminus T_{initial}$.

The cycle theory T_{cycle} of an agent is responsible for the behaviour of the agent, in that it induces a *cycle operational trace* of the agent, namely a (typically infinite) sequence of transitions

$$T_1(S_0, X_1, S_1, \tau_1), \ldots, T_i(S_{i-1}, X_i, S_i, \tau_i),$$
$$T_{i+1}(S_i, X_{i+1}, S_{i+1}, \tau_{i+1}), \ldots$$

(where each of the X_i may be empty), such that

- S_0 is the given initial state;
- for each $i \geq 1$, τ_i is given by the clock of the system, with the property that $\tau_i < \tau_{i+i}$;
- (*Initial Cycle Step*) $T^0_{cycle} \wedge now(\tau_1) \models_{pr} *T_1(S_0, X_1)$;

– (*Cycle Step*) for each $i \geq 1$
$\mathcal{T}^s_{cycle} \wedge T_i(S_{i-1}, X_i, S_i, \tau_i) \wedge now(\tau_{i+1}) \models_{pr} *T_{i+1}(S_i, X_{i+1})$
namely each (non-final) transition in a sequence is followed by the most preferred transition, as specified by $\mathcal{T}_{cycle}$.

If, at some stage, the most preferred transition determined by $\models_{pr}$ is not unique, we choose arbitrarily one.

Note that, for simplicity, the above definition of operational trace prevents the agent from executing transitions *concurrently*. However, a first level of concurrency can be incorporated within traces, by allowing all preferred transitions to be executed at every step. For this we would only need to relax the above definition of *incompatible* transitions to be restricted between any two transitions whose executions could interact with each other and therefore cannot be executed concurrently on the same state, e.g. the Plan Introduction and State Revision transitions. This would then allow several transitions to be chosen together as preferred next transitions and a concurrent model of operation would result by carrying out simultaneously the (non-interacting) state updates imposed by these transitions. Further possibilities of concurrency will be subject of future investigations.

In section 8 we will provide a simple extension of the notion of operational trace defined above.

6   Fixed Versus Flexible Behaviour

Cycle theories generalise fixed cycles in that the behaviour given by a fixed operational trace can be obtained via the behaviour given by a cycle operational trace, for some special cycle theories. This is shown by the following theorem, which refers to the notions of *fixed cycle* and *fixed operational trace* introduced in Section 4.

Theorem 1. *Let $T_1, \ldots, T_n$ be a fixed cycle, and let f_{T_i} be a given selection function for each $i = 1, \ldots, n$. Then there exists a cycle theory $\mathcal{T}_{cycle}$ which induces a cycle operational trace identical to the fixed operational trace induced by the fixed cycle.*

Proof. The proof is by construction as follows.

– $\mathcal{T}_{initial}$ consists of the rule
$*T_1(S_0, X) \leftarrow now(\tau)$
i.e. the initial transition is simply T_1.
– $\mathcal{T}_{basic}$ consists of the following rules, for each i with $2 \leq i \leq n$:
$*T_i(S', X') \leftarrow T_{i-1}(S, X, S', \tau), now(\tau'), X' = f_{T_i}(S', \tau')$.
In addition $\mathcal{T}_{basic}$ contains the rule
$*T_1(S', X') \leftarrow T_n(S, X, S', \tau), now(\tau'), X' = f_{T_1}(S', \tau')$.
– $\mathcal{T}_{behaviour}$ is empty.
– the auxiliary part contains the definitions of the given selection functions f_{T_i}, for each $i = 1, \ldots, n$.

The proof then easily follows by construction, since at each stage only one cycle step is enabled and no preference reasoning is required to choose the next transition to be executed.   □

It is clear that there are some (many) cycle theories that cannot be mapped onto any fixed cycles, e.g. the cycle theory given in the next Section. So, providing control via cycle theories is a genuine extension of providing control via conventional fixed cycles.

7   An Example

In this Section we exemplify the flexibility afforded by cycle theories through a simple example. Assume that the pool of transitions consists of GI, PI, AE and POI, as described in Section 3. We start from the cycle theory corresponding to the fixed cycle given by POI, GI, PI, AE which is constructed as follows (see Theorem 1).

(1) $\mathcal{T}_{initial}$ with the following rule
$$*POI(S_0, \{\}) \leftarrow$$
namely, the only way an agent can start is through a POI.

(2) $\mathcal{T}_{basic}$ with the following rules
$$*GI(S', \{\}) \leftarrow POI(S, \{\}, S', \tau)$$
$$*PI(S', Gs) \leftarrow GI(S, \{\}, S', \tau), Gs = f_{PI}(S', \tau'), now(\tau')$$
$$*AE(S', As) \leftarrow PI(S, Gs, S', \tau), As = f_{AE}(S', \tau'), now(\tau')$$
$$*POI(S', \{\}) \leftarrow AE(S, As, S', \tau)$$

(3) $\mathcal{T}_{behaviour}$ is empty.

A first simple improvement, providing a limited form of flexibility, consists in refining the rule $\mathcal{R}_{GI|PI}(\cdot)$ by adding the condition that the set of goals to plan for, which are selected by the corresponding selection function f_{PI}, is non-empty. This amounts at modifying the second rule of $\mathcal{T}_{basic}$ by adding the condition $Gs \neq \{\}$ to its body.

Similarly, AE is an option after PI if some actions can actually be selected for execution. This amounts at modifying the the third rule of $\mathcal{T}_{basic}$ by adding the condition $As \neq \{\}$ to its body.

In this case, we should provide further options for choosing the transition to be executed after GI and PI, respectively. To adhere with the given original cycle, these rules could be simply suitable rules named by $\mathcal{R}_{GI|AE}(S', As)$, $\mathcal{R}_{GI|POI}(S', \{\})$ and $\mathcal{R}_{PI|POI}(S', \{\})$, i.e. AE and POI are also an option after GI, and POI is also an option after PI. With this choice, the standard operational trace is recovered by adding to the $\mathcal{T}_{behaviour}$ part of the cycle theory the following rules
$$\mathcal{R}_{GI|PI}(S', Gs) \succ \mathcal{R}_{GI|AE}(S', As) \leftarrow$$
$$\mathcal{R}_{GI|AE}(S', As') \succ \mathcal{R}_{GI|POI}(S', \{\}) \leftarrow$$
$$\mathcal{R}_{GI|PI}(S', Gs') \succ \mathcal{R}_{GI|POI}(S', \{\}) \leftarrow$$
$$\mathcal{R}_{PI|AE}(S', As) \succ \mathcal{R}_{PI|POI}(S', \{\}) \leftarrow$$

The first rule states that PI has to be preferred over AE as the next transition to be applied after GI, whenever both PI and AE are enabled. Similarly for the other rules.

A more interesting, proper extension of the original (fixed) cycle amounts at adding further options to the transition which can follow any given transition. Imagine for instance that we want to express the behaviour of a *punctual* or *timely* agent. This agent should always prefer executing actions if there are actions in the plan which have become *urgent*. This can be declaratively formalised by adding to the $\mathcal{T}_{basic}$ part the rules

$$*AE(S', As') \leftarrow T(S, X, S', \tau), As' = f_{AE}(S', \tau'), now(\tau')$$

for each transition T in the pool, and by adding to the $\mathcal{T}_{behaviour}$ part the following rules named $\mathcal{P}^T_{AE \succ T'}$:

$$\mathcal{R}_{T|AE}(S', As') \succ \mathcal{R}_{T|T'}(S', X') \leftarrow urgent(As')$$

for each transition T and $T' \neq$ AE, where $urgent$ is defined in the auxiliary part of the theory with the intuitive meaning. In the rest of this Section, we use $\mathcal{T}^{fix}_{cycle}$ to refer to the cycle theory corresponding to the fixed cycle POI, GI, PI, AE, and we use $\mathcal{T}^{ext}_{cycle}$ to refer to the extended cycle theory.

As a concrete example, consider an agent aiding a businessman who, while on a business trip, can choose amongst three possible goals: return home (*home*), read news (*news*), and recharge his laptop battery (*battery*). Let us use first the cycle theory $\mathcal{T}^{fix}_{cycle}$.

Suppose that, initially (when $now(1)$ holds), the agent's state is empty, namely the (businessman's) agent holds no plan or goal, and that the initial POI does not add anything to the current state. Then GI is performed as the next transition in the trace:

$$GI(S_0, \{\}, S_1, 1),$$

and suppose also that the application of GI generates the agent's goal (added to S_1) $G_1 = home$. This goal may come along with a time parameter and some temporal constraints associated with it, e.g. the actual goal can be represented by $(home, t) \wedge t < 20$. Due to space limitations, we intentionally omit here the details concerning temporal parameters of goals and actions, and the temporal constraints associated with them. Since the state contains a goal to be planned for, suppose that the selection function f_{PI} selects this goal, and the PI transition is applied next, producing two actions *book_ticket* and *take_train*. Hence, the second transition of the trace is (when $now(3)$ holds)

$$PI(S_1, \{\}, S_2, 3)$$

where the new state S_2 contains the above actions.

Suppose now that the selection function f_{AE} selects the action *book_ticket* and hence that the next element of the trace is (when $now(4)$ holds)

$$AE(S_2, \{book\_ticket\}, S_3, 4). \tag{*}$$

In the original fixed cycle the next applicable transition is POI, and assume that this is performed at some current time, say 10. Hence the next element of the trace is (when $now(10)$ holds)

$$POI(S_3, \{\}, S_4, 10). \tag{**}$$

Imagine that this POI brings about the new knowledge that the laptop battery is low, suitably represented in the resulting state S_4. Then the next transition GI changes the state so that the goal *battery* is added, and then PI is performed to introduce a suitable plan to recharge the battery and so on.

Now suppose that we use $\mathcal{T}_{cycle}^{ext}$ instead and that the operational trace is identical up to the execution of the transition (*). At this point, the action *take_train* may have become *urgent*. Notice that it is likely that this same action was not urgent at time 3, when *book_ticket* was selected for execution, but has become urgent at time 10 (e.g. because the train is leaving at 11). Then, if we use $\mathcal{T}_{cycle}^{ext}$, the rule $\mathcal{P}_{AE \succ POI}^{AE}$ applies and the next element of the trace, replacing (**) above, becomes

$$AE(S_3, \{take\_train\}, S_4', 10).$$

This example shows how the use of cycle theories can lead to flexible behaviours. More flexibility may be achieved by allowing the agents to be interruptible, i.e. to be able to react to changes in the environment in which they are situated as soon as the perceive those changes. This added flexibility requires some further extensions, that we discuss in the next Section.

8   Interruptible Agents

In our approach we can provide a declarative specification of *interruptible* agents, i.e. agents that are able to dynamically modify their "normal" (either fixed or cycle) operational trace when they perceive changes in the environment in which they are situated.

In order to obtain interruptibility, we will make use of the POI transition as the means by which an agent can react to an interrupt. Referring to the example of the previous Section, assume that our agent can book the ticket only through its laptop and, by the time it decides to actually book the ticket, the laptop battery has run out. Then, the action of recharging the laptop battery should be executed as soon as possible in order to (possibly) achieve the initial goal. Indeed, executing the booking action before recharging would not be feasible at all.

In order to model the environment where the agent is situated, we assume the existence of an environmental knowledge base *Env* that it is not directly under the control of the agent, in that the latter can only dynamically assimilate the knowledge contained in *Env*. This knowledge base can be seen as an abstraction of the physical (as opposed to the mental) part of the agent (its *body*) which, e.g. through its sensors, perceives changes in the environment. We assume that, besides the knowledge describing the agent's percepts, *Env* models a special propositional symbol, referred to as *changed_env* which holds as soon as the body of the agent perceives any new, relevant changes in the environment. The way we model the reaction of the agent to the changes represented by *changed_env* becoming true, is through the execution of a POI. We also assume that the execution of a POI transition resets the truth value of *changed_env*, so that the agent may be later alerted of further changes in the environment.

The *Env* knowledge base becomes now part of the knowledge that the agent uses in order to decide the next step in its operational trace. This is formally specified through the notion of *cycle-env operational trace*, which extends the notion of cycle operational trace introduced in Section 5, by replacing the definitions of *Initial Cycle Step* and *Cycle Step* by the following new definitions:

(*Initial Cycle-env Step*): $\mathcal{T}_{cycle}^0 \wedge Env \wedge now(\tau_1) \models_{pr} *T_1(S_0, X_1)$;

(*Cycle-env Step*) for each $i \geq 1$

$$\mathcal{T}_{cycle}^s \wedge T_i(S_{i-1}, X_i, S_i, \tau_i) \wedge Env \wedge now(\tau_{i+1})$$
$$\models_{pr} *T_{i+1}(S_i, X_{i+1})$$

We can now define a notion of *interruptible agent* as follows. Let $\mathcal{T}_{cycle}$ be the cycle theory of the agent and let $T_1(\cdot), \ldots, T_i(\cdot), \ldots$ be a cycle operational trace of the agent. Let also $T_i(S_{i-1}, X_i, S_i, \tau_i)$ be an element of the given trace such that:

$Env \wedge now(\tau_i) \models \neg changed\_env$, and
$Env \wedge now(\tau_{i+1}) \models changed\_env$.

In other words, some changes have happened in the environment between the time of the execution of the transitions T_i and T_{i+1} in the trace. Then we say that the agent is interruptible if

$\mathcal{T}_{cycle} \wedge T_i(S_{i-1}, X_i, S_i, \tau_i) \wedge Env \wedge now(\tau_{i+1}) \models_{pr} *POI(S_i, \{\})$, i.e. as soon as the environment changes, in a cycle-env operational trace the next transition would be a POI.

It is worth noting that by interruptibility we do not mean here that the (executions of) transitions are interrupted, rather the trace is interrupted.

In order to make an agent interruptible, we need to extend both $\mathcal{T}_{basic}$ and $\mathcal{T}_{behaviour}$. In $\mathcal{T}_{basic}$, POI should be made an option after any other transition in the pool, which is achieved by adding the following rule $\mathcal{R}_{T|POI}(S, \{\})$, for any T:

$$*POI(S', \{\}) \leftarrow T(S, X', S', \tau).$$

In $\mathcal{T}_{behaviour}$, the following set of rules, where T, T' are transitions with $T' \neq$ POI, express that POI should be preferred over any other transition if the environment has actually changed:

$$\mathcal{R}_{T|POI}(S', \{\}) \succ \mathcal{R}_{T|T'}(S', X) \leftarrow changed\_env. \qquad (***)$$

Notice that, even if the above extensions are provided in the overall $\mathcal{T}_{cycle}$ theory, the interruptibility of the agent is still not guaranteed. For instance, $\mathcal{T}_{behaviour}$ could contain further rules which make a transition $T \neq$ POI preferable over POI even if *changed_env* holds. One way to achieve full interruptibility is by adding the condition $\neg changed\_env$ in the body of any rule in $\mathcal{T}_{behaviour}$ other than the rules (***) given above.

9   Patterns of Behaviour

In this section we show how different patterns of operation can arise from different cycle theories aiming to capture different profiles of operational behaviour by agents. We assume the agent is equipped with a set of transitions, as in the KGP model [10, 2] (see Section 3 for an informal description of these transitions):

- POI, *Passive Observation Introduction*
- AE, *Action Execution*
- GI, *Goal Introduction*
- PI, *Plan Introduction*
- RE, *Reactivity*
- SI, *Sensing Introduction*
- AOI, *Active Observation Introduction*
- SR, *State Revision*

In Section 7 we have given a simple example of a cycle theory describing a punctual, timely agent which attempts to execute its planned actions in time. This agent was obtained by adding some specific rules to $\mathcal{T}_{behaviour}$ of a given cycle theory. The same approach can be adopted to obtain different profiles.

For example, we can define a *focused or committed* agent, which, once chosen a plan to execute, prefers to continue with this plan (refining it and/or executing parts of it) until the plan is finished or it has become invalid, at which point the agent may consider other plans or other goals. Hence transitions that relate to an existing plan have preference over transitions that relate to other plans. This profile of behaviour can be captured by the following rules added to $\mathcal{T}_{behaviour}$ of an appropriate cycle theory:

$$\mathcal{R}_{T|AE}(S, As) \succ \mathcal{R}_{T|T'}(S, X) \leftarrow same\_plan(S, As)$$

for any T and any $T' \neq AE$, and

$$\mathcal{R}_{T|PI}(S, Gs) \succ \mathcal{R}_{T|T'}(S, X) \leftarrow same\_plan(S, Gs)$$

for any T and any $T' \neq PI$. These rules state that the agent prefers to execute actions or to reduce goals from the same plan as the actions that have just been executed. Here, the behaviour conditions are defined in terms of some predicate *same_plan* which, intuitively, checks that the selected inputs for AE and PI, respectively, belong to the *same plan* as the actions most recently executed within the latest AE transition.

Another example of behavioral profile is the *impatient* pattern, where actions that have been tried and failed are not tried again. This can be captured by rules of the form:

$$\mathcal{R}_{T|T'}(S, \_) \succ \mathcal{R}_{T|AE}(S, As) \leftarrow failed(S, As)$$

for any T and any $T' \neq AE$. In this way, AE is given less preference than any other transition T' after any transition T. Intuitively, As are *failed* actions. As a result of this priority rule it is possible that such failed actions would remain un-tried again (unless nothing else is enabled) until they are timed out and dropped by SR.

If we want to capture a *careful* behaviour where the agent revises its state when one of its goals or actions times out (being careful not to have in its state other goals or actions that are now impossible to achieve in time) we would have in $\mathcal{T}_{behaviour}$ the rule:

$$\mathcal{R}_{T|SR}(S, \{\}) \succ \mathcal{R}_{T|T'}(S, \_) \leftarrow timed\_out(S, \tau)$$

for any T and any $T' \neq SR$. In this way, the SR transition is preferred over all other transitions, where the behaviour condition $timed\_out(S, \tau)$ succeeds if some goal or action in the state S has timed out at time τ.

10   Conclusions and Ongoing Work

We have presented an approach providing declarative agent control, via logic programs with priorities. Our approach share the aims of 3APL [4], to make the agent cycle programmable and the selection mechanisms explicit, but goes beyond it. Indeed, the approach of [4] can be seen as relying upon a catalogue of fixed cycles together with the possibility of selecting amongst such fixed cycles according to some criteria, whereas we drop the concept of fixed cycle completely, and replace it with fully programmable cycle theories.

Our approach allows us to achieve flexibility and adaptability in the operation of an autonomous agent. It also offers the possibility to state and verify properties of agents behaviour formally. In this paper we have exemplified the first aspect via an example, and the second aspect via the property of "interruptibility" of agents. The identification and verification of more properties is a matter for future work.

Our approach also lends itself to achieving heterogeneity in the overall operational behaviour of different agents that can be specified within the proposed framework. Indeed, an advantage of control via cycle theories is that it opens up the possibility to produce a variety of patterns of operation of agents, depending on the particular circumstances under which the transitions are executed. This variety can be increased, and many different *patterns or profiles of behaviour* can be defined by varying the cycle theory, thus allowing agents with (possibly) the same knowledge and operating in the same environment to exhibit heterogeneous behaviour, due to their different cycle theories. We have given a number of examples of profiles of behaviour. A systematic study of behaviour parameterisation (perhaps linking with Cognitive Science) is a matter for future work, as well as the comparison on how different behaviours affect the agents' individual welfare in different contexts.

Acknowledgments

This work was partially funded by the IST programme of the EC, FET under the IST-2001-32530 SOCS project, within the Global Computing proactive initiative. The last two authors were also supported by the Italian MIUR programme "Rientro dei cervelli".

References

1. R.H. Bordini, A. L. C. Bazzan, R. O. Jannone, D. M. Basso, R. M. Vicari, and V. R. Lesser. AgentSpeak(XL): Efficient intention selection in bdi agents via decision-theoretic task scheduling. In C. Castelfranchi and W. Lewis Johnson, editors, *Proceedings of the First International Joint Conference on Autonomous Agents and Multiagent Systems (AAMAS-2002), Part III*, pages 1294–1302, Bologna, Italy, July 15–19 2002. ACM Press.

2. A. Bracciali, N. Demetriou, U. Endriss, A. Kakas, W. Lu, P. Mancarella, F. Sadri, K. Stathis, G. Terreni, and F. Toni. The KGP model of agency for GC: Computational model and prototype implementation. In *Proc. Global Computing 2004 Workshop*, LNCS. Springer Verlag, 2004.
3. G. Brewka. Reasoning with priorities in default logic. In *AAAI94*, pages 940–945. AAAI Press, 1994.
4. M. Dastani, F. S. de Boer, F. Dignum, W. van der Hoek, M. Kroese, and J. Ch. Meyer. Programming the deliberation cycle of cognitive robots. In *Proc. of 3rd International Cognitive Robotics Workshop (CogRob2002)*, Edmonton, Alberta, Canada, 2002.
5. Y. Dimopoulos and A. C. Kakas. Logic programming without negation as failure. In *Logic Programming, Proceedings of the 1995 International Symposium, Portland, Oregon*, pages 369–384, 1995.
6. FIPA Communicative Act Library Specification, August 2001. Published on August 10th, 2001, available for download from the FIPA website, http://www.fipa.org.
7. K. V. Hindriks, F. S. de Boer, W. van der Hoek, and J. Ch. Meyer. Agent programming in 3APL. *Autonomous Agents and Multi-Agent Systems*, 2(4):357–401, 1999.
8. A. C. Kakas, P. Mancarella, and P. M. Dung. The acceptability semantics for logic programs. In *Proceedings of the Eleventh International Conference on Logic Programming, Santa Marherita Ligure, Italy*, pages 504–519, 1994.
9. A. C. Kakas and P. Moraitis. Argumentation based decision making for autonomous agents. In J. S. Rosenschein, T. Sandholm, M. Wooldridge, and M. Yokoo, editors, *Proceedings of the Second International Joint Conference on Autonomous Agents and Multiagent Systems (AAMAS-2003)*, pages 883–890, Melbourne, Victoria, July 14–18 2003. ACM Press.
10. A.C. Kakas, P. Mancarella, F. Sadri, K. Stathis, and F. Toni. The KGP model of agency. In R. Lopez de Mantaras and L. Saitta, editors, *Proceedings of the Sixteenth European Conference on Artificial Intelligence, Valencia, Spain (ECAI 2004)*. IOS Press, August 2004.
11. R. A. Kowalski and F. Sadri. From logic programming towards multi-agent systems. *Annals of Mathematics and Artificial Intelligence*, 25(3/4):391–419, 1999.
12. R.A. Kowalski and F. Toni. Abstract argumentation. *Artificial Intelligence and Law Journal, Special Issue on Logical Models of Argumentation*, 4:275–296, 1996.
13. H. Prakken and G. Sartor. A system for defeasible argumentation, with defeasible priorities. In *International Conference on Formal and Applied Practical Reasoning*, volume 1085 of *Lecture Notes in Artificial Intelligence*, pages 510–524. Springer-Verlag, 1996.
14. A. S. Rao and M. Georgeff. BDI Agents: from theory to practice. In *Proceedings of the First International Conference on Multiagent Systems, San Francisco, California, USA*, pages 312–319, San Francisco, CA, June 1995.
15. Y. Shoham. Agent-oriented programming. *Artificial Intelligence*, 60(1):51–92, 1993.
16. Kostas Stathis, Antonis C. Kakas, Wenjin Lu, Neophytos Demetriou, Ulle Endriss, and Andrea Bracciali. PROSOCS: a platform for programming software agents in computational logic. pages 523–528, Vienna, Austria, April 13-16 2004. Austrian Society for Cybernetic Studies. Extended version to appear in a special issue of Applied Artificial Intelligence, Taylor & Francis, 2005.

Metareasoning for Multi-agent Epistemic Logics[*]

Konstantine Arkoudas and Selmer Bringsjord

RPI
{arkouk, brings}@rpi.edu

Abstract. We present an encoding of a sequent calculus for a multi-agent epistemic logic in Athena, an interactive theorem proving system for many-sorted first-order logic. We then use Athena as a metalanguage in order to reason about the multi-agent logic an as object language. This facilitates theorem proving in the multi-agent logic in several ways. First, it lets us marshal the highly efficient theorem provers for classical first-order logic that are integrated with Athena for the purpose of doing proofs in the multi-agent logic. Second, unlike model-theoretic embeddings of modal logics into classical first-order logic, our proofs are directly convertible into native epistemic logic proofs. Third, because we are able to quantify over propositions and agents, we get much of the generality and power of higher-order logic even though we are in a first-order setting. Finally, we are able to use Athena's versatile tactics for proof automation in the multi-agent logic. We illustrate by developing a tactic for solving the generalized version of the wise men problem.

1 Introduction

Multi-agent modal logics are widely used in Computer Science and AI. Multi-agent epistemic logics, in particular, have found applications in fields ranging from AI domains such as robotics, planning, and motivation analysis in natural language [1]; to negotiation and game theory in economics; to distributed systems analysis and protocol authentication in computer security [2,3]. The reason is simple—intelligent agents must be able to reason about knowledge. It is therefore important to have efficient means for performing machine reasoning in such logics. While the validity problem for most propositional modal logics is of intractable theoretical complexity[1], several approaches have been investigated in recent years that have resulted in systems that appear to work well in practice. These approaches include tableau-based provers, SAT-based algorithms, and translations to first-order logic coupled with the use of resolution-based automated theorem provers (ATPs). Some representative systems are FaCT [6], KSATC [7], TA [8], LWB [9], and MSPASS [10].

---

[*] This research was funded in part by the US Air Force Labs of Rome, NY.

[1] For instance, the validity problem for multi-agent propositional epistemic logic is PSPACE-complete [4]; adding a common knowledge operator makes the problem EXPTIME-complete [5].

J. Leite and P. Torroni (Eds.): CLIMA V, LNAI 3487, pp. 111–125, 2005.
© Springer-Verlag Berlin Heidelberg 2005

Translation-based approaches (such as that of MSPASS) have the advantage of leveraging the tremendous implementation progress that has occurred over the last decade in first-order theorem proving. Soundness and completeness are ensured by the soundness and completeness of the resolution prover (once the soundness and completeness of the translation have been shown), while a decision procedure is automatically obtained for any modal logic that can be translated into a decidable fragment of first-order logic, such as the two-variable fragment. Furthermore, the task of translating from a modal logic to the classical first-order setting is fairly straightforward (assuming, of course, that the class of Kripke frames captured by the modal logic is first-order definable [11]; modal logics such as the Gödel-Löb logic of provability in first-order Peano arithmetic would require translation into second-order classical logic). For instance, the well-known formula $[\Box P \wedge \Box (P \Rightarrow Q)] \Rightarrow \Box Q$ becomes

$$\forall w_1 \, . \, [(\forall w_2 \, . \, R(w_1, w_2) \Rightarrow P(w_2)) \wedge$$
$$(\forall w_2 \, . \, R(w_1, w_2) \Rightarrow P(w_2) \Rightarrow Q(w_2))] \Rightarrow (\forall w_2 \, . \, R(w_1, w_2) \Rightarrow Q(w_2))$$

Here the variables w_1 and w_2 range over possible worlds, and the relation R represents Kripke's accessibility relation. A constant propositional atom P in the modal language becomes a unary predicate $P(w)$ that holds (or not) for a given world w.

This is the (naive) classical translation of modal logic into first-order logic [4], and we might say that it is a *semantic* embedding, since the Kripke semantics of the modal language are explicitly encoded in the translated result. This is, for instance, the approach taken by McCarthy in his "Formalizing two puzzles involving knowledge" [12]. A drawback of this approach is that proofs produced in the translated setting are difficult to convert back into a form that makes sense for the user in the original modal setting (although alternative translation techniques such as the functional translation to path logic can rectify this in some cases [13]). Another drawback is that if a result is not obtained within a reasonable amount of time—which is almost certain to happen quite often when no decision procedure is available, as in first-order modal logics—then a batch-oriented ATP is of little help to the user due to its "low bandwidth of interaction" [14].

In this paper we explore another approach: We embed a multi-agent epistemic logic into many-sorted first-order logic in a proof-theoretic rather than in a model-theoretic way. [2] Specifically, we use the interactive theorem proving system Athena [15] to encode the formulas of the epistemic logic along with the inference rules of a sequent calculus for it. Hence first-order logic becomes our metalanguage and the epistemic logic becomes our object language. We then use standard first-order logic (our metalanguage) to reason about proofs in the object logic. In effect, we end up reasoning about reasoning—hence the term *metareasoning*. Since our metareasoning occurs at the standard first-order level, we are

---

[2] This paper treats a propositional logic of knowledge, but the technique can be readily applied to full first-order multi-agent epistemic logic, and indeed to hybrid multi-modal logics, e.g., combination logics for temporal and epistemic reasoning.

free to leverage existing theorem-proving systems for automated deduction. In particular, we make heavy use of Vampire [16] and Spass [17], two cutting-edge resolution-based ATPs that are seamlessly integrated with Athena.

Our approach has two additional advantages. First, it is trivial to translate the constructed proofs into modal form, since the Athena proofs are already *about proofs in the modal logic*. Second, because the abstract syntax of the epistemic logic is explicitly encoded in Athena, we can quantify over propositions, sequents, and agents. Accordingly, we get the generalization benefits of higher-order logic even in a first-order setting. This can result in significant efficiency improvements. For instance, in solving the generalized wise men puzzle it is necessary at some point to derive the conclusion $M_2 \vee \cdots \vee M_n$ from the three premises $\neg K_\alpha(M_1)$, $K_\alpha(\neg(M_2 \vee \cdots \vee M_n) \Rightarrow M_1)$, and

$$\neg(M_2 \vee \cdots \vee M_n) \Rightarrow K_\alpha(\neg(M_2 \vee \cdots \vee M_n))$$

where $M_1, \ldots, M_n$ are atomic propositions and α is an epistemic agent, $n > 1$. In the absence of an explicit embedding of the epistemic logic, this would have to be done with a tactic that accepted a list of propositions $[M_1 \cdots M_n]$ as input and performed the appropriate deduction dynamically, which would require an amount of effort quadratic in the length of the list. By contrast, in our approach we are able to formulate and prove a "higher-order" lemma stating

$$\forall\, P, Q, \alpha \;.\; \{\neg K_\alpha(P), K_\alpha(\neg Q \Rightarrow P), \neg Q \Rightarrow K_\alpha(\neg Q)\} \vdash Q$$

Obtaining the desired conclusion for any given $M_1, \ldots, M_n$ then becomes a matter of instantiating this lemma with $P \mapsto M_1$ and $Q \mapsto M_2 \vee \cdots \vee M_n$. We have thus reduced the asymptotic complexity of our task from quadratic time to constant time.

But perhaps the most distinguishing aspect of our work is our emphasis on *tactics*. Tactics are proof algorithms, which, unlike conventional algorithms, are guaranteed to produce sound results. That is, if and when a tactic outputs a result P that it claims to be a theorem, we can be assured that P is indeed a theorem. Tactics are widely used for proof automation in first- and higher-order proof systems such as HOL [18] and Isabelle [19]. In Athena tactics are called *methods*, and are particularly easy to formulate owing to Athena's Fitch-style natural deduction system and its assumption-base semantics [20]. A major goal of our research is to find out how easy—or difficult—it may be to automate multi-agent modal logic proofs with tactics. Our aim is not to obtain a completely automatic decision procedure for a certain logic (or class of logics), but rather to enable efficient interactive—i.e., semi-automatic—theorem proving in such logics for challenging problems that are beyond the scope of completely automatic provers. In this paper we formulate an Athena method for solving the generalized version of the wise men problem (for any given number of wise men). The relative ease with which this method was formulated is encouraging.

The remainder of this paper is structured as follows. In the next section we present a sequent calculus for the epistemic logic that we will be encoding. In Section 3 we present the wise men puzzle and formulate an algorithm for solving

$$\frac{\Gamma \vdash P \quad \Gamma \vdash Q}{\Gamma \vdash P \wedge Q}[\wedge\text{-}I] \quad \frac{\Gamma \vdash P \wedge Q}{\Gamma \vdash P}[\wedge\text{-}E_1] \quad \frac{\Gamma \vdash P \wedge Q}{\Gamma \vdash Q}[\wedge\text{-}E_2]$$

$$\frac{\Gamma \vdash P}{\Gamma \vdash P \vee Q}[\vee\text{-}I_1] \quad \frac{\Gamma \vdash Q}{\Gamma \vdash P \vee Q}[\vee\text{-}I_2]$$

$$\frac{\Gamma \vdash P_1 \vee P_2 \quad \Gamma, P_1 \vdash Q \quad \Gamma, P_2 \vdash Q}{\Gamma \vdash Q}[\vee\text{-}E]$$

$$\frac{\Gamma, P \vdash Q}{\Gamma \vdash P \Rightarrow Q}[\Rightarrow\text{-}I] \quad \frac{\Gamma \vdash P \Rightarrow Q \quad \Gamma \vdash P}{\Gamma \vdash Q}[\Rightarrow\text{-}E]$$

$$\frac{\Gamma \vdash \neg\neg P}{\Gamma \vdash P}[\neg\text{-}E] \quad \frac{\Gamma, P \vdash \bot}{\Gamma \vdash \neg P}[\neg\text{-}I] \quad \frac{}{\Gamma, P \vdash P}[Reflex]$$

$$\frac{\Gamma \vdash P}{\Gamma \cup \Gamma' \vdash P}[Dilution] \quad \frac{\Gamma \vdash P \wedge \neg P}{\Gamma \vdash \bot}[\bot\text{-}I] \quad \frac{}{\Gamma \vdash \top}[\top\text{-}I]$$

Fig. 1. Inference rules for the propositional connectives

the generalized version of it in the sequent calculus of Section 2. In Section 4 we discuss the Athena encoding of the epistemic logic and present the Athena method for solving the generalized wise men problem. Finally, in Section 5 we consider related work.

2   A Sequent Formulation of a Multi-agent Epistemic Logic

We will use the letters P, Q, R, ..., to designate arbitrary *propositions*, built according to the following abstract grammar:

$$P ::= A \mid \top \mid \bot \mid \neg P \mid P \wedge Q \mid P \vee Q \mid P \Rightarrow Q \mid K_\alpha(P) \mid C(P)$$

where A and α range over a countable set of atomic propositions ("atoms") and a primitive domain of *agents*, respectively. Propositions of the form $K_\alpha(P)$ and $C(P)$ are read as follows:

$K_\alpha(P)$: *agent α knows proposition P*

$C(P)$: *it is common knowledge that P holds*

By a *context* we will mean a finite set of propositions. We will use the letter Γ to denote contexts. We define a *sequent* as an ordered pair $\langle \Gamma, P \rangle$ consisting of

$$\frac{}{\Gamma \vdash [K\alpha(P \Rightarrow Q)] \Rightarrow [K\alpha(P) \Rightarrow K\alpha(Q)]}[K] \qquad \frac{}{\Gamma \vdash K\alpha(P) \Rightarrow P}[T]$$

$$\frac{\emptyset \vdash P}{\Gamma \vdash C(P)}[C\text{-}I] \qquad \frac{}{\Gamma \vdash C(P) \Rightarrow K\alpha(P)}[C\text{-}E]$$

$$\frac{}{\Gamma \vdash [C(P \Rightarrow Q)] \Rightarrow [C(P) \Rightarrow C(Q)]}[C_K] \qquad \frac{}{\Gamma \vdash C(P) \Rightarrow C(K\alpha(P))}[R]$$

Fig. 2. Inference rules for the epistemic operators

a context Γ and a proposition P. A more suggestive notation for such a sequent is $\Gamma \vdash P$. Intuitively, this is a judgment stating that P follows from Γ. We will write P, Γ (or Γ, P) as an abbreviation for $\Gamma \cup \{P\}$. The sequent calculus that we will use consists of a collection of inference rules for deriving judgments of the form $\Gamma \vdash P$. Figure 1 shows the inference rules that deal with the standard propositional connectives. This part is standard (e.g., it is very similar to the sequent calculus of Ebbinghaus et al. [21]). In addition, we have some rules pertaining to $K\alpha$ and C, shown in Figure 2.

Rule $[K]$ is the sequent formulation of the well-known *Kripke axiom* stating that the knowledge operator distributes over conditionals. Rule $[C_K]$ is the corresponding principle for the common knowledge operator. Rule $[T]$ is the "truth axiom": an agent cannot know false propositions. Rule $[C_I]$ is an introduction rule for common knowledge: if a proposition P follows from the empty set of hypotheses, i.e., if it is a tautology, then it is commonly known. This is the common-knowledge version of the "omniscience axiom" for single-agent knowledge which says that $\Gamma \vdash K\alpha(P)$ can be derived from $\emptyset \vdash P$. We do not need to postulate that axiom in our formulation, since it follows from $[C\text{-}I]$ and $[C\text{-}E]$. The latter says that if it is common knowledge that P then any (every) agent knows P, while $[R]$ says that if it is common knowledge that P then it is common knowledge that (any) agent α knows it. $[R]$ is a reiteration rule that allows us to capture the recursive behavior of C, which is usually expressed via the so-called "induction axiom"

$$C(P \Rightarrow E(P)) \Rightarrow [P \Rightarrow C(P)]$$

where E is the shared-knowledge operator. Since we do not need E for our purposes, we omit its formalization and "unfold" C via rule $[R]$ instead.

We state a few lemmas that will come handy later:

Lemma 1 (Cut). *If $\Gamma_1 \vdash P_1$ and $\Gamma_2, P_1 \vdash P_2$ then $\Gamma_1 \cup \Gamma_2 \vdash P_2$.*

Proof: Assume $\Gamma_1 \vdash P_1$ and $\Gamma_2, P_1 \vdash P_2$. Then, by $[\Rightarrow\text{-}I]$, we get $\Gamma_2 \vdash P_1 \Rightarrow P_2$. Further, by dilution, we have $\Gamma_1 \cup \Gamma_2 \vdash P_1 \Rightarrow P_2$ and $\Gamma_1 \cup \Gamma_2 \vdash P_1$. Hence, by $[\Rightarrow\text{-}E]$, we obtain $\Gamma_1 \cup \Gamma_2 \vdash P_2$. $\qquad\square$

The proofs of the remaining lemmas are equally simple exercises:

Lemma 2 (⇒-transitivity). *If $\Gamma \vdash P_1 \Rightarrow P_2$, $\Gamma \vdash P_2 \Rightarrow P_3$ then $\Gamma \vdash P_1 \Rightarrow P_3$.*

Lemma 3 (contrapositive). *If $\Gamma \vdash P \Rightarrow Q$ then $\Gamma \vdash \neg Q \Rightarrow \neg P$.*

Lemma 4. *(a)* $\emptyset \vdash (P_1 \vee P_2) \Rightarrow (\neg P_2 \Rightarrow P_1)$; *and (b)* $\Gamma \vdash C(P_2)$ *whenever* $\emptyset \vdash P_1 \Rightarrow P_2$ *and* $\Gamma \vdash C(P_1)$.

Lemma 5. *For all P, Q, and Γ, $\Gamma \vdash [C(P) \wedge C(Q)] \Rightarrow C(P \wedge Q)$.*

3   The Generalized Wise Men Puzzle

Consider first the three-men version of the puzzle:

> Three wise men are told by their king that at least one of them has a white spot on his forehead. In reality, all three have white spots on their foreheads. We assume that each wise man can see the others' foreheads but not his own, and thus each knows whether the others have white spots. Suppose we are told that the first wise man says, "I do not know whether I have a white spot," and that the second wise man then says, "I also do not know whether I have a white spot." Now consider the following question: Does the third wise man now know whether or not he has a white spot? If so, what does he know, that he has one or doesn't have one?

This version is essentially identical to the muddy-children puzzle, the only difference being that the declarations of the wise men are made sequentially, whereas in the muddy-children puzzle the children proclaim what they know (or not know) in parallel at every round.

In the generalized version of the puzzle we have an arbitrary number $n + 1$ of wise men $w_1, \ldots, w_{n+1}$, $n \geq 1$. They are told by their king that at least one them has a white spot on his forehead. Again, in actuality they all do. And they can all see one another's foreheads, but not their own. Supposing that each of the first n wise men, $w_1, \ldots, w_n$, sequentially announces that he does not know whether or not he has a white spot on his forehead, the question is what would the last wise man w_{n+1} report.

For all $n \geq 1$, it turns out that the last—$(n + 1)^{st}$—wise man knows he is marked. The case of two wise men is simple. The reasoning runs essentially by contradiction. The second wise man reasons as follows:

> Suppose I were not marked. Then w_1 would have seen this, and knowing that at least one of us is marked, he would have inferred that he was the marked one. But w_1 has expressed ignorance; therefore, I must be marked.

Consider now the case of $n = 3$ wise men w_1, w_2, w_3. After w_1 announces that he does not know that he is marked, w_2 and w_3 both infer that at least one of them is marked. For if neither w_2 nor w_3 were marked, w_1 would have seen this and would have concluded—and stated—that he was the marked one, since he knows that at least one of the three is marked. At this point the puzzle reduces to the two-men case: both w_2 and w_3 know that at least one of them is marked, and then w_2 reports that he does not know whether he is marked. Hence w_3 proceeds to reason as previously that he is marked.

In general, consider $n + 1$ wise men $w_1, \ldots, w_n, w_{n+1}, n \geq 1$. After the first j wise men $w_1, \ldots, w_j$ have announced that they do not know whether they are marked, for $j = 1, \ldots, n$, the remaining wise men $w_{j+1}, \ldots, w_{n+1}$ infer that at least one of them is marked. This holds for $j = n$ as well, which means that the last wise man w_{n+1} will infer (and announce, owing to his honesty) that he is marked.

The question is how to formalize this in our logic. Again consider the case of two wise men w_1 and w_2. Let $M_i, i \in \{1, 2\}$ denote the proposition that w_i is marked. For any proposition P, we will write $K_i(P)$ as an abbreviation for $K_{w_i}(P)$. We will only need three premises:

$$S_1 = C(\neg K_1(M_1))$$
$$S_2 = C(M_1 \vee M_2)$$
$$S_3 = C(\neg M_2 \Rightarrow K_1(\neg M_2))$$

The first premise says that it is common knowledge that the first wise man does not know whether he is marked. Although it sounds innocuous, note that a couple of assumptions are necessary to obtain this premise from the mere fact that w_1 has announced his ignorance. First, truthfulness—we must assume that the wise men do not lie, and further, that each one of them knows that they are all truthful. And second, each wise man must know that the other wise men will hear the announcement and believe it. Premise S_2 says that it is common knowledge that at least one of the wise men is marked. Observe that the announcement by the king is crucial for this premise to be justified. The two wise men can see each other and thus they individually know $M_1 \vee M_2$. However, each of them may not know that the other wise man knows that at least one of them is marked. For instance, w_1 may believe that he is not marked, and even though he sees that w_2 is marked, he may believe that w_2 does not know that at least one of them is marked, as w_2 cannot see himself. Finally, premise S_3 states that it is common knowledge that if w_2 is *not* marked, then w_1 will know it (because w_1 can see w_2). From these three premises we are to derive the conclusion $C(M_2)$—that it is common knowledge that w_2 is marked. Symbolically, we need to derive the judgment $\{S_1, S_2, S_3\} \vdash C(M_2)$. If we have encoded the epistemic propositional logic in a predicate calculus, then we can achieve this immediately by instantiating Lemma 7 below with $\alpha \mapsto w_1$, $P \mapsto M_1$ and $Q \mapsto M_2$—without performing any inference whatsoever. This is what we have done in Athena.

For the case of $n = 3$ wise men our set of premises will be:

$$S_1 = C(\neg K_1(M_1))$$
$$S_2 = C(M_1 \vee M_2 \vee M_3)$$
$$S_3 = C(\neg(M_2 \vee M_3) \Rightarrow K_1(\neg(M_2 \vee M_3)))$$
$$S_4 = C(\neg K_2(M_2))$$
$$S_5 = C(\neg M_3 \Rightarrow K_2(\neg M_3))$$

Consider now the general case of $n + 1$ wise men $w_1, \ldots, w_n, w_{n+1}$. For any $i = 1, \ldots, n$, define

$$S_1^i = C(\neg K_i(M_i))$$
$$S_2^i = C(M_i \vee \cdots \vee M_{n+1})$$
$$S_3^i = C(\neg(M_{i+1} \vee \cdots \vee M_{n+1}) \Rightarrow K_i(\neg(M_{i+1} \vee \cdots \vee M_{n+1})))$$

and $S_2^{n+1} = C(M_{n+1})$. The set of premises, Ω_{n+1}, can now be defined as

$$\Omega_{n+1} = \{C(M_1 \vee \cdots \vee M_{n+1})\} \bigcup_{i=1}^{n} \{S_1^i, S_3^i\}$$

Hence Ω_{n+1} has a total of $2n + 1$ elements. Note that S_2^1 is the commonly known disjunction $M_1 \vee \cdots \vee M_{n+1}$ and a known premise, i.e., a member of Ω_{n+1}. However, S_2^i for $i > 1$ is *not* a premise. Rather, it becomes derivable after the ith wise man has made his announcement. Managing the derivation of these propositions and eliminating them via applications of the cut is the central function of the algorithm below. Before we present the algorithm we state a couple of key lemmas.

Lemma 6. *Consider any agent α and propositions P, Q, and let R_1, R_2, R_3 be the following three propositions:*

1. $R_1 = \neg K_\alpha(P)$;
2. $R_2 = K_\alpha(\neg Q \Rightarrow P)$;
3. $R_3 = \neg Q \Rightarrow K_\alpha(\neg Q)$

Then $\{R_1 \wedge R_2 \wedge R_3\} \vdash Q$.

Proof. By the following sequent derivation:

1. $\{R_1 \wedge R_2 \wedge R_3\} \vdash R_1$		[*Reflex*], $\wedge$-E_1
2. $\{R_1 \wedge R_2 \wedge R_3\} \vdash R_2$		[*Reflex*], $\wedge$-E_1, $\wedge$-E_2
3. $\{R_1 \wedge R_2 \wedge R_3\} \vdash R_3$		[*Reflex*], $\wedge$-E_2
4. $\{R_1 \wedge R_2 \wedge R_3\} \vdash K_\alpha(\neg Q) \Rightarrow K_\alpha(P)$		2, [K], $\Rightarrow$-E
5. $\{R_1 \wedge R_2 \wedge R_3\} \vdash \neg Q \Rightarrow K_\alpha(P)$		3, 4, Lemma 2
6. $\{R_1 \wedge R_2 \wedge R_3\} \vdash \neg K_\alpha(P) \Rightarrow \neg\neg Q$		5, Lemma 3
7. $\{R_1 \wedge R_2 \wedge R_3\} \vdash \neg\neg Q$		6, 1, $\Rightarrow$-E
8. $\{R_1 \wedge R_2 \wedge R_3\} \vdash Q$		7, [$\neg$-E]

□

Lemma 7. *Consider any agent α and propositions P, Q. Define R_1 and R_3 as in Lemma 6, let $R_2 = P \vee Q$, and let $S_i = C(R_i)$ for $i = 1, 2, 3$. Then $\{S_1, S_2, S_3\} \vdash C(Q)$.*

Proof. Let $R'_2 = \neg Q \Rightarrow P$ and consider the following derivation:

1.	$\{S_1, S_2, S_3\} \vdash S_1$	[*Reflex*]
2.	$\{S_1, S_2, S_3\} \vdash S_2$	[*Reflex*]
3.	$\{S_1, S_2, S_3\} \vdash S_3$	[*Reflex*]
4.	$\emptyset \vdash (P \vee Q) \Rightarrow (\neg Q \Rightarrow P)$	Lemma 4a
5.	$\{S_1, S_2, S_3\} \vdash C((P \vee Q) \Rightarrow (\neg Q \Rightarrow P))$	4, [*C-I*]
6.	$\{S_1, S_2, S_3\} \vdash C(P \vee Q) \Rightarrow C(\neg Q \Rightarrow P)$	5, [C_K], [$\Rightarrow$-*E*]
7.	$\{S_1, S_2, S_3\} \vdash C(\neg Q \Rightarrow P)$	6, 2, [$\Rightarrow$-*E*]
8.	$\{S_1, S_2, S_3\} \vdash C(\neg Q \Rightarrow P) \Rightarrow C(K\alpha(\neg Q \Rightarrow P))$	[*R*]
9.	$\{S_1, S_2, S_3\} \vdash C(K\alpha(\neg Q \Rightarrow P))$	8, 7, [$\Rightarrow$-*E*]
10.	$\{R_1 \wedge K\alpha(\neg Q \Rightarrow P) \wedge R_3\} \vdash Q$	Lemma 6
11.	$\emptyset \vdash (R_1 \wedge K\alpha(\neg Q \Rightarrow P) \wedge R_3) \Rightarrow Q$	10, [$\Rightarrow$-*I*]
12.	$\{S_1, S_2, S_3\} \vdash C((R_1 \wedge K\alpha(\neg Q \Rightarrow P) \wedge R_3) \Rightarrow Q)$	11, [*C-I*]
13.	$\{S_1, S_2, S_3\} \vdash C(R_1 \wedge K\alpha(\neg Q \Rightarrow P) \wedge R_3) \Rightarrow C(Q)$	12, [C_K], [$\Rightarrow$-*E*]
14.	$\{S_1, S_2, S_3\} \vdash C(R_1 \wedge K\alpha(\neg Q \Rightarrow P) \wedge R_3)$	1, 3, 9, Lemma 5, [$\wedge$-*I*]
15.	$\{S_1, S_2, S_3\} \vdash C(Q)$	13, 14, [$\Rightarrow$-*E*]

□

Our method can now be expressed as follows:

$\Phi \leftarrow \{S_1^1, S_2^1, S_3^1\}$;
$\Sigma \leftarrow \Phi \vdash S_2^2$;
Use Lemma 7 to derive Σ;
If $n = 1$ **halt**
else
   For $i = 2$ **to** n **do**
     begin
       $\Phi \leftarrow \Phi \cup \{S_1^i, S_3^i\}$;
       $\Sigma' \leftarrow \{S_1^i, S_2^i, S_3^i\} \vdash S_2^{i+1}$;
       Use Lemma 7 to derive Σ';
       $\Sigma'' \leftarrow \Phi \vdash S_2^{i+1}$;
       Use the cut on Σ and Σ' to derive Σ'';
       $\Sigma \leftarrow \Sigma''$
   end

The loop variable i ranges over the interval $2, \ldots, n$. For any i in that interval, we write Φ^i and Σ^i for the values of Φ and Σ upon conclusion of the ith iteration of the loop. A straightforward induction on i will establish:

Lemma 8 (Algorithm correctness). *For any* $i \in \{2, \ldots, n\}$,

$$\Phi^i = \{C(M_1 \vee \cdots \vee M_{n+1})\} \bigcup_{j=1}^{i} \{S_1^j, S_3^j\}$$

while $\Sigma^i = \Phi^i \vdash S_2^{i+1}$.

Hence, $\Phi^n = \Omega_{n+1}$, and $\Sigma^n = \Phi^n \vdash S_2^{n+1} = \Omega_{n+1} \vdash S_2^{n+1} = \Omega_{n+1} \vdash C(M_{n+1})$, which is our goal.

It is noteworthy that no such correctness argument is necessary in the formulation of the algorithm as an Athena method, as methods are guaranteed to be sound. Their results are always logically entailed by the assumption base, assuming that our primitive methods are sound (see Chapter 8 of [20]).

4   Athena Implementation

In this section we present the Athena encoding of the epistemic logic and our method for solving the generalized version of the wise men puzzle (refer to the Athena web site [15] for more information on the language). We begin by introducing an uninterpreted domain of epistemic agents: (domain Agent). Next we represent the abstract syntax of the propositions of the logic. The following Athena datatype mirrors the abstract grammar for propositions that was given in the beginning of Section 2:

```
(datatype Prop
  True
  False
  (Atom Boolean)
  (Not Prop)
  (And Prop Prop)
  (Or Prop Prop)
  (If Prop Prop)
  (Knows Agent Prop)
  (Common Prop))
```

We proceed to introduce a binary relation sequent that may obtain between a finite set of propositions and a single proposition:

```
(declare sequent (-> ((FSet-Of Prop) Prop) Boolean))
```

Here FSet-Of is a unary sort constructor: for any sort T, (FSet-Of T) is a new sort representing the set of all finite sets of elements of T. Finite sets are built with two polymorphic constructors: the constant null, representing the empty set; and the binary constructor insert, which takes an element x of sort T and a finite set S (of sort (FSet-Of T)) and returns the set $\{x\} \cup S$. We also have all the usual set-theoretic operations available (union, intersection, etc.).

The intended interpretation is that if (sequent S P) holds for a set of propositions S and a proposition P, then the sequent $S \vdash P$ is derivable in the epistemic logic via the rules presented in Section 2. Accordingly, we introduce axioms capturing those rules. For instance, the conjunction introduction rule is represented by the following axiom:

```
(define And-I
  (forall ?S ?P ?Q
    (if (and (sequent ?S ?P)
             (sequent ?S ?Q))
        (sequent ?S (And ?P ?Q)))))
```

Note that the lowercase **and** above is Athena's built-in conjunction operator, and hence represents conjunction at the metalanguage level, whereas **And** represents the object-level conjunction operator of the epistemic logic.

The cut rule and the common knowledge introduction (necessitation) rule become:

```
(define cut
  (forall ?S1 ?S2 ?P ?Q
    (if (and (sequent ?S1 ?P)
             (sequent (insert ?P ?S2) ?Q))
        (sequent (union ?S1 ?S2) ?Q))))
```

```
(define common-intro-axiom
  (forall ?P ?S
    (if (sequent null ?P)
        (sequent ?S (Common ?P)))))
```

The remaining rules are encoded by similar first-order axioms.

We next proceed to derive several lemmas that are useful for the proof. Some of these lemmas are derived completely automatically via the ATPs that are integrated with Athena. For instance, the cut rule is proved automatically (in about 10 seconds). As another example, the following result—part (b) of Lemma 4—is proved automatically:

```
(forall ?S ?P1 ?P2
  (if (and (sequent null (If ?P1 ?P2))
           (sequent ?S (Common ?P1)))
      (sequent ?S (Common ?P2))))
```

Other lemmas are established by giving natural deduction proofs. For instance, the proof of Lemma 6 in Section 3 is transcribed virtually verbatim in Athena, and validated in a fraction of a second. (The fact that the proof is abridged— i.e., multiple steps are compressed into single steps—is readily handled by invoking ATPs that automatically fill in the details.) Finally, we are able to prove Lemma 7, which is the key technical lemma. Utilizing the higher-order character of our encoding, we then define a method **main-lemma** that takes an arbitrary list of agents $[a_1 \cdots a_n], n \geq 1$, and specializes Lemma 7 with $P \mapsto M_{a_1}$, $Q \mapsto M_{a_2} \vee \cdots \vee M_{a_n}$, and $\alpha \mapsto a_1$ (recall that for any agent α, $M\alpha$ signifies that α is marked). So, for instance, the application of **main-lemma** to the list $[a_1, a_2, a_3]$ would derive the conclusion $\{S_1, S_2, S_3\} \vdash C(M_{a_2} \vee M_{a_3})$, where $S_1 = C(\neg K_{a_1}(M_{a_1}))$, $S_2 = C(M_{a_1} \vee M_{a_2} \vee M_{a_3})$, and

$$S_3 = C(\neg(M_{a_2} \vee M_{a_3}) \Rightarrow K_{a_1}(\neg(M_{a_2} \vee M_{a_3})))$$

We also need a simple result **shuffle** asserting the equality $\Gamma, P_1, P_2 = \Gamma, P_2, P_1$ (i.e., $\Gamma \cup \{P_1\} \cup \{P_2\} = \Gamma \cup \{P_2\} \cup \{P_1\}$).

Using these building blocks, we express the tactic for solving the generalized wise men problem as the Athena method **solve** below. It takes as input a list of agents representing wise men, with at least two elements. Note that the for loop in the pseudocode algorithm has been replaced by recursion.

```
(define (solve wise-men)
  (dletrec
    ((loop (method (wise-men th)
             (dmatch wise-men
               ([_] (!claim th))
               ((list-of _ rest)
                 (dlet ((new-th (!main-lemma wise-men)))
                   (dmatch [th new-th]
                     ([[(sequent context Q2)
                        (sequent (insert Q1
                                   (insert Q2 (insert Q3 null))) P)]
                       (dlet ((cut-th
                                (!derive (sequent
                                           (union
                                             context
                                             (insert Q1 (insert Q3 null)))
                                           P)
                                         [th new-th shuffle cut])))
                         (!loop rest cut-th)))))))))))
    (dlet ((init (!prove-goal-2 wise-men)))
      (!loop (tail wise-men) init))))
```

Assuming that w1, w2, w3 are agents representing wise men, invoking the method solve with the list [w1 w2 w3]) as the argument will derive the appropriate result: $\Omega_3 \vdash$ (Common (isMarked w3)), where Ω_3 is the set of premises for the three-men case, as defined in the previous section.

5   Related Work

The wise men problem became a staple of epistemic AI literature after being introduced by McCarthy [12]. Formalizations and solutions of the two-wise-men problem are found in a number of sources [22, 23, 24], most of them in simple multi-agent epistemic logics (without common knowledge). Several variations have been given; e.g., Konolige has a version in which the third wise man states that he does not know whether he is marked, but that he would know if only the second wise man were wiser [25]. Ballim and Wilks [26] solve the three-men version of the puzzle using the "nested viewpoints" framework. Vincenzo Pallotta's solution [27] is similar but his ViewGen framework facilitates agent simulation. Kim and Kowalski [28] use a Prolog-based implementation of metareasoning to solve the same version of the problem using common knowledge. A more natural proof was given by Aiello et al. [29] in a rewriting framework.

The importance of reasoning about the intentional states of intelligent agents is widely recognized (see, for instance, the recent work by Dastani et al. on inferring trust [30]). Agent metareasoning and metaknowledge, in particular, is extensively discussed in "Logical foundations of Artifical Intelligence" by Genesereth and Nillson [24] (it is the subject of an entire chapter). They stress that the main advantage of an explicit encoding of the reasoning process is that it makes it possible to "create agents capable of reasoning in detail about the inferential abilities of and beliefs of other agents," as well as enabling introspection.[3]

The only work we are aware of that has an explicit encoding of an epistemic logic in a rich metalanguage is a recent project [32] that uses the Calculus of Constructions (Coq [33]). However, there are important differences. First, they encode a Hilbert proof system, which has an adverse impact on the readability and writability of proofs. The second and most important difference is our emphasis on reasoning efficiency. The seamless integration of Athena with state-of-the-art provers such as Vampire and Spass is crucial for automation, as it enables the user to skip tedious steps and keep the reasoning at a high level of detail. Another distinguishing aspect of our work is our heavy use of tactics. Athena uses a block-structured natural-deduction style not only for writing proofs but also for writing proof tactics ("methods"). Proof methods are much easier to write in this style, and play a key role in proof automation. Our emphasis on automation also differentiates our work from that of Basin et al. [34] using Isabelle, which only addresses proof presentation in modal logics, not automatic proof discovery.

References

1. Davis, E., Morgenstern, L.: Epistemic Logics and its Applications: Tutorial Notes. (www-formal.stanford.edu/leora/krcourse/ijcaitxt.ps)
2. Fagin, R., Halpern, J., Moses, Y., Vardi, M.: Reasoning about knowledge. MIT Press, Cambridge, Massachusetts (1995)
3. Meyer, J., Hoek, W.V.D.: Epistemic Logic for Computer Science and Artificial Intelligence. Volume 41 of Cambridge Tracts in Theoretical Computer Science. Cambridge University Press (1995)
4. Gabbay, D.M., Kurucz, A., Wolter, F., Zakharyaschev, M.: Many-dimensional modal logics: theory and applications. Volume 4 of Studies in Logic and the Foundations of Mathematics. Elsevier (1994)
5. Halpern, J., Moses, Y.: A guide to completeness and complexity for modal logics of knowledge and belief. Artificial Intelligence **54** (1992) 319–379
6. Horrocks, I.: Using an expressive description logic: FaCT or fiction? In: Sixth International Conference on Principles of Knowledge Representation and Reasoning. (1998) 636–647
7. Giunchiglia, E., Giunchiglia, F., Sebastiani, R., Tacchella, A.: More evaluation of decision procedures for modal logics. In Cohn, A.G., Schubert, L., Shapiro, S.C., eds.: 6th international conference on principles of knowledge representation and reasoning (KR'98), Trento (1998)
8. Hustadt, U., Schmidt, R.A.: On evaluating decision procedures for modal logic. In: Fifteenth International Joint Conference on Artificial Intelligence. (1997) 202–209

---

[3] In addition, Bringsjord and Yang [31] have claimed that the best of human reasoning is distinguished by a capacity for meta-reasoning, and have proposed a theory—mental metalogic—of human and machine reasoning that emphasizes this type of reasoning.

9. Heuerding, A.: LWBtheory: information about some propositional logics via the WWW. Logic Journal of the IGPL **4** (1996) 169–174
10. Schmidt, R.A.: MSPASS. http://www.cs.man.ac.uk/~schmidt/mspass/ (1999)
11. Fitting, M.: Basic modal logic. In Gabbay, D.M., Hogger, C.J., Robinson, J.A., eds.: Logical foundations. Volume 4 of Handbook of Logic in Artificial Intelligence and Logic Programming. Oxford Science Publications (1994)
12. McCarthy, J.: Formalization of two puzzles involving knowledge. In Lifschitz, V., ed.: Formalizing Common Sense: Papers by John McCarthy. Ablex Publishing Corporation, Norwood, New Jersey (1990)
13. Schmidt, R.A., Hustadt, U.: Mechanised reasoning and model generation for extended modal logics. In de Swart, H.C.M., Orlowska, E., Schmidt, G., Roubens, M., eds.: Theory and Applications of Relational Structures as Knowledge Instruments. Volume 2929 of Lecture Notes in Computer Science. Springer (2003) 38–67
14. Cyrluk, D., Rajan, S., Shankar, N., , Srivas, M.: Effective theorem proving for hardware verification. In: Theorem Provers in Circuit Design (TPCD '94). Volume 901 of Lecture Notes in Computer Science., Bad Herrenalb, Germany, Springer-Verlag (1994) 203–222
15. Arkoudas, K.: Athena. (http://www.pac.csail.mit.edu/athena)
16. Voronkov, A.: The anatomy of Vampire: implementing bottom-up procedures with code trees. Journal of Automated Reasoning **15** (1995)
17. Weidenbach, C.: Combining superposition, sorts, and splitting. In Robinson, A., Voronkov, A., eds.: Handbook of Automated Reasoning. Volume 2. North-Holland (2001)
18. Gordon, M.J.C., Melham, T.F.: Introduction to HOL, a theorem proving environment for higher-order logic. Cambridge University Press, Cambridge, England (1993)
19. Paulson, L.: Isabelle, A Generic Theorem Prover. Lecture Notes in Computer Science. Springer-Verlag (1994)
20. Arkoudas, K.: Denotational Proof Languages. (PhD dissertation, MIT, 2000)
21. Ebbinghaus, H.D., Flum, J., Thomas, W.: Mathematical Logic. 2nd edn. Springer-Verlag (1994)
22. Huth, M., Ryan, M.: Logic in Computer Science: modelling and reasoning about systems. Cambridge University Press, Cambridge, UK (2000)
23. Snyers, D., Thayse, A.: Languages and logics. In Thayse, A., ed.: From modal logic to deductive databases, John Wiley & Sons (1989) 1–54
24. Genesereth, M., Nilsson, N.: Logical Foundations of Artificial Intelligence. Morgan Kaufmann (1987)
25. Konolige, K.: A deduction model of belief. Research Notes in Artificial Intelligence. Pitman, London, UK (1986)
26. Ballim, A., Wilks, Y.: Artificial Believers. Lawrence Erlbaum Associates, Hillsdale, New Jersey (1991)
27. Pallotta, V.: Computational dialogue Models. In: 10th Conference of the European Chapter of the Association for Computational Linguistics EACL03. (2003)
28. Kim, J., Kowalski, R.: An application of amalgamated logic to multi-agent belief. In Bruynooghe, M., ed.: Second Workshop on Meta-Programming in Logic META90. (1990) 272–283
29. Aiello, L.C., Nardi, D., Schaerf, M.: Yet another solution to the three wisemen puzzle. In: Proceedings of the 3rd International Symposium on Methodologies for Intelligent Systems. (1988) 398–407
30. Dastani, M., Herzig, A., Hulstijn, J., van der Torre, L.: Inferring trust. In this volume.

31. Yang, Y., Bringsjord, S.: Mental Metalogic: A New, Unifying Theory of Human and Machine Reasoning. Erlbaum, Mahwah, NJ (2005)
32. Lescanne, P.: Epistemic logic in higher order logic: an experiment with COQ. Technical Report RR2001-12, LIP-ENS de Lyon (2001)
33. Coquand, T., Huet, G.: The Calculus of Constructions. Information and Computation **76** (1988) 95–120
34. Basin, D., Matthews, S., Viganò, L.: A modular presentation of modal logics in a logical framework. In Ginzburg, J., Khasidashvili, Z., Vogel, C., Lévy, J.J., Vallduví, E., eds.: The Tbilisi Symposium on Logic, Language and Computation: Selected Papers. CSLI Publications, Stanford, CA (1998) 293–307

Graded BDI Models for Agent Architectures⋆

Ana Casali[1], Lluís Godo[2], and Carles Sierra[2]

[1] Depto. de Sistemas e Informática,
Facultad de Cs. Exactas, Ingeniería y Agrimensura,
Universidad Nacional de Rosario,
Av Pellegrini 250, 2000 Rosario, Argentina
[2] Institut d'Investigació en Intel·ligència Artificial (IIIA) - CSIC,
Campus Universitat Autònoma de Barcelona s/n,
08193 Bellaterra, Catalunya, España

Abstract. In the recent past, an increasing number of multiagent systems (MAS) have been designed and implemented to engineer complex distributed systems. Several previous works have proposed theories and architectures to give these systems a formal support. Among them, one of the most widely used is the BDI agent architecture presented by Rao and Georgeff. We consider that in order to apply agents in real domains, it is important for the formal models to incorporate a model to represent and reason under uncertainty. With that aim we introduce in this paper a general model for graded BDI agents, and an architecture, based on multi-context systems, able to model these graded mental attitudes. This architecture serves as a blueprint to design different kinds of particular agents. We illustrate the design process by formalising a simple travel assistant agent.

1 Introduction

In the recent past, an increasing number of multiagent systems (MAS) have been designed and implemented to engineer complex distributed systems. Several previous works have proposed theories and architectures to give these systems a formal support. Agent theories are essentially specifications of agents' behaviour expressed as the properties that agents should have. A formal representation of the properties helps the designer to reason about the expected behaviour of the system [25]. Agent architectures represent a middle point between specification and implementation. They identify the main functions that ultimately determine the agent's behaviour and define the interdependencies that exist among them [25]. Agent theories based on an intentional stance are among the most common ones. Intentional systems describe entities whose behaviour can be predicted

---

⋆ A preliminary version of this paper, "Modelos BDI graduados para Arquitecturas de Agentes" (in Spanish), was presented at the Argentine Symposium on Artificial Intelligence (ASAI'04) and will appear in an especial issue of "Inteligencia Artificial" (Revista Iberoamericana de Inteligencia Artificial).

J. Leite and P. Torroni (Eds.): CLIMA V, LNAI 3487, pp. 126–143, 2005.
© Springer-Verlag Berlin Heidelberg 2005

by the method of attributing certain mentalistic attitudes such as knowledge, belief —*information attitudes*, desire, intention, obligation, commitment —*pro-attitudes*, among others [5]. A well-known intentional system formal approach is the BDI architecture proposed by Rao and Georgeff [20, 21]. This model is based on the explicit representation of the agent's beliefs (B) —used to represent the state of the environment, its desires (D) —used to represent the motivations of the agent, and its intentions (I) —used to represent the goals of the agent. This architecture has evolved over time and it has been applied in several of the most significant multiagent applications developed up to now.

Modelling different intentional notions by means of several modalities (B, D, I) can be very complex if only one logical framework is used. In order to help in the design of such complex logical systems Giunchiglia et.al. [9] introduced the notion of *multi-context system* (MCS for short). This framework allows the definition of different formal components and their interrelation. In our case, we propose to use separate contexts to represent each modality and formalise each context with the most appropriate logic apparatus. The interactions between the components are specified by using inter-unit rules, called *bridge rules*. These rules are part of the deduction machinery of the system. This approach has been used by Sabater et.al. [22] and Parsons et.al. [19] to specify several agent architectures and particularly to model some classes of BDI agents [17]. Indeed one advantage of the MCS logical approach to agency modelling is that it allows for rather affordable computational implementation. For instance, a portion of the framework described in [17] is being now implemented using a prolog multi-threaded architecture [8].

The agent architectures proposed so far mostly deal with two-valued information. Although the BDI model developed by Rao and Georgeff explicitly acknowledges that an agent's model of the world is incomplete, by modelling beliefs as a set of worlds that the agent knows that it might be in, it makes no use of quantified information about how possible a particular world is to be the actual one. Neither does it allow desires and intentions to be quantified. We think that taking into consideration this graded information could improve the agent's performance. There are a few works that partially address this issue and emphasize the importance of graded models. Notably, Parsons and Giorgini [17] consider the belief quantification by using Evidence Theory. In their proposal, an agent is allowed to express its opinion on the reliability of the agents it interacts with, and to revise its beliefs when they become inconsistent. They set out the importance of quantifying degrees in desires and intentions, but this is not covered by their work. Lang et al. [14] present an approach to a logic of desires, where the notion of hidden uncertainty of desires is introduced. Desires are formalized to support a realistic interaction between the concepts of preference and plausibility (or normality), both represented by a pre-order relation over the sets of possible worlds. Other works deal with reasoning about intentions in uncertain domains, as the proposal of Schut et al. [24]. They present an efficient intention reconsideration for agents that interact in an uncertainty environment in terms of dynamics, observability, and non-determinism.

All the above mentioned proposals model partial aspects of the uncertainty related to mental notions involved in an agent's architecture. We present in this paper a general model for a graded BDI agent, specifying an architecture able to deal with the environment uncertainty and with graded mental attitudes. In this sense, belief degrees represent to what extent the agent believes a formula is true. Degrees of positive or negative desire allow the agent to set different levels of preference or rejection respectively. Intention degrees give also a preference measure but, in this case, modelling the cost/benefit trade off of reaching an agent's goal. Then, Agents having different kinds of behaviour can be modeled on the basis of the representation and interaction of these three attitudes.

This paper is organised as follows: in Section 2, we introduce multi-context systems and the general multivalued logic framework for the graded contexts. Sections 3, 4, and 5 present the mental units of the graded BDI model, that is the contexts for beliefs (BC), desires (DC), and intentions (IC). Section 6 outlines two functional contexts for planning (PC) and communication (CC). In Section 7, we deal with bridge rules, we illustrate the overall reasoning process in Section 8, and finally, we present some conclusions and future lines of work.

2   Graded BDI Agent Model

The architecture presented in this paper is inspired by the work of Parsons et.al. [17] about multi-context BDI agents. Multi-context systems were introduced by Giunchiglia et.al. [9] to allow different formal (logic) components to be defined and interrelated. The MCS specification of an agent contains three basic components: units or contexts, logics, and bridge rules, which channel the propagation of consequences among theories. Thus, an agent is defined as a group of interconnected units: $\langle \{C_i\}_{i \in I}, \Delta_{br} \rangle$, where each context $C_i \in \{C_i\}_{i \in I}$ is the tuple $C_i = \langle L_i, A_i, \Delta_i \rangle$ where L_i, A_i and Δ_i are the language, axioms, and inference rules respectively. They define the logic for the context and its basic behaviour as constrained by the axioms. When a theory $T_i \in L_i$ is associated with each unit, the implementation of a particular agent is complete. Δ_{br} can be understood as rules of inference with premises and conclusions in different contexts, for instance:

$$\frac{C_1 : \psi, C_2 : \varphi}{C_3 : \theta}$$

means that if formula ψ is deduced in context C_1 and formula φ is deduced in context C_2 then formula θ is added to context C_3.

The deduction mechanism of these systems is based on two kinds of inference rules, internal rules Δ_i inside each unit, and bridge rules Δ_{br} outside. Internal rules allow to draw consequences within a theory, while bridge rules allow to embed results from a theory into another [7].

We have *mental* contexts to represent beliefs (BC), desires (DC) and intentions (IC). We also consider two *functional* contexts: for Planning (PC) and Communication (CC). The Planner is in charge of finding plans to change the current world into another world, where some goal is satisfied, and of computing the cost associated to the plans. The communication context is the agent's door to the external world, receiving and sending messages. In summary, the BDI agent model is defined as:

$$A_g = (\{BC, DC, IC, PC, CC\}, \Delta_{br})$$

Each context has an associated logic, that is, a logical language with its own semantics and deductive system. In order to represent and reason about graded notions of beliefs, desires and intentions, we decide to use a modal many-valued approach. In particular, we shall follow the approach developed by Hájek et al. in e.g. [12] and [10] where uncertainty reasoning is dealt with by defining suitable modal theories over suitable many-valued logics. The basic idea is the following. For instance, let us consider a Belief context where belief degrees are to be modeled as probabilities. Then, for each classical (two-valued) formula φ, we consider a modal formula $B\varphi$ which is interpreted as "φ is probable". This modal formula $B\varphi$ is then a *fuzzy* formula which may be more or less true, depending on the probability of φ. In particular, we can take as truth-value of $B\varphi$ precisely the probability of φ. Moreover, using a many-valued logic, we can express the governing axioms of probability theory as logical axioms involving modal formulae of the kind $B\varphi$. Then, the many-valued logic machinery can be used to reason about the modal formulae $B\varphi$, which faithfully respect the uncertainty model chosen to represent the degrees of belief.

In this proposal, for the mental contexts we choose the infinite-valued Łukasiewicz logic but another selection of many-valued logics may be done for each unit, according to the measure modeled in each case [1]. Therefore, in this kind of logical frameworks we shall have, besides the axioms of Łukasiewicz many-valued logic, a set of axioms corresponding to the basic postulates of a particular uncertainty theory. Hence, in this approach, reasoning about probabilities (or any other uncertainty models) can be done in a very elegant way within a uniform and flexible logical framework. The same many-valued logical framework may be used to represent and reason about degrees of desires and intentions, as will be seen in detail later on.

3   Belief Context

The purpose of this context is to model the agent's beliefs about the environment. In order to represent beliefs, we use modal many-valued formulae, following the above mentioned logical framework. We consider in this paper the particular

---

[1] The reason of using this many-valued logic is that its main connectives are based on the arithmetic addition in the unit interval $[0, 1]$, which is what is needed to deal with additive measures like probabilities. Besides, Łukasiewicz logic has also the *min* conjunction and *max* disjunction as definable connectives, so it also allows to define a logic to reason about degrees of necessity and possibility.

case of using probability theory as the uncertainty model. Other models might be used as well by just modifying the corresponding axioms.

3.1   The BC Language

To reason about the credibility of crisp propositions, we define a language for belief representation, following Godo et al.'s [10], based on Łukasiewicz logic. In order to define the basic crisp language, we start from a classical propositional language L, defined upon a countable set of propositional variables PV and connectives $(\neg, \rightarrow)$, and extend it to represent actions. We take advantage of Dynamic logic which has been used to model agent's actions in [23] and [16]. These actions, the environment transformations they cause, and their associated cost must be part of any situated agent's beliefs set.

The propositional language L is thus extended to L_D, by adding to it action modalities of the form $[\alpha]$ where α is an action. More concretely, given a set Π_0 of symbols representing elementary actions, the set Π of plans (composite actions) and formulae L_D is defined as follows:

- $\Pi_0 \subset \Pi$ (elementary actions are plans)
- if $\alpha, \beta \in \Pi$ then $\alpha; \beta \in \Pi$, (the concatenation of actions is also a plan)
- if $\alpha, \beta \in \Pi$ then $\alpha \cup \beta \in \Pi$ (non-deterministic disjunction)
- if $\alpha \in \Pi$ then $\alpha^* \in \Pi$ (iteration)
- If A is a formula, then $A? \in \Pi$ (test)

- if $p \in PV$, then $p \in L_D$
- if $\varphi \in L_D$ then $\neg\varphi \in L_D$
- if $\varphi, \psi \in L_D$ then $\varphi \rightarrow \psi \in L_D$
- if $\alpha \in \Pi$ and $\varphi \in L_D$ then $[\alpha]\varphi \in L_D$.

The interpretation of $[\alpha]A$ is *"after the execution of α, A is true"*

We define a modal language BC over the language L_D to reason about the belief on crisp propositions. To do so, we extend the crisp language L_D with a fuzzy unary modal operator B. If φ is a proposition in L_D, the intended meaning of $B\varphi$ is that "φ is believable". Formulae of BC are of two types:

- *Crisp (non B-modal):* they are the (crisp) formulae of L_D, built in the usual way, thus, if $\varphi \in L_D$ then $\varphi \in BC$.
- *B-Modal:* they are built from elementary modal formulae $B\varphi$, where φ is crisp, and truth constants $\bar{r}$, for each rational $r \in [0,1]$, using the connectives of Łukasiewicz many-valued logic:
  - If $\varphi \in L_D$ then $B\varphi \in BC$
  - If $r \in Q \cap [0,1]$ then $\bar{r} \in BC$
  - If $\Phi, \Psi \in BC$ then $\Phi \rightarrow_L \Psi \in BC$ and $\Phi \& \Psi \in BC$ (where $\&$ and $\rightarrow_L$ correspond to the conjunction and implication of Łukasiewicz logic)

Other Łukasiewicz logic connectives for the modal formulae can be defined from $\&$, $\rightarrow_L$ and $\bar{0}$: $\neg_L \Phi$ is defined as $\Phi \rightarrow_L \bar{0}$, $\Phi \wedge \Psi$ as $\Phi \& (\Phi \rightarrow_L \Psi)$, $\Phi \vee \Psi$ as $\neg_L(\neg_L\Phi \wedge \neg_L\Psi)$, and $\Phi \equiv \Psi$ as $(\Phi \rightarrow_L \Psi)\&(\Psi \rightarrow_L \Phi)$.

Since in Łukasiewicz logic a formula $\Phi \to_L \Psi$ is 1-true iff the truth value of Ψ is greater or equal to that of Φ, modal formulae of the type $\bar{r} \to_L B\varphi$ express that the probability of φ is at least r. Formulae of the type $\bar{r} \to_L \Psi$ will be denoted as (Ψ, r).

3.2   Belief Semantics

The semantics for the language BC is defined, as usual in modal logics, using a Kripke structure. We have added to such structure a ρ function in order to represent the world transitions caused by actions, and a probability measure μ over worlds. Thus, we define a BC probabilistic Kripke structure as a 4-tuple $K = \langle W, e, \mu, \rho \rangle$ where:

- W is a non-empty set of possible worlds.
- $e : V \times W \to \{0, 1\}$ provides for each world a Boolean (two-valued) evaluation of the propositional variables, that is, $e(p, w) \in \{0, 1\}$ for each propositional variable $p \in V$ and each world $w \in W$. The evaluation is extended to arbitrary formulae in L_D as described below.
- $\mu : 2^W \to [0, 1]$ is a finitely additive probability measure on a Boolean algebra of subsets of W such that for each crisp φ, the set $\{w \mid e(\varphi, w) = 1\}$ is measurable [12].
- $\rho : \Pi_0 \to 2^{W \times W}$ assigns to each elementary action a set of pairs of worlds denoting world transitions.

Extension of e to L_D formulae:
e is extended to L using classical connectives and to formulae with action modalities –as $[\alpha]\,A$, by defining $\rho(\alpha; \beta) = \rho(\alpha) \circ \rho(\beta)$, $\rho(\alpha \cup \beta) = \rho(\alpha) \cup \rho(\beta)$, $\rho(\alpha^*) = (\rho(\alpha))^*$ (ancestral relation) and $\rho(\varphi?) = \{(w, w) \mid e(\varphi, w) = 1\}$, and setting $e([\alpha]\,A, w) = min\,\{e(A, w_i) \mid (w, w_i) \in \rho(\alpha)\}$. Notice that $e([\alpha]\,A, w) = 1$ iff the evaluation of A is 1 in all the worlds w' that may be reached through the action α from w.

Extension of e to B-modal formulae:
e is extended to B-modal formulae by means of Łukasiewicz logic truth-functions and the probabilistic interpretation of belief as follows:

- $e(B\varphi, w) = \mu(\{w' \in W \mid e(\varphi, w') = 1\})$, for each crisp φ
- $e(\bar{r}, w) = r$, for all $r \in Q \cap [0, 1]$
- $e(\Phi \& \Psi, w) = \max(e(\Phi) + e(\Psi) - 1, 0)$
- $e(\Phi \to_L \Psi, w) = \min(1 - e(\Phi) + e(\Psi), 1)$

Finally, the truth degree of a formula Φ in a Kripke structure $K = \langle W, e, \mu, \rho \rangle$ is defined as $\|\Phi\|^K = \inf_{w \in W} e(\Phi, w)$.

3.3   BC Axioms and Rules

As mentioned in Section 2, to set up an adequate axiomatization for our belief context logic we need to combine axioms for the crisp formulae, axioms of

Łukasiewicz logic for modal formulae, and additional axioms for B-modal formulae according to the probabilistic semantics of the B operator. Hence, axioms and rules for the Belief context logic BC are as follows:

1. Axioms of propositional Dynamic logic for L_D formulae (see e.g. [11]).
2. Axioms of Łukasiewicz logic for modal formulae: for instance, axioms of Hájek's Basic Logic (BL) [12] plus the axiom: $\neg\neg\Phi \to \Phi$
3. Probabilistic axioms
   $B(\varphi \to \psi) \to_L (B\varphi \to B\psi)$
   $B\varphi \equiv \neg_L B(\varphi \wedge \neg\psi) \to_L B(\varphi \wedge \psi)$
   $\neg_L B\varphi \equiv B\neg\varphi$
4. Deduction rules for BC are: modus ponens, necessitation for $[\alpha]$ for each $\alpha \in \Pi$ (from φ derive $[\alpha]\varphi$), and necessitation for B (from φ derive $B\varphi$).

Deduction is defined as usual from the above axioms and rules and will be denoted by $\vdash_{BC}$. Notice that, taking into account Łukasiewicz semantics, the second *probabilistic axiom* corresponds to the finite additivity while the third one expresses that the probability of $\neg\varphi$ is 1 minus the probability of φ. Actually, one can show that the above axiomatics is sound and complete with respect to the intended semantics described in the previous subsection (cf. [12]). Namely, if T is a finite theory over BC and Φ is a (modal) formula, then $T \vdash \Phi$ iff $\|\Phi\|^K = 1$ in each BC probabilistic Kripke structure K model of T (i.e. K such that $\|\Psi\|^K = 1$ for all $\Psi \in T$).

4   Desire Context

In this context, we represent the agent's desires. Desires represent the *ideal* agent's preferences regardless of the agent's current perception of the environment and regardless of the cost involved in actually achieving them. We deem important to distinguish what is positively desired from what is not rejected. According to the works on bipolarity representation of preferences by Benferhat et.al. [2], positive and negative information may be modeled in the framework of possibilistic logic. Inspired by this work, we suggest to formalise agent's desires also as positive and negative. Positive desires represent what the agent would like to be the case. Negative desires correspond to what the agent rejects or does not want to occur. Both, positive and negative desires can be graded.

4.1   DC Language

The language DC is defined as an extension of a propositional language L by introducing two (fuzzy) modal operators D^+ and D^-. $D^+\varphi$ reads as "φ is positively desired" and its truth degree represents the agent's level of satisfaction would φ become true. $D^-\varphi$ reads as "φ is negatively desired" and its truth degree represents the agent's measure of disgust on φ becoming true. As in BC logic, we will use a modal many-valued logic to formalise graded desires. We use again Łukasiewicz logic as the base logic, but this time extended with a new connective Δ (known as Baaz's connective), considered also in [12]. For any modal Φ, if Φ has value < 1 then $\Delta\Phi$ gets value 0; otherwise, if Φ has value 1 then $\Delta\Phi$ gets value 1 as well. Hence $\Delta\Phi$ becomes a two-valued (Boolean) formula. Therefore, DC formulae are of two types:

- *Crisp (non modal):* formulae of L
- *Many-valued (modal):* they are built from elementary modal formulae $D^+\varphi$ and $D^-\varphi$, where φ is from L, and truth constants $\bar{r}$ for each rational $r \in [0,1]$:
  - If $\varphi \in L$ then $D^-\varphi, D^+\varphi \in DC$
  - If $r \in Q \cap [0,1]$ then $\bar{r} \in DC$
  - If $\Phi, \Psi \in DC$ then $\Phi \rightarrow_L \Psi \in DC$ and $\Phi \& \Psi \in DC$

As in BC, $(D\psi, \bar{r})$ denotes $\bar{r} \rightarrow_L D\psi$.

In this context the agent's preferences will be expressed by a theory T containing quantitative expressions about positive and negative preferences, like $(D^+\varphi, \alpha)$ or $(D^-\psi, \beta)$, as well as qualitative expressions like $D^+\psi \rightarrow_L D^+\varphi$ (resp. $D^-\psi \rightarrow_L D^-\varphi$), expressing that φ is at least as preferred (resp. rejected) as ψ. In particular $(D^+\phi_i, 1) \in T$ means that the agent has maximum preference in ϕ_i and is fully satisfied if it is true. While $(D^+\phi_j, \alpha) \notin T$ for any $\alpha > 0$ means that the agent is indifferent to ϕ_j and the agent doesn't benefit from the truth of ϕ_j. Analogously, $(D^-\psi_i, 1) \in T$ means that the agent absolutely rejects ϕ_i and thus the states where ψ_i is true are totally unacceptable. $(D^-\psi_j, \beta) \notin T$ for any $\beta > 0$ simply means that ψ_j is not rejected, the same applies to the formulae not explicitly included in T.

4.2   Semantics for DC

The degree of positive desire for (or level of satisfaction with) a disjunction of goals $\varphi \vee \psi$ is taken to be the minimum of the degrees for φ and ψ. Intuitively if an agent desires $\varphi \vee \psi$ then it is ready to accept the situation where the less desired goal becomes true, and hence to accept the minimum satisfaction level produced by one of the two goals. In contrast the satisfaction degree of reaching both φ and ϕ can be strictly greater than reaching one of them separately. These are basically the properties of the *guaranteed possibility* measures (see e.g. [1]). Analogously, we assume the same model for the degrees of negative desire or rejection, that is, the rejection degree of $\varphi \vee \phi$ is taken to be the minimum of the degrees of rejection for φ and for ψ separately, while nothing prevents the rejection level of $\varphi \wedge \psi$ be greater than both.

The DC models are Kripke structures $M_D = \langle W, e, \pi^+, \pi^- \rangle$ where W and e are defined as in the BL semantics and π^+ and π^- are preference distributions over worlds, which are used to give semantics to positive and negative desires:

- $\pi^+ : W \rightarrow [0,1]$ is a distribution of positive preferences over the possible worlds. In this context $\pi^+(w) < \pi^+(w')$ means that w' is more preferred than w.

 - $\pi^-: W \to [0, 1]$ is a distribution of negative preferences over the possible worlds: $\pi^-(w) < \pi^-(w')$ means that w' is more rejected than w.

We impose a consistency condition: $\pi^-(w) > 0$ implies $\pi^+(w) = 0$, that is, if w is rejected to some extent, it cannot be desired. And conversely. The truth evaluation e is extended to the non-modal formulae in the usual (classical) way. The extension to modal formulae uses the preference distributions for formulae $D^-\varphi$ and $D^+\varphi$, and for the rest of modal formulae by means of Łukasiewicz connectives, as in BC semantics, plus the unary connective Δ. The evaluation of modal formulae only depends on the formula itself –represented in the preference measure over the worlds where the formula is true– and not on the actual world where the agent is situated:

 - $e(D^+\varphi, w) = \inf\{\pi^+(w') \mid e(\varphi, w') = 1\}$
 - $e(D^-\varphi, w) = \inf\{\pi^-(w') \mid e(\varphi, w') = 1\}$
 - $e(\Delta\Phi, w) \begin{cases} 1, \text{ if } e(\Phi, w) = 1 \\ 0, \text{ otherwise.} \end{cases}$

As usual, by convention we take $\inf \emptyset = 1$ and thas $e(D^+\bot, w) = e(D^-\bot, w) = 1$ for all $w \in W$.

4.3   DC Axioms

In a similar way as in BC, to axiomatize the logical system DC we need to combine classical logic axioms for non-modal formulae with Łukasiewicz logic axioms extended with Δ for modal formulae. Also, additional axioms characterizing the behaviour of the modal operators D^+ and D^- are needed. Hence, we define the axioms and rules for the DC logic as follows:

1. Axioms of classical logic for the non-modal formulae.
2. Axioms of Łukasiewicz logic with Δ (cf. [12]) for the modal formulae.
3. Axioms for D^+ and D^- over Łukasiewciz logic:
   $D^+(A \vee B) \equiv D^+A \wedge D^+B$
   $D^-(A \vee B) \equiv D^-A \wedge D^-B$
   $\neg_L\Delta(D^+A \wedge D^-A) \to \neg_L(\nabla D^-A \& \nabla D^+A)$, where ∇ is $\neg_L\Delta\neg_L{}^2$.
   $D^+(\bot)$
   $D^-(\bot)$
4. Rules are: modus ponens, necessitation for Δ, and introduction of D^+ and D^- for implications: from $A \to B$ derive $D^+B \to_L D^+A$ and $D^-B \to_L D^-A$.

Notice that the two first axioms in item (3) define the behaviour of D^- and D^+ with respect to disjunctions, while the third axiom establishes that it is not possible to have at the same time positive and negative desires over the same

---

[2] Notice that $e(\nabla\Phi, w) = 1$ if $e(\Phi, w) > 0$, and $e(\nabla\Phi, w) = 0$ otherwise.

formula except if the formula is a contradiction. In that case notice that the antecedent of the axiom becomes false. Finally, the two inference rules state that the degree of desire is monotonically decreasing with respect to logical implication. This axiomatics is correct with respect to the above defined semantics, and the conjecture is that it is complete too.

5   Intention Context

In this context, we represent the agent's intentions. We follow the model introduced by Rao and Georgeff [20, 21], in which an intention is considered a fundamental pro-attitude with an explicit representation. Intentions, as well as desires, represent the agent's preferences. However, we consider that intentions cannot depend just on the benefit, or satisfaction, of reaching a goal φ –represented in $D^+\varphi$, but also on the world's state w and the cost of transforming it into a world w_i where the formula φ is true. By allowing degrees in intentions we represent a measure of the cost/benefit relation involved in the agent's actions towards the goal. The positive and negative desires are used as pro-active and restrictive tools respectively, in order to set intentions. Note that intentions depend on the agent's knowledge about the world, which may allow –or not– the agent to set a plan to change the world into a desired one. Thus, if in a theory T we have the formula $I\psi \rightarrow_L I\varphi$ then the agent may try φ before ψ and it may not try ϕ if $(I\phi, \delta)$ is a formula in T and $\delta < Threshold$. This situation may mean that the benefit of getting ϕ is low or the cost is high.

5.1   IC Language

We define its syntax in the same way as we did with BC (except for the dynamic logic part), starting with a basic language L and incorporating a modal operator I. We use Łukasiewicz multivalued logic to represent the degree of the intentions. As in the other contexts, if the degree of $I\varphi$ is δ, it may be considered that the truth degree of the expression "φ is intended" is δ. The intention to make φ true must be the consequence of finding a feasible plan α, that permits to achieve a state of the world where φ holds.

The value of $I\varphi$ will be computed by a bridge rule (see (3) in next Section 7), that takes into account the benefit of reaching φ and the cost, estimated by the Planner, of the possible plans towards it.

5.2   Semantics and Axiomatization for IC

The semantics defined in this context shows that the value of the intentions depends on the formula intended to bring about and on the benefit the agent gets with it. It also depends on the agent's knowledge on possible plans that may change the world into one where the goal is true, and their associated cost. This last factor will make the semantics and axiomatization for IC somewhat different from the presented for positive desires in DC.

The models for IC are Kripke structures $K = \langle W, e, \{\pi_w\}_{w \in W} \rangle$ where W and e are defined in the usual way, and for each $w \in W$, $\pi_w : W \to [0, 1]$ is a possibility distribution where $\pi_w(w') \in [0, 1]$ is the degree on which the agent may try to reach the state w' from the state w.

The truth evaluation $e : V \times W \to \{0, 1\}$ is extended to the non-modal formulae in the usual way. It is extended to modal formulae using Łukasiewicz semantics as $e(I\varphi, w) = N_w(\{w' \mid e(\varphi, w') = 1\})$, where N_w denotes the necessity measure associated to the possibility distribution π_w, defined as $N_w(S) = \inf\{1 - \pi_w(s) \mid s \notin S\}$. A sound and complete axiomatics for the I operator, is defined in a similar way as for the previous mental operators but now taking the axioms corresponding to necessity measures (cf. [12]), that is, the following axioms:

1. Axioms of classical logic for the non-modal formulae.
2. Axioms of Łukasiewicz logic for the modal formulae.
3. Axioms for I over Łukasiewciz logic:
   $I(\varphi \to \psi) \to (I\varphi \to I\psi)$
   $\neg I(\bot)$
   $I(\varphi \wedge \psi) \equiv (I\varphi \wedge I\psi)$
4. Deduction rules are modus ponens and necessitation for I (from φ derive $I\varphi$).

6 Planner and Communication Contexts

The nature of these contexts is functional. The Planner Context (PC) has to build plans which allow the agent to move from its current world to another, where a given formula is satisfied. This change will indeed have an associated cost according to the actions involved. Within this context, we propose to use a first order language restricted to Horn clauses (PL), where a theory of planning includes the following special predicates:

- $action(\alpha, P, A, c_\alpha)$ where $\alpha \in \Pi_0$ is an elementary action, $P \subset PL$ is the set of preconditions; $A \subset PL$ are the postconditions and $c_\alpha \in [0, 1]$ is the normalised cost of the action.
- $plan(\varphi, \alpha, P, A, c_\alpha, r)$ where $\alpha \in \Pi$ is a composite action representing the plan to achieve φ, P are the pre-conditions of α, A are the post-conditions $\varphi \in A$, c_α is the normalized cost of α and r is the belief degree (> 0) of actually achieving φ by performing plan α. We assume that only one instance of this predicate is generated per formula.
- $bestplan(\varphi, \alpha, P, A, c_\alpha, r)$ similar to the previous one, but only one instance with the best plan is generated.

Each plan must be feasible, that is, the current state of the world must satisfy the preconditions, the plan must make true the positive desire the plan is built for, and cannot have any negative desire as post-condition. These feasible plans are deduced by a bridge rule among the BC, DC and PC contexts (see (2) in the next Section 7).

The communication unit (CC) makes it possible to encapsulate the agent's internal structure by having a unique and well-defined interface with the environment. This unit also has a first order language restricted to Horn clauses. The theory inside this context will take care of the sending and receiving of messages to and from other agents in the Multi Agent society where our graded BDI agents live. Both contexts use resolution as a deduction method.

7   Bridge Rules

For our BDI agent model, we define a collection of basic bridge rules to set the interrelations between contexts. These rules are illustrated in figure 1. In this section we comment the most relevant ones.

The agent's knowledge about the world's state and about actions that change the world, is introduced from the belief context into the Planner as first order formulae $\lceil . \rceil$:

$$\frac{B : B\varphi}{P : \lceil B\varphi \rceil} \tag{1}$$

Then, from the positive desires, the beliefs of the agent, and the possible transformations using actions, the Planner can build plans. Plans are generated from actions, to fulfill positive desires, but avoiding negative desires. The following bridge rule among D, B, and P contexts does this:

$$\frac{\begin{array}{c} D : \nabla(D^+\varphi), D : (D^-\psi, threshold), P : action(\alpha, P, A, c), \\ B : (B([\alpha]\varphi), r), B : B(A \rightarrow \neg\psi) \end{array}}{P : plan(\varphi, \alpha, P, A, c, r)} \tag{2}$$

As we have previously mentioned, the intention degree trades off the benefit and the cost of reaching a goal. There is a bridge rule that infers the degree of $I\varphi$ for each plan α that allows to achieve the goal. This value is deduced from the degree of $D^+\varphi$ and the cost of a plan that satisfies desire φ. This degree is calculated by function f as follows:

$$\frac{D : (D^+\varphi, d), P : plan(\varphi, \alpha, P, A, c, r)}{I : (I\varphi, f(d, c, r))} \tag{3}$$

Different functions model different individual behaviours. For example, if we consider an *equilibrated agent*, the degree of the intention to bring about φ, under full belief in achieving φ after performing α, may depend equally on the satisfaction that it brings the agent and in the cost —considering the complement to 1 of the normalised cost. So the function might be defined as

$$f(d, c, r) = r(d + (1 - c))/2.$$

In fact, given the plan P for the goal φ, with desire level d and(normalized) cost c, we can think of $u = (d + (1 - c))/2$ as the utility of reaching φ by means of the plan P. The intention degree as computed above is thennothing but $r \cdot u$, that is, the utility u multiplied by the probability r of reaching φ after the plan is executed. This is actually the *expected utility* of reaching φ by means of the plan P if one considers a utility value of 0 when the plan P does not reach φ.

In BDI agents, bridge rules have been also used to determine the relationship between the mental attitudes and the actual behaviour of the agent. Well-established sets of relations for BDI agents have been identified [21]. If we use the *strong realism* model, the set of intentions is a subset of the set of desires, which in turn is a subset of the beliefs. That is, if an agent does not believe something, it will neither desire it nor intend it [20]:

$$\frac{B : \neg B\psi}{D : \neg D\psi} \text{ and } \frac{D : \neg D\psi}{I : \neg I\psi} \tag{4}$$

We also need bridge rules to establish the agent's interactions with the environment, meaning that if the agent intends φ at degree i_{max}, where i_{max} is the maximum degree of all the intentions, then the agent will focus on the plan -bestplan- that allows the agent to reach the most intended goal:

$$\frac{I : (I\varphi, i_{max}), P : bestplan(\varphi, \alpha, P, A, c_\alpha, r)}{C : C(does(\alpha))} \tag{5}$$

Through the comunication unit the agent perceives all the changes in the enviroment that are introduced by the following bridge rule in the belief context:

$$\frac{C : \beta}{B : B\beta} \tag{6}$$

Figure 1 shows the graded BDI agent proposed with the different contexts and the bridge rules relating them.

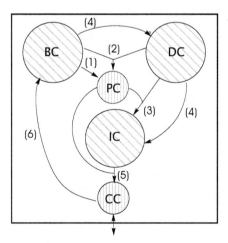

Fig. 1. Multicontext model of a graded BDI agent

8   Example of a Graded BDI Agent for Tourism

Suppose we want to instruct our travel agent to look for a one-week holiday destination package. We instruct the agent with two desires, first and more important, we want to rest, and second we want to visit new places (visitNP). We restrict its exploration range as we do not want to travel more than 1000 kms from Rosario, where we live. To propose a destination (plan) the agent will have to take into account the benefit (with respect to rest and to visitNP) and the cost of the travel. The agent will consult with a travel agency that will give a number of plans, that conveniently placed in the planner context will determine the final set of proposals. In this scenario we have the following theories in the BC, DC, and PC contexts (IC has no initial theory):

D *context:* The agent has the following positive and negative desires:

- $(D^+(rest), 0.8)$
- $(D^+(visitNP), 0.7)$
- $(D^+(rest \wedge visitNP), 0.9)$
- $(D^-(distance > 1000km), 0.9)$

B *context:* This theory contains knowledge about the relationship between possible actions the agent can take and formulae made true by their execution. In this case, actions would be *traveling* to different destinations. For this example we consider only six destinations:

$$\Pi_0 = \{CarlosPaz, Cumbrecita, Bariloche, VillaGesell, MardelPlata, PtoMadryn\}.$$

Then, we represent the agent's beliefs about visiting new places and resting. In particular, we may consider the degree of $B([\alpha]visitNP)$ as the probability of *visitNP* after traveling to α. According to the places we know in each destination and the remaining places to visit in each destination, we give our travel agent the following beliefs:

- (B([Cumbrecita]visitNP), 1)
- (B([Carlos Paz]visitNP), 0.3)
- (B([Bariloche]visitNP), 0.7)
- (B([Villa Gesell]visitNP), 0.6)
- (B([Mar del Plata]visitNP), 0.3)
- (B([Pto Madryn]visitNP), 1)

The agent needs to assess also beliefs about the possibility that a destination offers to rest. In this case the degree of $B([\alpha]Rest)$ is interpreted as the probability of resting in α. These beliefs are determined by the characteristics of the destination —beach, mountains, big or a small city, etc— and taking into account our personal views:

- (B([Cumbrecita]Rest), 1)
- (B([Carlos Paz]Rest), 0.8)

- (B([Bariloche]Rest), 0.6)
- (B([Villa Gesell]Rest), 0.8)
- (B([Mar del Plata]Rest), 0.5)
- (B([Pto Madryn]Rest), 0.7)

We assume here that, for each action α, the positive desires are stochastically independent, so we add to BC an appropriate inference rule:

$$\frac{(B[\alpha]Rest, r), (B[\alpha]visitNP, s)}{(B[\alpha](Rest \wedge visitNP), r \cdot s)}$$

P Context A series of elementary actions:

- action (Cumbrecita, {cost = 800},{dist =500 km}, 0.67)
- action (Carlos Paz, {cost = 500},{dist = 450 km}, 0.42)
- action (Bariloche, {cost = 1200},{dist = 1800 km},1)
- action (Pto Madryn, {cost = 1000},{dist =1700 km}, 0.83)
- action (Villa Gessell, {cost = 700},{dist =700 km}, 0.58)
- action (Mar del Plata, {cost = 600},{dist =850 km}, 0.5)

Once these theories are defined the agent is ready to reason in order to determine which Intention to adopt and which plan is associated with that intention. We follow give a brief schema of the different steps in this process:

1. *The desires are passed from DC to PC.*
2. *Within PC plans for each desire are found.*
   Starting from the positive desires the planner looks for a set of different destination plans, taking into consideration the beliefs of the agent about the possibilities of satisfying the goals rest and visitNP through the different actions. Using the restriction introduced by the negative desire: $(D^-(dist > 1000km), 0.9)$ the planner rejects plans to Bariloche and to Pto Madryn, because their post-conditions make true $(dist > 1000km)$ which is strongly rejected (0.9). Therefore, using the bridge rule (2), plans are generated for each desire. For instance, for the most preferred desire, i.e. $rest \wedge visitNP$ the following plans are generated:

   $plan(rest \wedge visitNP, Cumbrecita, \{cost = 800\}, \{dist = 500km\}, 0.67, 1)$
   $plan(rest \wedge visitNP, CarlosPaz, \{cost = 500\}, \{dist = 450km\}, 0.42, 0.24)$
   $plan(rest \wedge visitNP, VillaGessell, \{cost = 700\}, \{dist = 700km\}, 0.58, 0.48)$
   $plan(rest \wedge visitNP, MardelPlata, \{cost = 600\}, \{dist = 850km\}, 0.5, 0.15)$

3. *The plans determine the degree of intentions.*
   Using bridge rule (3) and the function f proposed for an *equilibrated* agent the I context calculates the intention degree for the different destinations. Since f is monotonically increasing with respect to d, it is enough to consider the most preferred desired, i.e. $rest \wedge visitNP$. Hence, $rest \wedge visitNP$ is preferred to a degree 0.9, using $f(d, b, c) = b(0.9 + (1 - c))/2$ we successively have for $\alpha \in \{Cumbrecita, CarlosPaz, VillaGessell, MardelPlata\}$:

$(I(rest \wedge visitNP), 0.615),$
$(I(rest \wedge visitNP), 0.1776),$
$(I(rest \wedge visitNP), 0.3168),$
$(I(rest \wedge visitNP), 0.105).$

We get a maximal degree of intention for $rest \wedge visitNP$ by the plan *cumbrecita*, of 0.615.

4. *A plan is adopted.*

Finally, by means of bridge rule (5), the action $\alpha = Cumbrecita$ is selected and passed to the Communication context CC.

9   Conclusions and Future Work

This paper has presented a BDI agent model that allows to explicitly represent the uncertainty of beliefs, desires and intentions. This graded architecture is specified using multicontext systems and is general enough to be able to specify different types of agents. In this work we have used a different context for each attitude: Belief, Desire and Intention. We used a specific logic for each unit, according to the attitude represented. The Łukasiewicz multivalued logic is the framework chosen to formalise the degrees and we added the corresponding axiomatic in order to represent the uncertainty behaviour as probability, necessity and possibility. Other measures of uncertainty might be used in the different units by simply changing the corresponding axiomatic. Adding concrete theories to each context, particular agents may be defined using our context blueprints. The agent's behaviour is then determined by the different uncertainty measures of each context, the specific theories established for each unit, and the bridge rules. An issue of current research is to look for possible alternative axiomatic modelings of desires and intentions, and their implications in the bridge rules which deal with them, and check how they can also influence the agent's behavior. Besides, the model introduced, based on a multicontext specification, can be easily extended to include other mental attitudes.

As for future work, we are considering two directions. On the one hand we want to extend our multicontext agent model to a multiagent scenario. We plan to do this by introducing a *social context* in the agent architecture to deal with all aspects of social relations with other agents. In particular to equip this social context with a good logical model of trust is very important to allow the agent to infer beliefs from other agents´ information. Interesting models of trust are Liau's logic of Belief, Information and Trust (BIT) [15] in the extension of this model described in [4] in this volume.

On the other hand, from an computational point of view, our idea is to implement each unit as prolog thread, equipped with its own meta-interpreter. The meta-interpreter purpose will be to manage inter-thread (inter-context) communication, i.e. all processes regarding bridge rule firing and assertion of bridge rule conclusions into the corresponding contexts. This implementation will support both, the generic definition of graded BDI agent architectures and the specific instances for particular types of agents. The implementation will also allow us to experiment and validate the formal model presented.

Acknowledgments. Lluis Godo acknowledges partial support by the Spanish project MULOG, TIN2004-07933-C03-01, and Carles Sierra acknowledges partial support by the Spanish project WEBI2, TIC2003-08763-C02-00.

References

1. Benferhat, S., Dubois, D., Kaci, S., Prade, H.: Bipolar Possibilistic Representations. In *Proceedings of the 18th Conference in Uncertainty in Artificial Intelligence (UAI 2002)*: pages 45-52. Morgan Kaufmann 2002.
2. Benferhat, S., Dubois, D., Kaci, S., Prade, H.: Bipolar representation and fusion of preferences in the possilistic Logic framework. In: *Proceedings of the 8th International Conference on Principle of Knowledge Representation and Reasoning (KR-2002)*, pages 421-448, 2002.
3. Cimatti, A., Serafini, L.: Multi-Agent Reasoning with Belief Contexts: the Approach and a Case Study. In: M. Wooldridge and N. R. Jennings, eds.: *Intelligent Agents: Proceedings of 1994 Workshop on Agent Theories, Architectures, and Languages*, number 890 in Lecture Notes in Computer Science, pages 71-5. Springer Verlag, 1995.
4. Dastani, M., Herzig, A., Hulstijn, J., van der Torre, L.: Inferring Trust. In this volume.
5. Dennet, D.C.: *The Intentional Stance*. MIT Press, Cambridge, MA, 1987.
6. Esteva, F., Garcia, P., Godo, L.: Relating and extending semantical approaches to possibilistic reasoning. *International Journal of Approximate Reasoning*, 10:311-344, 1994.
7. Ghidini, C., Giunchiglia, F.: Local Model Semantics, or Contextual Reasoning = Locality + Compatibility. *Artificial Intelligence*,127(2):221-259, 2001.
8. Giovannucci, A.: Towards Multi-Context based Agents Implementation. IIIA-CSIC Research Report, in preparation.
9. Giunchiglia, F., Serafini, L.: Multilanguage Hierarchical Logics (or: How we can do without modal logics). *Journal of Artificial Intelligence*, vol.65, pp. 29-70, 1994.
10. Godo, L., Esteva, F. and Hajek, P.: Reasoning about probabilities using fuzzy logic. *Neural Network World*, 10:811–824, 2000.
11. Goldblatt, R.: *Logics of Time and Computation*, CSLI Lecture Notes 7, 1992.
12. Hájek, P.: *Metamathematics of Fuzzy Logic*, volume 4 of Trends in Logic. Kluwer, 1998.
13. Jennings, N.R.: On Agent-Based Software Engineering. *Artificial Intelligence* 117(2), 277-296, 2000.
14. Lang, J., van der Torre, L., Weydert, E.: Hidden Uncertainty in the Logical Representation of Desires *International Joint Conference on Artificial Intelligence, IJCAI 03*, Acapulco, Mexico, 2003.
15. Liau, C.J.: Belief, Information Acquisition, and Trust in Multiagent Systems - a modal formulation. *Artificial Intelligence* 149, 31-60, 2003.
16. Meyer, J.J.: Dynamic Logic for Reasoning about Actions and Agents. *Workshop on Logic-Based Artificial Intelligence*, Washington, DC, June 14–16, 1999

17. Parsons, S., Sierra, C., Jennings, N.R.: Agents that reason and negotiate by arguing. *Journal of Logic and Computation*, 8(3): 261-292, 1998.
18. Parsons, S., Giorgini, P.: On using degrees of belief in BDI agents. *Proceedings of the International Conference on Information Processing and Management of Uncertainty in Knowledge-Based Systems*, Paris, 1998.
19. Parsons, S., Jennings, N.J., Sabater, J., Sierra, C.: Agent Specification Using Multi-context Systems. *Foundations and Applications of Multi-Agent Systems 2002:* 205-226, 2002.
20. Rao, A., Georgeff, M.: Modeling Rational Agents within a BDI-Architecture. *In proceedings of the 2nd International Conference on Principles of Knowledge Representation and Reasoning (KR-92)*, pages 473-484 (ed R. Fikes and E. Sandewall), Morgan Kaufmann, San Mateo, CA, 1991.
21. Rao, A., Georgeff, M.: BDI agents: From theory to practice. *In proceedings of the 1st International Conference on Multi-Agents Systems*, pp 312-319, 1995.
22. Sabater, J., Sierra, C., Parsons, S., Jennings, N.R.: Engineering executable agents using multi-context systems. *Journal of Logic and Computation* 12(3): 413-442 (2002).
23. Sierra, C., Godo,L., López de Màntaras, R., Manzano, M.: Descriptive Dynamic Logic and its Application to Reflective Architectures. *Future Generation Computer Systems*, 12, 157-171, 1996.
24. Schut, M., Wooldridge, M., Parsons, S.: Reasoning About Intentions in Uncertain Domains Symbolic and Quantitative Approaches to Reasoning with Uncertainty. *6th ECSQARU 2001, Proceedings*, pages 84-95, Toulouse, France, 2001.
25. Wooldridge, M., Jennings, N.R.: Intelligent Agents: theory and practice. *The Knowledge Engineering Review*, 10(2), 115-152, 1995.

Inferring Trust

Mehdi Dastani[1], Andreas Herzig[2], Joris Hulstijn[3], and Leendert van der Torre[4]

[1] Utrecht University, The Netherlands
mehdi@cs.uu.nl
[2] IRIT, Toulouse, France
herzig@irit.fr
[3] Vrije Universiteit, Amsterdam, The Netherlands
jhulstijn@feweb.vu.nl
[4] CWI, Amsterdam, The Netherlands
torre@cwi.nl

Abstract. In this paper we discuss Liau's logic of Belief, Inform and Trust (BIT), which captures the use of trust to infer beliefs from acquired information. However, the logic does not capture the derivation of trust from other notions. We therefore suggest the following two extensions. First, like Liau we observe that trust in information from an agent depends on the topic of the information. We extend BIT with a formalization of topics which are used to infer trust in a proposition from trust in another proposition, if both propositions have the same topics. Second, for many applications, communication primitives other than inform are required. We extend BIT with questions, and discuss the relationship with belief, inform and trust. An answer to a question can lead to trust, when the answer conforms to the beliefs of the agent.

1 Introduction

Trust is an issue which emerges in many subareas of artificial intelligence, such as in multiagent systems, reputation systems, e-institutions, and electronic commerce [1]. Liau [2] proposes an elegant, simple, but expressive modal logic as an extension of multi-agent epistemic logic. The three main ingredients are modal operators for belief (B), inform (I), and trust (T). The central axiom expresses that if an agent trusts another agent with respect to a proposition, and it has been informed by that agent that the proposition is true, then it believes that proposition.

The logic explains the consequences of trust, but it does not explain where trust comes from. The only optional axiom discussed by Liau that derives positive trust formulas is so-called transferability, which says that trust in one agent can lead to trust in another agent with respect to the same proposition. In this paper, we study two other ways in which trust can be derived. We do this by first enriching Liau's framework with topics and questions, and then by investigating the following issues.

1. How to use topics to infer trust? Like Liau we observe that trust in information depends on the topic of the information. We extend BIT with a

J. Leite and P. Torroni (Eds.): CLIMA V, LNAI 3487, pp. 144–160, 2005.
© Springer-Verlag Berlin Heidelberg 2005

formalization of topics. Topics can be used to infer trust in a proposition from trust in another proposition, if both propositions have the same topics.

2. How to use communication to infer trust? For many applications, communication primitives other than inform are required. We extend BIT with questions and discuss the relationship with belief, inform and trust. An answer to a question can also lead to trust, when an agent tests another agent by questioning him and the answer conforms to the beliefs of the agent.

We formalize topics and questions in terms of non-normal modal operators. To obtain a simple axiomatization of our semantically defined operators we re-formalize them in terms of operators from normal modal logic using a technique known as *simulation*. Moreover, Liau uses a non-normal modal logic to formalize trust, i.e., his notion of trust is not closed under tautologies, nor under conjunction nor implication: agent i does not necessarily trust that $\top$, trust that $\varphi \wedge \psi$ does not imply trust that φ, and validity of $\varphi \supset \psi$ does not entail that trust that φ implies trust that ψ. In order to work in a uniform and simple framework we also simulate the non-normal trust operator, using a combination of normal modal logic operators. The reductions or simulations use the fact that "normal modal logics can simulate all others" [3, 4].

The layout of this paper is as follows. In Section 2 we introduce the running example. In Section 3 we repeat and discuss Liau's BIT logic, and we formalize the running example in it. In Section 4 and 5 we introduce topics and questions, as well as the principles permitting to infer trust that can be based on them.

2   Running Example

We use the following example to motivate and illustrate our extensions of Liau's logic.

Agent i wants to know the interest rate, which is of vital importance for his portfolio management. He has found three web-services s_1, s_2 and s_3 that present financial information, but he does not know whether they deliver up to date information, or whether the information is correct at all. In other words, agent i does not know which web-service to trust. Suppose agent i knows the latest exchange rates for the euro against the dollar, and asks the web-services about this piece of information. If they do not provide the correct information, then the agent concludes that the web-services are not trustworthy. Otherwise, if they supply the correct exchange rate, then the agent trusts them with respect to financial information. Thus he then knows whom to ask about the interest rate, in order to use this piece of information in his portfolio management.[1]

---

[1] We assume that the web-service is not a strategic player, in the sense of Goffman's strategic interaction [5], that is, we assume that the web-service does not have something to gain by making you believe that it is trustworthy but not being so. In this sense this example is less complex than issues around trust found in electronic commerce.

In this paper, we ignore the dynamics and time aspects[2] involved in this example and discuss the formalization of three aspects of this example.

1. First we express the example in Liau's BIT logic. What can be said there is that
   - if the agent trusts the web-service, then he believes what he is being informed about;
   - if a web-service has informed the agent about something it believes to be false, then the agent does not trust the web-service.
2. To relate the question about exchange rates with the question about interest rates, we introduce the notion of topic. Both exchange and interest rates have the topic of financial information. So, when the web-service can be trusted on exchange rates, it can be trusted on the whole topic of financial information, and therefore it can be trusted on interest rates.
3. Based on the hypothesis that in general agents are not being informed by a web-service by accident, but are being informed as the result of a question being submitted to the web-service, we extend the system with a question operator. An agent can then infer trust in a web-service, in case the web-service has informed the agent in accordance with the agent's current beliefs.

3   BIT

In this section we repeat and discuss Liau's logic BIT [2], and we formalize the running example in it. Definition 1 presents the language of the basic BIT logic, where $B_i\varphi$ is read as 'agent i believes φ', $I_{ij}\varphi$ as 'agent i acquires information φ from agent j', and $T_{ij}\varphi$ as 'agent i trusts the judgment of agent j on the truth of φ'. In the rest of this paper, we read $I_{ij}\varphi$ as 'agent i is being informed φ by agent j' or 'agent i has been informed φ by agent j'. For the purpose of this paper, these three readings can be regarded as synonymous.

Definition 1 (BIT language). *Assume we have n agents and a set Φ_0 of countably many atomic propositions. The well formed formulae of the logic BIT is the least set containing Φ_0 that is closed under the following formation rules:*

   - *if φ is a wff, then so are $\neg\varphi$, $B_i\varphi$, $I_{ij}\varphi$ and $T_{ij}\varphi$ for all $1 \leq i \neq j \leq n$, and*
   - *if φ and ψ are wffs, then so is $\varphi \vee \psi$.*

As usual, other classical boolean connectives are defined as abbreviations.

Definition 2 presents the axiomatic system for basic BIT. Beliefs are represented by a normal KD45 modal operator; inform by a normal KD modal operator, and trust by a non-normal modal operator.

---

[2] We do not discuss the state transitions based on communication actions such as inform and question.

Definition 2 (BIT). *The basic BIT logic contains the following axioms and is closed under the following set of inference rules:*

P *propositional tautologies*

B1 $[B_i\varphi \land B_i(\varphi \supset \psi)] \supset B_i\psi$

B2 $\neg B_i \bot$

B3 $B_i\varphi \supset B_i B_i\varphi$

B4 $\neg B_i\varphi \supset B_i \neg B_i\varphi$

I1 $[I_{ij}\varphi \land I_{ij}(\varphi \supset \psi)] \supset I_{ij}\psi$

I2 $\neg I_{ij} \bot$

C1 $(B_i I_{ij}\varphi \land T_{ij}\varphi) \supset B_i\varphi$

C2 $T_{ij}\varphi \supset B_i T_{ij}\varphi$

R1 *(Modus Ponens, MP): from* $\vdash \varphi$ *and* $\vdash \varphi \supset \psi$ *infer* $\vdash \psi$

R2 *(Generalization, Gen): from* $\vdash \varphi$ *infer* $\vdash B_i\varphi$ *and* $\vdash I_{ij}\varphi$

R3 *from* $\vdash \varphi \equiv \psi$ *infer* $\vdash T_{ij}\varphi \equiv T_{ij}\psi$

Liau discusses several possible extensions of the basic BIT logic: additional axiom C3 is called symmetric trust, C4 is called transferability, C5 is called cautious trust, and axiom C6 is called the ideal environment assumption.

C3 $T_{ij}\varphi \supset T_{ij}\neg\varphi$ (symmetric trust)

C4 $B_i T_{jk}\varphi \supset T_{ik}\varphi$ (transferability)

C5 $T_{ij}\varphi \supset B_i[(I_{ij}\varphi \supset B_j\varphi) \land (B_j\varphi \supset \varphi)]$ (cautious trust)

C6 $I_{ij}\varphi \equiv B_i I_{ij}\varphi$ (ideal environment)

To understand Liau's logic, first observe that an agent can trust another agent, without believing that the other agent is sincere and competent, as in other logics of trust, see for example [6]. This is expressed by the central axiom (C1), which is weaker than the inference from a combination of sincerity $I_{ij}\varphi \supset B_j\varphi$ and competence $B_j\varphi \supset \varphi$ by the trusted agent, which are the respective constituents of cautious trust in C5.

Secondly, observe that the logic is focussed on the formalization of consequences of trust, not on how trust is derived. That is, axiom C1 characterizes how trust in a proposition may lead to a belief in that proposition (in case of an inform), but little is said about the derivation of trust. Axiom C3 relates trust in a proposition to trust in its negation, and axiom C4 derives trust in an agent from trust in another agent. There are no axioms that derive trust from an inform, or that relate trust in a proposition to trust in another proposition, except for the negation in C3.

Thirdly, it should be observed that the fact that the trust operator is non-normal, means that using axiom C1 we can derive $B_i\varphi$ from $B_i I_{ij}(\varphi \land \psi)$ and $T_{ij}\varphi$, but we cannot derive $B_i\varphi$ from $B_i I_{ij}\varphi$ and $T_{ij}(\varphi \land \psi)$. There are good reasons for this, for which we refer to Liau's paper. Liau presents the following standard semantics for his logic. We do not mention the semantic constraints for the additional C3-C6.

Definition 3 (Semantics BIT). *A BIT model is a tuple*

$$\langle W, \pi, (B_i)_{1 \leq i \leq n}, (I_{ij})_{1 \leq i \neq j \leq n}, (T_{ij})_{1 \leq i \neq j \leq n} \rangle$$

where W is a set of possible worlds, $\pi : \Phi_0 \to 2^W$ is a truth assignment mapping each atomic proposition to the set of worlds in which it is true, $(B_i)_{1 \leq i \leq n} \subseteq W \times W$ are serial, transitive and Euclidian binary relations on W, $(I_{ij})_{1 \leq i \neq j \leq n} \subseteq W \times W$ are serial binary relations on W, and $(T_{ij})_{1 \leq i \neq j \leq n}$ are binary relations between W and the power set of W. Moreover, the satisfaction relation is defined as follows.

1. $M, w \models p$ *iff* $w \in \pi(p)$
2. $M, w \models \neg\varphi$ *iff* $M, w \not\models \varphi$
3. $M, w \models \varphi \vee \psi$ *iff* $M, w \models \varphi$ *or* $M, w \models \psi$
4. $M, w \models B_i\varphi$ *iff for all* $u \in B_i(w)$, $M, u \models \varphi$
5. $M, w \models I_{ij}\varphi$ *iff for all* $u \in I_{ij}(w)$, $M, u \models \varphi$
6. $M, w \models T_{ij}\varphi$ *iff* $|\varphi| = \{u \in W \mid M, u \models \varphi\} \in T_{ij}(w)$, *where $|\varphi|$ is called the truth set of φ.*

The corresponding constraints for axioms C1 and C2 are:

m1 *For all $S \in T_{ij}(w)$, if $(B_i \circ I_{ij})(w) \subseteq S$, then $B_i(w) \subseteq S$, where '$\circ$' denotes the composition operator between two binary operations;*

m2 $T_{ij}(w) = \cap_{u \in B_i(w)} T_{ij}(u)$.

The logic may seem relatively simple, but – although Liau does not discuss such applications – we can already use the logic to reason about relatively complex phenomena such as trust in the ignorance of agents $T_{ij}(\neg B_j\varphi \wedge \neg B_j\neg\varphi)$ or some aspects of trusted third parties $(B_i I_{ij} T_{jk}\varphi \wedge T_{ij} T_{jk}\varphi) \supset T_{ik}\varphi$.

The following example formalizes some aspects of the running example.

Example 1. Assume a finite set of atomic propositions $i(0.0), \ldots, i(10.0)$ denoting interest rates, and a finite set of atomic propositions $e(0.50), \ldots, e(2.00)$ denoting exchange rates, where the interval and step size are chosen arbitrarily. Moreover, let the set of agents be $\{i, s_1, s_2, s_3\}$. From axiom C1, by contraposition we have the following set of instances, for $s \in \{s_1, s_2, s_3\}$ and $r \in \{0.50, \ldots, 2.00\}$, which states that if an agent i believes that a web-service s has informed him about an exchange rate which i does not believe, then agent i will not trust that web-service.

$$B_i I_{is} e(r) \wedge \neg B_i e(r) \supset \neg T_{is} e(r)$$

Moreover, axiom C1 also implies the following set of instances, for $s \in \{s_1, s_2, s_3\}$ and $r \in \{0.0, \ldots, 10.0\}$, which states that if an agent i believes that the web-service s has informed him about the interest rates, and i trusts s, then agent i believes the interest rates.

$$B_i I_{is} i(r) \wedge T_{is} i(r) \supset B_i i(r)$$

Finally, if agent i trusts the web-service s with respect to some interest or exchange rates, then i also trusts s with respect to other rates. This can be 'hard-coded' with the following set of assumptions, for $s \in \{s_1, s_2, s_3\}$, $r_1, r_3 \in \{i(0.0), \ldots, i(10.0)\}$ and $r_2, r_4 \in \{e(0.50), \ldots, e(2.00)\}$.

$$T_{is}i(r_1) \vee T_{is}e(r_2) \supset T_{is}i(r_3) \wedge T_{is}e(r_4)$$

Hence Liau's logic already allows to infer new beliefs via trust, and to infer distrust. What it does not allow is to infer trust, which is what the rest of the paper is about.

4   Topics

For trust it matters what a formula "is about": its topic. Agents have a certain area of expertise or competence. If they are trustworthy on some formulas, then they are likely to be trustworthy on other formulas that have the same topic. That will lead to a principle of inference that, for example, trust in one financial rate implies trust in another financial rate. We formalize a principle of *topical trust*. Liau already recognizes the need for topical trust, as his third item for further research:

> "A special case of symmetric trust, called topical trust, is considered without standard axiomatization. This problem may be remedied by introducing the topics of propositions into the language. For example, in a logic of aboutness [7], a sorted binary predicate $A(t,\text{'}p\text{'})$ is used to denote "sentence 'p' is about topic t". If our BIT language is extended with such a predicate, then we can formulate axioms as: $A(t,\text{'}\varphi\text{'}) \supset T_{ij}\varphi$ when j is specialized at topic t, or more strongly, as $(A(t_1,\text{'}\varphi\text{'}) \vee \ldots \vee A(t_k,\text{'}\varphi\text{'})) \equiv T_{ij}\varphi$ when the set of topics at which an agent is specialized are $[t_1, \ldots, t_k]$. However, further research is needed to see how the semantics can be changed to accommodate this syntactic extension."

Our extension of BIT logic with topics is loosely inspired by a proposal of Herzig and Longin. Whereas Herzig and Longin formalize the notion of topics in the metalanguage, we will formalize it using standard normal modal operators.

4.1   Herzig and Longin

The conceptual model of Herzig and Longin [8] is visualized in Figure 1. It contains a meta theory with the following three relations:

- A competence function that relates agents to topics, namely those topics in which the agent is an expert.
- A subject function that relates propositions to topics, namely those topics that the propositions are about.
- A scope function that relates actions (such as inform) to topics. Actions which are affected by the topic of proposition are listed here.

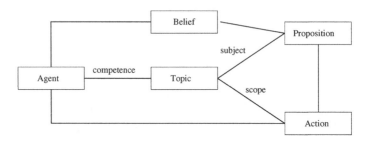

Fig. 1. Conceptual Model of Trust

These concepts enable one to formulate principles of belief update. Informally, they can be expressed as follows:

- If a formula φ holds, and an agent is informed about a proposition which does not share any topic with φ, then φ persists;
- If an agent j is competent on a topic and φ belongs to that topic, then an inform by agent j that φ implies belief that φ.

The first principle is not relevant for this paper, because the BIT logic only considers the state of the world at one moment. An extension with time is very interesting, but beyond the scope of this paper. The second principle implies that if an agent is competent on a proposition φ and all topics of proposition ψ are also topics of φ, then the agent is competent on ψ, too. It is the latter issue which we formalize in the BIT logic, simply replacing belief in competence by trust. This move disregards the distinction between the two, in the sense that belief in someone's competence may lead to trust, but this need not always be the case and more importantly, trust can be based on other reasons than belief in competence. Note that both Demolombe and Herzig and Longin take a syntactic approach. Aboutness $A(t,'p')$ and 'subject' are relations between formulas and some set of objects $t_1, ..., t_n$ called topics with no additional structure. By contrast we handle topics in the semantics.

4.2   Simulation

In this section we formalize the trust and topic operators, using a technique called *simulation*. This means that – typically complex – operators are defined in terms of standard normal modal operators. For example, the simulation of the non-normal trust operator in normal modal logic means that the trust operator is defined using normal operators, but that the operator itself behaves like a non-normal operator.

The advantages of simulation are twofold. First, the advantage of classical simulations such as the simulation of various kinds of non-normal modal logics in [3, 4] is that theorem provers of normal modal logic can be used for proving theorems of non-normal modal logic. This advantage also holds for the simulation of the non-normal trust operator in normal modal logic. This means, among other things, that it becomes easier to have a theorem prover test specifications written in the extended BIT logic. Second, the advantage that motivates the simulation in this paper is that such a simulation gives us a direct axiomatization of the logic, which would not be obtained if the operators were only defined semantically. In that case, additional axioms would have to be given to characterize the semantic notions.

Consider the trust operator, which is a non-normal modal operator. This operator can be simulated using three standard normal modal operators $\Box^1_{ij}$, $\Box^2$ and $\Box^3$ [4]

$$T_{ij}\varphi \equiv \Diamond^1_{ij}(\Box^2\varphi \wedge \Box^3\neg\varphi)$$

where $\Diamond\varphi$ abbreviates $\neg\Box\neg\varphi$ as usual.

To understand the reduction remember that truth of $T_{ij}\varphi$ in a world w of a model M means that there is a truth set (neighborhood) $S \in T_{ij}(w)$ such that $M, w' \models \varphi$ for every $w' \in S$, and $M, w'' \not\models \varphi$ for every $w'' \notin S$. Thus $\Diamond^1_{ij}$ enables us to refer to the existence of a truth set (neighborhood), $\Box^2$ is used to express the truth of φ in S, and $\Box^3$ expresses the falsehood of φ outside S.

4.3   Topic as Enumeration of Options

In this paper, we assume that propositions have topics and that topics are shared by all agents[3]. For example, the proposition $i(5.0)$ has financial information as its topic. Moreover, in the Herzig-Longin approach propositions can belong to two or more topics, though this does not play a role in the example. Consequently, a complication of the formalization of topics is that we not only have to state which topics there are, but that these are all the topics available. It is only by making explicit all given topics, that we can quantify over topics. For this reason, we introduce both an operator topic and an operator all_topics. We identify a topic with the set of atomic propositions that have this topic as a subject (see above). For example, the topic financial information is identified with the set

$$\{i(0.0), \ldots, i(10.0), e(0.50), \ldots, e(2.00)\}$$

Such a topic set will be represented by a formula like

$$\mathsf{topic}(i(0.0) \times \ldots \times i(10.0) \times e(0.50) \times \ldots \times e(2.00))$$

in which '$\times$' is used to separate alternative options. Our encoding is as follows.

Definition 4 (Topics). *The language of BIT with topics is the language of BIT, together with clause*

– *if φ is a sentence of BIT, then so are $\Box^1\varphi$, $\Box^2\varphi$, $\Box^3\varphi$ and $\Box^4\varphi$.*

Moreover, we add the following abbreviations:

– $\varphi_1 \times \ldots \times \varphi_n \equiv \Diamond^2(\Box^3\varphi_1 \wedge \Box^4\neg\varphi_1) \wedge \ldots \wedge \Diamond^2(\Box^3\varphi_n \wedge \Box^4\neg\varphi_n) \wedge$
$\Box^2((\Box^3\varphi_1 \wedge \Box^4\neg\varphi_1) \vee \ldots \vee (\Box^3\varphi_n \wedge \Box^4\neg\varphi_n))$

---

[3] We assume here that topics are shared by all agents to simplify our presentation.

- $\text{topic}(\varphi_1 \times \ldots \times \varphi_n) \equiv \Diamond^1(\varphi_1 \times \ldots \times \varphi_n)$
- $\text{all\_topics}((\varphi_{1,1} \times \ldots \times \varphi_{1,n}); \ldots ; (\varphi_{k,1} \times \ldots \times \varphi_{k,m})) \equiv$
  $\square^1((\varphi_{1,1} \times \ldots \times \varphi_{1,n}) \vee \ldots \vee (\varphi_{k,1} \times \ldots \times \varphi_{k,m}))$
- $\text{topic\_contained}(\varphi, \psi) \equiv \square^1(\Diamond^2(\square^3\varphi \wedge \square^4\neg\varphi) \supset \Diamond^2(\square^3\psi \wedge \square^4\neg\psi))$

The topic notation with $\times$ may be read as a representation of a set. That is, due to the properties of the modal logic we have for example that $p \times q \times r$ implies $q \times p \times r$ or $p \times p \times q \times r$, but it does not imply for example $p \times q$.

The operator topic represents the set of propositions having the same topic; all_topics states furthermore that these are all topics available, and topic_contained formalizes the fact that all topics of the first element are also a topic of the second element. In our example $\text{topic\_contained}(i(1.0), e(2.00))$ holds. In example 2 an explanation is given. So $\text{topic\_contained}(\varphi, \psi)$ expresses that for every ($\square^1$) topic, if formula φ has that topic ($\Diamond^2(\square^3\varphi \wedge \square^4\neg\varphi)$), then formula ψ has that topic too. It is the latter abbreviation which will be used to formulate a topic-based trust inference principle.

We assume that topics are treated as axioms, in the sense that they are known by all agents, and distribute over inform and trust operators. We therefore accept the following principles:

$$\text{topic}(\varphi_1 \times \ldots \times \varphi_n) \equiv B_i\text{topic}(\varphi_1 \times \ldots \times \varphi_n)$$
$$\text{topic}(\varphi_1 \times \ldots \times \varphi_n) \equiv I_{ij}\text{topic}(\varphi_1 \times \ldots \times \varphi_n)$$
$$\text{topic}(\varphi_1 \times \ldots \times \varphi_n) \equiv T_{ij}\text{topic}(\varphi_1 \times \ldots \times \varphi_n)$$

The semantics of BIT with topics extends the semantics of BIT with four binary accessibility relations that correspond to $\square^1$ to $\square^4$, that are interpreted in the usual way. The distribution of topic operators over the BIT modalities is characterized by the fact that in each world, the relevant accessibility relations are the same. Due to space limitations we do not give the details.

It may seem that our encoding of the topic operators is rather complicated, compared to for example [7], but the advantage is that we have a standard semantics. Moreover, an important advantage is that we can use the same methodology for questions too (see section 5).

4.4   Comparison with Janin and Walukiewicz

The encoding of the topic operator is a further extension of the simulation of non-normal modal operators mentioned above. This extension can be understood by analogy to work by Janin and Walukiewicz [9]. They define $a \rightarrow S =_{def} \bigwedge_{\varphi \in S} \Diamond^a\varphi \wedge \square^a \bigvee_{\varphi \in S} \varphi$, where a is an index of a modal operator and S is set of formulas [9]. It means that world w satisfies formula $a \rightarrow S$ when any formula of S is satisfied by at least one a-successor of w, and all a-successors of w satisfy at least one formula of S. Classical modal operators are written as $\Diamond^a\varphi \equiv a \rightarrow \{\varphi, \top\}$ and $\square^a p \equiv a \rightarrow \{\varphi\} \vee a \rightarrow \emptyset$. This is essentially the definition of bisimulation,[4] so the representation reflects the essence of modal logic. As

---

[4] This insight is attributed to Alexandru Baltag by Yde Venema.

we indicated above, we use the ×-notation instead of sets, so $S = \{p, q, r\}$ is represented by $p \times q \times r$. Like sets we have iteration and associativity, i.e., we can derive for example $p \times q \times q \times r$. However, also note that if modalities $\Box^a$ and $\Diamond^a$ are normal, then we can derive weakening: $(p \wedge q) \times r \to p \times r$. Since we do not like this property for topics, we use non-normal modal operators – to be precise, non-monotonic ones – that do not satisfy weakening. So, in our reduction of topics, we combine two ideas:

(a) $\Box\varphi \equiv \Diamond^2(\Box^3\varphi \wedge \Box^4\neg\varphi)$ (simulation, as before)

(b) $a \to S \equiv \bigwedge_{\varphi \in S} \Diamond^a\varphi \wedge \Box^a \bigvee_{\varphi \in S} \varphi$ (Janin and Walukiewicz)

These are combined using the definition of modality 2 according to (b), substituting $(\Box^3\varphi \wedge \Box^4\neg\varphi)$ for φ and substituting '2' for a, which gives us $\bigwedge_{\varphi \in S} \Diamond^2(\Box^3\varphi \wedge \Box^4\neg\varphi) \wedge \Box^2 \bigvee_{\varphi \in S}(\Box^3\varphi \wedge \Box^4\neg\varphi)$, which corresponds to the topic definition above. Since this only defines one topic, we still have to represent that "there is a topic", for which we use $\Diamond^1$.

4.5   Topics and Trust

Now we can formalize the intuition that if a proposition is trusted, then also all other propositions are trusted which are based on the same topics. We call it *topic-based trust transfer* ($T3$).

$$\Diamond^1(\Diamond^2(\Box^3\varphi \wedge \Box^4\neg\varphi)) \wedge \mathsf{topic\_contained}(\varphi, \psi) \supset (T_{ij}\varphi \supset T_{ij}\psi) \qquad (T3)$$

We formalize the running example with topics. Since there is only one topic, the example is relatively simple.

Example 2. The topic financial information (f) is defined as follows.

$$f \equiv (i(0.0) \times \ldots \times i(10.0) \times e(0.50) \times \ldots \times e(2.00)) \qquad \mathsf{topic}(f) \qquad \mathsf{all\_topics}(f)$$

In the first treatment of the example, the trust inference was 'hard coded'. Now, we use axiom $T3$ to derive: $T_{is}i(r_1) \vee T_{is}e(r_2) \supset (T_{is}i(r_3) \wedge T_{is}e(r_4))$. In particular, from $\mathsf{topic}(f)$ we can derive $\Diamond^1(\Diamond^2(\Box^3 i(r_1) \wedge \Box^4\neg i(r_1)))$ and from $\mathsf{topic}(f)$ and $\mathsf{all\_topics}(f)$ we can infer $\mathsf{topic\_contained}(i(r_1), i(r_3))$. Using axiom $T3$, we can infer $T_{is}i(r_1) \supset T_{is}i(r_3)$. Similarly, we can infer $T_{is}i(r_1) \supset T_{is}e(r_4)$ and therefore $T_{is}i(r_1) \vee T_{is}e(r_2) \supset T_{is}i(r_3) \wedge T_{is}e(r_4)$. So the property that was postulated in Example 1, is now derived from our topic construction.

Finally, we note that Liau does not discuss the possibility to add $(T_{ij}\varphi \wedge T_{ij}\psi) \supset T_{ij}(\varphi \vee \psi)$, which at first hand looks reasonable, in particular when φ and ψ belong to the same topics. Such an axiom can be formalized with our topics. Also, by contraposition we can derive $\mathsf{topic\_contained}(\varphi, \psi) \supset (\neg T_{ij}\psi \supset \neg T_{ij}\varphi)$. In other words, if all topics of φ are a topic of ψ, distrust in ψ transfers to distrust in φ.

5   Questions

In this section, the logic of Liau is extended with questions, because of their specific relation to trust. Questions have been studied extensively as part of the semantics of natural language. In this paper we use the semantics of questions and answers of Groenendijk and Stokhof [10]. The idea is as follows. Conceptually, a question expresses a 'gap' in the information of the asker, to be filled by an answer of the right type. For example, a 'when'-question asks for a time or date. So a question specifies what its possible answers are. In the semantics, that means that a question separates the set of possible worlds into disjoint subsets, each of which correspond to a complete answer to the question. The resulting structure is a partition [10]. Technically, a partition is equivalent to an equivalence relation, called an *indistinguishability relation*: the agent does not distinguish between worlds that satisfy the same answer to a question. For a yes/no question there are two sets of worlds in the partition: worlds that correspond to the answer "yes", and worlds that correspond to the answer "no". For an alternative question like "Which color is the traffic light?", the partition corresponds to three possible answers: "red", "yellow" and "green". For an open question like "Who are coming to the party?", which asks about groups of people coming to the party, we would get possible answers ranging from "Nobody will come", "John will come", "Mary will come" and "John and Mary will come", up to ""Everybody will come". In other words, open questions are treated as alternative questions, where each selection from a contextually relevant set corresponds to one alternative.

Like in the case of topics, this conceptualization of questions can be encoded using the symbol '×' to separate alternatives. We denote a question by an expression $\mathsf{question}_{ij}(\varphi_1 \times \ldots \times \varphi_n)$, where $\varphi_1...\varphi_n$ are the alternative answers. For example, "Which color is the traffic light?" is encoded by $\mathsf{question}_{ij}($'*traffic_light_is_red* × *traffic_light_is_yellow* × *traffic_light_is_green*$)$. Note that yes/no questions are a special case of alternative questions.

In some of the trust derivation cases, we need to express the fact that a possible answer was, either explicitly or implicitly, asked for. We use the Q_{ij}-operator for this. Expression $Q_{ij}\varphi$ means that agent i has posed a question to agent j for which φ is a possible answer. In other words, $Q_{ij}\varphi$ holds in case $\mathsf{question}_{ij}(\psi_1 \times \ldots \times \psi_n)$ has been explicitly or implicitly posed by agent i to agent j, for $\varphi \equiv \psi_k$ and $1 \leq k \leq n$.

Definition 5 (Questions). *The language of BIT with topics and questions, is the language of BIT with topics, together with the following clause:*

- *if φ is a sentence of BIT with topics, then so is $\square_{ij}\varphi$, for $1 \leq i \neq j \leq n$.*

Moreover, we add the following abbreviations:

- $\mathsf{question}_{ij}(\varphi_1 \times \ldots \times \varphi_n) = \Diamond_{ij}(\varphi_1 \times \ldots \times \varphi_n)$
- $Q_{ij}\varphi = \Diamond_{ij}\Diamond^2(\square^3\varphi \wedge \square^4\neg\varphi)$

The definition is analogous to the simulation of topics by a range of normal modal operators. The semantics of the BIT logic with topics and questions, extends the semantics of the BIT logic with topics, with a suitable accessibility relation corresponding to $\square_{ij}$. In the semantics $\lozenge_{ij}$ or equivalently question$_{ij}$ expresses the existence of a neighborhood corresponding to the answers to a question from agent i to j. The operators $\lozenge^2$ and $\square^3$, $\square^4$ are again used to express the properties of the $\times$-notation for alternatives. Note that like trust, but unlike topics, the semantics of questions is made relative to agents i and j. This expresses the intuition that topics are part of the general logical language, which is shared by all agents, whereas the questions that have been asked are particular for specific agents.

In a way, this provides only a minimal semantics. It does not express Groenendijk and Stokhof's idea of a partition. In case we want to model that answers to a question must be exclusive, and that the presented answers cover the whole logical space, i.e., that a question partitions the logical space, then we add the following axioms:

$$\text{question}_{ij}(\varphi_1 \times \ldots \times \varphi_n) \supset (\varphi_i \wedge \varphi_j \supset \bot), \text{ for all } 1 \leq i \neq j \leq n$$
$$\text{question}_{ij}(\varphi_1 \times \ldots \times \varphi_n) \supset (\varphi_1 \vee \ldots \vee \varphi_n \equiv \top)$$

5.1   Questions and Trust

The specific relation between questions and trust that we like to formalize in this section is based on the following intuition. If agent i has deliberately posed a question to an agent j to which agent i already believes the answer, and agent j has provided information that corresponds to the initial beliefs of agent i, then agent i will trust the second agent j. Otherwise, if agent j has provided the wrong answer, i.e. the information does not correspond to i's initial beliefs, then agent i will not trust agent j. This intuition is formalized by the following axioms which we call *question-based trust derivation* and *question-based distrust derivation* respectively.

$$(Q_{ij}\varphi \wedge B_i\varphi \wedge B_iI_{ij}\varphi) \supset T_{ij}\varphi$$
$$(Q_{ij}\varphi \wedge B_i\neg\varphi \wedge B_iI_{ij}\varphi) \supset \neg T_{ij}\varphi$$

Here, the combination of $Q_{ij}\varphi$ and $B_iI_{ij}\varphi$ is meant to express that $I_{ij}\varphi$ is a relevant response of agent j to a question posed by agent i. This reading may be problematic for a setting in which different questions can be posed, with the same kinds of answers. For example an answer "at five" may be relevant to both "When does the bus come?" and 'When does the train come?". However, these problems are not essential for the phenomenon of inferring trust.

Using these axioms, we can formalize our running example.

Example 3. Agent i asks a web-service s the exchange rate: question$_{is}(e(0.50) \times \ldots \times e(2.00))$ which implies $Q_{is}e(0.50) \wedge \ldots \wedge Q_{is}e(2.00)$. If the agent believes for example that the exchange is 1, $B_ie(1)$, and the web-service gives the correct answer, i.e., $B_iI_{is}e(1)$, then using the question-based trust creation axiom we can derive $T_{is}e(1)$. Similarly, in case the agent's beliefs do not correspond to the answer, for example $B_ie(5)$ and therefore $B_i\neg e(1)$ because exchange rates are unique, we derive $\neg T_{is}e(1)$ by question-based distrust creation.

5.2   Questions and Topics

Questions turn out to be very similar to topics. In the example, the topic 'financial information' corresponds to a combination of the questions "What is the current interest rate?" and "What is the current exchange rate?". In natural language semantics, relations between topics and questions have long been known. Van Kuppevelt [11] even defines topics in terms of the questions that are currently under discussion. By asking a question, the asker can manipulate the current topic of the conversation. As we noted above, topics are the same for all worlds and all agents. By contrast, we can use Q_{ij} to express the particular 'questions under discussion' for agents i and j. Under such an interpretation, it would make sense that questions were closed under topic: $Q_{ij}\varphi \land$ topic_contained$(\varphi, \psi) \supset Q_{ij}\psi$. However, under such an implicit 'questions under discussion' interpretation, the question operator cannot be used to model that an agent explicitly asked for some information. But this is exactly the interpretation we need in the running example. We therefore use an intermediate step, first using question-based trust creation, and then applying the topic-based trust transfer principle.

Example 4. We would like to prove the following.

$$(B_i e(r) \land \text{question}_{is}(\dots \times e(r) \times \dots) \land I_{is} e(r) \land$$
$$\text{topic\_contained}(e(r), i(r')) \land I_{is} i(r')) \supset B_i i(r')$$

Suppose $(B_i e(r) \land \text{question}_{is}(\dots \times e(r) \times \dots) \land I_{is} e(r) \land$ topic_contained$(e(r), i(r')) \land I_{is} i(r'))$. First, derive $Q_{is} e(r)$ by the definition of Q_{ij}, and subsequently $T_{is} e(r)$ by the principle of question-based trust creation. Second, derive $T_{is} i(r')$ from $(T_{is} e(r) \land \text{topic\_contained}(e(r), i(r'))$ by topic-based trust transfer, and third, derive $B_i i(r')$ from $(I_{is} i(r') \land T_{is} i(r'))$ by Liau's trust-based belief creation axiom C1. From these three formulas the desired implication can be obtained by principles of classical logic.

6   Further Research

6.1   Other Communicative Primitives

Suppose communication primitives proposal$_{ij}\varphi$ and request$_{ij}\varphi$ are added to the logic, to express that agent i received a proposal or request from j. Like an inform, an agent will only accept a proposal when it trusts the agent's capabilities. And like a question, a request either indicates trust in the other agent's capabilities, or, analogous to our running example, a request is used to test the agent's capabilities. Once accepted, a proposal or request expresses a commitment of one of the participants to achieve some future state of affairs. Therefore we would have to further extend the logic with a 'see-to-it that' operator $E_i\varphi$ [12]. In that case, i's acceptance of a proposal by j can be expressed by an inform that i trusts the sender j to achieve the content of the proposal: $I_{ji}T_{ij}E_j\varphi$.

Similarly, an acceptance of a request, is an inform that the accepter will achieve the content of the request: $I_{ji}E_i\varphi$. Thus in case of a proposal the sender will act upon acceptance, while in case of a request the receiver will act after having accepted.

$$\text{proposal}_{ij}\varphi \wedge I_{ji}T_{ij}E_j\varphi \supset E_j\varphi$$
$$\text{request}_{ij}\varphi \wedge I_{ji}E_i\varphi \supset E_i\varphi$$

6.2   Control Procedures

Trust can be based on personal relationships between agents, on past experiences, or on a reputation that has been passed on by other trusted agents. In the absence of such direct trust in the other party, an agent has to rely on institutional control procedures to make sure that other agents will keep their part of the deal. Examples are banks to guarantee payment, or a bill of lading to guarantee shipping. However, if an agent does not understand a control mechanism, or does not trust the institutions that guarantee it, the mechanism is useless. Therefore one should also model trust in the control procedures. The general idea can be summarized as follows [1].

$$\text{Transaction Trust} = \text{Party Trust} + \text{Control Trust}$$

If we further analyze control trust, it comes down to two aspects. First, the agent must understand the workings of the control mechanism. For example, agent i understands that, within a shipment institution s, a bill of lading 'counts as' evidence of the goods having been shipped. A bill of lading is a specific kind of inform act. In BIT we write $I_{is}bill \supset I_{is}shipped$. Second, the agent must trust the institution s that guarantees the control mechanism. This can be expressed in BIT too: $T_{is}shipped$. Together, these rules implicate, that whenever the agent receives a bill of lading, it will trust that the goods have been shipped: $I_{is}bill \supset B_i shipped$. This translation is promising, but rather simplified. Further relations between Liau's BIT logic and evidential norms need to be investigated.

7   Related Research

The notion of trust has been studied extensively in the social sciences. For an overview of research on trust in the context of electronic commerce and multi-agent systems, see Tan and Thoen [1, 13]. Generally, trust is studied in relation to a transaction. Mayer et al. give the following definition of trust: "The willingness of a party to be vulnerable to the actions of another party based on the expectation that the other party will perform a particular action important to the trustor, irrespective of the ability to monitor or control that other party [14]". Note that risk is involved for the truster. A similar sentiment is found in the definition by Gambetta "Trust is the subjective probability by which an individual A expects that another individual B performs a given action on which its welfare depends" [15]. Both these definitions indicate that trust is subjective, and directed towards another agent. Trust reflects an interpersonal relation, that can be generalized to machines. This aspect is nicely reflected in the logic of Liau.

Aboutness and topicality have received a lot of attention in linguistics. A topic and its subtopics can be used to identify the structure of a text. For example, Grosz and Sidner [16] relate the topic of a discourse (also called *center* or *focus of attention*) to the intention that is intended to be conveyed by the author. More technical research on aboutness is done in the context of information retrieval [17]. Clearly, in information retrieval it matters under what circumstances we can say that two documents are "about the same topic".

A notion that is very similar to trust is found in the so called BAN logics [18], used to define authentication policies in computer security. Although there is no explicit notion of trust in these logics, sharing a secret key counts as a proof of being trusted. The primitives of BAN logic are as follows: i *sees* X, which means that agent i received a message containing X. This is similar to Liau's inform; j *said* X, which means that agent j actually sent a message containing X, and that in case j is to be trusted, X ought to be believed by i; i *controls* X, which can be interpreted as saying that agent i is trusted as an authority on X. This notion might be developed towards our use of topics. In BAN logics it is often used to represent trusted third parties, like authentication services; *fresh* X, which means that X has not been sent previously, and $i \xleftrightarrow{K} j$, which means that agent i and j are entitled to use the same secret key K. Sharing a key counts as a proof of being trusted. There are several differences between BAN logics and Liau's BIT logic and the way they are used. An obvious difference is the use of keys, which is absent from Liau. Another difference concerns the perspective: Liau's logic takes the viewpoint of an individual agent: under what circumstances can I believe the content of a message? BAN takes the bird's eye view of a designer: how should I design my protocol to avoid secrets getting lost? The underlying logic is also different.

Finally, trust has been studied extensively in the context of a 'Grid'-like architecture for the sharing of resources and services [19]. Much of this work is applied. However, the underlying formal models that are developed in the context of such research [20] deserve to be compared with the BIT logic proposed here. Other formalizations in terms of modal logic also exist [21].

8   Conclusion

Trust plays an important role in advanced computer systems such as trust management systems in computer security [22] and reputation systems as used for example in eBay [23]. These applications define a much more precise notion of trust than the notion of trust used in social theories. Moreover, intelligent agents use trust mechanisms to reason about other agents, for example in cooperation, coordination, or electronic commerce. Agents that reason about their relations with other agents, such as agents reasoning about possible cooperation strategies, can benefit from reasoning about trust explicitly. Liau's logic does not tell us much about the inner structure of trust, which may even be considered as a black box, but it does explain the relation between trust and other concepts, in particular the relation between trust, belief and information actions.

This paper presents two extensions to Liau's BIT logic, which allow the derivation of trust. First, we extend the logic with topics. In this way, we can express that from trust in the truth of one proposition, we can infer trust in the truth of other propositions that are related by topic.

Second, we extend the logic with questions. In this way, we can express that informs are explicitly asked for, or else are implicitly considered relevant by an agent. There are two kinds of trust inference principles. We might say that by selecting another agent to ask a question, you indicate that you will trust this other agent. Thus, questions imply trust. On the other hand, questions may be asked strategically. In our running example the agent deliberately asked for a question with a known answer, in order to infer if the replying agent could be trusted on propositions of a related topic.

A question concerns the applicability of trust principles. We have already seen two alternative principles regarding trust and questions. It also seems reasonable to restrict the trust derivation axiom to situations in which the agent is relatively ignorant. In an exam situation, the teacher knows the answers to all the questions he asks. But a correct answer to the first question will not necessarily make the teacher trust the student about the answers to the remaining questions. This just shows that the social context in which trust is applied, needs to be modeled very carefully.

There are several important properties of trust which remain undiscussed. The logic does not capture the element of risk. In the running example, trusting the web-service is risky, because the portfolio management of the agent depends on it. Note that without such a risk, the agent would not go through the trouble of testing the services with the question about exchange rates.

We briefly indicated how the logic might be further extended with requests and proposals. This however, would require a shift from an epistemic notion of trust, about beliefs, to a more practical notion of trust, about actions. We also discussed how the logic is related to more general transaction models of trust, which involve control mechanisms guaranteed by an institution. More research is needed to connect these models with work on institutional norms.

References

[1] Tan, Y.H., Thoen, W.: Formal aspects of a generic model of trust for electronic commerce. In: 33rd Hawaii International Conference on System Sciences (HICSS'00). (2000) p. 6006

[2] Liau, C.J.: Belief, information acquisition, and trust in multi-agent systems – a modal formulation. Artificial Intelligence **149** (2003) 31–60

[3] Gasquet, O., Herzig, A.: From classical to normal modal logics. In Wansing, H., ed.: Proof Theory of Modal Logics. Volume 2 of Applied Logic Series. Kluwer (1996) 293–311

[4] Kracht, M., Wolter, F.: Normal monomodal logics can simulate all others. Journal of Symbolic Logic **64** (1999) 99–138

[5] Goffman, E.: Strategic interaction. University of Pennsylvania Press, Pennsylvania (1969)

[6] Demolombe, R.: To trust information sources: a proposal for a modal logical framework. In Castelfranchi, C., Tan, Y.H., eds.: Trust and Deception in Virtual Societies. Kluwer (2001) 111–124

[7] Demolombe, R., Jones, A.: On sentences of the kind "sentence 'p' is about topic t". In: Logic, language and reasoning: Essays in Honour of Dov Gabbay. Kluwer Academic, Dordrecht (1999) 115–133

[8] Herzig, A., Longin, D.: Belief dynamics in cooperative dialogues. Journal of Semantics **17** (2000) 91–118

[9] Janin, D., Walukiewicz, I.: Automata for the modal mu-calculus and related results. In: Proceedings of the 20th International Symposium on Mathematical Foundations of Computer Science (MFCS'95). LNCS 969, Springer Verlag (1995) 552–562

[10] Groenendijk, J., Stokhof, M.: Questions. In Van Benthem, J., Ter Meulen, A., eds.: Handbook of Logic and Language. North-Holland, Elsevier (1996) 1055–1124

[11] van Kuppevelt, J.: Discourse structure, topicality and questioning. Journal of Linguistics **31** (1995) 109–149

[12] Horty, J.: Agency and Deontic Logic. Oxford University Press (2001)

[13] Tan, Y.H., Thoen, W.: An outline of a trust model for electronic commerce. Applied Artificial Intelligence **14** (2000) 849–862

[14] Mayer, R., Davis, J., Schoorman, F.: An integrative model of organizational trust. Academy of Management Review **20** (1995) 709–734

[15] Gambetta, D.: Can we trust trust? In: Trust. Basil Blackwell, New York (1988) 213–237

[16] Grosz, B., Sidner, C.: Attentions, intentions and the structure of discourse. Computational Linguistics **12** (1986) 175–204

[17] Huibers, T.: An Axiomatic Theory for Information Retrieval. PhD thesis, Utrecht University (1996)

[18] Burrows, M., Abadi, M., Needham, R.: A logic of authentication. ACM Transactions on Computer Systems **8** (1990) 18–36

[19] Foster, I., Kesselman, C., Tuecke, S.: The anatomy of the Grid: Enabling scalable virtual organizations. .International Journal of High Performance Computing Applications **15** (2001) 200–222

[20] Carbone, M., Nielsen, M., Sassone, V.: A formal model for trust in dynamic networks. In: International Conference on Software Engineering and Formal Methods (SEFM'03), IEEE (2003) 54–63

[21] Jones, A., Firozabadi, B.S.: On the characterisation of a trusting agent - aspects of a formal approach. In Castelfranchi, C., Tan, Y., eds.: Trust and Deception in Virtual Societies. Kluwer Academic Publishers (2001) 157–168

[22] Blaze, M., Feigenbaum, J., Lacy, J.: Decentralized trust management. In: IEEE Symposium on Security and Privacy. IEEE (1996) 164–173

[23] Dellarocas, C.: The digitization of word-of-mouth: Promise and challenges of online feedback mechanisms. Management Science **49** (2004) 1407–1424

Coordination Between Logical Agents

Chiaki Sakama[1] and Katsumi Inoue[2]

[1] Department of Computer and Communication Sciences,
Wakayama University,
Sakaedani, Wakayama 640 8510, Japan
sakama@sys.wakayama-u.ac.jp
[2] National Institute of Informatics,
2-1-2 Hitotsubashi, Chiyoda-ku, Tokyo 101 8430, Japan
ki@nii.ac.jp

Abstract. In this paper we suppose an agent that has a knowledge base written in logic programming and sets of beliefs under the answer set semantics. We then consider the following two problems: given two logic programs P_1 and P_2, which have the sets of answer sets $\mathcal{AS}(P_1)$ and $\mathcal{AS}(P_2)$, respectively; (i) find a program Q which has the set of answer sets such that $\mathcal{AS}(Q) = \mathcal{AS}(P_1) \cup \mathcal{AS}(P_2)$; (ii) find a program R which has the set of answer sets such that $\mathcal{AS}(R) = \mathcal{AS}(P_1) \cap \mathcal{AS}(P_2)$. A program Q satisfying the condition (i) is called *generous coordination* of P_1 and P_2; and R satisfying (ii) is called *rigorous coordination* of P_1 and P_2. Generous coordination retains all of the original belief sets of each agent, but admits the introduction of additional belief sets of the other agent. By contrast, rigorous coordination forces each agent to give up some belief sets, but the result remains within the original belief sets for each agent. We provide methods for constructing these two types of coordination and discuss their properties.

1 Introduction

In multi-agent systems different agents may have different sets of beliefs, and agents negotiate and accommodate themselves to reach acceptable agreements. We call a process of forming such agreements between agents *coordination*. The problem is how to settle an agreement acceptable to each agent. The outcome of coordination is required to be consistent and is desirable to retain original information of each agent as much as possible.

Suppose an agent that has a knowledge base as a logic program whose semantics is given as the collection of *answer sets* [7]. Answer sets represent sets of literals corresponding to beliefs which can be built by a rational reasoner on the basis of a program [2]. An agent may have (conflicting) alternative sets of beliefs, which are represented by multiple answer sets of a program. Different agents have different collections of answer sets in general. We then capture coordination between two agents as the problem of finding a new program which has the meaning balanced between two programs. Consider, for instance, a logic

J. Leite and P. Torroni (Eds.): CLIMA V, LNAI 3487, pp. 161–177, 2005.
© Springer-Verlag Berlin Heidelberg 2005

program P_1 which has two answer sets S_1 and S_2; and another logic program P_2 which has two answer sets S_2 and S_3. Then, we want to find a new program which is a result of coordination between P_1 and P_2. In this paper, we consider two different solutions: one is a program Q which has three answer sets S_1, S_2, and S_3; the other is a program R which has the single answer set S_2.

These two solutions provide different types of coordination — the first one retains all of the original belief sets of each agent, but admits the introduction of additional belief sets of the other agent. By contrast, the second one forces each agent to give up some belief sets, but the result remains within the original belief sets for each agent. These two types of coordination occur in real life. For instance, suppose the following scenario: to decide the Academy Award of Best Pictures, each member of the Academy nominates films. Now there are three members — p_1, p_2, and p_3, and each member can nominate at most two films: p_1 nominates f_1 and f_2, p_2 nominates f_2 and f_3, and p_3 nominates f_2. At this moment, three nominees f_1, f_2, and f_3 are fixed. The situation is represented by three programs:

$$P_1 : \quad f_1 \,;\, f_2 \leftarrow,$$
$$P_2 : \quad f_2 \,;\, f_3 \leftarrow,$$
$$P_3 : \quad f_2 \leftarrow,$$

where ";" represents disjunction. Here, P_1 has two answer sets: $\{f_1\}$ and $\{f_2\}$; P_2 has two answer sets: $\{f_2\}$ and $\{f_3\}$; P_3 has the single answer set: $\{f_2\}$. The three nominees correspond to the answer sets: $\{f_1\}$, $\{f_2\}$, and $\{f_3\}$. A program having these three answer sets is the first type of coordination. After final voting, the film f_2 is supported by three members and becomes the winner of the Award. That is, the winner is represented by the answer set $\{f_2\}$. A program having this single answer set is the second type of coordination. Thus, these two types of coordination happen in different situations, and it is meaningful to develop computational logic for these coordination between agents.

The problem is then how to build a program which realizes such coordination. Formally, the problems considered in this paper are described as follows.

Given: two programs P_1 and P_2;

Find: (1) a program Q satisfying $\mathcal{AS}(Q) = \mathcal{AS}(P_1) \cup \mathcal{AS}(P_2)$;

(2) a program R satisfying $\mathcal{AS}(R) = \mathcal{AS}(P_1) \cap \mathcal{AS}(P_2)$,

where $\mathcal{AS}(P)$ represents the set of answer sets of a program P. The program Q satisfying (1) is called *generous coordination* of P_1 and P_2; and the program R satisfying (2) is called *rigorous coordination* of P_1 and P_2. We develop methods for computing these two types of coordination and verify the results.

The rest of this paper is organized as follows. Section 2 presents definitions and terminologies used in this paper. Section 3 introduces a framework of coordination between logic programs. Section 4 provides methods for computing coordination and addresses their properties. Section 5 discusses related issues and Section 6 summarizes the paper.

2 Preliminaries

In this paper, we suppose an agent that has a knowledge base written in logic programming. An agent is then identified with its logic program and we use those terms interchangeably throughout the paper.

A *program* considered in this paper is an *extended disjunctive program* (EDP) which is a set of *rules* of the form:

$$L_1 ; \cdots ; L_l \leftarrow L_{l+1}, \ldots, L_m, \textit{not}\, L_{m+1}, \ldots, \textit{not}\, L_n \quad (n \geq m \geq l \geq 0)$$

where each L_i is a positive/negative literal, i.e., A or $\neg A$ for an atom A, and *not* is *negation as failure* (NAF). *not* L is called an *NAF-literal*. The symbol ";" represents disjunction. The left-hand side of the rule is the *head*, and the right-hand side is the *body*. For each rule r of the above form, $head(r)$, $body^+(r)$, $body^-(r)$, and $not\_body^-(r)$ denote the sets of (NAF-)literals $\{L_1, \ldots, L_l\}$, $\{L_{l+1}, \ldots, L_m\}$, $\{L_{m+1}, \ldots, L_n\}$, and $\{\textit{not}\, L_{m+1}, \ldots, \textit{not}\, L_n\}$, respectively. A disjunction of literals and a conjunction of (NAF-)literals in a rule are identified with its corresponding sets of (NAF-)literals. A rule r is often written as $head(r) \leftarrow body^+(r)$, $not\_body^-(r)$ or $head(r) \leftarrow body(r)$ where $body(r) = body^+(r) \cup not\_body^-(r)$. A rule r is *disjunctive* if $head(r)$ contains more than one literal. A rule r is an *integrity constraint* if $head(r) = \emptyset$; and r is a *fact* if $body(r) = \emptyset$. A program P is *NAF-free* if $body^-(r) = \emptyset$ for any rule r in P. A program with variables is semantically identified with its ground instantiation, and we handle propositional and ground programs throughout the paper.

The semantics of EDPs is given by the *answer set semantics* [7]. Let Lit be the set of all ground literals in the language of a program. A set $S(\subset Lit)$ *satisfies* a ground rule r if $body^+(r) \subseteq S$ and $body^-(r) \cap S = \emptyset$ imply $head(r) \cap S \neq \emptyset$. In particular, S satisfies a ground integrity constraint r with $head(r) = \emptyset$ if either $body^+(r) \not\subseteq S$ or $body^-(r) \cap S \neq \emptyset$. S satisfies a ground program P if S satisfies every rule in P. When $body^+(r) \subseteq S$ (resp. $head(r) \cap S \neq \emptyset$), it is also written as $S \models body^+(r)$ (resp. $S \models head(r)$).

Let P be an NAF-free EDP. Then, a set $S(\subset Lit)$ is a *(consistent) answer set* of P if S is a minimal set such that

1. S satisfies every rule from the ground instantiation of P,
2. S does not contain a pair of complementary literals L and $\neg L$ for any $L \in Lit$.

Next, let P be any EDP and $S \subset Lit$. For every rule r in the ground instantiation of P, the rule $r^S : head(r) \leftarrow body^+(r)$ is included in the *reduct* P^S if $body^-(r) \cap S = \emptyset$. Then, S is an *answer set* of P if S is an answer set of P^S. An EDP has none, one, or multiple answer sets in general. The set of all answer sets of P is written as $\mathcal{AS}(P)$. A program P is *consistent* if it has a consistent answer set. In this paper, we assume that a program is consistent unless stated otherwise.

A literal L is a consequence of *credulous reasoning* in a program P (written as $L \in crd(P)$) if L is included in some answer set of P. A literal L is a consequence of *skeptical reasoning* in a program P (written as $L \in skp(P)$) if L is included in every answer set of P. Clearly, $skp(P) \subseteq crd(P)$ holds for any P. Two programs

P_1 and P_2 are said to be *AS-combinable* if every set in $\mathcal{AS}(P_1) \cup \mathcal{AS}(P_2)$ is minimal under set inclusion.

Example 2.1. Given two programs:

$$P_1 : \quad p ; q \leftarrow,$$
$$p \leftarrow q,$$
$$q \leftarrow p,$$
$$P_2 : \quad p \leftarrow not\, q,$$
$$q \leftarrow not\, p,$$

where $\mathcal{AS}(P_1) = \{\{p, q\}\}$ and $\mathcal{AS}(P_2) = \{\{p\}, \{q\}\}$. Then, $crd(P_1) = skp(P_1) = \{p, q\}$; $crd(P_2) = \{p, q\}$ and $skp(P_2) = \emptyset$. P_1 and P_2 are not AS-combinable because the set $\{p, q\}$ is not minimal in $\mathcal{AS}(P_1) \cup \mathcal{AS}(P_2)$.

Technically, when two programs P_1 and P_2 are not AS-combinable, we can make them AS-combinable by introducing the rule $\overline{L} \leftarrow not\, L$ for every $L \in Lit$ to each program, where $\overline{L}$ is a newly introduced atom associated uniquely with each L.

Example 2.2. In the above example, put $P_1' = P_1 \cup Q$ and $P_2' = P_2 \cup Q$ with

$$Q : \quad \overline{p} \leftarrow not\, p,$$
$$\overline{q} \leftarrow \;\; not\, q.$$

Then, $\mathcal{AS}(P_1') = \{\{p, q\}\}$ and $\mathcal{AS}(P_2') = \{\{p, \overline{q}\}, \{\overline{p}, q\}\}$, so P_1' and P_2' are AS-combinable.

3   Coordination Between Programs

Given two programs, coordination provides a program which is a reasonable compromise between agents. In this section, we introduce two different types of coordination under the answer set semantics.

Definition 3.1. Let P_1 and P_2 be two programs. A program Q satisfying the condition $\mathcal{AS}(Q) = \mathcal{AS}(P_1) \cup \mathcal{AS}(P_2)$ is called *generous coordination* of P_1 and P_2; a program R satisfying the condition $\mathcal{AS}(R) = \mathcal{AS}(P_1) \cap \mathcal{AS}(P_2)$ is called *rigorous coordination* of P_1 and P_2.

Generous coordination retains all of the answer sets of each agent, but admits the introduction of additional answer sets of the other agent. By contrast, rigorous coordination forces each agent to give up some answer sets, but the result remains within the original answer sets for each agent.

Technically, generous coordination requires two programs P_1 and P_2 to be AS-combinable, since answer sets of Q are all minimal. Thus, when we consider generous coordination between two programs, we assume them to be AS-combinable.

Generous coordination between programs that are not AS-combinable is possible by making them AS-combinable in advance using the program transformation presented in Section 2.

Definition 3.2. For two programs P_1 and P_2, let Q be a result of generous coordination, and R a result of rigorous coordination. We say that generous (resp. rigorous) coordination *succeeds* if $\mathcal{AS}(Q) \neq \emptyset$ (resp. $\mathcal{AS}(R) \neq \emptyset$); otherwise, it *fails*.

Generous coordination always succeeds whenever both P_1 and P_2 are consistent. On the other hand, when $\mathcal{AS}(P_1) \cap \mathcal{AS}(P_2) = \emptyset$, rigorous coordination fails as two agents have no common belief sets. Note that generous coordination may produce a collection of answer sets which contradict with one another. But this does not cause any problem as a collection of answer sets represents (conflicting) alternative belief sets of each agent.

As we assume consistent programs, the next result holds by the definition.

Proposition 3.1 *When generous/rigorous coordination of two programs succeeds, the result of coordination is consistent.*

Coordination changes the consequences of credulous/skeptical reasoning by each agent.

Proposition 3.2 *Let P_1 and P_2 be two programs.*

1. *If Q is a result of generous coordination,*
   (a) $crd(Q) = crd(P_1) \cup crd(P_2)$;
   (b) $skp(Q) = skp(P_1) \cap skp(P_2)$;
   (c) $crd(Q) \supseteq crd(P_i)$ for $i = 1, 2$;
   (d) $skp(Q) \subseteq skp(P_i)$ for $i = 1, 2$.
2. *If R is a result of rigorous coordination,*
   (a) $crd(R) \subseteq crd(P_1) \cup crd(P_2)$;
   (b) $skp(R) \supseteq skp(P_1) \cup skp(P_2)$ if $\mathcal{AS}(R) \neq \emptyset$;
   (c) $crd(R) \subseteq crd(P_i)$ for $i = 1, 2$;
   (d) $skp(R) \supseteq skp(P_i)$ for $i = 1, 2$ if $\mathcal{AS}(R) \neq \emptyset$.

Proof. 1.(a) A literal L is included in an answer set in $\mathcal{AS}(P_1) \cup \mathcal{AS}(P_2)$ iff L is included in an answer set in $\mathcal{AS}(P_1)$ or included in an answer set in $\mathcal{AS}(P_2)$. (b) L is included in every answer set in $\mathcal{AS}(P_1) \cup \mathcal{AS}(P_2)$ iff L is included in every answer set in $\mathcal{AS}(P_1)$ and also included in every answer set in $\mathcal{AS}(P_2)$. The results of (c) and (d) hold by (a) and (b), respectively.

2.(a) If L is included in an answer set in $\mathcal{AS}(P_1) \cap \mathcal{AS}(P_2)$, L is included in an answer set in $\mathcal{AS}(P_i)$ $(i = 1, 2)$. (b) If L is included in every answer set of either P_1 or P_2, L is included in every answer set in $\mathcal{AS}(P_1) \cap \mathcal{AS}(P_2)$ if the intersection is nonempty. The results of (c) and (d) hold by (a) and (b), respectively. $\square$

Example 3.1. Let $\mathcal{AS}(P_1) = \{\{a, b, c\}, \{b, c, d\}\}$ and $\mathcal{AS}(P_2) = \{\{b, c, d\}, \{c, e\}\}$, where $crd(P_1) = \{a, b, c, d\}$, $skp(P_1) = \{b, c\}$, $crd(P_2) = \{b, c, d, e\}$, and $skp(P_2) = \{c\}$. Generous coordination Q of P_1 and P_2 has the answer sets $\mathcal{AS}(Q) = \{\{a, b, c\}, \{b, c, d\}, \{c, e\}\}$ where $crd(Q) = \{a, b, c, d, e\}$ and $skp(Q) = \{c\}$. Rigorous coordination R has the answer sets $\mathcal{AS}(R) = \{\{b, c, d\}\}$ where $crd(R) = skp(R) = \{b, c, d\}$. The above relations are verified for these sets.

Generous coordination merges credulous consequences of P_1 and P_2, while restricts skeptical consequences to those that are common between two programs. As a result, it increases credulous consequences and decreases skeptical consequences. This reflects the situation that accepting opinions of the other agent increases alternative choices while weakening the original argument of each agent. By contrast, rigorous coordination reduces credulous consequences, but increases skeptical consequences in general. This reflects the situation that excluding opinions of the other agent costs abandoning some of one's alternative beliefs, which results in strengthening some original argument of each agent.

Definition 3.3. For two programs P_1 and P_2, let Q be a result of generous coordination, and R a result of rigorous coordination. When $\mathcal{AS}(Q) = \mathcal{AS}(P_1)$ (resp. $\mathcal{AS}(R) = \mathcal{AS}(P_1)$), P_1 *dominates* P_2 under generous (resp. rigorous) coordination.

Proposition 3.3 *Let P_1 and P_2 be two programs. When $\mathcal{AS}(P_1) \subseteq \mathcal{AS}(P_2)$, P_2 dominates P_1 under generous coordination, and P_1 dominates P_2 under rigorous coordination.*

When P_2 dominates P_1 under generous coordination, we can easily have a result of generous coordination as $Q = P_2$. Similarly, when P_1 dominates P_2 under rigorous coordination, a result of rigorous coordination becomes $R = P_1$.

In cases where one agent dominates the other one, or when coordination fails, the results of coordination are trivial and uninteresting. Then, the problem of interest is the cases where $\mathcal{AS}(P_1) \not\subseteq \mathcal{AS}(P_2)$ and $\mathcal{AS}(P_2) \not\subseteq \mathcal{AS}(P_1)$ for computing generous/rigorous coordination; and $\mathcal{AS}(P_1) \cap \mathcal{AS}(P_2) \neq \emptyset$ for computing rigorous coordination. In the next section, we present methods for computing these two coordination.

4   Computing Coordination

4.1   Computing Generous Coordination

We first present a method of computing generous coordination between two programs.

Definition 4.1. Given two programs P_1 and P_2,

$$P_1 \oplus P_2 = \{ head(r_1) ; head(r_2) \leftarrow body_*(r_1), body_*(r_2) \mid r_1 \in P_1, r_2 \in P_2 \},$$

where $head(r_1); head(r_2)$ is the disjunction of $head(r_1)$ and $head(r_2)$, $body_*(r_1) = body(r_1) \setminus \{ not\, L \mid L \in T \setminus S \}$ and $body_*(r_2) = body(r_2) \setminus \{ not\, L \mid L \in S \setminus T \}$ for any $S \in \mathcal{AS}(P_1)$ and $T \in \mathcal{AS}(P_2)$.

The program $P_1 \oplus P_2$ is a collection of rules which are obtained by combining a rule of P_1 and a rule of P_2 in every possible way. In $body_*(r_1)$ every NAF-literal $not\, L$ such that $L \in T \setminus S$ is dropped because the existence of this may prevent the derivation of some literal in $head(r_2)$ after combination.

Example 4.1. Consider two programs:

$$P_1 : \quad p \leftarrow not\, q,$$
$$q \leftarrow not\, p,$$
$$P_2 : \quad \neg p \leftarrow not\, p,$$

where $\mathcal{AS}(P_1) = \{\{p\}, \{q\}\}$ and $\mathcal{AS}(P_2) = \{\{\neg p\}\}$. Then, $P_1 \oplus P_2$ becomes

$$p; \neg p \leftarrow not\, q,$$
$$q; \neg p \leftarrow not\, p.$$

Note that $not\, p$ from the rule of P_2 is dropped in the resulting rules because of the existence of $\{p\}$ in $\mathcal{AS}(P_1)$.

By the definition, $P_1 \oplus P_2$ is computed in time $|P_1| \times |P_2| \times |\mathcal{AS}(P_1)| \times |\mathcal{AS}(P_2)|$, where $|P|$ represents the number of rules in P and $|\mathcal{AS}(P)|$ represents the number of answer sets in P.

The program $P_1 \oplus P_2$ generally contains useless or redundant literals/rules, and the following program transformations are helpful to simplify the program.

- (elimination of tautologies: TAUT)
  Delete a rule r from a program if $head(r) \cap body^+(r) \neq \emptyset$.
- (elimination of contradictions: CONTRA)
  Delete a rule r from a program if $body^+(r) \cap body^-(r) \neq \emptyset$.
- (elimination of non-minimal rules: NONMIN)
  Delete a rule r from a program if there is another rule r' in the program such that $head(r') \subseteq head(r)$, $body^+(r') \subseteq body^+(r)$ and $body^-(r') \subseteq body^-(r)$.
- (merging duplicated literals: DUPL)
  A disjunction $(L; L)$ appearing in $head(r)$ is merged into L, and a conjunction (L, L) or $(not\, L, not\, L)$ appearing in $body(r)$ is merged into L or $not\, L$, respectively.

These program transformations all preserve the answer sets of an EDP [3].

Example 4.2. Given two programs:

$$P_1 : \quad p \leftarrow q,$$
$$r \leftarrow,$$
$$P_2 : \quad p \leftarrow not\, q,$$
$$q \leftarrow r,$$

$P_1 \oplus P_2$ becomes

$$p\,;\, p \leftarrow q,\, not\, q,$$
$$p\,;\, q \leftarrow q,\, r,$$
$$p\,;\, r \leftarrow not\, q,$$
$$r\,;\, q \leftarrow r.$$

The first rule is deleted by CONTRA, the second rule and the fourth rule are deleted by TAUT. After such elimination, the resulting program contains the third rule only.

Now we show that $P_1 \oplus P_2$ realizes generous coordination of P_1 and P_2.

Lemma 4.1 *Let P_1 and P_2 be two NAF-free AS-combinable programs. Then, S is an answer set of $P_1 \oplus P_2$ iff S is an answer set of either P_1 or P_2.*

Proof. Suppose that S is an answer set of P_1. Then, S satisfies any rule $head(r_1) \leftarrow body(r_1)$ in P_1, thereby satisfies any rule $head(r_1); head(r_2) \leftarrow body(r_1), body(r_2)$ in $P_1 \oplus P_2$. (Note: $body_*(r_i) = body(r_i)$ for NAF-free programs.) To see that S is an answer set of $P_1 \oplus P_2$, suppose that there is a minimal set $T \subset S$ which satisfies every rule in $P_1 \oplus P_2$. Since S is an answer set of P_1, there is a rule r_1' in P_1 which is not satisfied by T. For this rule, $T \not\models head(r_1')$ and $T \models body(r_1')$ hold. Then, for any rule $head(r_1'); head(r_2) \leftarrow body(r_1'), body(r_2)$ in $P_1 \oplus P_2$, $T \models head(r_2)$ or $T \not\models body(r_2)$. Since every rule in P_2 is combined with r_1', it holds that $T \models head(r_2)$ or $T \not\models body(r_2)$ for every r_2 in P_2. Then, T satisfies P_2. As P_2 is consistent, it has an answer set $T' \subseteq T$. This contradicts the assumption that P_1 and P_2 are AS-combinable, i.e., $T' \not\subseteq S$. Hence, S is an answer set of $P_1 \oplus P_2$. The case that S is an answer set of P_2 is proved in the same manner.

Conversely, suppose that S is an answer set of $P_1 \oplus P_2$. Then, S satisfies any rule $head(r_1); head(r_2) \leftarrow body(r_1), body(r_2)$ in $P_1 \oplus P_2$. Then $S \models body(r_1), body(r_2)$ implies $S \models head(r_1); head(r_2)$. If $S \not\models head(r_1)$ for some rule $r_1 \in P_1$, $S \models head(r_2)$ for any $r_2 \in P_2$. Then, $S \models body(r_2)$ implies $S \models head(r_2)$ for any $r_2 \in P_2$, so that S satisfies every rule in P_2. Else if $S \not\models head(r_2)$ for some rule $r_2 \in P_2$, $S \models head(r_1)$ for any $r_1 \in P_1$. Then, $S \models body(r_1)$ implies $S \models head(r_1)$ for any $r_1 \in P_1$, so that S satisfies every rule in P_1. Else if $S \models head(r_1)$ for every $r_1 \in P_1$ and $S \models head(r_2)$ for every $r_2 \in P_2$, S satisfies both P_1 and P_2. Thus, in every case S satisfies either P_1 or P_2. Suppose that S satisfies P_1 but it is not an answer set of P_1. Then, there is an answer set T of P_1 such that $T \subset S$. By the if-part, T becomes an answer set of $P_1 \oplus P_2$. This contradicts the assumption that S is an answer set of $P_1 \oplus P_2$. Similar argument is applied when S satisfies P_2. $\square$

Theorem 4.2. *Let P_1 and P_2 be two AS-combinable programs. Then, $\mathcal{AS}(P_1 \oplus P_2) = \mathcal{AS}(P_1) \cup \mathcal{AS}(P_2)$.*

Proof. Suppose $S \in \mathcal{AS}(P_1)$. Then, S is an answer set of P_1^S, so that S is an answer set of $P_1^S \oplus P_2^T$ for any $T \in \mathcal{AS}(P_2)$ (Lemma 4.1). (Note: as P_1 and P_2 are AS-combinable, the reducts P_1^S and P_2^T are also AS-combinable.) For any rule $head(r_1); head(r_2) \leftarrow body^+(r_1), body^+(r_2)$ in $P_1^S \oplus P_2^T$, it holds that $body^-(r_1) \cap S = body^-(r_2) \cap T = \emptyset$. On the other hand, for any rule $head(r_1); head(r_2) \leftarrow body_*(r_1), body_*(r_2)$ in $P_1 \oplus P_2$, $head(r_1); head(r_2) \leftarrow body^+(r_1), body^+(r_2)$ is in $(P_1 \oplus P_2)^S$ iff $(body^-(r_1) \setminus \{ L \mid L \in T \setminus S' \}) \cap S = \emptyset$ and $(body^-(r_2) \setminus \{ L \mid L \in S' \setminus T \}) \cap S = \emptyset$ for any $S' \in \mathcal{AS}(P_1)$ and $T \in \mathcal{AS}(P_2)$. Here it holds that $(body^-(r_1) \setminus \{ L \mid L \in T \setminus S' \}) \cap S \subseteq body^-(r_1) \cap S$ and $(body^-(r_2) \setminus \{ L \mid L \in S' \setminus T \}) \cap S \subseteq body^-(r_2) \cap T \cap S \subseteq body^-(r_2) \cap T$. Hence, $P_1^S \oplus P_2^T \subseteq (P_1 \oplus P_2)^S$. Suppose any rule $head(r_1); head(r_2) \leftarrow body^+(r_1), body^+(r_2)$ in $(P_1 \oplus P_2)^S \setminus (P_1^S \oplus P_2^T)$. Since S satisfies any rule r_1 in P_1, $S \models body^+(r_1), body^+(r_2)$ implies $S \models head(r_1); head(r_2)$. Thus, the answer set S of $P_1^S \oplus P_2^T$ satisfies every rule in $(P_1 \oplus P_2)^S \setminus (P_1^S \oplus P_2^T)$. By $P_1^S \oplus P_2^T \subseteq (P_1 \oplus P_2)^S$, S becomes an answer set of $(P_1 \oplus P_2)^S$ and $S \in \mathcal{AS}(P_1 \oplus P_2)$. The case of $S \in \mathcal{AS}(P_2)$ is proved in the same manner.

Conversely, suppose $S \in \mathcal{AS}(P_1 \oplus P_2)$. Then, S satisfies any rule $head(r_1); head(r_2) \leftarrow body_*(r_1), body_*(r_2)$ in $P_1 \oplus P_2$, so $S \models body_*(r_1), body_*(r_2)$ implies $S \models head(r_1); head(r_2)$. If $S \not\models head(r_1)$ for some rule $r_1 \in P_1$, $S \models head(r_2)$ for any $r_2 \in P_2$. Then, $S \models body_*(r_2)$ implies $S \models head(r_2)$ for any $r_2 \in P_2$, so $S \models head(r_2)$ or $S \not\models body_*(r_2)$. As $S \not\models body_*(r_2)$ implies $S \not\models body(r_2)$, it holds that $S \models head(r_2)$ or $S \not\models body(r_2)$ for any $r_2 \in P$. Hence, S satisfies every rule in P_2. Else if $S \not\models head(r_2)$ for some rule $r_2 \in P_2$, it is shown in a similar manner that S satisfies every rule in P_1. Else if $S \models head(r_1)$ for every $r_1 \in P_1$ and $S \models head(r_2)$ for every $r_2 \in P_2$, S satisfies both P_1 and P_2. Thus, in every case S satisfies either P_1 or P_2. Suppose that S satisfies P_1 but it is not an answer set of P_1. Then, there is an answer set T of P_1 such that $T \subset S$. By the if-part, T becomes an answer set of $P_1 \oplus P_2$. This contradicts the assumption that S is an answer set of $P_1 \oplus P_2$. Similar argument is applied when S satisfies P_2. □

Example 4.3. In Example 4.1, $\mathcal{AS}(P_1 \oplus P_2) = \{\{p\}, \{q\}, \{\neg p\}\}$, thereby $\mathcal{AS}(P_1 \oplus P_2) = \mathcal{AS}(P_1) \cup \mathcal{AS}(P_2)$.

4.2 Computing Rigorous Coordination

Next we present a method of computing rigorous coordination between two programs.

Definition 4.2. Given two programs P_1 and P_2,

$$P_1 \otimes P_2 = \bigcup_{S \in \mathcal{AS}(P_1) \cap \mathcal{AS}(P_2)} R(P_1, S) \cup R(P_2, S),$$

where $\mathcal{AS}(P_1) \cap \mathcal{AS}(P_2) \neq \emptyset$ and

$$R(P, S) = \{ head(r) \cap S \leftarrow body(r), not\, (head(r) \setminus S) \mid r \in P \text{ and } r^S \in P^S \}$$

and $not\, (head(r) \setminus S) = \{ not\, L \mid L \in head(r) \setminus S \}$.

When $\mathcal{AS}(P_1) \cap \mathcal{AS}(P_2) = \emptyset$, $P_1 \otimes P_2$ is undefined.[1]

Intuitively, the program $P_1 \otimes P_2$ is a collection of rules which may be used for constructing answer sets that are common between P_1 and P_2. In $R(P, S)$ any literal in $head(r)$ which does not contribute to the construction of the answer set S is shifted to the body as NAF-literals. $P_1 \otimes P_2$ may contain redundant rules, which are eliminated using program transformations given in the previous subsection.

Example 4.4. Consider two programs:

$$P_1 : \quad p \leftarrow not\, q,\, not\, r,$$
$$q \leftarrow not\, p,\, not\, r,$$
$$r \leftarrow not\, p,\, not\, q,$$
$$P_2 : \quad p\,;\, q\,;\, \neg r \leftarrow not\, r,$$

where $\mathcal{AS}(P_1) = \{\{p\}, \{q\}, \{r\}\}$, $\mathcal{AS}(P_2) = \{\{p\}, \{q\}, \{\neg r\}\}$, and $\mathcal{AS}(P_1) \cap \mathcal{AS}(P_2) = \{\{p\}, \{q\}\}$. Then, $P_1 \otimes P_2$ becomes

$$p \leftarrow not\, q,\, not\, r,$$
$$q \leftarrow not\, p,\, not\, r,$$
$$p \leftarrow not\, r,\, not\, q,\, not\, \neg r,$$
$$q \leftarrow not\, r,\, not\, p,\, not\, \neg r.$$

Here, the third and the fourth rules can be eliminated by NONMIN.

By the definition, $P_1 \otimes P_2$ is computed in time $(|P_1| + |P_2|) \times |\mathcal{AS}(P_1) \cap \mathcal{AS}(P_2)|$ where $|\mathcal{AS}(P_1) \cap \mathcal{AS}(P_2)|$ represents the number of answer sets in $\mathcal{AS}(P_1) \cap \mathcal{AS}(P_2)$.

$P_1 \otimes P_2$ realizes rigorous coordination of P_1 and P_2.

Lemma 4.3 *Let P be a program. Then, S is an answer set of P iff S is an answer set of $R(P, S)$.*

Proof. S is an answer set of P iff S is an answer set of P^S
iff S is a minimal set such that $body^+(r) \subseteq S$ implies $head(r) \cap S \neq \emptyset$ for every rule $head(r) \leftarrow body^+(r)$ in P^S (∗). By the definition of $R(P, S)$, the rule $head(r) \leftarrow body^+(r)$ is in P^S iff the corresponding rule $head(r) \cap S \leftarrow body^+(r)$ is in $R(P, S)^S$ (because $body^-(r) \cap S = \emptyset$ and $(head(r) \setminus S) \cap S = \emptyset$). Hence, the statement (∗) holds iff S is a minimal set such that $body^+(r) \subseteq S$ implies $head(r) \cap S \neq \emptyset$ for every rule $head(r) \cap S \leftarrow body^+(r)$ in $R(P, S)^S$
iff S is a minimal set which satisfies every rule $head(r) \cap S \leftarrow body^+(r)$ in $R(P, S)^S$
iff S is an answer set of $R(P, S)$. □

---

[1] Technically, $P_1 \otimes P_2$ is set as $\{p \leftarrow not\, p\}$ for any atom p.

Theorem 4.4. *Let P_1 and P_2 be two programs. Then, $\mathcal{AS}(P_1 \otimes P_2) = \mathcal{AS}(P_1) \cap \mathcal{AS}(P_2)$.*

Proof. Suppose $S \in \mathcal{AS}(P_1) \cap \mathcal{AS}(P_2)$. Then, S satisfies any rule $head(r) \leftarrow body(r)$ in P_1 and P_2, so that S satisfies the corresponding rules $head(r) \cap T \leftarrow body(r), not\,(head(r) \setminus T)$ in $R(P_1, T) \cup R(P_2, T)$ for any $T \in \mathcal{AS}(P_1) \cap \mathcal{AS}(P_2)$. Thus, S satisfies $P_1 \otimes P_2$. Suppose that S is not an answer set of $P_1 \otimes P_2$. Then, there is a minimal set $U \subset S$ which satisfies every rule in $P_1 \otimes P_2$. In this case, U satisfies $R(P_1, S)$. By Lemma 4.3, however, S is a minimal set which satisfies $R(P_1, S)$. Contradiction. Hence, S is an answer set of $P_1 \otimes P_2$.

Conversely, suppose $S \in \mathcal{AS}(P_1 \otimes P_2)$. Then, S is a minimal set which satisfies every rule $head(r) \cap T \leftarrow body(r), not\,(head(r) \setminus T)$ in $R(P_1, T) \cup R(P_2, T)$ for any $T \in \mathcal{AS}(P_1) \cap \mathcal{AS}(P_2)$. By Lemma 4.3, T is also a minimal set which satisfies both $R(P_1, T)$ and $R(P_2, T)$, so that there is a literal $L \in S \setminus T$ and a literal $M \in T \setminus S$. However, any rule in $R(P_1, T) \cup R(P_2, T)$ has the head $head(r) \cap T$, so that no literal $L \in S \setminus T$ is included in the head. Thus, L is not included in the answer set S, thereby $S \setminus T = \emptyset$. As both T and S are minimal, $T \setminus S = \emptyset$. Hence, $T = S$ and $S \in \mathcal{AS}(P_1) \cap \mathcal{AS}(P_2)$. □

Example 4.5. In Example 4.4, $\mathcal{AS}(P_1 \otimes P_2) = \{\{p\}, \{q\}\}$, thereby $\mathcal{AS}(P_1 \otimes P_2) = \mathcal{AS}(P_1) \cap \mathcal{AS}(P_2)$.

4.3   Algebraic Properties

In this subsection, we provide properties of the operations $\oplus$ and $\otimes$.

Proposition 4.5 *For programs P_1, P_2, and P_3, the operations $\oplus$ and $\otimes$ have the following properties:*

(i) $P_1 \oplus P_2 = P_2 \oplus P_1$ and $P_1 \otimes P_2 = P_2 \otimes P_1$;
(ii) $(P_1 \oplus P_2) \oplus P_3 = P_1 \oplus (P_2 \oplus P_3)$ if P_1, P_2 and P_3 are NAF-free;
(iii) $(P_1 \otimes P_2) \otimes P_3 = P_1 \otimes (P_2 \otimes P_3)$.

Proof. The results of (i) and (ii) are straightforward. To see (iii), $\mathcal{AS}(P_1 \otimes P_2) = \mathcal{AS}(P_1) \cap \mathcal{AS}(P_2)$ holds by Theorem 4.4. Then, both $(P_1 \otimes P_2) \otimes P_3$ and $P_1 \otimes (P_2 \otimes P_3)$ consist of rules in $R(P_1, S) \cup R(P_2, S) \cup R(P_3, S)$ for every $S \in \mathcal{AS}(P_1) \cap \mathcal{AS}(P_2) \cap \mathcal{AS}(P_3)$. □

The operation $\oplus$ is not associative in general when programs contain NAF, but it holds the relation $\mathcal{AS}((P_1 \oplus P_2) \oplus P_3) = \mathcal{AS}(P_1 \oplus (P_2 \oplus P_3))$. $\oplus$ is also *idempotent*, $P \oplus P = P$ if NONMIN and DUPL are applied to $P \oplus P$ and P. $\otimes$ is not idempotent but the relation $\mathcal{AS}(P \otimes P) = \mathcal{AS}(P)$ holds. By the definition, $P \otimes P$ has the effect of extracting rules used for constructing answer sets of P.

By Proposition 4.5, when rigorous coordination are done among more than two agents, the order of computing coordination does not affect the result of final outcome. This is also the case for generous coordination when programs are NAF-free.

Two types of coordination are mixed among agents. In this case, the absorption laws and the distribution laws do not hold in general, i.e.,

$$P_1 \oplus (P_1 \otimes P_2) \neq P_1 \text{ and } P_1 \otimes (P_1 \oplus P_2) \neq P_1;$$
$$P_1 \oplus (P_2 \otimes P_3) \neq (P_1 \oplus P_2) \otimes (P_1 \oplus P_3) \text{ and}$$
$$P_1 \otimes (P_2 \oplus P_3) \neq (P_1 \otimes P_2) \oplus (P_1 \otimes P_3),$$

Note that programs are generally different, but the following relations hold by the definitions:

$$\mathcal{AS}(P_1 \oplus (P_1 \otimes P_2)) = \mathcal{AS}(P_1 \otimes (P_1 \oplus P_2)) = \mathcal{AS}(P_1),$$
$$\mathcal{AS}(P_1 \oplus (P_2 \otimes P_3)) = \mathcal{AS}((P_1 \oplus P_2) \otimes (P_1 \oplus P_3)),$$
$$\mathcal{AS}(P_1 \otimes (P_2 \oplus P_3)) = \mathcal{AS}((P_1 \otimes P_2) \oplus (P_1 \otimes P_3)).$$

5 Discussion

When a set of answer sets is given, it is not difficult to construct a program which has exactly those answer sets. Given a set of answer sets $\{S_1, \ldots, S_m\}$, first compute the disjunctive normal form: $S_1 \vee \cdots \vee S_m$, then convert it into the conjunctive normal form: $R_1 \wedge \cdots \wedge R_n$. The set of facts $\{R_1, \ldots, R_n\}$ then has the answer sets $\{S_1, \ldots, S_m\}$. This technique is also used for computing coordination between programs. For instance, suppose two programs:

$$
\begin{aligned}
P_1 : \quad & sweet \leftarrow strawberry, \\
& strawberry \leftarrow, \\
P_2 : \quad & red \leftarrow strawberry, \\
& strawberry \leftarrow,
\end{aligned}
$$

where $\mathcal{AS}(P_1) = \{\{sweet, strawberry\}\}$ and $\mathcal{AS}(P_2) = \{\{red, strawberry\}\}$.

To get generous coordination which has the answer sets $\mathcal{AS}(P_1) \cup \mathcal{AS}(P_2)$, taking the DNF of each answer set produces

$$(sweet \wedge strawberry) \vee (red \wedge strawberry).$$

Converting it into the CNF, it becomes

$$(sweet \vee red) \wedge strawberry.$$

As a result, the set of facts

$$
\begin{aligned}
Q : \quad & sweet \,; red \leftarrow, \\
& strawberry \leftarrow
\end{aligned}
$$

is a program which is generous coordination of P_1 and P_2. On the other hand, the program $P_1 \oplus P_2$ becomes

$$sweet\,;\,red \leftarrow strawberry,$$
$$strawberry \leftarrow,$$

after eliminating duplicated literals and redundant rules.

These two programs have the same meaning but have different syntax. Then, a question is which one is more preferable as a result of coordination? Our answer is $P_1 \oplus P_2$. The intuition behind this selection is that we would like to include as much information as possible from the original programs. Comparing Q with $P_1 \oplus P_2$, information of dependency between $sweet$ (or red) and $strawberry$ is lost in Q.[2] Generally speaking, if there exist different candidates for coordination between two programs, a program which is syntactically closer to the original ones is preferred. Then, a question is how to measure such "syntactical closeness" between programs? One solution we have in mind is, as illustrated above, using dependency relations between literals. We prefer a result of coordination which inherits dependency relations from the original programs as much as possible.

More precisely, suppose the *dependency graph* of a program P in which each node represents a ground literal and there is a directed edge from L_1 to L_2 (we say L_1 *depends on* L_2) iff there is a ground rule in P such that L_1 appears in the head and L_2 appears in the body of the rule. Let (L_1, L_2) be a pair of ground literals such that L_1 depends on L_2 in the dependency graph of a program. Let $\delta(P)$ be the collection of such pairs in P. For two programs P_1 and P_2, suppose that two different programs P_3 and P_4 are obtained as candidates for coordination. Then, we say that P_3 is *preferable* to P_4 if

$$\Delta(\delta(P_3), \delta(P_1) \cup \delta(P_2)) \subset \Delta(\delta(P_4), \delta(P_1) \cup \delta(P_2)),$$

where $\Delta(S, T)$ represents the symmetric difference between two sets S and T, i.e., $(S \setminus T) \cup (T \setminus S)$. Applying to the above example, $\delta(P_1) = \{(sweet, strawberry)\}$, $\delta(P_2) = \{(red, strawberry)\}$, $\delta(Q) = \emptyset$, and $\delta(P_1 \oplus P_2) = \{(sweet, strawberry), (red, strawberry)\}$. Then, $\Delta(\delta(P_1 \oplus P_2), \delta(P_1) \cup \delta(P_2)) \subset \Delta(\delta(Q), \delta(P_1) \cup \delta(P_2))$, so we conclude that $P_1 \oplus P_2$ is preferable to Q. Further elaboration would be considered to reflect syntactical closeness, but we do not pursue this issue further here.

Coordination supposes that different programs have equal standings and combines those programs while maximally keeping original information from them. The problem of combining logical theories has been studied by several researchers in different contexts. Baral *et al.* [1] introduce algorithms for combining logic programs by enforcing satisfaction of integrity constraints. For instance, suppose two programs:

$$P_1 : \quad p(x) \leftarrow not\,q(x),$$
$$q(b) \leftarrow r(b),$$
$$q(a) \leftarrow,$$
$$P_2 : \quad r(a) \leftarrow,$$

---

[2] Technically, the program Q is obtained by unfolding rules in $P_1 \oplus P_2$ [3, 11].

together with the integrity constraints:

$$IC: \quad \leftarrow p(a), r(a),$$
$$\leftarrow q(a), r(a).$$

They combine P_1 and P_2 and produce a new program which satisfies IC as follows:

$$P_3: \quad p(x) \leftarrow not\, q(x),\ x \neq a,$$
$$q(b) \leftarrow r(b),$$
$$q(a) \vee r(a) \leftarrow .$$

By contrast, $(P_1 \cup IC) \oplus P_2$ in our framework becomes[3]

$$p(x)\,;\, r(a) \leftarrow not\, q(x),$$
$$q(b)\,;\, r(a) \leftarrow r(b),$$
$$q(a)\,;\, r(a) \leftarrow,$$

after eliminating tautologies. Comparing two results, the program P_3 has two answer sets $\{p(b), q(a)\}$ and $\{p(b), r(a)\}$; by contrast, $(P_1 \cup IC) \oplus P_2$ has two answer sets: $\{p(b), q(a)\}$ and $\{r(a)\}$. Thus, the answer sets of P_3 do not coincide with those of the original programs. Indeed, they request that every answer set of a resulting program to be a subset of an answer set of $P_1 \cup P_2$. This is in contrast to our approach where we request the result of coordination to keep (part of) the answer sets of the original programs. Another important difference is that algorithms in [1] are not applicable to unstratified logic programs, while our method is applied to every extended disjunctive program.

The problem of *program composition* has been studied by several researchers (e.g., [4, 6, 12]). It combines different programs into one. The problem is then how to provide the meaning of a program in terms of those components. Brogi *et al.* [4] introduce three meta-level operations for composing normal logic programs: union, intersection, and restriction. The union simply puts two programs together, and the intersection combines two programs by merging pair of rules with unifiable heads. For instance, given two programs:

$$P_1: \quad likes(x, y) \leftarrow not\, bitter(y),$$
$$hates(x, y) \leftarrow sour(y);$$
$$P_2: \quad likes(Bob, y) \leftarrow sour(y),$$

the program $P_1 \cap P_2$ consists of the single rule:

$$likes(Bob, y) \leftarrow not\, bitter(y),\ sour(y).$$

The restriction allows one to filter out some rules from a program. They employ Fitting's 3-valued fixpoint semantics and show how one can compute the

---

[3] Here IC is included in P_1 as we handle integrity constraints as a part of a program.

semantics of the composed program in terms of the original programs. In the context of normal open logic programs, Verbaeten *et al.* [12] introduce a variant of the well-founded semantics, and identify conditions for two programs P_1 and P_2 to satisfy the equality $Mod(P_1 \cup P_2) = Mod(P_1) \cap Mod(P_2)$ where $Mod(P)$ is the set of models of P. Etalle and Teusink [6] consider three-valued completion semantics for program composition as the union of normal open programs. Comparing these three studies with ours, both program operations and underlying semantics are different from ours. Moreover, the goal of program composition is to compute the meaning of the whole program in terms of its subprograms; on the other hand, our goal is to construct a program whose answer sets are the union/intersection of the original programs.

Combination of propositional theories has been studied under the names of *merging* [8] or *arbitration* [9]. The goal of these research is to provide a new theory which is consistent and preserves as much information as possible from their sources. Merging is different from coordination presented in this paper. For instance, two theories $P_1 = \{ p \leftarrow \}$ and $P_2 = \{ q \leftarrow \}$ are merged into $P_3 = \{ p \leftarrow , \ q \leftarrow \}$. By contrast, generous coordination of P_1 and P_2 becomes $P_1 \oplus P_2 = \{ p \, ; q \leftarrow \}$. Thus, in contrast to generous coordination, merging does not preserve answer sets of the original programs. In merging different beliefs by different agents are mixed together as far as they are consistent, which makes it difficult to distinguish the original beliefs of one agent after merging. This implies the problem that original beliefs of one agent are hard to recover when one of the information sources turns out incorrect. For instance, suppose an agent has the program $P_4 = \{ p \, ; q \leftarrow \}$ and new information $P_1 = \{ p \leftarrow \}$ arrives. If P_4 and P_1 are merged, the result becomes $P_5 = \{ p \leftarrow \}$. Later, it turns out that the fact p in P_1 does not hold. At this stage, the agent cannot recover the original program P_4 from P_5. By contrast, if generous coordination is done, it becomes $P_4 \oplus P_1 = P_4$ and the original information P_4 is kept.

Ciampolini *et al.* [5] introduce a language for coordinating logic-based agents. They handle two types of coordination: collaboration and competition. Their goal is to solve these different types of queries using abduction, and not to construct a program as a result of coordination. Recently, Meyer *et al.* [10] introduce a logical framework for negotiating agents. They introduce two different modes of negotiation: concession and adaptation. They characterize such negotiation by rational postulates and provide methods for constructing outcomes. Those postulates are not generally applied to nonmonotonic theories, and in this sense coordination considered in this paper is beside the subject of those postulates.

Coordination introduced in this paper is naive in the sense that it just takes the union/intersection of different collections of answer sets. We can develop variants of coordination by introducing strategies that depend on situations. For instance, when there are more than two agents, it is considered to take the *majority* into account as in [8]. Given collections of answer sets by three agents, $\{ S_1, S_2, S_3 \}$, $\{ S_2, S_4 \}$, and $\{ S_1, S_5 \}$, such majority principle allows us to build $\{ S_1, S_2 \}$ as a result of coordination, whose member is supported by more than one agent. Priorities between agents are also considerable. In the above example, if the second agent is most reliable, we can have a choice to take S_4 into account. We can also consider finer grains of compositions such as having $S_1 \cup S_2$ or $S_1 \cap S_2$ as a result of coordination from two answer sets S_1 and S_2 (where $S_1 \cup S_2$ is assumed consistent). Detailed studies on such variants are left to further research.

6 Concluding Remarks

This paper has studied coordination between logical agents. Given multiple agents as logic programs, two different types of coordination have been introduced and their computational methods have been provided. We have verified that the proposed methods realize generous/rigorous coordination between logic programs. Our coordination framework provides a compositional semantics of multiple agents and serves as a declarative basis for accommodation in multi-agent systems. From the viewpoint of answer set programming, the process of computing coordination is considered as a program development under a specification that requests a program reflecting the meanings of two or more programs. This relates to the issue of program composition under the answer set semantics. This paper considered the answer set semantics but a similar framework would be developed under different semantics (though computational methods are likely to be different).

There is still room for improvement in computing generous/rigorous coordination. The operations $\oplus$ and $\otimes$ introduced in this paper require computation of answer sets of original programs, but it is much better if coordination can be constructed by purely syntactic manipulation without computing those answer sets. Further, the operation $\oplus$ produces a disjunctive program even when the original programs are non-disjunctive programs. The resulting disjunctive program is reduced to a non-disjunctive one if it is *head-cycle-free*, but this is not the case in general. At the moment, we do not have solutions for these problems. In future work, we will refine our framework and also investigate other types of coordination and collaboration as well as their characterization in terms of computational logic.

References

1. C. Baral, S. Kraus, and J. Minker. Combining multiple knowledge bases. *IEEE Transactions of Knowledge and Data Engineering* 3(2):208–220, 1991.
2. C. Baral and M. Gelfond. Logic programming and knowledge representation. *Journal of Logic Programming* 19/20:73–148, 1994.
3. S. Brass and J. Dix. Characterizations of the disjunctive stable semantics by partial evaluation. *Journal of Logic Programming* 32(3):207–228, 1997.
4. A. Brogi, S. Contiero, and F. Turini. Composing general logic programs. *Proc. 4th International Conference on Logic Programming and Nonmonotonic Reasoning, Lecture Notes in Artificial Intelligence* 1265, pp. 273–288, Springer, 1997.

5. A. Ciampolini, E. Lamma, P. Mello, F. Toni, and P. Torroni. Cooperation and competition in ALIAS: a logic framework for agents that negotiate. *Annals of Mathematics and Artificial Intelligence* 37(1/2), pp. 65–91, 2003.

6. S. Etalle and F. Teusink. A compositional semantics for normal open programs. *Proceedings of the Joint International Conference and Symposium on Logic Programming*, pp. 468–482, MIT Press, 1996.

7. M. Gelfond and V. Lifschitz. Classical negation in logic programs and disjunctive databases. *New Generation Computing* 9(3/4):365–385, 1991.

8. S. Konieczny and R. Pino-Pérez. On the logic of merging. *Proceedings of the 6th International Conference on Principles of Knowledge Representation and Reasoning*, pp. 488–498, Morgan Kaufmann, 1998.

9. P. Liberatore and M. Schaerf. Arbitration (or how to merge knowledge bases). *IEEE Transactions on Knowledge and Data Engineering* 10(1):76–90, 1998.

10. T. Meyer, N. Foo, R. Kwok, and D. Zhang. Logical foundation of negotiation: outcome, concession and adaptation. *Proceedings of the 19th National Conference on Artificial Intelligence*, pp. 293–298, MIT Press, 2004.

11. C. Sakama and H. Seki. Partial deduction in disjunctive logic programming. *Journal of Logic Programming* 32(3):229–245, 1997.

12. S. Verbaeten, M. Denecker, and D. De. Schreye. Compositionality of normal open logic programs. *Proceedings of the 1997 International Symposium on Logic Programming*, pp. 371–385, MIT Press, 1997.

A Computational Model for Conversation Policies for Agent Communication

Jamal Bentahar[1], Bernard Moulin[1], John-Jules Ch. Meyer[2],
and Brahim Chaib-draa[1]

[1] Laval University, Department of Computer Science and Software Engineering, Canada
jamal.bentahar.1@ulaval.ca
{bernard.moulin, brahim.chaib-draa}@ift.ulaval.ca
[2] University Utrecht, Department of Computer Science, The Netherlands
jj@cs.uu.nl

Abstract. In this paper we propose a formal specification of a persuasion protocol between autonomous agents using an approach based on social commitments and arguments. In order to be flexible, this protocol is defined as a combination of a set of conversation policies. These policies are formalized as a set of dialogue games. The protocol is specified using two types of dialogue games: entry dialogue game and chaining dialogue games. The protocol terminates when exit conditions are satisfied. Using a tableau method, we prove that this protocol always terminates. The paper addresses also the implementation issues of our protocol using logical programming and an agent-oriented platform.

1 Introduction

Research in agent communication has received much attention during the past years [9; 13; 14]. Agent communication protocols specify the rules of interaction governing a dialogue between autonomous agents in a multi-agent system. These protocols are patterns of behavior that restrict the range of allowed follow-up utterances at any stage during a dialogue. Unlike protocols used in distributed systems, agent communication protocols must take into account the fact that artificial agents are autonomous and proactive. These protocols must be flexible enough and must also be specified using expressive formalisms. Indeed, logic-based protocols seem an interesting way for specifying these protocols [3; 16].

On the one hand, conversation policies [18] and dialogue games [12; 21] aim at offering more flexible protocols [20]. This is achieved by combining different policies and games to construct complete and more complex protocols. In this paper we argue that conversation policies and dialogue games are related and can be used together to specify agent communication. Conversation policies are declarative specifications that govern communication between autonomous agents. We propose to formalize these policies as a set of dialogue games. Dialogue games are interactions between players, in which each player moves by performing utterances according to a pre-defined set of roles. Indeed, protocols specified using, for example, finite state machines are not flexible in the sense that agents must respect the whole protocol from the beginning to

J. Leite and P. Torroni (Eds.): CLIMA V, LNAI 3487, pp. 178–195, 2005.
© Springer-Verlag Berlin Heidelberg 2005

the end. Thus, we propose to specify these protocols by small conversation policies that can be logically put together using a combination of dialogue games.

On the other hand, in the last years, some research works addressed the importance of social commitments in the domain of agent communication [4; 5; 11; 20; 24; 27]. These works showed that social commitments are a powerful representation to model multi-agent interactions. Commitments provide a basis for a normative framework that makes it possible to model agents' communicative behaviors. This framework has the advantage of being expressive because all speech act types can be represented by commitments [11]. Commitment-based protocols enable the content of agent interactions to be represented and reasoned about [17; 28]. In opposition to the BDI mental approach, the commitment-approach stresses the importance of conventions and the public aspects of dialogue. A speaker is committed to a statement when he makes this statement or when he agreed upon this statement made by another participant. In fact, we do not speak here about the expression of a belief, but rather about a particular relationship between a participant and a statement. What is important in this approach is not that an agent agrees or disagrees upon a statement, but rather the fact that the agent *publicly expresses* agreement or disagreement, and acts accordingly.

In this paper we present a persuasion dialogue which is specified using conversation policies, dialogue games and a framework based on commitments. In addition, in order to allow agents to effectively reason on their communicative actions, our framework is also based on an argumentative approach. In our framework the agent's reasoning capabilities are linked to their ability to argue. In this paper *we consider conversation policies as units specified by dialogue games whose moves are expressed in terms of actions that agents apply to commitments and arguments.* Indeed, the paper presents three results: 1- A new formal language for specifying a persuasion dialogue as a combination of conversation policies. 2- A termination proof of the dialogue based on a tableau method [10]. 3- An implementation of the specification using an agent oriented and logical programming.

The paper is organized as follows. In Section 2, we introduce the main ideas of our approach based on commitments and arguments. In Section 3 we address the specification of our persuasion protocol based on this approach. We present the protocol form, the specification of each dialogue game and the protocol dynamics. We also present our termination proof. In Section 4 we describe the implementation of a prototype allowing us to illustrate how the specification of dialogue games is implemented. In Section 5 we compare our protocol to related work. Finally, in Section 6 we draw some conclusions and we identify some directions for future work.

2 Commitment and Argument Approach

2.1 Social Commitments

A social commitment *SC* is a public commitment made by an agent (the *debtor*), that some fact is true or that something will be done. This commitment is directed toward a set of agents (*creditors*) [8]. A commitment is an obligation in the sense that the debtor must respect and behave in accordance with this commitment. A representation of this notion as directed obligations using a deontic logic is proposed in [19]. Commitments are social in the sense that they are expressed publicly. Consequently, they are different from the private mental states like beliefs, desires and intentions. In order to model the dynamics of conversations, we interpret a speech act *SA* as an action performed on a commitment or on its content [4]. A speech act is an abstract act that an agent, the speaker, performs when producing an utterance *U* and addressing it to another agent, the addressee. In the dialogue games that we specify in Section 3, the actions that an agent can perform on a commitment are: $Act \in \{Create,$ *Withdraw*}. The actions that an agent can perform on a commitment content are: *Act-content* $\in \{Accept, Refuse, Challenge, Defend, Attack, Justify\}$. In our framework, a speech act is interpreted either as an action applied to a commitment when the speaker is the debtor, or as an action applied to its content when the speaker is the debtor or the creditor [4]. Formally, a speech act can be defined as follows:

Definition 1. $SA(Ag_1, Ag_2, U) =_{def} Act(Ag_1, SC(Ag_1, Ag_2, p))$
$$| Act\text{-}content(Ag_k, SC(Ag_i, Ag_j, p))$$

where $i, j \in \{1, 2\}$ and $(k = i$ or $k = j)$, *p is the commitment content.* The definiendum $SA(Ag_1, Ag_2, U)$ is defined by the definiens $Act(Ag_1, SC(Ag_1, Ag_2, p))$ as an action performed by the debtor Ag_1 on its commitment. The definiendum is defined by the definiens $Act\text{-}content(Ag_k, SC(Ag_i, Ag_j, p))$ as an action performed by an agent Ag_k (the debtor or the creditor) on the commitment content.

2.2 Argumentation and Social Commitments

An argumentation system essentially includes a logical language *L*, a definition of the argument concept, and a definition of the attack relation between arguments. Several definitions were also proposed to define arguments. In our model, we adopt the following definitions from [15]. Here Γ indicates a knowledge base with deductive closure. $\vdash$ Stands for classical inference and $\equiv$ for logical equivalence.

Definition 2. *An argument is a pair* (H, h) *where h is a formula of L and H a sub-set of Γ such that : i) H is consistent, ii) $H \vdash h$ and iii) H is minimal, so no subset of H satisfying both i and ii exists. H is called the support of the argument and h its conclusion. We use the notation*: $H = Support(Ag, h)$ *to indicate that agent Ag has a support H for h.*

Definition 3. *Let* (H_1, h_1), (H_2, h_2) *be two arguments.* (H_1, h_1) *attacks* (H_2, h_2) *iff h_1 $\equiv \neg h_2$.*

In fact, before committing to some fact *h* being true (i.e. before creating a commitment whose content is *h*), the speaker agent must use its argumentation system to build an argument (H, h). On the other side, the addressee agent must use its own argumentation system to select the answer it will give (i.e. to decide about the appropriate manipulation of the content of an existing commitment). For example, an agent Ag_1 accepts the commitment content *h* proposed by another agent if Ag_1 has an argument for *h*. If Ag_1 has an argument neither for *h*, nor for $\neg h$, then it challenges *h*.

In our framework, we distinguish between arguments that an agent has (private arguments) and arguments that this agent used in its conversation (public arguments). Thus, we use the notation: $S = Create\_Support(Ag_1, SC(Ag_1, Ag_2, p))$ to indicate the set of commitments S *created* by agent Ag_1 to support the content of $SC(Ag_1, Ag_2, p)$. This support relation is transitive i.e.:

$(SC(Ag_1, Ag_2, p_2) \in Create\_Support(Ag, SC(Ag_1, Ag_2, p_1))$

$\wedge SC(Ag_1, Ag_2, p_1) \in Create\_Support(Ag, SC(Ag_1, Ag_2, p_0)))$

$SC(Ag_1, Ag_2, p_2) \in Create\_Support(Ag, SC(Ag_1, Ag_2, p_0))$

Other details about our commitment and argument approach are described in [4]. Surely, an argumentation system is essential to help agents to act on commitments and on their contents. However, reasoning on other social attitudes should be taken into account in order to explain the agents' decisions. In our persuasion protocol we use the agents' trustworthiness to decide, in some cases, about the acceptance of arguments [6].

3 Conversation Policies for Persuasion Dialogue

3.1 Protocol Form

Our persuasion protocol is specified as a set of conversation policies. In order to be flexible, these policies are defined as initiative/reactive dialogue games. In accordance with our approach, the game moves are considered as actions that agents apply to commitments and to their contents. A dialogue game is specified as follows:

$$Action\_Ag_1 \xrightarrow{\quad Cond \quad} Action\_Ag_2$$

This specification indicates that if an agent Ag_1 performs the action $Action\_Ag_1$, and that the condition $Cond$ is satisfied, then the interlocutor Ag_2 will perform the action $Action\_Ag_2$. The condition $Cond$ is expressed in terms of the possibility of generating an argument from the agent's argumentation system and in terms of the interlocutor's trustworthiness. We use the notation: $p \triangle Arg\_Sys(Ag_1)$ to denote the fact that a propositional formula p can be generated from the argumentation system of Ag_1 denoted $Arg\_Sys(Ag_1)$. The formula $\neg(p \triangle Arg\_Sys(Ag_1))$ indicates the fact that p cannot be generated from Ag_1's argumentation system. A propositional formula p can be generated from an agent's argumentation system, if this agent can find an argument that supports p. To simplify the formalism, we use the notation $Act'(Ag_x, SC(Ag_i, Ag_j, p))$ to indicate the action that agent Ag_x performs on the commitment $SC(Ag_i, Ag_j, p)$ or on its content ($Act' \in \{Create, Withdraw, Accept, Challenge, Refuse\}$). For the actions related to the argumentation relations, we write $Act\text{-}Arg(Ag_x, [SC(Ag_n, Ag_m, q)], SC(Ag_i, Ag_j, p))$. This notation indicates that Ag_x defends (resp. attacks or justifies) the content of $SC(Ag_i, Ag_j, p)$ by the content of $SC(Ag_n, Ag_m, q)$ ($Act\text{-}Arg \in \{Defend, Attack, Justify\}$). The commitment that is written between square brackets [ ] is the support of the argument. In a general way, we use the notation $Act'(Ag_x, S)$ to indicate the action that Ag_x performs on the set of commitments S or on the contents of these commitments, and the notation $Act\text{-}Arg(Ag_x, [S], SC(Ag_i, Ag_j, p))$

to indicate the argumentation-related action that Ag_x performs on the content of $SC(Ag_i, Ag_j, p)$ using the contents of S as support. We also introduce the notation *Act-Arg(Ag_x, [S], S')* to indicate that Ag_x performs an argumentation-related action on the contents of a set of commitments S' using the contents of S as supports.

We distinguish two types of dialogue games: *entry game* and *chaining games*. The entry game allows the two agents to *open* the persuasion dialogue. The chaining games make it possible to construct the conversation. The protocol terminates when the exit conditions are satisfied (Figure 1).

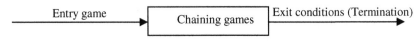

Fig. 1. The general form of the protocol

3.2 Dialogue Games Specification

A Entry Game

The conversational policy that describes the entry conditions in our persuasion protocol about a propositional formula p is described by the entry dialogue game as follows (*Specification 1*):

$$Create(Ag_1, SC(Ag_1, Ag_2, p)) \overset{a_1}{\underset{c_1}{\xleftarrow{\quad b_1 \quad}}}$$

$Accept(Ag_2, SC(Ag_1, Ag_2, p)) \longrightarrow Termination$

$Challenge(Ag_2, SC(Ag_1, Ag_2, p)) \longrightarrow Information$-$seeking\ Dialogue$

$Refuse(Ag_2, SC(Ag_1, Ag_2, p)) \longrightarrow Persuasion\ Dialogue$

where a_1, b_1 and c_1 are three conditions specified as follows:
$a_1 = p \triangle Arg\_Sys(Ag_2)$
$b_1 = \neg(p \triangle Arg\_Sys(Ag_2)) \wedge \neg(\neg p \triangle Arg\_Sys(Ag_1))$
$c_1 = \neg p \triangle Arg\_Sys(Ag_2)$

If Ag_2 has an argument for p then it accepts p (the content of $SC(Ag_1, Ag_2, p)$) and the conversation terminates as soon as it begins (Condition a_1). If Ag_2 has neither an argument for p nor for $\neg p$, then it challenges p and the two agents open an information-seeking dialogue (condition b_1). The persuasion dialogue starts when Ag_2 refuses p because it has an argument against p (condition c_1).

B Defense Game

Once the two agents opened a persuasion dialogue, the initiator must defend its point of view. Thus, it must play a defense game. Our protocol is specified in such a way that the *persuasion dynamics* starts by playing a defense game. We have (*Specification 2*):

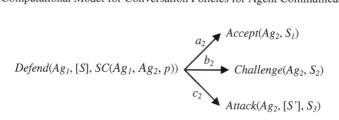

where:

$S = \{SC(Ag_1, Ag_2, p_i)/i=0,...,n\}$, p_i are propositional formulas.

$\hbar_{i=1}^{3} S_i = S$, $S_i \hbar S_j = \varnothing$, $i, j = 1,...,3 \& i \neq j$

By definition, $Defend(Ag_1, [S], SC(Ag_1, Ag_2, p))$ means that Ag_1 creates S in order to defend the content of $SC(Ag_1, Ag_2, p)$. Formally:

$Defend(Ag_1, [S], SC(Ag_1, Ag_2, p)) =_{def} (Create(Ag_1, S)$
$\wedge S = Create\_Support(Ag_1, SC(Ag_1, Ag_2, p)))$

We consider this definition as an *assertional* description of the *Defend* action.

This specification indicates that according to the three conditions (a_2, b_2 and c_2), Ag_2 can accept a subset S_1 of S, challenge a subset S_2 and attack a third subset S_3. Sets S_i and S_j are mutually disjoint because Ag_2 cannot, for example, both accept and challenge the same commitment content. *Accept*, *Challenge* and *Attack* a set of commitment contents are defined as follows:

$Accept(Ag_2, S_1) =_{def} (\forall i, SC(Ag_1, Ag_2, p_i) \in S_1 \quad Accept(Ag_2, SC(Ag_1, Ag_2, p_i)))$
$Challenge(Ag_2, S_2) =_{def} (\forall i, SC(Ag_1, Ag_2, p_i) \in S_2 \quad Challenge(Ag_2, SC(Ag_1, Ag_2, p_i)))$
$Attack(Ag_2, [S'], S_3) =_{def} \forall i, SC(Ag_1, Ag_2, p_i) \in S_3 \quad \exists S'_j \subseteq S':$
$$Attack(Ag_2, [S'_j], SC(Ag_1, Ag_2, p_i))$$

where: $\hbar_{j=0}^{m} S'_j = S'$. This indication means that any element of S' is used to attack one or more elements of S_3.

The conditions a_2, b_2 and c_2 are specified as follows:

$a_2 = \forall i, SC(Ag_1, Ag_2, p_i) \in S_1 \quad p_i \triangle Arg\_Sys(Ag_2)$
$b_2 = \forall i, SC(Ag_1, Ag_2, p_i) \in S_2 \quad (\neg(p_i \triangle Arg\_Sys(Ag_2)) \wedge \neg(\neg p_i \triangle Arg\_Sys(Ag_2)))$
$c_2 = \forall i, SC(Ag_1, Ag_2, p_i) \in S_3 \quad \exists S'_j \subseteq S', Content(S'_j) = Support(Ag_2, \neg p_i)$

where $Content(S'_j)$ indicates the set of contents of the commitments S'_j.

C Challenge Game

The challenge game is specified as follows (*Specification 3*):

$$Challenge(Ag_1, SC(Ag_2, Ag_1, p)) \xrightarrow{a_3} Justify(Ag_2, [S], SC(Ag_2, Ag_1, p))$$

where the condition a_3 is specified as follows:

$a_3 = (Content(S) = Support(Ag_2, p))$

In this game, the condition a_3 is always true. The reason is that in accordance with the commitment semantics, an agent must always be able to defend the commitment it created [5].

D Justification Game

For this game we distinguish two cases:

Case1. $SC(Ag_1, Ag_2, p) \notin S$

In this case, Ag_1 justifies the content of its commitment $SC(Ag_1, Ag_2, p)$ by creating a set of commitments S. As for the Defend action, Ag_2 can accept, challenge and/or attack a subset of S. The specification of this game is as follows (*Specification 4*):

$$Justify(Ag_1, [S], SC(Ag_1, Ag_2, p)) \quad \overset{a_4}{\underset{c_4}{\xleftarrow{b_4}}} \quad \begin{array}{l} Accept(Ag_2, S_1) \\ Challenge(Ag_2, S_2) \\ Attack(Ag_2, [S'], S_3) \end{array}$$

where:

$S = \{SC(Ag_1, Ag_2, p_i)/i=0,...,n\}$, p_i are propositional formulas.

$\hbar^{3}_{i=1} S_i = S$, $S_i \hbar S_j = \emptyset$, $i, j = 1,...,3 \ \& \ i \neq j$

$a_4 = a_2, b_4 = b_2, c_4 = c_2$

Case2. $\{SC(Ag_1, Ag_2, p)\} = S$

In this case, the justification game has the following specification (*Specification 5*):

$$Justify(Ag_1, [S], SC(Ag_1, Ag_2, p)) \quad \overset{a'_4}{\underset{b'_4}{<}} \quad \begin{array}{l} Accept(Ag_2, SC(Ag_1, Ag_2, p)) \\ Refuse(Ag_2, SC(Ag_1, Ag_2, p)) \end{array}$$

Ag_1 justifies the content of its commitment $SC(Ag_1, Ag_2, p)$ by itself (i.e. by p). This means that p is part of Ag_1's knowledge. Only two moves are possible for Ag_2: 1) *accept* the content of $SC(Ag_1, Ag_2, p)$ if Ag_1 is a trustworthy agent for Ag_2 (a'_4), 2) if not, *refuse* this content (b'_4). Ag_2 cannot attack this content because it does not have an argument against p. The reason is that Ag_1 plays a justification game because Ag_2 played a challenge game.

Like the definition of the *Defend* action, we define the *Justify* action as follows:

$Justify(Ag_1, [S], SC(Ag_1, Ag_2, p)) =_{def} (Create(Ag_1, S)$
$\qquad\qquad\qquad\qquad \wedge S = Create\_Support(Ag_1, SC(Ag_1, Ag_2, p)))$

This means that Ag_1 creates the set S of commitments to support the commitment $SC(Ag_1, Ag_2, p)$.

E Attack Game

The attack game is specified as follows (*Specification 6*):

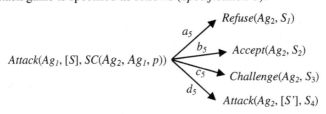

$$Attack(Ag_1, [S], SC(Ag_2, Ag_1, p)) \quad \overset{a_5}{\underset{d_5}{\overset{b_5}{\underset{c_5}{<}}}} \quad \begin{array}{l} Refuse(Ag_2, S_1) \\ Accept(Ag_2, S_2) \\ Challenge(Ag_2, S_3) \\ Attack(Ag_2, [S'], S_4) \end{array}$$

where:

$S=\{SC(Ag_1,Ag_2,p_i)/i=0,...,n\}$, p_i are propositional formulas.

$\hbar_{i=1}^4 S_i = S$, $Card(S_1)=1$, $S_i \hbar S_j = \varnothing$, $i,j = 1,...,4$ & $i \neq j$

Formally, the *Attack* action is defined as follows:

$Attack(Ag_1, [S], SC(Ag_2, Ag_1, p)) =_{def} (Create(Ag_1, SC(Ag_1, Ag_2, \neg p)) \wedge Create(Ag_1, S)$
$\wedge S = Create\_Support(Ag_1, SC(Ag_1, Ag_2, \neg p)))$

This means that by attacking $SC(Ag_2, Ag_1, p)$, Ag_1 creates the commitment $SC(Ag_1, Ag_2, \neg p)$ and the set S to support this commitment.

The conditions a_5, b_5, c_5 and d_5 are specified as follows:

$a_5 = \exists i: SC(Ag_2, Ag_1, p_i) \in Create\_Support(Ag_2, SC(Ag_2, Ag_1, \neg q))$
where $S_1 = \{SC(Ag_1, Ag_2, q)\}$
$b_5 = \forall i, SC(Ag_1, Ag_2, p_i) \in S_2 \qquad p_i \triangle Arg\_Sys(Ag_2)$
$c_5 = \forall i, SC(Ag_1, Ag_2, p_i) \in S_3 \qquad (\neg(p_i \triangle Arg\_Sys(Ag_2)) \wedge \neg(\neg p_i \triangle Arg\_Sys(Ag_2)))$
$d_5 = \forall i, SC(Ag_1, Ag_2, p_i) \in S_4 \qquad \exists S'_j \subseteq S': Content(S'_j) = Support(Ag_2, \neg p_i)$
$\wedge \nexists k: SC(Ag_2, Ag_1, p_k) \in Create\_Support(Ag_2, SC(Ag_2, Ag_1, \neg p_i))$

Ag_2 refuses Ag_1's argument if Ag_2 already attacked this argument. In other words, Ag_2 refuses Ag_1's argument if Ag_2 cannot attack this argument since it *already* attacked it, and it cannot accept it or challenge it since it has an argument against this argument. We have only one element in S_1 because we consider a refusal move as an exit condition. The acceptance and the challenge actions of this game are the same as the acceptance and the challenge actions of the defense game. Finally, Ag_2 attacks Ag_1's argument if Ag_2 has an argument against Ag_1's argument, and if Ag_2 did not attack Ag_1's argument before. In d_5, the universal quantifier means that Ag_2 attacks all Ag_1's arguments for which it has an against-argument. The reason is that Ag_2 must act on all commitments created by Ag_1. The temporal aspect (the past) of a_5 and d_5 is implicitly integrated in $Create\_Support(Ag_2, SC(Ag_2, Ag_1, \neg q))$ and $Create\_Support(Ag_2, SC(Ag_2, Ag_1, \neg p_i))$.

F Termination

The protocol terminates either by a final acceptance or by a refusal. There is a final acceptance when Ag_2 accepts the content of the initial commitment $SC(Ag_1, Ag_2, p)$ or when Ag_1 accepts the content of $SC(Ag_2, Ag_1, \neg p)$. Ag_2 accepts the content of $SC(Ag_1, Ag_2, p)$ iff it accepts all the supports of $SC(Ag_2, Ag_1, p)$. Formally:

$Accept(Ag_2, SC(Ag_1, Ag_2, p)) \Leftrightarrow$
$\qquad [\forall i, SC(Ag_1, Ag_2, p_i) \in Create\_Support(Ag_1, SC(Ag_1, Ag_2, p))$
$\qquad\qquad Accept(Ag_2, SC(Ag_2, Ag_2, p_i))]$

The acceptance of the supports of $SC(Ag_1, Ag_2, p)$ by Ag_2 does not mean that they are accepted directly after their creation by Ag_1, but it can be accepted after a number of challenge, justification and attack games. When Ag_2 accepts definitively, then it withdraws all commitments whose content was attacked by Ag_1. Formally:

$Accept(Ag_2, SC(Ag_1, Ag_2, p)) \qquad [\forall i, \forall S, Attack(Ag_1, [S], SC(Ag_2, Ag_1, p_i))$
$\qquad\qquad Withdraw(Ag_2, SC(Ag_2, Ag_1, p_i))]$

On the other hand, Ag_2 refuses the content of $SC(Ag_1, Ag_2, p)$ iff it refuses one of the supports of $SC(Ag_1, Ag_2, p)$. Formally:

$Refuse(Ag_2, SC(Ag_1, Ag_2, p)) \Leftrightarrow$

$$[\exists i: SC(Ag_1, Ag_2, p_i) \in Create\_Support(Ag_1, SC(Ag_1, Ag_2, p))$$
$$\wedge Refuse(Ag_2, SC(Ag_1, Ag_2, p_i))]$$

3.3 Protocol Dynamics

The persuasion dynamics is described by the chaining of a finite set of dialogue games: acceptance move, refusal move, defense, challenge, attack and justification games. These games can be combined in a sequential and parallel way (Figure 2).

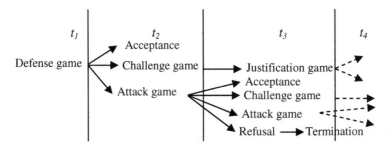

Fig. 2. The persuasion dialogue dynamics

After Ag_1's defense game at moment t_1, Ag_2 can, at moment t_2, accept a part of the arguments presented by Ag_1, challenge another part, and/or attack a third part. These games are played in parallel. At moment t_3, Ag_1 answers the challenge game by playing a justification game and answers the attack game by playing an acceptance move, a challenge game, another attack game, and/or a final refusal move. The persuasion dynamics continues until the exit conditions become satisfied (final acceptance or a refusal). From our specifications, it follows that our protocol plays the role of the dialectical proof theory of the argumentation system.

Indeed, our persuasion protocol can be described by the following BNF grammar:

Persuasion protocol : *Defense game ~ Dialogue games*
Dialogue games : (*Acceptance move*
        // (*Challenge game ~ Justification game ~ Dialogue games*)
        // (*Attack game ~ Dialogue games*))
        | *refusal move*

where: "~" is the sequencing symbol, "//" is the possible parallelization symbol. Two games *Game1* and *Game 2* are possibly parallel (i.e. *Game1* // *Game2*) iff an agent can play the two games in parallel or only one game (*Game1* or *Game2*).

3.4 Termination Proof

Theorem. The protocol dynamics always terminates.

Proof. To prove this theorem, we use a tableau method [10]. The idea is to formalize our specifications as tableau rules and then to prove the finiteness of the tableau. Tableau rules are written in such a way that premises appear above conclusions. Using a tableau method means that the specifications are conducted in a top-down fashion. For example, specification 2 (p 3.2) can be expressed by the following rules:

$$R1: \frac{Defend(Ag_1,[S],SC(p))}{Accept(Ag_2,S_1)} \quad R2: \frac{Defend(Ag_1,[S],SC(p))}{Challenge(Ag_2,S_1)}$$

$$R3: \frac{Defend(Ag_1,[S],SC(p))}{Attack(Ag_2,[S'],S_1)}$$

We denote the formulas of our specifications by σ, and we define E the set of σ. We define an ordering $\hbar$ on E and we prove that $\hbar$ has no infinite ascending chains. Intuitively, this relation is to hold between σ_1 and σ_2 if it is possible that σ_1 is an ancestor of σ_2 in some tableau. Before defining this ordering, we introduce some notations: $Act^*(Ag, [S], S')$ with $Act^* \in \{Act', Act\text{-}Arg\}$ is a formula. We notice that formulas in which there is no support $[S]$, can be written as follows: $Act^*(Ag, [\phi], S')$. $\sigma[S] \rightarrow_R \sigma[S']$ indicates that the tableau rule R has the formula $\sigma[S]$ as premise and the formula $\sigma[S']$ as conclusion, with $\sigma[S] = Act^*(Ag, [S], S')$. The size $|S|$ is the number of commitments in S.

Definition 4. *Let $\sigma[S_i]$ be a formula and E the set of $\sigma[S_i]$. The ordering $\hbar$ on E is defined as follows. We have $\sigma[S_0] \, \hbar \, \sigma[S_1]$ if:*
$|S_1| < |S_0|$ *or*
For all rules Ri such that $\sigma[S_0] \rightarrow_{R0} \sigma[S_1] \rightarrow_{R1} \sigma[S_2]... \rightarrow_{Rn} \sigma[S_n]$ we have $|S_n| = 0$.

Intuitively, in order to prove that a tableau system is finite, we need to prove the following:
1- if $\sigma[S_0] \rightarrow_R \sigma[S_1]$ then $\sigma[S_0] \, \hbar \, \sigma[S_1]$.
2- $\hbar$ has no infinite ascending chains (i.e. the inverse of $\hbar$ is well-founded).

Property 1 reflects the fact that applying tableau rules results in shorter formulas, and property 2 means that this process has a limit. The proof of 1 proceeds by a case analysis on R. Most cases are straightforward. We consider here the case of $R3$. For this rule we have two cases. If $|S_1| < |S_0|$, then $\sigma[S_0] \, \hbar \, \sigma[S_1]$. If $|S_1| \geq |S_0|$, the rules corresponding to the attack specification can be applied. The three first rules are straightforward since $S_2 = \phi$. For the last rule, we have the same situation that $R3$. Suppose that there is no path in the tableau $\sigma[S_0] \rightarrow_{R0} \sigma[S_1] \rightarrow_{R1} \sigma[S_2]... \rightarrow_{Rn} \sigma[S_n]$ such that $|S_n| = 0$. This means that i) the number of arguments that agents have is infinite or that ii) one or several arguments are used several times. However, situation i is not possible because the agents' knowledge bases are finite sets, and situation ii is not allowed in our protocol.

Because the definition of $\hbar$ is based on the size of formulas and since $|S_0| \in N$ ($<$ ∞) and $<$ is well-founded in N, it follows that there is no infinite ascending chains of the form $\sigma[S_0] \, \hbar \, \sigma[S_1]...$

4 Implementation

In this section we describe the implementation of the different dialogue games using the $Jack^{TM}$ platform [25]. We chose this language for three main reasons:
1- It is an agent-oriented language offering a framework for multi-agent system development. This framework can support different agent models.
2- It is built on top of and fully integrated with the Java programming language. It includes all components of Java and it offers specific extensions to implement agents' behaviors.
3- It supports logical variables and cursors. These features are particularly helpful when querying the state of an agent's beliefs. Their semantics is mid-way between logic programming languages with the addition of type checking Java style and embedded SQL.

4.1 General Architecture

Our system consists of two types of agents: conversational agents and trust model agents. These agents are implemented as $Jack^{TM}$ agents, i.e. they inherit from the basic class $Jack^{TM}$ Agent. Conversational agents are agents that take part in the persuasion dialogue. Trust model agents are agents that can inform an agent about the trustworthiness of another agent.

According to the specification of the justification game, an agent Ag_2 can play an acceptance or a refusal move according to whether it considers that its interlocutor Ag_1 is trustworthy or not. If Ag_1 is unknown for Ag_2, Ag_2 can ask agents that it considers trustworthy for it to offer a trustworthiness assessment of Ag_1. From the received answers, Ag_2 can build a *trustworthiness graph* and measure the trustworthiness of Ag_1. This trustworthiness model is described in detail in [6].

4.2 Implementation of the Dialogue Games

To be able to take part in a persuasion dialogue, agents must possess knowledge bases that contain arguments. In our system, these knowledge bases are implemented as $Jack^{TM}$ beliefsets. *Beliefsets* are used to maintain an agent's beliefs about the world. These beliefs are represented in a first order logic and tuple-based relational model. The logical consistency of the beliefs contained in a *beliefset* is automatically maintained. The advantage of using *beliefsets* over normal Java data structures is that *beliefsets* have been specifically designed to work within the agent-oriented paradigm.

Our knowledge bases (KBs) contain two types of information: arguments and beliefs. Arguments have the form ([*Support*], *Conclusion*), where *Support* is a set of propositional formulas and *Conclusion* is a propositional formula. Beliefs have the form ([*Belief*], *Belief*) i.e. *Support* and *Conclusion* are identical. The meaning of the propositional formulas (i.e. the ontology) is recorded in a *beliefset* whose access is shared between the two agents.

To open a dialogue game, an agent uses its argumentation system. The argumentation system allows this agent to seek in its knowledge base an argument for a given conclusion or for its negation (*"against argument"*). For example, before creating a commitment $SC(Ag_1, Ag_2, p)$, agent Ag_1 must find an argument for p. This enables us to respect the commitment semantics by making sure that agents can always defend the content of their commitments.

Agent communication is done by sending and receiving messages. These messages are *events* that extend the basic *Jack^{TM} event*: *MessageEvent* class. *MessageEvents* represent events that are used to communicate with other agents. Whenever an agent needs to send a message to another agent, this information is packaged and sent as a *MessageEvent*. A *MessageEvent* can be sent using the primitive: *Send(Destination, Message)*. In our protocol, *Message* represents the action that an agent applies to a commitment or to its content, for example: *Create(Ag_1, SC(Ag_1, Ag_2, p))*, etc.

Our dialogue games are implemented as a set of *events* (*MessageEvents*) and *plans*. A plan describes a sequence of actions that an agent can perform when an event occurs. Whenever an event is posted and an agent chooses a task to handle it, the first thing the agent does is to try to find a plan to handle the event. Plans are methods describing what an agent should do when a given event occurs.

Each dialogue game corresponds to an event and a plan. These games are not implemented within the agents' program, but as event classes and plan classes that are external to agents. Thus, each conversational agent can instantiate these classes. An agent Ag_1 starts a dialogue game by generating an event and by sending it to its interlocutor Ag_2. Ag_2 executes the plan corresponding to the received event and answers by generating another event and by sending it to Ag_1. Consequently, the two agents can communicate by using the same protocol since they can instantiate the same classes representing the events and the plans. For example, the event *Event_Attack_Commitment* and the plan *Plan_ev_Attack_commitment* implement the defense game. The architecture of our conversational agents is illustrated in Figure 3.

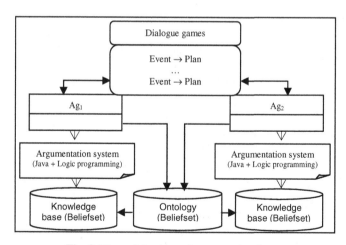

Fig. 3. The architecture of conversational agents

To start the entry game, an agent (initiator) chooses a goal that it tries to achieve. This goal is to persuade its interlocutor that a given propositional formula is true. For this reason, we use a particular event: *BDI Event (Belief-Desire-Intention)*. BDI events model goal-directed behavior in agents, rather than plan-directed behavior. What is important is the desired outcome, not the method chosen to achieve it. This type of events allows an agent to pursue long term goals.

4.3. Example

In this section we present a simple example dialogue that illustrates some notions presented in this paper.

Ag_1: Newspapers can publish information I (p).

Ag_2: I don't agree with you.

Ag_1: They can publish information I because it is not private (q), and any public information can be published (r).

Ag_2: Why is information I public?

Ag_1: Because it concerns a Minister (s), and information concerning a Minister are public (t).

Ag_2: Information concerning a Minister is not necessarily public, because information I is about the health of Minister (u), and information about the health remains private (v).

Ag_1: I accept your argument.

This example was also studied in [2] in a context of strategical considerations for argumentative agents. The letters on the left of the utterances are the propositional formulas that represent the propositional contents. Agent Ag_1's KB contains: ([q, r], p), ([s, t], q) and ([u], u). Agent Ag_2's KB contains: ([$\neg t$], $\neg p$), ([u, v], $\neg t$), ([u], u) and ([v], v). The combination of the dialogue games that allows us to describe the persuasion dialogue dynamics is as follows:

Ag_1 creates $SC(Ag_1, Ag_2, p)$ to achieve the goal of persuading Ag_2 that p is true. Ag_1 can create this commitment because it has an argument for p. Ag_2 refuses $SC(Ag_1, Ag_2, p)$ because it has an argument against p. Thus, the entry game is played and the persuasion dialogue is opened. Ag_1 defends $SC(Ag_1, Ag_2, p)$ by creating $SC(Ag_1, Ag_2, q)$ and $SC(Ag_1, Ag_2, r)$. Ag_2 accepts $SC(Ag_1, Ag_2, r)$ because it has an argument for r and challenges $SC(Ag_1, Ag_2, q)$ because it has no argument for q or against q. Ag_1

plays a justification game to justify $SC(Ag_1, Ag_2, q)$ by creating $SC(Ag_1, Ag_2, s)$ and $SC(Ag_1, Ag_2, t)$. Ag_2 accepts the content of $SC(Ag_1, Ag_2, s)$ and attacks the content of $SC(Ag_1, Ag_2, t)$ by creating $SC(Ag_2, Ag_1, u)$ and $SC(Ag_2, Ag_1, v)$. Finally, Ag_1 plays acceptance moves because it has an argument for u and it does not have arguments against v and the dialogue terminates. Indeed, before accepting v, Ag_1 challenges it and Ag_2 defends it by itself (i.e. ([$SC(Ag_2, Ag_1, v)$, $SC(Ag_2, Ag_1, v)$]])). Then, Ag_1 accepts this argument because it considers Ag_2 trustworthy. This notion of agent trust and its role as an acceptance criteria of arguments are detailed in [6]. Ag_1 updates its KB by removing the attacked argument and including the new argument. Figure 4 illustrates the screen shot of this example generated by our prototype. In this figure commitments are described only by their contents and the identifiers of the two agents are the two first arguments of the exchanged communicative actions. The contents are specified using a predicate language that the two agents share (the ontology).

Fig. 4. The example screen shot

5 Related Work

In this section, we compare our protocol with some proposals that have been put forward in two domains: dialogue modeling and commitment based protocols.

1- *Dialogue modeling*. In [1] and [22] Amgoud, Parsons and their colleagues studied argumentation-based dialogues. They proposed a set of atomic protocols which can be combined. These protocols are described as a set of dialogue moves using Walton and Krabbe's classification and formal dialectics. In these protocols, agents can argue about the truth of propositions. Agents can communicate both propositional statements and arguments about these statements. These protocols have the advantage of taking into account the capacity of agents to reason as well as their attitudes (confident, careful, etc.). In addition, Prakken [23] proposed a framework for protocols for dynamic disputes, i.e., disputes in which the available information can change during the conversation. This framework is based on a logic of defeasible argumentation and is formulated for dialectical proof theories. Soundness and completeness of these protocols have also been studied. In the same direction, Brewka [7] developed a formal model for argumentation processes that combines nonmonotonic logic with protocols for dispute. Brewka pays more attention to the speech act aspects of disputes and he formalizes dispositional protocols in situation calculus. Such a logical formalization of protocols allows him to define protocols in which the legality of a move can be disputed. Semantically, Amgoud, Parsons, Prakken and Brewkas' approaches use a defeasible logic. Therefore, it is difficult, if not impossible, to formally verify the proposed protocols.

There are many differences between our protocol and the protocols proposed in the domain of dialogue modeling: 1. Our protocol uses not only an argumentative approach, but also a public one. Locutions are formalized not as agents' private attitudes (beliefs, intentions, etc.), but as social commitments. In opposition of private mental attitudes, social commitments can be verified. 2. Our protocol is based on a combination of dialogue games instead of simple dialogue moves. Using our dialogue game specifications enables us to specify the entry and the exit conditions more clearly. In addition, computationally speaking, dialogue games provide a good balance between large protocols that are very rigid and atomic protocols that are very detailed. 3. From a theoretical point of view, Amgoud, Parsons, Prakken and Brewkas' protocols use moves from formal dialectics, whereas our protocol uses actions that agents apply on commitments. These actions capture the speech acts that agents perform when conversing (see Definition 1). The advantage of using these actions is that they enable us to better represent the persuasion dynamics considering that their semantics is defined in an unambiguous way in a temporal and dynamic logic [5]. Specifying protocols in this logic allows us to formally verify these protocols using model checking techniques. 4. Amgoud, Parsons and Prakkens' protocols use only three moves: assertion, acceptance and challenge, whereas our protocol uses not only creation, acceptance, refusal and challenge actions, but also attack and defense actions in an explicit way. These argumentation relations allow us to directly illustrate the concept of dispute in this type of protocols. 5. Amgoud, Parsons, Prakken and Brewka use an acceptance criterion directly related to the argumentation system, whereas we use an acceptance criteria for conversational agents (supports of arguments and trustworthiness). This makes it possible to decrease the computational complexity of the protocol for agent communication.

2- *Commitment-based protocols*. Yolum and Singh [28] developed an approach for specifying protocols in which actions' content is captured through agents' commitments. They provide operations and reasoning rules to capture the evolution of commitments. In a similar way, Fornara and Colombetti [17] proposed a method to define interaction protocols. This method is based on the specification of an interaction diagram (ID) specifying which actions can be performed under given conditions. These approaches allow them to represent the interaction dynamics through the allowed operations. Our protocol is comparable to these protocols because it is also based on commitments. However, it is different in the following respects. The choice of the various operations is explicitly dealt with in our protocol by using argumentation and trustworthiness. In commitment-based protocols, there is no indication about the combination of different protocols. However, this notion is essential in our protocol using dialogue games. Unlike commitment-based protocols, our protocol plays the role of the dialectical proof theory of an argumentation system. This enables us to represent different dialogue types as studied in the philosophy of language. Finally, we provide a termination proof of our protocol whereas this property is not yet studied in classical commitment-based protocols.

6   Conclusion and Future Work

The contribution of this paper is the proposition of a logical language for specifying persuasion protocols between agents using an approach based on commitments and arguments. This language has the advantage of expressing the public elements and the reasoning process that allows agents to choose an action among several possible actions. Because our protocol is defined as a set of conversation policies, this protocol has the characteristic to be more flexible than the traditional protocols such as those used in FIPA-ACL. This flexibility results from the fact that these policies can be combined to produce complete and more complex protocols. We formalized these conversation policies as a set of dialogue games, and we described the persuasion dynamics by the combination of five dialogue games. Another contribution of this paper is the tableau-based termination proof of the protocol. We also described the implementation of this protocol. Finally, we presented an example to illustrate the persuasion dynamics by the combination of different dialogue games.

   As an extension of this work, we intend to specify other protocols according to Walton and Krabbe's classification [27] using the same framework. Another interesting direction for future work is verifying these protocols using model checking techniques. The method we are investigating is an automata theoretic approach based on a tableau method [10]. This method can be used to verify the temporal and dynamic aspects of our protocol. Finally, we intend to extend our implementation using ideas from the agent programming language 3APL, namely the concept of cognitive agents. An important characteristic of this language that is interesting for us is its dynamic logic semantics [26] because our protocol is based on an action theory and the semantics of our approach is also based on dynamic logic [5].

Acknowledgements. We'd like to deeply thank the three anonymous reviewers for their valuable comments and suggestions. We'd also like to thank Rance Cleaveland and Girish Bhat for their interesting explanations on the tableau method.

References

1. Amgoud, L., Maudet, N., and Parsons, S. Modelling dialogues using argumentation. In Proc. of 4th Int. Conf. on Multi Agent Systems (2000) 31-38.
2. Amgoud, L., and Maudet, N. Strategical considerations for argumentative agents. In Proc. of 10th Int. Workshop on Non-Monotonic Reasoning (2002) 409-417.
3. Baldoni, M., Baroglio, C., Martelli, A., Patti, V., Schifanella, C. Verifying protocol conformance for logic-based communicating agents. In Proc. of 5th Int. Workshop on Computational Logic in Multi-Agent Systems (2004) 82-97.
4. Bentahar, J., Moulin, B., and Chaib-draa, B. Commitment and argument network: a new formalism for agent communication. In [13] (2004) 146-165.
5. Bentahar, J., Moulin, B., Meyer, J-J. Ch., and Chaib-draa, B. A logical model for commitment and argument network for agent communication (extended abstract). In 3rd Int. J. Conf. on Autonomous Agents and Multi-Agent Systems AAMAS (2004) 792-799.
6. Bentahar, J., Moulin, B., and Chaib-draa, B. Specifying and implementing a persuasion dialogue game using commitment and argument network. In I. Rahwan, P. Moraitis and C. Reed (Eds.), Argumentation in Multi-Agent Systems, LNAI 3366, Springer, (2005). (in press).
7. Brewka, G. Dynamic argument systems: A formal model of argumentation processes based on situation calculus. Journal of Logic and Computation, 11(2) (2001) 257-282.
8. Castelfranchi, C. Commitments: from individual intentions to groups and organizations. In Proc. of Int. Conf. on Multi Agent Systems (1995) 41-48.
9. Chaib-draa, B., and Dignum, F. Trends in agent communication languages. In Computational Intelligence, (18)2 (2002) 89-101.
10. Cleaveland, R. Tableau-based model checking in the propositional mu-calculus. In Acta Informatica, 27(8) (1990) 725-747.
11. Colombetti, M. A commitment-based approach to agent speech acts and conversations. In Proc. of Int. Autonomous Agent Workshop on Conversational Policies (2000) 21-29.
12. Dastani, M., Hulstijn, J., and der Torre, L.V. Negotiation protocols and dialogue games. In Proc. of Belgium/Dutch AI Conference (2000) 13-20.
13. Dignum, F. (Ed.). Advances in Agent Communication. Int. Workshop on Agent Communication Languages. LNAI 2922, Springer, (2004).
14. Dignum, F., and Greaves, M. (Eds.). Issues in agent communication. LNAI 1916, Springer (2000).
15. Elvang-Goransson, M., Fox, J., and Krause, P. Dialectic reasoning with inconsistent information. In Proc. of 9th Conf. on Uncertainty in Artificial Intelligence (1993) 114-121.
16. Endriss, U., Maudet, N., Sadri, F., and Toni, F. Logic_based agent communication protocols. In [13] (2004) 91-107.
17. Fornara, N. and Colombetti, M. Protocol specification using a commitment based ACL. In [13] (2004) 108-127.
18. Greaves, M., Holmback, H., and Bradshaw, J. What is a conversation policy? In [14] (2000) 118-131.
19. Herrestad, H. and Krogh, C. Obligations directed from bearers to counterparties. In Proc. of 5th Int. Conf. on Artificial Intelligence and Law (1995) 210-218.

20. Maudet, N., and Chaib-draa, B. Commitment-based and dialogue-game based protocols, new trends in agent communication languages. In Knowledge Engineering Review, 17(2), Cambridge University Press (2002) 157-179.
21. McBurney, P., and Parsons, S. Games that agents play: A formal framework for dialogues between autonomous agents. In Journal of Logic, Language, and Information, 11(3) (2002) 1-22.
22. Parsons, S., Wooldridge, M., and Amgoud, L. On the outcomes of formal inter-agent dialogues. In Proc. of 2nd Int. J. Conf. on Autonomous Agents and Multi-Agent Systems (2003) 616-623.
23. Prakken, H. Relating protocols for dynamic dispute with logics for defeasible argumentation. In Synthese (127) (2001) 187-219.
24. Singh, M.P. A social semantics for agent communication language. In [14] (2000) 31-45.
25. The Agent Oriented Software Group. Jack 4.1. 2004. www.agent-software.com/
26. van Riemsdijk, M.B., de Boer, F.S., and Meyer, J-J. Ch. Dynamic logic for plan revision in intelligent agents. In Proc. of 5th Int. Workshop on Computational Logic in Multi-Agent Systems (2004) 196-211.
27. Walton, D.N., and Krabbe, E.C.W. Commitment in dialogue: basic concepts of interpersonal reasoning. State University of New York Press, NY (1995).
28. Yolum, P. and Singh, M.P. Flexible protocol specification and execution: applying event calculus planning using commitments. In Proc. of 1st Int. J. Conf. on Autonomous Agents and Multi-Agent Systems (2002) 527-534.

Verifying Protocol Conformance for Logic-Based Communicating Agents*

Matteo Baldoni, Cristina Baroglio, Alberto Martelli,
Viviana Patti, and Claudio Schifanella

Dipartimento di Informatica — Università degli Studi di Torino,
C.so Svizzera, 185 — I-10149 Torino (Italy)
{baldoni,baroglio,mrt,patti,schi}@di.unito.it

Abstract. Communication plays a fundamental role in multi-agents systems. One of the main issues in the design of agent interaction protocols is the verification that a given protocol implementation is "conformant" w.r.t. the abstract specification of it. In this work we tackle those aspects of the conformance verification issue, that regard the dependence/independence of conformance from the agent private state in the case of logic, individual agents, set in a multi-agent framework. We do this by working on a specific agent programming language, DyLOG, and by focussing on interaction protocol specifications described by AUML sequence diagrams. By showing how AUML sequence diagrams can be translated into regular grammars and, then, by interpreting the problem of conformance as a problem of language inclusion, we describe a method for automatically verifying a form of "structural" conformance; such a process is shown to be decidable and an upper bound of its complexity is given. We also give a set of properties that describes the influence of the agent private information on the conformance of its communication policies to protocol specifications.

1 Introduction

Multi-agent systems (MASs) often comprise heterogeneous components, different in the way they represent knowledge about the world and about other agents, as well as in the mechanisms used for reasoning about it. Notwithstanding heterogeneity, agents must cooperate, to execute a common task or compete for shared resources; interoperation is, normally, ruled by a set of shared *interaction protocols*. The design and implementation of interaction protocols are crucial steps in the development of a MAS. Following the development process, described in [21], for interaction protocol engineering, two different kinds of test are to be executed. The first consists in verifying the consistency of an *abstract protocol*

---

* This research is partially supported by MIUR Cofin 2003 "Logic-based development and verification of multi-agent systems (MASSiVE)" national project and by the European Commission and by the Swiss Federal Office for Education and Science within the 6th Framework Programme project REWERSE number 506779.

J. Leite and P. Torroni (Eds.): CLIMA V, LNAI 3487, pp. 196–212, 2005.
© Springer-Verlag Berlin Heidelberg 2005

definition w.r.t. the original *requirements*, derived from the analysis phase, that it should embody. This verification, often called *validation test*, is typically done by means of model-checking techniques. A different problem is the one that we face in this work, which amounts to verify if a given *implementation*, which is an agent interaction policy, respects a given *abstract protocol definition*. This problem is known as *conformance testing*. Moreover, since the specific implementations[1] normally use the agent's private information (the agent's "state"), e.g. for deciding which utterances to articulate, one further question that arises is: to which extent does the agent internal state influence the conformance of an implementation to a given protocol specification? Indeed, depending on the result of tests on the agent's *internal state*, different executions could occur, only part of them being correct w.r.t. the specifications. Merely in the case in which the "structure" of the conversation policy is such that it is bound to produce correct conversations, conformance is not influenced at all by the agent's internal state (we will discuss this issue in Section 3).

In this work we tackle the problem of conformance verification for two specific languages: we use Agent UML (AUML for short, first specified in [27]) as the interaction protocol specification language and DyLOG [3, 5] as the conversation policy implementation language. In the literature one can, actually, find many formal techniques for protocol specification. A non-exhaustive list includes finite state automata [6, 24], petri nets [23, 11], temporal logic [15, 16] and UML-based languages. All these proposals are currently being studied and no definitive standard emerged yet. The reason for choosing AUML is that, despite its yet incomplete formal semantics (a proposal for a semantics based on petri nets can be found in [10]), this language bears some relevant advantages: it is based on the widespread and well-known UML standard, it is intuitive and easy to learn, there are graphical editors for the generation of code, and AUML sequence diagrams have been adopted by FIPA to represent agent interaction protocols. On the other hand, DyLOG is a logic language for programming agents, based on reasoning about actions and change in a modal framework, that allows the inclusion of a set of conversation policies, in the specification of an agent. The language refers to a mentalistic approach, where speech acts are represented as atomic actions with preconditions and effects on the executor's mental state. It allows the specification of *individual agents*, situated in a multi-agent context, each having a personal view of the world. The use of a declarative language is helpful because it allows the proof of properties of the *specific implementation* in a straightforward way. In particular, a language that explicitly represents and uses the agent internal state, is useful for proving to which extent certain properties depend on the agent mental state or on the semantics of the speech acts. For instance, in our work we perform hypothetical reasoning about the effects of conversations on the agent mental state, in order to find conversation plans which are proved to respect the implemented protocols, achieving at the same time some desired goal. The DyLOG language is briefly introduced in Section 2, for a thorough description of it see [5].

---

[1] In Java, in a logic language, etc.

Our goal for this work is, then, to study under which conditions a DyLOG implementation can be declared as being conformant to an AUML specification. To this aim, we will introduce different levels of abstraction w.r.t. the agent mental state by defining three degrees of conformance (*agent conformance, agent strong conformance,* and *protocol conformance*). We will describe their relations and, by interpreting the problem of conformance verification as a problem of inclusion of a context-free language (CFL) into a regular language, we will show a method for automatically verifying the strongest degree of conformance; an upper bound to its complexity is also given. When this kind of conformance holds, the implemented policy respects the specification whatever the rational effects of the speech acts are, whatever the agent mental state is.

As a last observation about AUML, some authors, who work on protocol validation, criticize the choice of this formalism because its lack of a formal semantics makes it difficult to validate the designed protocols w.r.t. the original specifications. They also criticize the choice of a mentalistic approach (á la FIPA) because at the level of protocol validation this approach has shown relevant flaws. The dissatisfaction to the mentalistic approach is mostly due to the difficulty of verifying that an agent acts according to a commonly agreed semantics, because it is not possible to have access to the agents' private mental state [30], a problem known as *semantics verification*. Some authors have proposed a *social approach* to agent communication [29], where communicative actions affect the "social state" of the system, rather than the internal states of the agents. The social state records the social facts, like the *permissions* and the *commitments* of the agents, which are created and modified along the interaction. The social approach overcomes the semantics verification problem by exploiting a set of established commitments between the agents, that are stored as part of the MAS social state. In this framework it is possible to formally prove the correctness of public interaction protocols with respect to the specifications outcoming from the analysis phases; such proof can be obtained, for instance, by means of model checking techniques [22, 25, 28, 30, 18, 7] (but not only, e.g., [9]).

Nevertheless, AUML is being used, more and more often, in MAS development because it is intuitive for designers that have a background in UML and in the object-oriented approach, and for this reason it has an appeal for the deployment of agent systems in the industry world. Moreover, when developing the single agents, besides verifying that the agent respects the social commitments, it is important to study properties of their implementations and, in particular, to understand if and to which extent such properties depend on the agent's internal state (in the case of communication, on the semantics of the speech acts).

2   Specification of Communication in DyLOG

DyLOG [5] is a high-level logic programming language for modeling rational agents, based upon a modal logic of actions and mental attitudes where modalities are used for representing actions as well as beliefs that are in the agent's mental state. It accounts both for atomic and complex actions, or procedures, for specifying the agent behavior. A DyLOG agent can be provided with a *communication kit* that specifies its communicative behavior [3], defined in terms of interaction protocols, i.e. conversation policies that build on FIPA-like speech acts. The communication theory is a homogeneous component of the general agent theory; in particular, both the conversational policies, that guide the agent's communicative behavior, and the other policies, defining the agent's behavior, are represented by procedure definitions (represented by *axiom schema*). DyLOG agents can reason about their communicative behavior answering to queries like "given a protocol and a set of desiderata, is there a conversation, that respects the protocol, which also satisfies the desired conditions on the final mental state?".

2.1   The DyLOG Language in Brief

In DyLOG atomic actions are either world actions, affecting the world, or mental actions, i.e. sensing or communicative actions which only affect the agent beliefs. The set of atomic actions consists of the set $\mathcal{A}$ of the world actions, the set $\mathcal{C}$ of communicative acts, and the set $\mathcal{S}$ of sensing actions. For each atomic action a and agent ag_i we introduce the modalities $[a^{ag_i}]$ and $\langle a^{ag_i} \rangle$. $[a^{ag_i}]\alpha$ means that α holds after every execution of action a by agent ag_i; $\langle a^{ag_i} \rangle \alpha$ means that there is a possible execution of a (by ag_i) after which α holds. We use the modality $\square$ to denote *laws*, i.e. formulas that hold always (after every action sequence). Our formalization of complex actions draws considerably from dynamic logic for the definition of action operators like sequence, test and non-deterministic choice. However, differently than [26], we refer to a *Prolog-like* paradigm: procedures are defined by means of (possibly recursive) Prolog-like clauses. For each procedure p, the language contains also the universal and existential modalities $[p]$ and $\langle p \rangle$. The mental state of an agent is described by a consistent set of *belief formulas* (we call it *belief state*). We use the modal operator $\mathcal{B}^{ag_i}$ to model the beliefs of agent ag_i. The modality $\mathcal{M}^{ag_i}$ is defined as the dual of $\mathcal{B}^{ag_i}$ and means that ag_i considers φ possible. A mental state contains what ag_i (dis)believes about the world and about the other agents (nested beliefs are needed for reasoning on how other agents beliefs can be affected by communicative actions). Formally it is a complete and consistent set of rank 1 and 2 belief fluents, where a *belief fluent* F is a belief formula $\mathcal{B}^{ag_i}L$ or its negation. L denotes a *belief argument*, i.e. a *fluent literal* l (f or $\neg f$) or a belief fluent of rank 1 ($\mathcal{B}l$ or $\neg \mathcal{B}l$).

All the modalities of the language are normal; $\square$ is reflexive and transitive, its interaction with action modalities is ruled by $\square\varphi \supset [a^{ag_i}]\varphi$. The epistemic modality $\mathcal{B}^{ag_i}$ is serial, transitive and euclidean. A non-monotonic solution to the persistency problem is given, which consists in maximizing assumptions about fluents after the execution of action sequences, based on an abductive framework.

2.2   The Communication Kit in Brief

The *behavior* of an agent ag_i is specified by a domain description, which includes, besides a specification of the agent *belief state*: (i) *action and precondition laws* for describing the atomic world actions in terms of their preconditions and their affects on the agent's mental state, (ii) *sensing axioms* for describing atomic sensing actions, (iii) *procedure axioms* for describing complex behaviors, (iv) a *communication kit* that describes the agent communicative behavior by means of further axioms and laws of the kind mentioned above. In fact a *communication kit* consists of (i') a set of action and preconditions laws modeling a predefined set of primitive speech acts the agent can perform/recognize (ii') a set of sensing axioms for defining special sensing actions for getting new information by external communications (iii') a set of procedure axioms for specifying interaction protocols, which can be seen as a library of conversation policies the agent can follow when engaging a conversations with others.

Interaction Protocols are represented as procedures that build upon individual speech acts and specify conversation policies for guiding the agent communicative behavior. They are expressed by *axiom schema* of form:

$$\langle p_0 \rangle \varphi \subset \langle p_1; p_2; \ldots; p_m \rangle \varphi \tag{1}$$

p_0 is a procedure name and the p_i's ($i = 1, \ldots, m$) are either procedure names, atomic actions, or test actions (actions of the form $Fs?$, where Fs is a belief fluent conjunction); intuitively, the ? operator corresponds to checking the value of a fluent conjunction in the current state while the ; is the sequencing operator of dynamic logic. Since each agent has a subjective perception of the communication with other agents, given a protocol specification we expect to have as many procedural representations as the possible roles in the conversation.

The axiom schema used to define procedures have the form of *inclusion axioms*, which were the subject of previous work [4, 2], in which the class of multimodal logics, characterized by axioms that have the general form $\langle s_1 \rangle \ldots \langle s_m \rangle \varphi \subset \langle t_1 \rangle \ldots \langle t_n \rangle \varphi$, where $\langle s_i \rangle$ and $\langle t_i \rangle$ are modal operators, has been analyzed. These axioms have interesting computational properties because they can be considered as *rewriting rules*. In [14] this kind of axioms is used for defining *grammar logics* and some relations between formal languages and such logics are analyzed.

A speech act c in $\mathcal{C}$ has form speech_act(ag_s, ag_r, l), where ag_s (sender) and ag_r (receiver) are agents and l is the message content. Effects and preconditions are modeled by a set of effect and precondition laws. In particular, *effects* on ag_i's belief state of an action c are expressed by *action laws* of form:

$$\Box(\mathcal{B}^{ag_i} L_1 \wedge \ldots \wedge \mathcal{B}^{ag_i} L_n \supset [c^{ag_i}] \mathcal{B}^{ag_i} L_0) \tag{2}$$

$$\Box(\mathcal{M}^{ag_i} L_1 \wedge \ldots \wedge \mathcal{M}^{ag_i} L_n \supset [c^{ag_i}] \mathcal{M}^{ag_i} L_0) \tag{3}$$

Law (2) means that, after any sequence of actions ($\Box$), if the set of fluent literals $L_1 \wedge \ldots \wedge L_n$ (representing the preconditions of the action c) is believed by ag_i then, after the execution of c, L_0 (the effect of c) is also believed by ag_i. Notice that our representation of speech acts models only the dynamics of the mental state of the agent the we are implementing. Executing a speech act may cause an agent to have new beliefs (in its mental state), that are assumptions on what the others believe but the agent cannot be sure that the others actually have those beliefs. Law (3) states that when the preconditions of c are unknown to ag_i, after the execution of c, it will consider unknown also its effects. *Precondition laws* specify mental conditions that make an action in $\mathcal{C}$ executable in a state. They have form:

$$\Box(\mathcal{B}^{ag_i} L_1 \land \ldots \land \mathcal{B}^{ag_i} L_n \supset \langle c^{ag_i} \rangle \top) \tag{4}$$

ag_i can execute c when its precondition fluents are in ag_i's belief state.

Get message actions are formalized as sensing actions, i.e. knowledge producing actions whose outcome cannot be predicted before the execution. In fact, from the perspective of the individual agent, expecting a message corresponds to query for an external input, thus it is natural to think of it as a special case of sensing. A get_message action is defined by the *inclusion axiom schema*:

$$[\text{get\_message}(ag_i, ag_j, l)]\varphi \equiv [\bigcup_{\text{speech\_act} \in \mathcal{C}_{\text{get\_message}}} \text{speech\_act}(ag_j, ag_i, l)]\varphi \tag{5}$$

Intuitively, $\mathcal{C}_{\text{get\_message}}$ is a finite set of speech acts, which are all the possible communications that ag_i could expect from ag_j in the context of a given conversation. Hence, the information that can be obtained is calculated by looking at the effects of the speech acts in $\mathcal{C}_{\text{get\_message}}$ on ag_i's mental state.

As a finale comment, in the operational interpretation of the language, (1) is handled as a rewriting rule. From a declarative semantics point of view, the rule is an axiom schema of the logic, hence its form. Intuitively, the set of formulas of kind (2), (3) and (4) define the theory, while those of form (1) and (5) define the characteristics of the multi-modal logic in which the formulas are interpreted.

Example 1. The following procedure axioms represent an implementation of the protocol in Fig. 1 as the conversation policy that the customer agent (*cus*) must use for interacting with the service provider (*sp*). Axioms implementing the query subprotocol follow. Since the AUML protocol contains two roles, the customer and the provider, the implementation must contain two views as well but for brevity we report only the view of the customer (get_cinema_ticket$_C$). Similarly for the subprotocol for querying information: yes_no_query$_Q$ implements the role of the querier and yes_no_query$_I$ the one of the responder[2].

(a) $\langle \text{get\_cinema\_ticket}_C(cus, sp, movie)\rangle\varphi \subset$
    $\langle \text{yes\_no\_query}_Q(cus, sp, available(movie));$
    $\mathcal{B}^{cus} available(movie)?; \text{get\_info}(cus, sp, cinema(c));$
    $\text{yes\_no\_query}_I(cus, sp, pay\_by(credit\_card));$
    $\mathcal{B}^{cus} pay\_by(credit\_card)?; \text{inform}(cus, sp, cc\_number);$
    $\text{get\_info}(cus, sp, booked(movie))\rangle\varphi$

(b) $\langle \text{get\_cinema\_ticket}_C(cus, sp, movie)\rangle\varphi \subset$
    $\langle \text{yes\_no\_query}_Q(cus, sp, available(movie)); \mathcal{B}^{cus} available(movie)? ;$
    $\text{get\_info}(cus, sp, cinema(c));$
    $\text{yes\_no\_query}_I(cus, sp, pay\_by(credit\_card)); \neg\mathcal{B}^{cus} pay\_by(credit\_card)?\rangle\varphi$

---

[2] The subscripts next to the protocols names are a writing convention for representing the role that the agent plays: Q stands for *querier*, I stands for *informer*, C for *customer*.

(c) $\langle \text{get\_cinema\_ticket}_C(cus, sp, movie) \rangle \varphi \subset$
$\quad \langle \text{yes\_no\_query}_Q(cus, sp, available(movie)); \neg \mathcal{B}^{cus} available(movie)? \rangle \varphi$

(d) $[\text{get\_info}(cus, sp, Fluent)]\varphi \equiv [\text{inform}(sp, cus, Fluent)]\varphi$

Protocol $\text{get\_cinema\_ticket}_C$ works as follows: agent cus begins the interaction. After checking if the requested movie is available by the yes_no_query_Q protocol, it waits for an information (get_info) from the provider (sp) about which cinema shows it. Then, the provider asks for a payment by credit card by using the yes_no_query_I protocol. If the answer if positive cus communicates the credit card number and the confirmation of the ticket booking is returned to it, otherwise clause (b) is selected, ending the conversation. Clause (c) tackles the case in which the movie is not available; clause (d) describes get_info, which is a get_message action. In the following the get_answer and get_start definitions are instances of axiom schema (5): the right hand side of get_answer represents all the possible answers expected by cus from sp about $Fluent$, during a conversation ruled by yes_no_query_Q.

(e) $\langle \text{yes\_no\_query}_Q(cus, sp, Fluent) \rangle \varphi \subset$
$\quad \langle \text{queryIf}(cus, sp, Fluent); \text{get\_answer}(cus, sp, Fluent) \rangle \varphi$

(f) $[\text{get\_answer}(cus, sp, Fluent)]\varphi \equiv [\text{inform}(sp, cus, Fluent) \cup$
$\quad \text{inform}(sp, cus, \neg Fluent) \cup \text{refuseInform}(sp, cus, Fluent)]\varphi$

(g) $\langle \text{yes\_no\_query}_I(cus, sp, Fluent) \rangle \varphi \subset \langle \text{get\_start}(cus, sp, Fluent);$
$\quad \mathcal{B}^{cus} Fluent?; \text{inform}(cus, sp, Fluent) \rangle \varphi$

(h) $\langle \text{yes\_no\_query}_I(cus, sp, Fluent) \rangle \varphi \subset \langle \text{get\_start}(cus, sp, Fluent);$
$\quad \mathcal{B}^{cus} \neg Fluent?; \text{inform}(cus, sp, \neg Fluent) \rangle \varphi$

(i) $\langle \text{yes\_no\_query}_I(cus, sp, Fluent) \rangle \varphi \subset \langle \text{get\_start}(cus, sp, Fluent);$
$\quad \mathcal{U}^{cus} Fluent?; \text{refuseInform}(cus, sp, Fluent) \rangle \varphi$

(j) $[\text{get\_start}(cus, sp, Fluent)]\varphi \equiv [\text{queryIf}(sp, cus, Fluent)]\varphi$

Given a set Π_C of action and precondition laws defining the agent ag_i's primitive speech acts, a set Π_{Sget} of axioms for the reception of messages, and a set Π_{CP}, of procedure axioms for specifying conversation protocols, we denote by CKit^{ag_i} the *communication kit* of an agent ag_i, that is the triple $(\Pi_C, \Pi_{CP}, \Pi_{Sget})$.

A *domain description* (DD) for agent ag_i, is a triple $(\Pi, \text{CKit}^{ag_i}, S_0)$, where CKit^{ag_i} is ag_i's communication kit, S_0 is the initial set of ag_i's belief fluents, and Π is a tuple (Π_A, Π_S, Π_P), where Π_A is the set of ag_i's world action and precondition laws, Π_S is a set of axioms for ag_i's sensing actions, Π_P a set of axioms that define the complex non-communicative behavior of the agent.

From a DD with the specifications of the interaction protocols and of the relevant speech acts, a *planning* activity can be triggered by *existential queries* of form $\langle p_1 \rangle \langle p_2 \rangle \ldots \langle p_m \rangle Fs$, where each p_k $(k = 1, \ldots, m)$ may be an atomic or complex action (a primitive speech act or an interaction protocol), executed by our agent, or an external[3] speech act, that belongs to CKit^{ag_i}. In [3] we

---

[3] By the word *external* we denote a speech act in which our agent plays the role of the receiver.

presented a goal-directed proof procedure for the language based on negation as failure (NAF) which allows query of form $\langle p_1 \rangle \langle p_2 \rangle \ldots \langle p_m \rangle Fs$ to be proved from a given domain description and returns as answer an action sequence. A query of the form $\langle p_1; p_2; \ldots; p_n \rangle Fs$, where p_i, $1 \leq i \leq n$ $(n \geq 0)$, is either a world action, or a sensing action, or a procedure name, or a test, succeeds if it is possible to execute $p_1, p_2, \ldots, p_n$ (in the order) starting from the current state, in such a way that Fs holds at the resulting state. In general, we will need to establish if a goal holds at a given state. Hence, we will write:

$$a_1, \ldots, a_m \vdash \langle p_1; p_2; \ldots; p_n \rangle Fs \text{ with answer (w.a.) } \sigma$$

to mean that the query $\langle p_1; p_2; \ldots; p_n \rangle Fs$, i.e. $\langle p_1 \rangle \langle p_2 \rangle \ldots \langle p_n \rangle Fs$, can be proved from the DD $(\Pi, \mathsf{CKit}^{ag_i}, S_0)$ at the state $a_1, \ldots, a_m$ with answer σ, where σ is an action sequence $a_1, \ldots, a_m, \ldots a_{m+k}$ which represents the state resulting by executing $p_1, \ldots, p_n$ in the current state $a_1, \ldots, a_m$. ε denotes the initial state.

3   Protocol Conformance

In AUML a protocol is specified by means of sequence diagrams [27], which model the interactions among the participants as message exchanges, arranged in time sequences. The vertical (time) dimension specifies when a message is sent (expected), the horizontal dimension expresses the participants and their roles. The current proposal [17], enriches the set of possible operators of the language; particularly interesting is the possibility of representing loops, calls to subprotocols, and exit points. Generally speaking, given a protocol implementation it would be nice to have a means for automatically verifying its *conformance* to the desired AUML specification. The technique that we follow consists in turning this problem into a problem of formal language inclusion. To this aim, given a sequence diagram, we define a formal grammar which generates a language, that is the set of all the conversations allowed by the diagram itself. The algorithm used to this purpose is described in Section 3.1. On the other hand, given a DyLOG implementation of a protocol, we define a language that is compared to the previously obtained one: if the language obtained from the implementation is included in the one obtained from the sequence diagram we conclude that a type of conformance holds. We, actually, define three degrees of conformance (*agent conformance*, *agent strong conformance*, and *protocol conformance*), characterized by different levels of abstraction from the agent private mental state, which correspond to different ways of extracting the language from the implementation. These definitions allow us to define which parts of a protocol implementation must fit the specification and to describe in a modular way how the implementation can be enriched with respect to the specification, without compromising the conformance. Such an enrichment is important when using logic agents, that support sophisticated forms of reasoning.

3.1   Turning an AUML Sequence Diagram into a Linear Grammar

In the following we show how it is possible to translate an AUML sequence diagram, as defined in [17], into a grammar. Using the notation of [20], a grammar G is a tuple (V, T, P, S), where V is a set of variables, T a set of terminals, P of production rules, and S is the start symbol. By $L(G)$ we will denote the language generated by grammar G, i.e. the set of sentences in T^* that are generated starting from S, by applying rules in P.

On the side of sequence diagrams we focus on the operators used to specify FIPA protocols, which are: message, alternative, loop, exit, and reference to a sub-protocol (see top of Fig. 1).

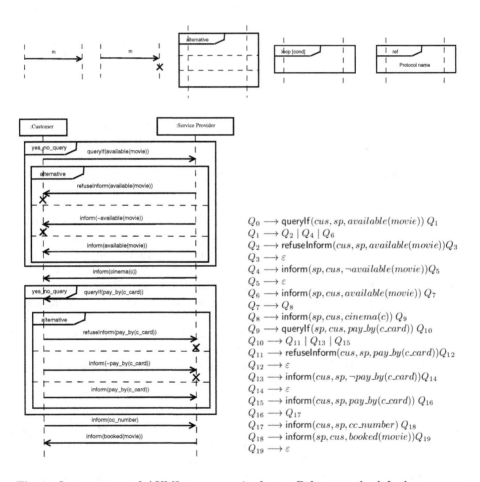

$$Q_0 \longrightarrow \mathsf{queryIf}(cus, sp, available(movie))\ Q_1$$
$$Q_1 \longrightarrow Q_2 \mid Q_4 \mid Q_6$$
$$Q_2 \longrightarrow \mathsf{refuseInform}(cus, sp, available(movie))Q_3$$
$$Q_3 \longrightarrow \varepsilon$$
$$Q_4 \longrightarrow \mathsf{inform}(sp, cus, \neg available(movie))Q_5$$
$$Q_5 \longrightarrow \varepsilon$$
$$Q_6 \longrightarrow \mathsf{inform}(sp, cus, available(movie))\ Q_7$$
$$Q_7 \longrightarrow Q_8$$
$$Q_8 \longrightarrow \mathsf{inform}(sp, cus, cinema(c))\ Q_9$$
$$Q_9 \longrightarrow \mathsf{queryIf}(sp, cus, pay\_by(c\_card))\ Q_{10}$$
$$Q_{10} \longrightarrow Q_{11} \mid Q_{13} \mid Q_{15}$$
$$Q_{11} \longrightarrow \mathsf{refuseInform}(cus, sp, pay\_by(c\_card))Q_{12}$$
$$Q_{12} \longrightarrow \varepsilon$$
$$Q_{13} \longrightarrow \mathsf{inform}(cus, sp, \neg pay\_by(c\_card))Q_{14}$$
$$Q_{14} \longrightarrow \varepsilon$$
$$Q_{15} \longrightarrow \mathsf{inform}(cus, sp, pay\_by(c\_card))\ Q_{16}$$
$$Q_{16} \longrightarrow Q_{17}$$
$$Q_{17} \longrightarrow \mathsf{inform}(cus, sp, cc\_number)\ Q_{18}$$
$$Q_{18} \longrightarrow \mathsf{inform}(sp, cus, booked(movie))Q_{19}$$
$$Q_{19} \longrightarrow \varepsilon$$

Fig. 1. On top a set of AUML operators is shown. Below, on the left the sequence diagram, representing the interaction protocol between a cinema booking service and a customer, is reported with its corresponding production rules

Algorithm 1 (Generating $G_{p_{AUML}}$) The grammar construction is done in the following way. We will denote by the variable *last* the most recently created variable. Initially T and P are empty. Define the start symbol as Q_0, initialize *last* to Q_0 and $V := \{Q_0\}$, then, we apply the translation rules described by cases hereafter, according to the sequence given by the AUML diagram:

- given a *message arrow*, labeled by m, create a new variable Q_{new}, $V := V \cup \{Q_{new}\}$, $T := T \cup \{m\}$, $P := P \cup \{last \longrightarrow mQ_{new}\}$, finally, set $last := Q_{new}$;
- given an *exit operator*, add to P a production $last \longrightarrow \epsilon$, $last :=\perp$ (undefined).
- given an *alternative* operator with n branches, apply to each branch the grammar construction algorithm, so obtaining a grammar $G'_i = (V'_i, T'_i, P'_i, S'_i)$ with $last'_i$ being the last variable used inside that branch. Let us assume that $V'_1 \cap \ldots \cap V'_n \cap V = \emptyset$ (it is sufficient to rename all variables in the V''_i's), then create a new variable Q_{new}. $V := V \cup V'_1 \cup \ldots \cup V'_n \cup \{Q_{new}\}$, $T := T \cup T'_1 \cup \ldots T'_n$, $P := P \cup P'_1 \cup \{last \longrightarrow S'_1\} \cup \ldots \cup P'_n \cup \{last \longrightarrow S'_n\}$, moreover $P := P \cup \{last'_i \longrightarrow Q_{new}\}$ for each $i \in [1,n]$ such that $last'_i \neq \perp$, and finally we set *last* to Q_{new};
- given a *loop*, apply the grammar construction algorithm to its body, so obtaining a grammar $G' = (V', T', P', S')$ with a value for $last'$. Let us assume that $V' \cap V = \emptyset$, then create Q_{new}, $V := V \cup V' \cup \{Q_{new}\}$, $T := T \cup T'$, $P := P \cup P' \cup \{Q_{last} \longrightarrow S', last \longrightarrow Q_{new}\}$ if $last' \neq \perp$ then $P := P \cup \{last' \longrightarrow last\}$, and $last := Q_{new}$;
- given a *subprotocol reference*, apply the grammar construction algorithm to the called subprotocol, so obtaining a grammar $G' = (V', T', P', S')$ with a value for $last'$. Let us assume that $V' \cap V = \emptyset$, then increment *new*, create Q_{new}, $V := V \cup V' \cup \{Q_{new}\}$, $T := T \cup T'$, $P := P \cup P' \cup \{Q_{last} \longrightarrow S'\}$, if $last' \neq \perp$ then $P := P \cup \{last' \longrightarrow Q_{new}\}$, and $last := Q_{new}$;

Proposition 1. *The set of conversations allowed by an AUML sequence diagram is a regular language.*

Proof. The Algorithm 1 produces a *right linear grammars* (variables appear only at the rigth end of productions), so the generated language is *regular* [20]. □

By this translation we give to the set of conversations encoded by the sequence diagram a structural semantics (although no semantics is given to the single speech acts). The grammar could, then, be translated into a finite-state automaton, another formal tool often used to represent interaction protocols, as mentioned in the introduction. As a last observation, the produced grammar may contain redundancies and could be simplified using standard algorithms [20].

Consider, as an example, the sequence diagram in Fig. 1: it represents an interaction protocol with two agent roles (Customer, *cus*, and Service Provider, *sp*): the protocol rules the interaction of a cinema booking service with each of its customers, and will be used as a running example along the paper. Suppose, now, to have a DyLOG implementation of the specification given by the diagram. The technique that we apply for verifying if it is conformant (w.r.t. the definitions given in Section 3) to the specifications, intuitively works as follows. If we can prove that all the conversations produced by the implementation belong to the language generated by the grammar into which the specification can be translated (see Fig. 1), then the implementation can be considered conformant.

3.2   Three Degrees of Conformance

We have shown how AUML sequence diagrams can be translated into regular grammars. By interpreting the problem of conformance as a problem of formal language inclusion, we will describe a method for automatically verifying the strongest of the three degrees of conformance (protocol conformance). The verification of protocol conformance is shown to be decidable and an upper bound of its complexity is given.

Definition 1 (Agent conformance). *Let $D = (\Pi, \mathsf{CKit}^{ag_i}, S_0)$ be a domain description, $\mathsf{p}_{dylog} \in \mathsf{CKit}^{ag_i}$ be an implementation of the interaction protocol p_{AUML} defined by means of an AUML sequence diagram. Moreover, let us define the set*

$$\Sigma(S_0) = \{\sigma \mid (\Pi, \mathsf{CKit}^{ag_i}, S_0) \vdash \langle \mathsf{p}_{dylog} \rangle \top \ w.\ a.\ \sigma\}$$

We say that the agent described by means of D is conformant to the sequence diagram p_{AUML} if and only if

$$\Sigma(S_0) \subseteq L(G_{\mathsf{p}_{AUML}}) \tag{6}$$

In other words, the agent conformance property holds if we can prove that every conversation, that is an instance of the protocol implemented in our language (an execution trace of p_{dylog}), is a legal conversation according to the grammar that represents the AUML sequence diagram p_{AUML}; that is to say that conversation is also generated by the grammar $G_{\mathsf{p}_{AUML}}$.

The agent conformance depends on the initial state S_0. Different initial states can determine different possible conversations (execution traces). One can define a notion of agent conformance that is independent from the initial state.

Definition 2 (Agent strong conformance). *Let $D = (\Pi, \mathsf{CKit}^{ag_i}, S_0)$ be a domain description, let $\mathsf{p}_{dylog} \in \mathsf{CKit}^{ag_i}$ be an implementation of the interaction protocol p_{AUML} defined by means of an AUML sequence diagram. Moreover, let us define the set*

$$\Sigma = \bigcup_S \Sigma(S)$$

where S ranges over all possible initial states. We say that the agent described by means of D is strongly conformant to the sequence diagram p_{AUML} if and only if

$$\Sigma \subseteq L(G_{\mathsf{p}_{AUML}}) \tag{7}$$

The agent strong conformance property holds if we can prove that every conversation for every possible initial state is a legal conversation. It is obvious by definition that agent strong conformance (7) implies agent conformance (6).

Agent strong conformance, differently than agent conformance, does not depend on the initial state but it still depends on the set of speech acts defined in CKit^{ag_i}. In fact, an execution trace σ is built taking into account test actions and the semantics of the speech acts (defined by executability precondition laws and action laws).

A stronger notion of conformance should require that a DyLOG implementation is conformant to an AUML sequence diagram *independently from the semantics of the speech acts*. In other world, we would like to prove a sort of "structural" conformance of the implemented protocol w.r.t. the corresponding AUML sequence diagram. In order to do this, we define a formal grammar from the DyLOG implementation of a conversation protocol. In this process, the particular form of axiom, namely *inclusion axiom*, used to define protocol clauses in a DyLOG implementation, comes to help us.

Algorithm 2 (Generating $G_{p_{dylog}}$) Given a domain description $(\Pi, \mathsf{CKit}^{ag_i}, S_0)$ and a conversation protocol $p_{dylog} \in \mathsf{CKit}^{ag_i} = (\Pi_C, \Pi_{CP}, \Pi_{Sget})$, we define the grammar $G_{p_{dylog}} = (T, V, P, S)$, where:

- T is the set of all terms that define the speech acts in Π_C;
- V is the set of all the terms that define a conversation protocol or a get message action in Π_{CP} or Π_{Sget};
- P is the set of production rules of the form $p_0 \longrightarrow p_1 p_2 \ldots p_n$ where $\langle p_0 \rangle \varphi \subset \langle p_1; p_2; \ldots; p_n \rangle \varphi$ is an axiom that defines either a conversation protocol (that belongs to Π_{CP}) or a get message action (that belongs to Π_{Sget}). Note that, in the latter case, we add a production rule for each alternative speech act in $C_{\mathsf{get\_message}}$ see (5), moreover, the test actions $Fs?$ are not reported in the production rules;
- the start symbol S is the symbol p_{dylog}.

Let us define $L(G_{p_{dylog}})$ as the language generated by means of the grammar $G_{p_{dylog}}$.

Proposition 2. *Given a domain description $(\Pi, \mathsf{CKit}^{ag_i}, S_0)$ and a conversation protocol $p_{dylog} \in \mathsf{CKit}^{ag_i} = (\Pi_C, \Pi_{CP}, \Pi_{Sget})$, $L(G_{p_{dylog}})$ is a context-free language.*

Proof. The proposition follows from the fact that $G_{p_{dylog}}$ is a context-free grammar (CFG).

Intuitively, the language $L(G_{p_{dylog}})$ represents all the possible sequences of speech acts (conversations) allowed by the DyLOG protocol p_{dylog} independently from the evolution of the mental state of the agent. For example, clause (a) of get_cinema_ticket$_C$ presented in the previous section is represented as follows:

get_cinema_ticket$_C(cus, sp, movie) \longrightarrow$
 yes_no_query$_Q(cus, sp, available(movie))$
 get_info$(cus, sp, cinema(c))$
 yes_no_query$_I(cus, sp, pay\_by(credit\_card))$
 $inform(cus, sp, cc\_number)$
 get_info$(cus, sp, booked(movie))$

Definition 3 (Protocol conformance). *Given a domain description $DD =$ $(\Pi, \mathsf{CKit}^{ag_i}, S_0)$, let $\mathsf{p}_{dylog} \in \mathsf{CKit}^{ag_i}$ be an implementation of the interaction protocol p_{AUML} defined by means of an AUML sequence diagram. We say that p_{dylog} is conformant to the sequence diagram p_{AUML} if and only if*

$$L(G_{\mathsf{p}_{dylog}}) \subseteq L(G_{\mathsf{p}_{AUML}}) \tag{8}$$

We then interpret the verification of conformance as a containment of formal languages problem; in particular, that a CFL is included in a regular language. By doing so, we verify the structural matching of the implementation to the specification.

Proposition 3. Protocol conformance *(8) implies agent strong conformance (7) and the latter implies agent conformance (6).*

Proof. It is sufficient to prove that $\Sigma \subseteq L(G_{\mathsf{p}_{dylog}})$. We give a sketch of proof. Actually, let us consider the application of proof rule (1) and (4) in the proof of $(\Pi, \mathsf{CKit}^{ag_i}, S_0) \vdash_{ps} \langle \mathsf{p}_{dylog} \rangle \top$ w.a. σ, it is possible to build a derivation $\mathsf{p}_{dylog} \Rightarrow_* \sigma$ where each derivation step is determined by selecting the production rule that is obtained from the inclusion axiom of the the corresponding rule (1) and (4) that has been applied. This shows that $\sigma \in L(G_{\mathsf{p}_{dylog}})$. The second part of the proposition trivially derives from definitions.

Proposition 4. *Protocol conformance is decidable.*

Proof. Equation (8) is equivalent to $L(G_{\mathsf{p}_{dylog}}) \cap \overline{L(G_{\mathsf{p}_{AUML}})} = \emptyset$. Now, $L(G_{\mathsf{p}_{dylog}})$ is a CFL while $L(G_{\mathsf{p}_{AUML}})$ is a regular language. Since the complement of a regular language is still regular, $\overline{L(G_{\mathsf{p}_{AUML}})}$ is a regular language. The intersection of a CFL and a regular language is a CFL. For CFLs, the emptyness is decidable [20].

Proposition 4 tells us that an algorithm for verifying protocol conformance exists. In [13, 8] a procedure to verify the containment property of a CFL in a regular language is given, that takes $O(|P_{G_{\mathsf{p}_{dylog}}}| \cdot |V_{G_{\mathsf{p}_{AUML}}}|^3)$ time and $O(|P_{G_{\mathsf{p}_{dylog}}}| \cdot |V_{G_{\mathsf{p}_{AUML}}}|^2)$ space.

Example 2. Let us consider the $\mathsf{yes\_no\_query}_I$ DyLOG procedure, presented in Section 2.2, clauses (g)-(j). In the case in which *Fluent* holds *available(movie)*, Algorithm 2 produces the following grammar $G_{\mathsf{yes\_no\_query}_{I\,dylog}}$:

$\mathsf{yes\_no\_query}_I(cus, sp, available(movie)) \longrightarrow$
    $\mathsf{get\_start}(cus, sp, available(movie))\ \mathsf{refuseInform}(cus, sp, available(movie))$
$\mathsf{yes\_no\_query}_I(cus, sp, available(movie)) \longrightarrow$
    $\mathsf{get\_start}(cus, sp, available(movie))\ \mathsf{inform}(cus, sp, available(movie))$
$\mathsf{yes\_no\_query}_I(cus, sp, available(movie)) \longrightarrow$
    $\mathsf{get\_start}(cus, sp, available(movie))\ \mathsf{inform}(cus, sp, \neg available(movie))$
$\mathsf{get\_start}(cus, sp, available(movie)) \longrightarrow$
    $\mathsf{queryIf}(cus, sp, available(movie))$

It is easy to see that the language produced by it is the following and that it contains three possible conversations:

$L(G_{\mathsf{yes\_no\_query}_{I_{dylog}}}) = \{$

queryIf$(cus, sp, available(movie))$refuseInform$(cus, sp, available(movie))$,

queryIf$(cus, sp, available(movie))$inform$(cus, sp, available(movie))$,

queryIf$(cus, sp, available(movie))$inform$(cus, sp, \neg available(movie))$ $\}$

The grammar $G_{\mathsf{yes\_no\_query}_{I_{AUML}}}$, obtained starting from the AUML specification of the protocol, is similar to the one shown in Fig. 1, productions from Q_1 through Q_7, where Q_7 produces ε instead of Q_8. The language $L(G_{\mathsf{yes\_no\_query}_{I_{AUML}}})$ contains the same conversations of $L(G_{\mathsf{yes\_no\_query}_{I_{dylog}}})$, therefore the *protocol conformance* trivially holds. This is a structural conformance, in the sense that no information about the agent private state is taken into account nor the semantics of the speech acts is.

Now, the speech acts might have different semantics (different preconditions or effects); for instance, we can imagine two *inform* implementations, the first can be executed when the informer knows a certain fact, the other when it knows a fact and it believes that the querier does not know it. Depending on its semantics, an *inform* act might or might not be executed in a given agent mental state. Thus, generally, the interaction dynamics of the speech act semantics and the agent belief states might enable or disable conversations even when using the same agent policy. Nervethless, since protocol conformance holds, by Proposition 3 we can state that the obtained conversations will *always* be legal w.r.t. the AUML specification; the private information of the agent and the semantics of the speech acts will, at most, reduce the set of possible conversations but they will never introduce new, uncorrect sequences.

4   Conclusions and Related Work

In this work we face the problem of verifying if the implementation of an interaction protocol as an internal policy of a logic-based agent is conformant to the protocol abstract specification, in the special case of DyLOG agents implementing AUML specifications. We have taken advantage from the logical representation of protocols in DyLOG as inclusion axioms, by interpreting the conformance problem as a problem of language inclusion.

Verifying the conformance of protocol implementations is a crucial problem in an AOSE perspective, that can be considered as a part of the process of engineering interaction protocols sketched in [21]. In this perspective the techniques discussed along our paper, actually, suggest a straightforward *methodology* for directly implementing protocols in DyLOG so that conformance to the AUML specification is respected. In fact, we can build our implementation starting from the grammar $G_{\mathsf{p}_{AUML}}$, and applying the inverse of the process that we described for passing from a DyLOG implementation to the grammar $G_{\mathsf{p}_{dylog}}$. In this way we can obtain a skeleton of a DyLOG implementation of p_{AUML} that is to be completed by adding the desired ontology for the speech acts and customized with tests. Such an implementation trivially satisfies protocol conformance and, then, all the other degrees of conformance.

The problem of checking the agent conformance to a protocol in a logical framework has been faced also in [12]. In [12] agent communication strategies and protocol specification are both represented by means of sets of *if-then rules* in a logic-based language, which relies on abductive logic programming. A notion of weak conformance is introduced, which allows to check if the possible moves that an agent can make, according to a given communication strategy, are legal w.r.t. the protocol specification. The conformance test is done by disregarding any condition related to the agent private knowledge, which is not considered as relevant in order to decide weak conformance. On this respect, our notion of conformance is similar to the notion of agent weak conformance described above. However, our approach allows to tackle a broader class of protocols: we are not restricted to protocols that sequentially alternate the dialogue moves of the agents. Furthermore, while in [12] conformance avoids to deal with the dialogue history, our notion of conformance takes into account the whole context of the conversation, due to the fact that it considers sequences of dialogue acts. This can be done thanks to the modal logic framework, which allows to naturally deal with contexts.

Moreover, our framework allows us to give a finer notion of conformance, for which we can distinguish different degrees of abstraction with respect to the agent private mental state. This allows us to decide which parts of a protocol implementation must fit the protocol specification and to describe in a modular way how the protocol implementation can be enriched with respect to the protocol specification, without compromising the conformance. Such an enrichment is important when using logic agents, whose ability of reasoning about the properties of the interactions among agents before they actually occur, may be a powerful tool for supporting MAS designers.

So far we have focussed on the conformance of the policies of a single agent to a protocol specification. A current research issue that we are studying concerns the conditions by which our notion of conformance can be proved compositional. Intuitively, given two agent policies that are conformant to the same protocol and that encode the different roles foreseen by it, it would be interesting to prove that the actual interaction of the two agents will also be conformant.

Some authors (e.g. [29]) have proposed a different approach to agent communication, the *social* approach, in which communicative actions affect the "social state" of the system, rather than the internal states of the agents. The social state records the social facts, like the *permissions* and the *commitments* of the agents, which are created and modified along the interaction. Different approaches enable different types of properties to be proved [19]. For instance the mental approach is not well suited for the verification of *open* multi-agent systems, where the history of communications is observable, but the internal states of the single agents may not be accessed [29]. Therefore the social approach is taken in works such as the one in [1], where an open society of agents is considered and the problem of verifying on the fly the compliance of the agents' behavior to protocols specified in a logic-based formalism (Social Integrity Constraints) is addressed by taking the point of view of an external entity that detects faulty behaviors.

Acknowledgement. The authors would like to thank Dr. Giuseppe Berio for the discussion about Agent UML.

References

1. M. Alberti, D. Daolio, P. Torroni, M. Gavanelli, E. Lamma, and P. Mello. Specification and verification of agent interaction protocols in a logic-based system. In H. Haddad, A. Omicini, R. L. Wainwright, and L. M. Liebrock, editors, *Proc. of the 2004 ACM Symposium on Applied Computing, SAC 2004*, pages 72–78, Nicosia, Cyprus, 2004. ACM.
2. M. Baldoni. Normal Multimodal Logics with Interaction Axioms. In D. Basin, M. D'Agostino, D. M. Gabbay, S. Matthews, and L. Viganò, editors, *Labelled Deduction*, volume 17 of *Applied Logic Series*, pages 33–53. Applied Logic Series, Kluwer Academic Publisher, 2000.
3. M. Baldoni, C. Baroglio, A. Martelli, and V. Patti. Reasoning about self and others: communicating agents in a modal action logic. In C. Blundo and C. Laneve, editors, *Theoretical Computer Science, 8th Italian Conference, ICTCS'2003*, volume 2841 of *LNCS*, pages 228–241, Bertinoro, Italy, October 2003. Springer.
4. M. Baldoni, L. Giordano, and A. Martelli. A Tableau Calculus for Multimodal Logics and Some (un)Decidability Results. In H. de Swart, editor, *Proc. of TABLEAUX'98*, volume 1397 of *LNAI*, pages 44–59. Springer-Verlag, 1998.
5. M. Baldoni, L. Giordano, A. Martelli, and V. Patti. Programming Rational Agents in a Modal Action Logic. *Annals of Mathematics and Artificial Intelligence, Special issue on Logic-Based Agent Implementation*, 41(2-4):207–257, 2004.
6. M. Barbuceanu and M.S. Fox. Cool: a language for describing coordination in multiagent systems. In *the 1st Int. Conf. on Multi-Agent Systems (ICMAS-95)*. AAAI Press, 1995.
7. J. Bentahar, B. Moulin, J. J. Ch. Meyer, and B. Chaib-Draa. A computational model for conversation policies for agent communication. In this volume.
8. A. Bouajjani, J. Esparza, A. Finkel, O. Maler, P. Rossmanith, B. Willems, and P. Wolper. An efficient automata approach to some problems on context-free grammars. *Information Processing Letters*, 74(5–6):221–227, 2000.
9. A. Bracciali, P. Mancarella, K. Stathis, and F. Toni. On modelling declaratively multiagent systems. In Leite et al. [25], pages 76–92.
10. L. Cabac and D. Moldt. Formal semantics for auml agent interaction protocol diagrams. In *Proc. of AOSE 2004*, 2004.
11. R. S. Cost, Y. Chen, T. Finin, Y. Labrou, and Y. Peng. Modeling agent conversation with colored petri nets. In *Autonomous Agents Workshop on Conversation Policies*, 1999.
12. U. Endriss, N. Maudet, F. Sadri, and F. Toni. Logic-based agent communication protocols. In F. Dignum, editor, *Advances in agent communication languages*, volume 2922 of *Lecture Notes in Artificial Intelligence (LNAI)*, pages 91–107. Springer-Verlag, 2004.

13. J. Esparza, P. Rossmanith, and S. Schwoon. A uniform framework for problems on context-free grammars. *EATCS Bulletin*, 72:169–177, October 2000.
14. L. Fariñas del Cerro and M. Penttonen. Grammar Logics. *Logique et Analyse*, 121-122:123–134, 1988.
15. M. Finger, M. Fisher, and R. Owens. Metatem: modeling reactive systems using executable temporal logic. In *the Int. Conf. on Industrial and Engineering Applications of Artificial Intelligence and Expert Systems (IEA-AIE)*, 1993.
16. M. Fisher and M.J. Wooldridge. Specifying and executing protocols for cooperative actions. In *the Int. Working Conf. on Cooperative Knowledge-Based Systems (CKBS-94)*, 1994.
17. Foundation for InteroPerable Agents. Fipa modeling: Interaction diagrams. Technical report, 2003. Working Draft Version 2003-07-02.
18. L. Giordano, A. Martelli, and C. Schwind. Verifying communicating agents by model checking in a temporal action logic. In J. Alferes and J. Leite, editors, *9th European Conference on Logics in Artificial Intelligence (JELIA'04)*, volume 3229 of *LNAI*, pages 57–69, Lisbon, Portugal, Sept. 2004. Springer-Verlag.
19. F. Guerin and J. Pitt. Verification and Compliance Testing. In H.P. Huget, editor, *Communication in Multiagent Systems*, volume 2650 of *LNAI*, pages 98–112. Springer-Verlag, 2003.
20. J. E. Hopcroft and J. D. Ullman. *Introduction to automata theory, languages, and computation*. Addison-Wesley Publishing Company, 1979.
21. M. P. Huget and J.L. Koning. Interaction Protocol Engineering. In H.P. Huget, editor, *Communication in Multiagent Systems*, volume 2650 of *LNAI*, pages 179–193. Springer-Verlag, 2003.
22. M. Kacprzak, A. Lomuscio, and W. Penczek. Verification of multiagent systems via unbounded model checking. In *Proc. of the 3rd Int. Joint Conf. on Autonomous Agents and Multiagent Systems (AAMAS04)*, New York, NY, USA, 2004.
23. J.-L. Koning, G. Franois, and Y. Demazeau. Formalization and pre-validation for interaction protocols in multiagent systems. In *the 13th European Conference on Artificial Intelligence (ECAI-98)*, 1998.
24. K. Kuwabara, T. Ishida, and N. Osato. Agentalk : describing multiagent coordination protocols with inheritance. In *7th Int. Conf. on Tools for Artificial Intelligence (ICTAI-95)*, 1995.
25. J. Leite, A. Omicini, P. Torroni, and P. Yolum, editors. *Int. Workshop on Declarative Agent Languages and Technology*, New York City, NY, USA, July 2004. Volume 3476 of *LNAI*. Springer-Verlag, 2005.
26. H. J. Levesque, R. Reiter, Y. Lespérance, F. Lin, and R. B. Scherl. GOLOG: A Logic Programming Language for Dynamic Domains. *J. of Logic Programming*, 31:59–83, 1997.
27. J. Odell, H. V. D. Parunak, and B. Bauer. Extending UML for agents. In *Proceedings of the Agent-Oriented Information System Workshop at the 17th National Conference on Artificial Intelligence*. 2000.
28. L. R. Pokorny and C. R. Ramakrishnan. Modeling and verification of distributed autonomous agents using logic programming. In Leite et al. [25], pages 172–187.
29. M. P. Singh. A social semantics for agent communication languages. In *Proc. of IJCAI-98 Workshop on Agent Communication Languages*, Berlin, 2000. Springer.
30. C. Walton. Model checking agent dialogues. In Leite et al. [25], pages 156–171.

An Application of Global Abduction
to an Information Agent
Which Modifies a Plan Upon Failure
- Preliminary Report -

Ken Satoh

National Institute of Informatics,
2-1-2 Hitotsubashi, Chiyoda-ku, Tokyo, 101-8430, Japan
ksatoh@nii.ac.jp

Abstract. This paper proposes an implementation of an information agent in a new form of abductive logic programming called *global abduction* [11]. We consider an information agent which performs not only information gathering, but also actions which update the outside world. However, since the success of the actions is not guaranteed, the agent might encounter a failure of some action. In this case, the agent needs to modify an alternative plan with consideration to the side-effects caused by the already-executed actions. In this paper, we solve the problem of such plan modification by using global abduction. Global abduction is a new form of abduction whose abducibles can be referred to in any search path once abduced. This mechanism is used to propagate information about already-executed actions so that we can modify an alternative plan to accommodate side-effects caused by the already-executed actions.

1 Introduction

Thanks to the Internet, human activity within cyber-space has become accelerated and sometimes beyond one's ability to control. Therefore, support by information agents has become very important. However, current research on information agents is mainly limited to "information gathering" which aids one element of human activity within the cyber-space. Another important aspect of information manipulation is updating outside information sources such as making online-reservations or ordering a product online. The most distinguishing property of such updating actions is that they may include side-effects to the outside world and therefore these updates may influence the agents' subsequent activity.

To make things more complicated, there are a lot of uncertainties on the success of such updates. In other words, even though agents can make a plan to achieve a given goal, they cannot guarantee that the plan will always be successful since they may rely on some assumptions about the outside world. For example, suppose that an agent makes a schedule for a user's trip abroad. The

J. Leite and P. Torroni (Eds.): CLIMA V, LNAI 3487, pp. 213–229, 2005.
© Springer-Verlag Berlin Heidelberg 2005

agent would create a plan to ask an airplane company to make a reservation of a flight and to ask a hotel to make a reservation for the accommodation. However, one of these reservations might fail since we do not know whether there are any vacancies on the flight or the hotel. This means that there might be a failure of information manipulation activity and therefore, we need to modify the plan upon failure. However, already-executed actions might cause side-effects and we need to care about such side-effects when we consider an alternative plan.

In this paper, we use the following motivating example:

1. An agent is asked to buy a good book on the subject of computers using a credit card "card1" or "card2".
2. We assume that the bank account associated with the credit card might not contain enough money to buy the book.
3. The agent makes a plan which consists of logging-in to a site selling books and searching for a book on the subject of computers, and purchasing a copy with a credit card.
4. The agent logs in to a site selling books (called "amazon") with a user ID associated with a credit card.
5. Suppose that the agent logs in as the user of credit card "card1".
6. The agent asks for a good book on the subject of computers to the "amazon" site and the site returns information about a book (named "linux").
7. The agent tries to purchase a copy of the book using the credit card "card1".
8. It turns out that the bank account for "card1" cannot be used because the account does not contain enough money to buy the book.
9. The agent backtracks to make an alternative plan to purchase the book by using the other credit card "card2".
10. However, the agent has to log-in with a user ID associated with "card2". We assume that the system does not allow double logging-in and so, the agent must log-out first and then log-in to "amazon" again as the user of "card2".
11. Since the agent already knows about a good book on computers ("linux"), the agent avoids searching for the book again.
12. The agent directly proceeds to purchase the book by using the credit card "card2".

The characteristics of a problem class considered in this paper are as follows:

- There is a failure in the plan (authorization of "card1") which could not have been anticipated when the plan was first executed.
- An agent makes actions with side-effects (an agent logs-in as the user of "card1").
- An agent changes the plan on the fly when failure occurs.
- An agent must consider the side-effects from the already-executed actions when changing the plan (an agent logs-out as the user of "card1" and then logs-in as another user associated with "card2").
- An agent can make use of these side-effects in the changed plan (a result of search of a book on the computer is reused).

There are many research issues involved in making an agent do tasks such as the above.

- How to propagate the information gained from already-executed actions in one plan to alternative plans?
- How to identify the exact situation when the failure in execution of the plan occurs?
  (In the working example, the agent itself had to figure out whether the agent had already logged in or not.)
- How to make a new plan at the failure point?
  (e.g. what does the agent do in order to purchase the book when it turns out that "card1" is not authorized?)
- What are the semantics for this agent's behaviour in order to consider the correctness of the agent's internal mechanism?

We solve the above problem by introducing a new form of abduction in logic programming called *global abduction* [11]. In the previous abductive logic programming framework (see [6] for a comprehensive survey), we use abduction to complement unknown information when the derivation of a goal needs such hypotheses. However, these hypotheses are valid only in the derivation path to achieve the goal and there is no influence on the other search path. We call this type of abduction *local abduction*.

For global abduction, we introduce a *global belief state*, a store of global information, which can be accessed from any search path, and two annotations, announce(P) and hear(P). announce(P) asserts a ground literal P in the global belief state. After announce(P) is executed, P becomes true globally as if it was asserted in the beginning of the execution. This means P is abduced not only in the search path where the announcement is done, but also propagated to the other search paths as if it were true in the beginning. hear(P) is used to see the truth value of P in a global belief state. If P has already been announced in the global belief state by announce(P), hear(P) is succeeded. If the complement of P has already been announced in the global belief state, hear(P) fails. Otherwise, the execution related with hear(P) is suspended and other derivation path will be traversed.

Using *global abduction*, we can solve the above problem class as follows.

- How to propagate already-executed actions in one plan to another plan? ⇒ These actions are regarded as abducibles for global abduction. Every time an action with side-effects is performed, information about such actions is propagated to other alternative plans by *announcing* these abducibles.
- How to identify the exact situation when the failure in execution of the plan occurs? ⇒ By *hearing* abducibles representing already-executed actions, we can detect these actions and simulate these actions in alternative paths to modify a new plan.
- How to make a new plan at the failure point? ⇒ We consider an alternative plan by backtracking to the choice point and modify the alternative plan if necessary according to the side effects of the already-executed actions.

– What are the semantics for this agent behaviour to talk about the correctness of the agent's internal mechanism? ⇒ We use the semantics of global
abduction called **"all's well that ends well (AWW) principle"** which
means that if we add the last set of abduced atoms to the initial program,
the same result is derived by the usual SLDNF procedure.

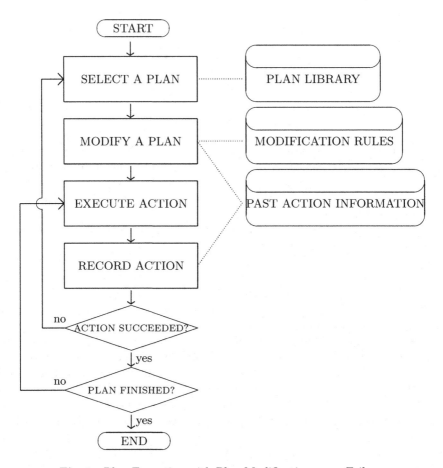

Fig. 1. Plan Execution with Plan Modification upon Failure

One of the key ideas presented in this paper is plan modification. In Fig. 1, we
show how to execute a plan with plan modification upon failure. We select a plan
from a plan-library to achieve a given goal. Then, we check whether there exist
the past executed actions. If such past actions exist, we modify the plan according
to plan modification rules. After a modification, we execute a modified plan and
record actions during the plan execution. If an action in the plan fails, then
we select another plan and modify the plan according to the already-executed
actions. We iterate through the above process until all the execution of actions
in the plan are performed. This is a different modification method from the

one considered in [9]. In [9], they consider generating a modified plan from the current plan using action-effect rules while we use plan modification rules which directly modify a plan without action-effect rules.

We implement this idea by global abduction in logic programming. We backtrack to the choice point upon failure of actions and then consider an alternative plan. However, there might be some side-effects which influence the alternative plan. If so, we modify an alternative plan to accommodate these side-effects. To check such side-effects, we announce the already-executed actions in other alternative paths by global abduction. Then, in other alternative paths, we refer to these actions using hearing literals, and consider a modification of alternative plans.

The structure of the paper is as follows. In Section 2, we review (slightly modified) framework of global abduction and show a solution of the motivating example using global abduction. Then, we review semantics of the framework and a correct proof procedure of the framework w.r.t. the semantics. In Section 3, we show an execution trace of the motivating example. In Section 4, we discuss the related works, and we summarize our contributions and discuss future research in Section 5.

2   Global Abduction

We give an adapted formalization of global abduction used for a solution of the working example. The difference between global abduction in [11] and this paper is that we introduce a "cut" operator[1] and omit integrity constraints and impose an evaluation strategy of goals which are used in PROLOG; a depth-first search with right-to-left evaluation of the body of the rule and top-to-bottom trial over rules.

2.1   Framework of Global Abduction

Definition 1. *A global abductive framework* GA *is the following tuple* $\langle \mathcal{B}, \mathcal{P} \rangle$ *where*

- $\mathcal{B}$ *is a set of predicates called* belief predicates.
  Let A *be an atom with belief predicate. We call* A *a* positive belief literal, *or a* belief atom *and* $\neg A$ *a* negative belief literal. *We call a literal of the above form* belief literal. *Let* Q *be a belief literal. We introduce annotated literals* announce(Q) *and* hear(Q) *called* announcing literal *and* hearing literal *respectively. We say that* announce(Q) *contains* Q *and* hear(Q) *contains* Q.
- $\mathcal{P}$ *is a set of rules of the form:*

$$H\colon -B_1, B_2, ..., B_n.$$

---

[1] Note that in [11], we show how to implement "cut" in global abduction with integrity constraints. Thus, the introducing "cut" does not cause any extra control mechanism. In this paper, however, we omit the detail for simplicity.

where

- *H is an* ordinary *atom which is neither an annotated literal, an equality literal nor a belief literal.*
- *each of $B_1, ..., B_n$ is an ordinary atom, or an annotated literal, or an equality literal of the form $t = s$, or a disequality literal of the form $t \neq s$ or '!' (called a cut operator).*

We call H a head denoted as $head(R)$ and $B_1, ..., B_n$ a body denoted as $body(R)$. If there are no atoms in the body, $body(R) = \emptyset$.

Intuitively, annotated literals have the following meaning.

- For global abduction, we introduce a *global belief state*, a store of global information, which can be accessed from any search path.
- Announcing literal announce(L) is an assertion of a ground positive/negative belief L to the global belief state. This means while we traverse a search space to achieve a goal, some of the facts are added by the program itself. Then, from another search path, we can access this addition using a hearing literal. Therefore, L is "globally" abduced by announce(L).
- Hearing literal hear(L) is a check of a ground positive/negative belief L in the current belief state. If L is included in the current belief state, hear(L) coincides with the truth value of L w.r.t. the current belief state. Else if L is not included in the current belief state, the truth value of hear(L) is undefined and the evaluation is postponed.

The following program shows a solution to the motivating example of book purchase[2]

Example 1. Rules for plan generation:

```
plan(Genre,card1,Plan):-
    modify_plan(
        [login(id1),book_search(Genre,Book),purchase(Book,card1)],
        Plan).
plan(Genre,card2,Plan):-
    modify_plan(
        [login(id2),book_search(Genre,Book),purchase(Book,card2)],
        Plan).
```

The above rules represent two alternative plans that an agent logs in either as id1 (associated with card1) or id2 (associated with card2) and then searches for a book on the genre specified as Genre. However, we have to check whether there were any previous actions which influence the current plan. If so, we make a plan modification according to the following rules.

---

[2] Note that a string starting with an upper case is a variable and a string starting with an lower case is a constant.

Rules for Plan Modification

```
modify_plan([],[]):-!.

modify_plan([login(ID)|Plan],[login(ID)|RevisedPlan]):-
   hear(logged_in(ID1)),ID=/=ID1,hear(logged_out(ID1)),!,
   modify_plan(Plan,RevisedPlan).
modify_plan([login(ID)|Plan],[logout(ID1),login(ID)|RevisedPlan]):-
   hear(logged_in(ID1)),ID=/=ID1,!,
   modify_plan(Plan,RevisedPlan).
modify_plan([login(ID)|Plan],[login(ID)|RevisedPlan]):-!,
   modify_plan(Plan,RevisedPlan).

modify_plan([book_search(Genre,Book)|Plan],RevisedPlan):-
   hear(book_searched(Genre,Book)),!,
   modify_plan(Plan,RevisedPlan).
modify_plan([book_search(Genre,Book)|Plan],
            [book_search(Genre,Book)|RevisedPlan]):-!,
   modify_plan(Plan,RevisedPlan).

modify_plan([purchase(Book,Card)|Plan],
            [purchase(Book,Card)|RevisedPlan]):-!,
   modify_plan(Plan,RevisedPlan).
```

For a plan for the login action, we firstly ensure that the agent currently does not log in as another ID. If there is a history that the agent logged in, we also check that the agent has already logged out. If so (in the second rule), there is no modification in a plan so that the agent directly logs in, otherwise (in the third rule), we add the logout action before logging in. If there is no such history (in the fourth rule), we do not need to change the plan [3]

The fifth and sixth rules are for an action of searching for a book. The fifth rule is a deletion of redundant search of a book. If a book has already been searched for the genre Genre, the agent no longer searches for another book for the genre. We use a hearing literal for book_searched(Genre,Book) for such a check. If a book has already been searched for, we modify the plan by deleting the action of search. Otherwise, we do not need to change the plan. Note that since we adopt the top-bottom trial strategy, we should check in the first place whether the search of a book has been done so that we can guaranteed that there has been no such search when we execute the sixth rule.

The seventh rule is for an action of buying a book. We could put another rule to avoid the redundant purchase like search action, but we omit the rule for simplicity.

---

[3] Precisely speaking, if we have a history of multiple log-ins, we need to keep a correspondence between log-in's and log-out's. However, we do not consider here for simplicity.

Rules for execution:

```
execute([]):-!.
execute([login(ID)|Plan]):-
   login(ID),execute(Plan).
execute([logout(ID)|Plan]):-
   logout(ID),execute(Plan).
execute([book_search(Genre,Book)|Plan]):-
   book_search(Genre,Book),execute(Plan).
execute([purchase(Book,Card)|Plan]):-
   purchase(Book,Card),execute(Plan).
```

Rule for logging-in amazon site:

```
login(ID):-!,
   announce(action(login(ID))@amazon),announce(logged_in(ID)).
```

announce(action(login(ID))@amazon) expresses that an action of logging-in to amazon as ID and its history is recorded as logged_in(ID) by announcing it by global abduction.

Rule for logging-out from amazon site:

```
logout(ID):-!,
   announce(action(logout(ID))@amazon),announce(logged_out(ID)).
```

Rule for searching books:

```
book_search(Genre,Book):-
   hear(book_search(Genre,Book)@amazon),!,
   announce(book_searched(Genre,Book)).
```

In this action, the search command is dispatched to amazon site and wait till the site returns a book information. When the information is returned, the agent announces it by global abduction of book_searched(Genre,Book).

Rule for purchasing a book:

```
purchase(X,CARD):-
   hear(authorize(CARD)@checker),!,
   announce(action(purchase(X,CARD))@amazon).
```

The above rule checks whether the credit card CARD is authorized or not, if not, it simply fails and otherwise, we submit a purchase command to amazon.

2.2   Semantics for Global Abduction

In this subsection, we briefly explain the semantics of global abduction. Readers who would like to know the detail of the semantics, see [11].

We use the three-valued semantics of logic programs [1, 10] since the truth value of the belief literals can be undefined when the current belief state does not decide their truth values. We extend the three-valued least model so that the semantic of the global abduction are indexed w.r.t. a belief state. A belief state BS is the set of belief literals which represents agent's belief. We define truth-values of belief literals w.r.t. BS as follows:

- If a literal L in BS, L is said to be true w.r.t. BS.
- If the complement of a literal L in BS, L is said to be false w.r.t. BS.
- Otherwise L is said to be undefined w.r.t. BS.

Let $\mathcal{P}$ be sets of rules. We firstly replace $\mathtt{announce}(L)$ and $\mathtt{hear}(L)$ by a corresponding belief literal L. We denote a set of ground rules obtained by replacing all the variables in every rule of the resulting program by every term in the language as $\Pi_{\mathcal{P}}$. Then, we translate $\Pi_{\mathcal{P}}$ into another program $\Pi_{\mathcal{P}}^{BS}$ which is reduced by BS as follows.

- We delete every rule in the program $\Pi_{\mathcal{P}}$ which contains a false belief literal w.r.t. BS in the body.
- We delete every true literal w.r.t. BS and replace every undefined literal w.r.t. BS by a special atom $\mathtt{undef}$ in the body of the remaining rules.

We assume that the truth value of $\mathtt{undef}$ is always "*undefined*".

We also drop the "cut" operator since it does not influence the correctness of the program. Then, the reduced program $\Pi_{\mathcal{P}}^{BS}$ is a normal logic program which may have $\mathtt{undef}$ in the body. Then, we follow the three-valued least model semantics [1] to give the truth value of an ordinary ground atom. We say that the three-valued least model of $\Pi_{\mathcal{P}}^{BS}$ is the *assumption-based three-valued least model of $\mathcal{P}$ w.r.t. BS*.

2.3   Proof Procedure

In this section we give a proof procedure which is correct in the above semantics. The execution of global abductive framework is based on *process reduction*. Intuitively, processes are created when a choice point of computation is encountered like case splitting. A process terminates successfully if all the computation is done and the belief literals used in the process are not contradictory with the last belief state. As the subsequent theorem shows, if we reflect the last belief state BS to the program $\mathcal{P}$ by considering $\Pi_{\mathcal{P}}^{BS}$, then the same result is obtained by usual SLDNF procedure. Therefore, we call this principle *"all's well that ends well (AWW)"* principle in that we talk about the correctness at the last belief state when we get an answer.

In the procedure, we reduce an active process into a new process. Reduction for an ordinary atom is a usual goal reduction in logic programming and reduction for an announcing literal corresponds with an update of the belief state and reduction for a hearing literal corresponds with an inquiry to the belief state.

Updating the belief state by an announcing literal may result in the suspension of the current executed process and change of the execution to an alternative process.

Preliminary Definitions

We define the following for explanation of the proof procedure.

Definition 2. *A* process *is the following tuple* $\langle GS, BA, ANS \rangle$ *which consists of*

- *GS: a set of atoms to be proved called a* goal set.
- *BA: a set of ground belief literals called* belief assumptions.
- *ANS: a set of instantiations of variables in the initial query.*

A process expresses an execution status in a path in the search tree. The intuitive meaning of the above objects is as follows:

- GS expresses the current status of computation.
- BA is a set of belief assumptions used during a process.
- ANS gives an answer for variables in the initial query.

We use the following two sets for process reduction.

Definition 3.

- *A process set* PS *is a set of processes.*
- *A current belief state* CBS *is a belief state.*

PS is a set of processes which express all the alternative computations considered so far, and CBS is the current belief state which expresses the agent's current belief.

Definition 4. *Let* $\langle GS, BA, ANS \rangle$ *be a process and* CBS *be a current belief state. A process is* active *w.r.t.* CBS *if for every* $L \in BA$, L *is true in* CBS *and a process is* suspended *w.r.t.* CBS *otherwise.*

If BA contradicts CBS, the execution of process is considered to be useless at the current belief state and therefore, the process will be suspended.

Description of Proof Procedure

In the following reduction, we specify only changed PS, CBS as $NewPS$, $NewCBS$; otherwise each PS, CBS is unchanged. We modified the proof procedure in [11] to impose a PROLOG-like evaluation strategy in order to use "cut" operator.

Initial Step: Let GS be the initial goal set.

We give $\langle GS, \emptyset, ANS \rangle$ to the proof procedure where ANS is a set of variables in GS. That is, $PS = \{\langle GS, \emptyset, ANS \rangle\}$. and let CBS be the initial set of belief literals.

Iteration Step: Do the following.

Case 1 If there is an active process $\langle \emptyset, BA, ANS' \rangle$ w.r.t. CBS in PS, return instantiation for variables ANS' and the current belief state CBS.

Case 2 If PS is empty, return "failure".

Case 3 Select the most recently added active process $\langle GS, BA, ANS \rangle$ w.r.t. CBS from PS and select a left-most literal L (an ordinary atom, or an equality atom, or a disequality atom, or an annotated literal or "cut" operator) in GS which satisfies one of the conditions in the following subcase. If there is no such process, return "floundering".

Let $PS' = PS - \{\langle GS, BA, ANS \rangle\}$ and $GS' = GS - \{L\}$.

Case 3.1 If L is an ordinary atom,

append the following processes to PS' to from $NewPS$:

$\{\langle (\{body(R)\} \cup GS')\theta, BA, ANS\theta \rangle |$
$R \in \mathcal{P}$ and $\exists$most general unifier(mgu) θ s.t. $head(R)\theta = L\theta\}$
in the order of matched rules in the program.

Case 3.2 If L is an equality atom $t = s$,

Case 3.2.1 if there is an mgu θ between t and s, then $NewPS = \{\langle GS'\theta, BA, ANS\theta \rangle\} \cup PS'$

Case 3.2.2 else if there is no such mgu, then $NewPS = PS'$.

Case 3.3 If L is an disequality atom $t \neq s$, and t and s are ground terms,

Case 3.3.1 if t and s are different ground terms then $NewPS = \{\langle GS', BA, ANS \rangle\} \cup PS'$

Case 3.3.2 else if t and s are identical terms, then $NewPS = PS'$.

Case 3.4 If L is a hearing literal **hear**(Q) and there is a ground instance of Q in CBS, then $NewPS = \{\langle GS', BA \cup \{Q\}, ANS \rangle\} \cup PS'$.

Case 3.5 If L is a ground announcing literal **announce**(A), then $NewPS = \{\langle GS', BA \cup \{A\}, ANS \rangle\} \cup PS'$, and $NewCBS = CBS\backslash\{\overline{A}\} \cup \{A\}$.

Case 3.6 If L is the "cut" operator "!", then we delete all alternatives reduced to the body of alternative rules competing with the rule which contains the above cut.

"All's Well that Ends Well (AWW)" Principle

The following theorem shows correctness of the above procedure. The theorem intuitively means that when we receive an answer of execution, the answer is correct in the assumption-based three-valued model w.r.t. the program and the final belief state. This is an idea of *AWW principle*.

Let ANS' be an instantiation of the variables and GS be the initial goal. We write $GS \circ ANS'$ as the goal obtained from GS by replacing variables in GS by corresponding term in ANS'. Let M be the assumption-based least three-valued model of the program w.r.t. a belief state. and $\{L_1, ..., L_n\}$ be a set of ground literals. We write $M \models \{L_1, ..., L_n\}$ if L_i is true in M.

Theorem 1. *Let GA be a global abductive framework $\langle \mathcal{B}, \mathcal{P} \rangle$. Let GS be an initial goal set. Suppose that an instantiation of the variables ANS' and the current belief state CBS are returned. Let M be the assumption-based three-valued model of $\mathcal{P}$ w.r.t. CBS. Then, $M \models GS \circ ANS'$.*

A proof of Theorem 1 can be found in [11].

3   Execution of Global Abduction

We show an execution trace of Example 1 using the above proof procedure. Since no belief literal changes its truth-value once announced in the example, we omit belief assumptions of a process, and show only goal sets.

1. The agent starts from the following initial goal meaning that the agent firstly makes a plan and then executes the plan.
   ```
   plan(computer,Card,Plan),execute(Plan)
   ```
2. The goal is reduced to two alternative plans. Firstly, the agent considers the following goal of a plan using the credit card card1.
   ```
   modify_plan(
       [login(id1),book_search(computer,Book),purchase(Book,card1)],
       Plan),
   execute(Plan)
   ```
3. To check whether the agent should modify the plan related with logging-in action, the agent checks the three rules for the logging-in action, but since there is no information that the agent logged-in, the first and the second rules are suspended and the third rule is selected and the plan is not modified.
   ```
   !,modify_plan(
       [book_search(computer,Book),purchase(Book,card1)],
       RevisedPlan),
   execute([login(id1)|RevisedPlan])
   ```
4. By executing a cut "!", the suspended goals associated with the first and the second rules of logging-in is deleted.
   ```
   modify_plan(
       [book_search(computer,Book),purchase(Book,card1)],
       RevisedPlan), execute([login(id1)|RevisedPlan])
   ```
5. To check whether the agent has to modify the plan related with searching for a book, the agent first checks by using hearing literal in the first rule of searching for books whether a book search has been already performed or not. This time there is no such information about the current belief state, and so, the first rule of searching for books is suspended and the second rule is used to reduced the goal.
   ```
   !,modify_plan([purchase(Book,card1)],RevisedPlan1),
   execute([login(id1),book_search(computer,Book)|RevisedPlan1])
   ```
6. By executing a cut "!", the suspended goals associated with the first rule of searching for books is deleted.
   ```
   modify_plan([purchase(Book,card1)],RevisedPlan1),
   execute([login(id1),book_search(computer,Book)|RevisedPlan1])
   ```
7. Since there is no modification rule of the purchase action, we reduce the goal without any modification of the action.
   ```
   execute(
       [login(id1),book_search(computer,Book),purchase(Book,card1)])
   ```
8. The agent logs in as id1.
   ```
   login(id1),
       execute([book_search(computer,Book),purchase(Book,card1)])
   ```

9. The agent executes an action of logging-in by sending a login command to amazon, and announcing a history of the logging-in as id1.

```
!,announce(action(login(id1))@amazon),announce(logged_in(id1)),
execute([book_search(computer,Book),purchase(Book,card1)])
```

10. The agent executes a book-search action.

```
book_search(computer,Book),execute([purchase(Book,card1)])
```

11. To search for a book, the agent asks amazon whether there is a good book on computer by the hearing predicate of

```
            book_search(computer,Book)@amazon,
```

and then announces a history that the agent knows about a good book on computer.

```
hear(book_search(computer,Book)@amazon),
!,announce(book_searched(computer,Book)),
execute([purchase(Book,card1)])
```

12. We assume that amazon returns a book linux. Then, the agent purchases the book with card1.

```
purchase(linux,card1),execute([])
```

13. To purchase the book titled linux, the agent needs to ask a checker agent in order to confirm that card1 is authorized.

```
hear(authorize(card1)@checker),
!,announce(action(purchase(linux,card1))@amazon),
execute([])
```

14. Suppose that this plan is failed because the payment of card1 is not authorized.

15. The agent backtracks to the other alternative plan in that the agent uses card2. So, the agent checks whether there is a need of modification of an alternative plan by the already-executed action.

```
modify_plan(
  [login(id2),book_search(computer,Book),purchase(Book,card2)],
  Plan), execute(Plan)
```

16. The agent checks whether he has already logged in and logged out.

```
hear(logged_in(ID1)),id2=/=ID1,hear(logged_out(ID1)),
!,modify_plan(
  [book_search(computer,Book),purchase(Book,card2)],
  RevisedPlan), execute([login(id2)|RevisedPlan])
```

17. The above goal is suspended since there is no information about hear(logged_out(id1)) and the agent checks the second rule for logging-in.

```
hear(logged_in(ID1)),id2=/=ID1,
!,modify_plan(
  [book_search(computer,Book),purchase(Book,card2)],
  RevisedPlan), execute([logout(ID1),login(id2)|RevisedPlan])
```

18. In this case, since the agent has not logged out from amazon site, the agent adds the action of logging-out as id1 before logging-in as id2. **This expresses a plan modification mechanism with the consideration of already-executed action.** By the cut operation, the first alternative is removed.

```
modify_plan(
  [book_search(computer,Book),purchase(Book,card2)],
  RevisedPlan), execute([logout(id1),login(id2)|RevisedPlan])
```

19. The agent checks whether he has already known a good book on computer by using the hearing predicate.
```
hear(book_searched(computer,Book)),
!,modify_plan([purchase(Book,card2)],RevisedPlan),
execute([logout(id1),login(id2)|RevisedPlan])
```

20. This time the agent has already known a good book linux so, we remove the book-search action from the plan. **This also represents a plan modification mechanism with the consideration of already-executed action. In this case, in stead of adding an action, we delete a redundant action.**
```
modify_plan([purchase(linux,card2)],RevisedPlan),
execute([logout(id1),login(id2)|RevisedPlan])
```

21. Since there is no modification rule of the purchase action, we reduce the goal without any modification of the action.
```
execute([logout(id1),login(id2),purchase(linux,card2)])
```

22. The agent logs out from amazon by id1.
```
logout(id1),execute([login(id2),purchase(linux,card2)])
```

23. The agent executes an action of logout by sending a logout command to amazon, and announcing a history of the logging-out as id1.
```
!,announce(action(logout(id1))@amazon),announce(logged_out(id1)),
execute([login(id2),purchase(linux,card2)])
```

24. The agent logs into amazon as id2.
```
login(id2),execute([purchase(linux,card2)])
```

25. The agent executes an action of logging-in by sending a login command to amazon, and announcing a history of the logging-in as id2.
```
!,announce(action(login(id2))@amazon),announce(logged_in(id2)),
execute([purchase(linux,card2)])
```

26. Thanks to plan modification, the agent no longer needs to search for a book again and he can proceed to the action of purchase of the book.
```
purchase(linux,card2),execute([])
```

27. To purchase a book linux, the agent needs to ask a checker agent to confirm that card2 is authorized.
```
hear(authorize(card2)@checker),
!,announce(action(purchase(linux,card2))@amazon),
execute([])
```

28. Suppose that authorizing the card is succeeded, then the agent dispatches a purchase command to amazon with the credit card card2.
```
announce(action(purchase(linux,card2))@amazon),execute([])
```

29. Finally, there is no action which should be performed and the agent accomplishes the purchase of the book.

4   Related Work

There are some previously published works on information manipulation [7, 2] which consider not only information gathering (or in other words, sensing) but also actions.

Golden [2] handles information under the open-world assumption and introduces "local closed world information" (LCW) which temporarily make a closed world assumption which can be later revoked. They show how LCW can avoid redundant information gathering. However, they do not consider any replanning upon failure.

Knoblock [7] discusses replanning in information gathering. However, he only considers actions with regard to information access to other servers without side-effects. A replan is only for accessing other information sources upon failure caused by a system-down of one information sources and therefore, it does not perform any complex replanning.

There are a lot of works relating with cognitive robotics [3, 8, 12, 13] which could be applied to the example considered here. Although the above works are aimed at rigorous semantics, they do not seem to care about efficiency very seriously and the replanning is usually made from scratch again after identifying the current situation. As pointed out in the Introduction, our framework of plan modification is different from the one considered in [9]. In [9], they consider a modified plan from the existing plan using action-effect rules whereas we use plan modification rules which can directly modify rules. Therefore, the argument in [9] on the replanning from scratch and plan modification is not applied here.

Hayashi et al. [4, 5] give a framework for agents which perform planning, make actions with side effects and repair plans on the fly in a Hierarchical Task Network (HTN) planning. In their work, every time an action with side effects is performed,

- for an undoable action, undoing action sequences will be inserted in the beginning of every alternative plan,
- alternative plans which is incompatible with side effects will be deleted,
- and if there are alternative plans with the same action in the beginning, the action will be deleted in these plans to avoid redundant action.

The difference between their work and ours is that they only consider undoing of the action or deletion of redundant action in the beginning of alternative plans for a modification of actions, whereas we can be more flexible in a plan modification by accommodating side-effects using hearing predicates.

5   Conclusion

The contribution of the paper is to show a basic mechanism using global abduction of an information agent which modifies an alternative plan to accommodate side-effects by already-executed actions.

We need to pursue the following future research.

- We would like to define an action language which is automatically translated to a logic program with global abduction. This language will be a general framework for replanning.
- We would like to apply this solution to various information activities to assess its feasibility.
- We would like to relax the constraint of the evaluation strategy (a depth-first search with right-to-left evaluation of the body of the rule and top-to-bottom trial over rules) of the framework.

Acknowledgements. This research is partly supported by Grants-in-Aid for Scientific Research from JSPS, No. 16200010. I thank Hideaki Takeda from NII for suggesting the motivating example on information agents. I also thank Bob Kowalski, Fariba Sadri, Paolo Torroni, Evelina Lamma and Nigel Collier and anonymous referees for constructive comments on the paper.

References

1. Fitting, M. C., "A Kripke/Kleene Semantics for Logic Programs", Journal of Logic Programming, Vol 2. pp. 295 – 312 (1985).
2. Golden, K., Etzioni, O., and Weld, D., "Omnipotence Without Omniscience: Efficient Sensor Management for Planning", Proc. of AAAI-94, pp. 1048 – 1054 (1994).
3. Levesque, H, Reiter R., Lesperance, Y., Lin F., and Scherl R., "GOLOG: A Logic Programming Language for Dynamic Domains", Journal of Logic Programming, 31, pp. 59 – 84 (1997).
4. Hayashi, H., Cho, K., and Ohsuga, A., "Mobile Agents and Logic Programming", Proc. of Mobile Agents 2002, pp. 32 – 46 (2002).
5. Hayashi H., Cho K., and Ohsuga A., "A New HTN Planning Framework for Agents in Dynamic Environments", Computational Logic in Multi-Agent Systems, CLIMA IV, Revised selected and invited papers, LNAI 3259, pp. 108 – 133 (2004).
6. Kakas, A. C., Kowalski, R., and Toni, F., "The Role of Abduction in Logic Programming", Handbook of Logic in Artificial Intelligence and Logic Programming 5, pages 235-324, D.M. Gabbay, C.J. Hogger and J.A. Robinson eds., Oxford University Press (1998)
7. Knoblock, C. A., "Planning, Executing, Sensing, and Replanning for Information Gathering", Proc. of IJCAI'95, pp. 1686 – 1693 (1995).
8. Kowalski, R.A., and Sadri, F., "From Logic Programming towards Multi-agent Systems", Annals of Mathematics and Artificial Intelligence, Vol. 25, pp. 391 – 419 (1999).
9. Nebel, B., Koehler, J., "Plan Reuse Versus Plan Generation: A Theoretical and Empirical Analysis", Artif. Intell., 76(1-2), pp. 427 – 454 (1995).
10. Przymusinski, T., "The Well-Founded Semantics Coincides with the Three-Valued Stable Semantics", *Fundamenta Informaticae* 13 (4), pp. 445 – 463 (1990).
11. Satoh, K., "All's Well that Ends Well – A Proposal of Global Abduction –", Proceedings of the Tenth International Workshop on Non-Monotonic Reasoning, pp. 360 – 367 (2004).

12. Shanahan, M. P., "Reinventing Shakey", Jack Minker (ed.), Logic-Based Artificial Intelligence, Kluwer Academic, pp. 233–253 (2000)
13. Thielscher, M., "The Qualification Problem: A Solution to the Problem of Anomalous Models", Artificial Intelligence, Vol. 131, No. 1–2, pp. 1–37 (2001).

Planning Partially for Situated Agents

Paolo Mancarella[1], Fariba Sadri[2], Giacomo Terreni[1], and Francesca Toni[1,2]

[1] University of Pisa, Pisa, Italy
{paolo, terreni, toni}@di.unipi.it
[2] Department of Computing, Imperial College London, UK
{fs, ft}@doc.ic.ac.uk

Abstract. In recent years, within the planning literature there has been a departure from approaches computing *total plans* for given goals, in favour of approaches computing *partial plans*. Total plans can be seen as (partially ordered) sets of actions which, if executed successfully, would *lead* to the achievement of the goals. Partial plans, instead, can be seen as (partially ordered) sets of actions which, if executed successfully, would *contribute* to the achievement of the goals, subject to the achievement of further *sub-goals*. Planning partially (namely computing partial plans for goals) is useful (or even necessary) for a number of reasons: (i) because the planning agent is resource-bounded, (ii) because the agent has incomplete and possibly incorrect knowledge of the environment in which it is situated, (iii) because this environment is highly dynamic. In this paper, we propose a framework to design situated agents capable of planning partially. The framework is based upon the specification of planning problems via an abductive variant of the event calculus.

1 Introduction

Conventional GOFAI planners and planning techniques (e.g. [1]) rely upon a number of assumptions: (i) that the planning agent can devote as many resources as required to the planning task, and thus it can keep on planning until a *total plan* for some given goals is obtained, (ii) that the knowledge of the agent is complete and correct at the planning time, and (iii) that the environment in which the agent is situated will not change between the planning time and the time of execution of the plan, and thus the plan will be directly executable, thus leading to achieving the goals it is meant to achieve. These assumptions are unrealistic in most cases where planning is used, e.g. when the planning agent is a robot in a dynamic physical environment.

A number of approaches have been proposed in the literature to cope with the limitations of GOFAI planners, starting from early work on hierarchical planning. In this paper, we present an approach to planning whereby the planning agent generates possibly *partial plans*, namely (partially ordered) sets of actions which, if executed successfully, would *contribute* to the achievement of the goals, subject to the achievement of further *sub-goals*. A partial plan, like a hierarchical plan, is obtained by decomposition of *top-level goals*. A partial plan

J. Leite and P. Torroni (Eds.): CLIMA V, LNAI 3487, pp. 230–248, 2005.
© Springer-Verlag Berlin Heidelberg 2005

consists of sub-goals, that still need to be planned for, and *actions*, that can be directly executed, subject to their *preconditions* holding. Preconditions are also part of partial plans, and they need planning for before the actions can be executed. Within our approach, the decomposition of top-level goals, sub-goals and preconditions into total plans is interleaved with the observation of the environment in which the agent is situated, via a *sensing* capability of the agent. Sensed changes in the environment are assimilated within the planning knowledge base of the agent. Currently, this assimilation is done rather straightforwardly, by adding the sensed information to the planning knowledge base and, if inconsistent with it, by "dropping" (implicitly) the existing beliefs in this knowledge base that lead to the inconsistency. Thus, our approach relies upon full trust upon the sensing capability of the agent. Observations from the environment in turn might lead to the need to revise the currently held partial plan, because as a consequence of the observations the agent notices that some top-level goals, sub-goals or preconditions already hold, or that they need to be re-planned for, or that they will never hold.

We adopt a novel variant of the event calculus [10], based upon abduction, to represent the planning knowledge base of agents, which allows to perform partial planning and to assimilate observations from the environment (in the simple manner described above). We represent top-level goals, sub-goals, preconditions and actions in the language of the event calculus. We impose a *tree structure* over top-level goals, sub-goals, preconditions and actions to support the revision of partial plans after observations and because of the passage of time. We define the behaviour of the planning agent via a *sense − revise − plan − execute* life-cycle, which relies upon *(state) transitions* (for sensing, revision, planning and action execution) and *selection functions* to select intelligently top-level goals, sub-goals and preconditions to plan for and actions to be executed. A variant of the approach described here has been used within KGP agents [7, 2] and realized within the prototype implementation $PROSOCS$ [19] of KGP agents.

The paper is organised as follows. In section 2 we give some background on abductive logic programming with constraints, since the event calculus-based planning knowledge base of agents we adopt is a theory in this framework. In section 3 we give the planning knowledge base. In section 4 we define our partial plans and the cycle of planning agents. In section 5 we define the individual transitions. In section 6 we define the selection functions. In section 7 we give a simple example. In section 8 we evaluate our approach against related work and conclude.

2   Background: Abductive Logic Programming with Constraints

We briefly recall the framework of Abductive Logic Programming (ALP) for knowledge representation and reasoning [8], which underlies our planning technique. An *abductive logic program* is a triple $\langle P, A, I \rangle$ where:

- *P* is a *normal logic program*, namely a set of rules (clauses) of the form $H \leftarrow L_1, \ldots, L_n$ with H atom, $L_1, \ldots, L_n$ literals, and $n \geq 0$. Literals can be positive, namely atoms, or negative, namely of the form *not B*, where B is an atom. The negation symbol *not* indicates *negation as failure*. All variables in H, L_i are implicitly universally quantified, with scope the entire rule. H is called the *head* and $L_1, \ldots L_n$ is called the *body* of a rule. If $n = 0$, then the rule is called a *fact*.
- *A* is a set of *abducible predicates* in the language of P, not occurring in the head of any clause of P (without loss of generality, see [8]). Atoms whose predicate is abducible are referred to as *abducible atoms* or simply *abducibles*.
- *I* is a set of *integrity constraints*, that is, a set of sentences in the language of P. All the integrity constraints in this paper will have the implicative form $L_1, \ldots, L_n \Rightarrow A_1 \vee \ldots \vee A_m$ $(n \geq 0, m > 1)$ where L_i are literals[1], A_j are atoms (possibly the special atom *false*). All variables in the integrity constraints are implicitly universally quantified from the outside, except for variables occurring only in the *head* $A_1 \vee \ldots \vee A_m$, which are implicitly existentially quantified with scope the head. $L_1, \ldots, L_n$ is referred to as the *body*.

Given an abductive logic program $\langle P, A, I \rangle$ and a formula (*query/observation/goal*) Q, which is an (implicitly existentially quantified) conjunction of literals in the language of the abductive logic program, the purpose of abduction is to find a (possibly minimal) set of (ground) abducible atoms Δ which, together with P, "entails" (an appropriate ground instantiation of) Q, with respect to some notion of "entailment" that the language of P is equipped with, and such that this extension of P "satisfies" I (see [8] for possible notions of integrity constraint "satisfaction"). Here, the notion of "entailment" depends on the semantics associated with the logic program P (there are many different possible choices for such semantics [8]). More formally and concretely, given a query Q, a set of (ground) abducible atoms Δ, and a variable substitution θ for the variables in Q, the pair (Δ, θ) is a *(basic) abductive answer* for Q, with respect to an abductive logic program $\langle P, A, I \rangle$, iff $P \cup \Delta \models_{LP} Q\theta$, and $P \cup \Delta \models_{LP} I$, where $\models_{LP}$ is a chosen semantics for logic programming. In this paper, we will not commit to any such semantics.

The framework of ALP can be usefully extended to handle constraint predicates in the same way Constraint Logic Programming (CLP) [6] extends logic programming. This extension allows to deal with non-ground abducibles, needed to support our planning approach. The CLP framework is defined over a particular structure $\Re$ consisting of domain $D(\Re)$ and a set of constraint predicates which includes equality, together with an assignment of relations on $D(\Re)$ for each constraint predicate. The structure is equipped with a notion of $\Re$-satisfiability. In this paper, the constraint predicates will be $<, \leq, >, \leq, =, \neq$, but we will not commit to any concrete structure for their interpretation. Given a (set of) constraints C, $\models_\Re C$ will stand for C is $\Re$-satisfiable, and $\sigma \models_\Re C$, for some grounding σ of the variables of C over $D(\Re)$, will stand for C is $\Re$-satisfied via σ.

---

[1] If $n = 0$, then $L_1, \ldots, L_n$ represents the special atom *true*.

The rules of a constraint logic program P take the same form as the rules in conventional logic programming, but with constraints occurring in the body of rules. Similarly, P and I in an abductive logic program might have constraints in their bodies. The semantics of a logic program with constraints is obtained by combining the logic programming semantics $\models_{LP}$ and $\Re$-satisfiability [6]. Below, we will refer to such a combined semantics as $\models_{LP(\Re)}$.

The notion of basic abductive answer can be extended to incorporate constraint handling as follows. Given a query Q (possibly with constraints), a set Δ of (possibly non-ground) abducible atoms, and a set C of (possibly non-ground) constraints, the pair (Δ, C) is an *abductive answer with constraints* for Q, with respect to an abductive logic program with constraints $\langle P, A, I \rangle$, with the constraints interpreted on $\Re$, iff for all groundings σ for the variables in Q, Δ, C such that $\sigma \models_\Re C$ then, (i) $P \cup \Delta\sigma \models_{LP(\Re)} Q\sigma$, and (ii) $P \cup \Delta\sigma \models_{LP(\Re)} I$.

In the sequel, we will use the following extended notion of abductive answer. Given an abductive logic program (with constraints) $\langle P, A, I \rangle$, a query Q (with constraints), an initial set of (possibly non-ground) abducible atoms Δ_0 and an initial set of (possibly non-ground) constraint atoms C_0, an *abductive answer* for Q, with respect to $\langle P, A, I \rangle$, Δ_0, C_0, is a pair (Δ, C) such that $\Delta \cap \Delta_0 = \{\}$, $C \cap C_0 = \{\}$, and $(\Delta \cup \Delta_0, C \cup C_0)$ is an abductive answer with constraints for Q, with respect to $\langle P, A, I \rangle$.

In abductive logic programming (with constraints), abductive answers are computed via *abductive proof procedures*, which typically extend SLD-resolution, providing the computational backbone underneath most logic programming systems, in order to check and enforce integrity constraint satisfaction, the generation of abducible atoms, and the satisfiability of constraint atoms (if any). There are a number of such procedures in the literature, e.g. CIFF [4, 3]. Any such (correct) procedure could be adopted to obtain a concrete planning system based upon our approach. Within KGP agents [7, 19] we have adopted CIFF to perform the planning tasks along the lines described in this paper.

3   Representing a Planning Domain

In our framework, a planning problem is specified within the framework of the event calculus (EC) for reasoning about actions, events and changes [10], in terms of an abductive logic program with constraints $KB_{plan} = \langle P_{plan}, A_{plan}, I_{plan} \rangle$ and an ordinary logic program KB_{pre}. The EC allows to represent a wide variety of phenomena, including operations with indirect effects, non-deterministic operations, and concurrent operations [15]. A number of abductive variants of the EC have been proposed to deal with planning problems. Here, we propose a novel variant KB_{plan}, somewhat inspired by the $\mathcal{E}$-language of [9], to allow situated agents to generate partial plans in a dynamic environment. In a nutshell, the conventional EC allows to write meta-logic programs which "talk" about object-level concepts of *fluents*, *operations*, and *time points*. We allow fluents to be positive, indicated e.g. as F, or negative, indicated e.g. as $\neg F$. Fluent literals will be indicated e.g. as L. The main meta-predicates of the formalism are: $holds\_at(L, T)$ (a fluent literal L holds at a time T), $clipped(T_1, F, T_2)$ (a fluent F is clipped - from holding to not holding - between a time T_1 and a time T_2), $declipped(T_1, F, T_2)$ (a fluent F is declipped - from not holding to holding - between a time T_1 and a time T_2), $initially(L)$ (a fluent literal L holds at the initial time, say time 0), $happens(O, T)$ (an operation/action O happens at a time T), $initiates(O, T, F)$ (a fluent F starts to hold after an operation O at time T) and $terminates(O, T, F)$ (a fluent F ceases to hold after an operation O at time T). Roughly speaking, in a planning setting the last two predicates represent the cause-effects links between operations and fluents in the modelled world. We will also use a meta-predicate $precondition(O, L)$ (the fluent literal L is one of the preconditions for the executability of the operation O). In our novel variant we also use *executed* and *observed* predicates to deal with dynamic environments and the *assume_holds* predicate to allow for partial planning.

We now give KB_{plan}. P_{plan} consists of domain-independent and domain-dependent rules. The basic *domain-independent rules*, adapted from the original EC, are:

$$holds\_at(F, T_2) \leftarrow happens(O, T_1), initiates(O, T_1, F),$$
$$T_1 < T_2, \neg\, clipped(T_1, F, T_2)$$
$$holds\_at(\neg F, T_2) \leftarrow happens(O, T_1), terminates(O, T_1, F),$$
$$T_1 < T_2, \neg\, declipped(T_1, F, T_2)$$
$$holds\_at(F, T) \leftarrow initially(F), 0 < T, \neg\, clipped(0, F, T)$$
$$holds\_at(\neg F, T) \leftarrow initially(\neg F), 0 < T, \neg\, declipped(0, F, T)$$
$$clipped(T_1, F, T_2) \leftarrow happens(O, T), terminates(O, T, F), T_1 \leq T < T_2$$
$$declipped(T_1, F, T_2) \leftarrow happens(O, T), initiates(O, T, F), T_1 \leq T < T_2$$

The *domain-dependent rules* define the *initiates*, *terminates*, and *initially* predicates. We show a simple example for such rules within the *blocks-world* domain.

Example 1. The domain dependent rules for the $mv(X, Y)$ operation in the block world domain, whose effects are to move block X onto block Y, are the following:

$$initiates(mv(X, Y), T, on(X, Y))$$
$$terminates(mv(X, Y), T, clear(Y))$$
$$terminates(mv(X, Y), T, on(X, Z)) \leftarrow holds\_at(on(X, Z), T), Y \neq Z$$
$$initiates(mv(X, Y), T, clear(Z)) \quad \leftarrow holds\_at(on(X, Z), T), Y \neq Z$$

namely the $mv(X, Y)$ operation *initiates* block X to be on block Y and *terminates* Y being clear. Moreover, if block X was on a block Z, the operation mv *terminates* this relation and *initiates* block Z being clear.

The conditions for the rules defining *initiates* and *terminates* can be seen as preconditions for the effects of the operation (e.g. mv in the earlier example) to be established. Conditions for the executability of operations are specified within KB_{pre}, which consists of a set of rules defining the predicate *precondition*.

Example 2. The preconditions for the executability of operation $mv(X, Y)$ are that both X and Y are clear, namely:

$$precondition(mv(X, Y), clear(X)) \qquad precondition(mv(X, Y), clear(Y))$$

□

In order to accommodate (partial) planning we will assume that the domain-independent part in P_{plan} also contains the rules:

$$happens(O,T) \leftarrow assume\_happens(O,T)$$
$$holds\_at(L,T) \leftarrow assume\_holds(L,T)$$
i.e. an operation can be made to happen and a fluent can be made to hold simply by assuming them, where $assume\_happens$ and $assume\_holds$ are the only predicates in A_{plan} in KB_{plan}. This supports partial planning as follows. We will see that actions in our specification amount to atoms in the abducible predicate $assume\_happens$: thus, abducing an atom in this predicate amounts to planning to execute the corresponding action. Moreover, as yet unplanned for, sub-goals in our specification of partial plans amount to atoms in the abducible predicate $assume\_holds(L,T)$: abducing an atom in this predicate indicates that further planning is needed for the corresponding sub-goal.

I_{plan} in KB_{plan} contains the following domain-independent integrity constraints:

$$holds\_at(F,T), holds\_at(\neg F,T) \Rightarrow false$$
$$assume\_happens(A,T), not\ executed(A,T), time\_now(T') \Rightarrow T > T'$$
namely a fluent and its negation cannot hold at the same time and when assuming (planning) that an action will happen, we need to enforce it to be executable in the future.

As we will see in section 4, a concrete planning problem is influenced (amongst other things) by a *narrative* of events, which, unlike KB_{plan} and KB_{pre}, changes over the life-cycle of the agent. We refer to the agent's representation of this narrative as KB_0. We assume that KB_0 represents events via predicates $executed$ and $observed$, e.g., the KB_0 of an agent in the blocks-world domain with a and b as two blocks, might contain:

$$executed(mv(a,b),3) \quad observed(\neg on(b,a),10) \quad observed(ag,mv(c,d),3,5)$$
namely the agent has *executed* a $mv(a,b)$ operation at time 3, the agent has *observed* that $\neg on(b,a)$ holds at time 10 and the agent has observed at time 5 that another agent ag has moved block c onto block d at time 3. Observations are drawn, via specific sensing capabilities of agents, from the environment in which they are situated, and are recorded in KB_0, as are records of actions executed by the agent itself. To allow agents to draw conclusions, via the EC, from the contents of KB_0 the following *bridge rules* are also contained in the domain independent rules of P_{plan}:

$$clipped(T_1,F,T_2) \quad \leftarrow observed(\neg F,T), T_1 \leq T < T_2$$
$$declipped(T_1,F,T_2) \leftarrow observed(F,T), T_1 \leq T < T_2$$
$$holds\_at(F,T_2) \qquad \leftarrow observed(F,T_1), T_1 \leq T_2, \neg\ clipped(T_1,F,T_2)$$
$$holds\_at(\neg F,T_2) \qquad \leftarrow observed(\neg F,T_1), T_1 \leq T_2, \neg\ declipped(T_1,F,T_2)$$
$$happens(O,T) \qquad \leftarrow executed(O,T)$$
$$happens(O,T) \qquad \leftarrow observed(A,O,T',T)$$

Note that we assume that the value of a fluent literal is changed according to observations only from the moment the observations are made, and actions by other agents have effects only from the time observations are made that they have been executed, rather than from the execution time itself. These choices are dictated by the rationale that observations can only have effects from the moment the planning agent makes them.

4   Representing Planning Problems and the Life-Cycle of Agents

Given a planning domain and a set of (top-level) goals *Goals* held by the agent, each of the form $holds\_at(L, T)$, we represent a *partial plan* for *Goals* as a triple $\langle Strategy, Parent, TC \rangle$, where

- *Strategy* is a set of *subgoals* and *preconditions*, each of the form $holds\_at(L, T)$, and of *actions*, each of the form $assume\_happens(L, T)$; each T of goals, subgoals, preconditions and actions is existentially quantified in the context of the goals and the partial plan; each such T is unique as we shall see in section 5; thus, such time variable uniquely identifies goals, subgoals, preconditions and actions;
- *Parent* is a function from *Strategy* to *Goals* ∪ *Strategy*, inducing a *tree structure* over the *Goals* and the *Strategy*; the root of this tree is the special symbol ⊥, its children are all the goals in *Goals*, and the children of any other node in the tree is the set of all subgoals/preconditions/actions which are mapped, via *Parent*, onto the node; as we shall see in section 5, preconditions can only be children of actions, whereas subgoals and actions can be children of goals, subgoals or preconditions;
- *TC* is a set of *temporal constraints* over the times of goals, subgoals, preconditions and actions in *Strategy*, namely constraint atoms in the language of KB_{plan}.

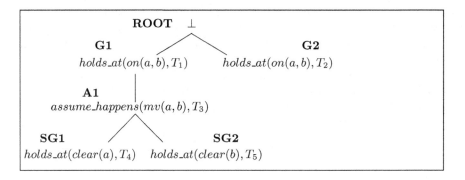

Above we show a simple tree structure (where a Gn represents a goal, an SGn represents a subgoal and an An represents an action) for the blocks world domain, for the example given later in Section 7, to which we remand for details.

In the sequel, we will refer to any of goals, subgoals, preconditions and actions as *nodes*. Moreover, with an abuse of notation, we will represent nodes N in *Goals* and *Strategy* as pairs $\langle holds\_at(L, T), Pt \rangle$ and $\langle assume\_happens(O, T), Pt \rangle$, where $Pt = Parent(N)$, and we will omit mentioning *Parent* in partial plans.

Given a planning domain, we represent a concrete planning problem, at a certain time τ (to be interpreted as the current time), via a notion of *state* defined below. Then, the planning process amounts to a sequence of such states, at incremental times, corresponding to the agent's life-cycle.

Definition 1. *An agent's state at time τ is a tuple $\langle KB_0, \Sigma, Goals, Strategy, TC \rangle$, where*

- KB_0 *is the recorded set of observations and executed operators (up until τ);*
- Σ *is the set of all bindings $T = X$, where T is the time variable associated with some action recorded as having been executed by the agent itself within KB_0, with the associated execution time X;*
- *Goals is the set of (currently unachieved) goals, held by the agent at time τ;*
- $\langle Strategy, TC \rangle$ *is a partial plan for Goals, held by the agent at time τ;*

Below, by the tree corresponding to a state we mean the tree corresponding to the *Goals* and *Strategy* in the state, and to a node of the tree to indicate an element of *Strategy* $\cup$ *Goals*, thus excluding $\bot$.

We now introduce the concepts of *initial state* and *final state*. An initial state is a state of the form $\langle \{\}, \{\}, Goals, \{\}, TC \rangle$, where TC are the given temporal constraints for *Goals*. The tree Tr_S corresponding to an initial state S is a two-level tree with root $\bot$ and all the goals in *Goals* as the children of $\bot$.

A final state can be either a *success state* or a *failure state*. A success state is a state of the form $\langle KB_0, \Sigma, \{\}, \{\}, TC \rangle$.

A failure state is a state of the form: $\langle KB_0, \Sigma, \oslash, \{\}, TC \rangle$, where the symbol $\oslash$ indicates that there is no way to achieve *one* of the initial goals. [2]

In our framework, an agent which wants to plan in order to achieve its goals behaves according to a *life-cycle* which is an adaptation of the classical *sense - plan - execute* cycle. Concretely, such a life-cycle can be seen as the repetition of a sequence of steps

$$sense - revise - plan - execute$$

starting from an initial state until a final state is reached. In the next section we show the specification of the various steps, in the form of *state transitions*. Thus, the life-cycle of the planning agent can be equated to a sequence of states, each at a specific time τ. The corresponding tree varies during the life-cycle of the agent, by inserting and deleting nodes, as specified in the next section.

We will use the following notation. Given a state S, with its corresponding tree Tr_S:

- the set of *siblings* of a node $N \in Tr_S$ of the form $\langle \_, Pt \rangle$ is the set $Siblings(N, Tr_S) = \{N' \in Tr_S \mid N' = \langle \_, Pt \rangle\}$.
- the set of *preconditions* of an action A of the form $\langle assume\_happens(O, T), Pt \rangle$ is the set $Pre(A, Tr_S) = \{P \in Tr_S \mid P = \langle \_, A \rangle\}$.

---

[2] This is an arbitrary decision, and we could have defined a failure state as one where there is no way to achieve all the goals, and a success state as one where at least one goal can be achieved.

5   Transitions Specification

Here we give the specification of the state transitions determining the life-cycle of the planning agent. We refer to these transitions as the *sensing transition*, the *planning transition*, the *execution transition*, and the *revision transition*. The planning and execution transitions take inputs that are computed via *selection functions*, defined in section 6.

5.1   Sensing Transition

Given a state $S = \langle KB_0, \Sigma, Goals, Strategy, TC \rangle$ at a time τ, the application of a sensing transition at τ leads to a state $S' = \langle KB_0', \Sigma, Goals, Strategy, TC \rangle$, where KB_0' is obtained from KB_0 by adding any observations on fluent literals at τ and any observations at τ that an operation has been executed by another agent (at an earlier time). These observations are obtained by calling the *sensing capability* of the agent at time τ which we refer to as $\models_{Env}^{\tau}$, which accesses the environment of the agent.

Definition 2. *Given a state* $S = \langle KB_0, \Sigma, Goals, Strategy, TC \rangle$ *at a time* τ, *if*
$$\models_{Env}^{\tau} l_1 \wedge \ldots \wedge l_n \wedge a_1 \wedge \ldots \wedge a_m$$
where $n + m \geq 0$, *each* l_i *is a fluent literal and each* a_j *is an operation* o_j *executed by agent* ag_j *at some earlier time* τ_j, *then the* sensing transition *leads to a state* $S' = \langle KB_0', \Sigma, Goals, Strategy, TC \rangle$ *where:*

$$KB_0' = KB_0 \cup \{observed(l_1, \tau) \cup \ldots \cup observed(l_n, \tau)\}$$
$$\cup \{observed(ag_1, o_1, \tau_1, \tau), \ldots, observed(ag_m, o_m, \tau_m, \tau)\}.$$

5.2   Planning Transition

The planning transition relies upon a *planning selection function* $SelP(S, \tau)$ which, given as input a state S at time τ returns a (single) goal, subgoal or precondition to be planned for. The extension whereby multiple goals, subgoals and preconditions are returned by the selection function is straightforward. In this section, we assume that such a selection function is given (a possible specification is provided in the next section).

We introduce the following useful notation which will be helpful in defining the planning transition. Let $S = \langle KB_0, \Sigma, Goals, Strategy, TC \rangle$ be a state. Then:

- for any set $X \subseteq Goals \cup Strategy$, by $X(\Sigma)$ we denote the set obtained by applying to each element of X the instantiations provided by Σ;
- given a node $G \in Goals \cup Strategy$, by $Rest(G)$ we denote the set $Rest(G) = Strategy(\Sigma) \cup Goals(\Sigma) - G(\Sigma)$;
- given a node $N \in Goals \cup Strategy$, we denote by $\mathcal{A}(N)$ the *abducible version* of N, namely
$$\mathcal{A}(N) = \begin{cases} assume\_happens(O, T) & \text{if } N = \langle assume\_happens(O, T), \_\rangle \\ assume\_holds(L, T) & \text{if } N = \langle holds\_at(L, T), \_\rangle \end{cases}$$
This notation is lifted to any set X of nodes as usual, i.e. $\mathcal{A}(X) = \bigcup_{N \in X} \mathcal{A}(N)$.

Intuitively, given a state $S = \langle KB_0, \Sigma, Goals, Strategy, TC \rangle$, the planning transition builds a (partial) plan for a given goal, subgoal or precondition G in terms of an abductive answer, as defined in section 2, and updates the state accordingly. More precisely, an abductive answer is computed with respect to:

- the abductive logic program with constraints KB_{plan}, as defined in Section 3;
- the initial query Q given by G;
- the initial set of abducibles Δ_0 given by the abducible version of the current tree (except for G), namely $\mathcal{A}(Rest(G))$;
- the initial set of constraints C_0 given by the current set of constraints in the state, along with the instantiations in Σ, namely $TC \cup \Sigma$.

Once such abductive answer, say (Δ, C'), is obtained, the planning transition leads to a new state $S' = \langle KB_0, \Sigma, Goals, Strategy', TC' \rangle$ where $Strategy'$ is $Strategy$ augmented with the actions, goals and preconditions derived from Δ, and TC' is TC augmented with C' and with suitable equalities on the time variables of the preconditions of actions added to the state. We assume that the abducibles in Δ do not share time variables[3]. This is formalised in the next definition.

Definition 3. *Given a state $S = \langle KB_0, \Sigma, Goals, Strategy, TC \rangle$ at a time τ and the node $G = SelP(S, \tau)$, let (Δ, C') be an abductive answer for the query G with respect to the abductive logic program (with constraints) KB_{plan}, and initial sets $\Delta_0 = \mathcal{A}(Rest(G))$ and $C_0 = TC \cup \Sigma$. Then, the planning transition leads to a state $S' = \langle KB_0, \Sigma, Goals, Strategy', TC' \rangle$ where $Strategy'$ and TC' are obtained by augmenting $Strategy$ and TC as follows:*

- *for each $assume\_holds(L, T) \in \Delta$, $\langle holds\_at(L, T), G \rangle$ is added in $Strategy'$*
- *for each $assume\_happens(O, T) \in \Delta$*
  - *$A = \langle happens(O, T), G \rangle$ is added in $Strategy'$, and*
  - *for each P such that $precondition(happens(O, T), P) \in KB_{pre}$, let T_p be a fresh time variable; then:*
    $\langle holds\_at(P, T_P), A \rangle$ is added in $Strategy'$, and
    $T_P = T$ is added in TC'
  - *C' is added in TC'*

Note that this transition enforces that preconditions of actions hold at the time of the execution of the actions, by adding such preconditions to $Strategy'$ so that they will need planning for. Note also that, when introducing preconditions, we need to make sure that their time variable is new, and relate this, within TC', to the time variable of the action whose preconditions we are enforcing.

5.3   Execution Transition

Similarly to the planning transition, the execution transition relies upon an *execution selection function* $SelE(S, \tau)$ which, given a state S and a time τ,

---

[3] Notice that this is not a restrictive assumption, since shared variables can be renamed and suitable equalities can be added to the constraints in C'.

returns a (single) action to be executed (a possible specification of this selection function is provided in the next section). The extension to the case of multiple actions is straightforward.

Definition 4. *Given a state $S = \langle KB_0, \Sigma, Goals, Strategy, TC \rangle$ at a time τ and an action A of the form $\langle assume\_happens(O, T), Pt \rangle$ such that $A = SelE(S, \tau)$, then the* execution transition *leads to a state $S' = \langle KB'_0, \Sigma', Goals, Strategy, TC \rangle$ where:*

- $KB'_0 = KB_0 \cup \{executed(O, \tau)\}$
- $\Sigma' = \Sigma \cup \{T = \tau\}$

Note that we are implicitly assuming that actions are ground except for their time variable. The extension to deal with other variables in actions is straightforward.

Executed actions are eliminated from states by the revision transition, presented next.

5.4   Revision Transition

To specify the revision transition we need to introduce some useful concepts. A node is said to be *obsolete* wrt a state S at a time τ for any of the following reasons:

- The node is a goal, subgoal or precondition node and the node itself is achieved.
- The parent of the node is obsolete wrt S and τ. Indeed, if a node is obsolete there is no reason to plan for or execute any of its children (or descendants).

Thus, obsolete nodes amount to achieved goals, subgoals and preconditions and actions that have been introduced for them (and thus become redundant).

Definition 5. *Given a state $S = \langle KB_0, \Sigma, Goals, Strategy, TC \rangle$ at a time τ, we define the set of* obsolete nodes $Obsolete(S, \tau)$ *as the set composed of each node $N \in Strategy \cup Goals$ of the form $N = \langle X, Pt \rangle$ such that:*

- $Pt \in Obsolete(S, \tau)$ *or*
- $X = holds\_at(L, T) and P_{plan} \cup KB_0 \models_{LP(\Re)} \Sigma \wedge holds\_at(L, T) \wedge T \leq \tau \wedge TC$

A node is *timed out* wrt a state S at a time τ for any of the following reasons:

- It has not been achieved yet, and there is no way to achieve it in the future due to temporal constraints.
- Its parent or one of its siblings is timed out wrt S and τ. Indeed, if either the parent or a sibling of the node is timed out, there is no reason to keep the node for later planning. This condition is not imposed if the node is a top-level goal because top-level goals do not influence each other (except via possible temporal constraints on their time variables).

Definition 6. *Given a state $S = \langle KB_0, \Sigma, Goals, Strategy, TC \rangle$ at a time τ, we define the set of* timed out nodes $TimedOut(S, \tau)$ *as the set composed of each node $N \in Strategy \cup Goals$ of the form $\langle holds\_at(L,T), Pt \rangle$ such that:*

- $N \notin Obsolete(S, \tau)$ and $\not\models_{\Re} \Sigma \wedge TC \wedge T > \tau$ or
- $Pt \in TimedOut(S, \tau)$ or
- $N \notin Goals$ and there exists $N' \in Siblings(N)$ such that $N' \in TimedOut(S, \tau))$.

Using the above definitions we now define the revision transition which, roughly speaking, removes obsolete and timed out nodes.

Definition 7. *Given a state $S = \langle KB_0, \Sigma, Goals, Strategy, TC \rangle$ at a time τ, the* revision transition *leads to a state $S' = \langle KB_0, \Sigma, Goals', Strategy', TC \rangle$ where, for each $N \in Strategy' \cup Goals'$:*

- $N \notin TimedOut(S, \tau)$, and
- if $N = \langle assume\_happens(O, T), \_ \rangle$ then it is not the case that executed$(O, \tau') \in KB_0$ and $T = \tau' \in \Sigma$, and
- if $N \in Obsolete(S, \tau)$ then $Parent(N) = \langle assume\_happens(O, T), \_ \rangle$, and
- $Parent(N) \in Goals' \cup Strategy'$.

Intuitively, each timed out node, each obsolete node and each executed action has to be eliminated from the tree. The only exception is represented by preconditions. Indeed, obsolete precondition at revision time are not eliminated because they must hold at execution time. If an obsolete precondition p for an action a is eliminated at revision time due to the fact that it holds at that time, something could happen later on (e.g. an external change or an action performed by some other agent or by the agent itself) that invalidates p so that it does not hold when a is executed. Note that we could also impose for the temporal constraints to be simplified at revision time, but this is not necessary to guarantee the correctness of our approach.

6   Selection Functions

The planning and execution transitions require a *selection function* each. Here, we give possible definitions for these functions. Note that we use the term function loosely, as the selection randomly returns one of possibly several candidates.

6.1   Planning Selection Function

Given a state $S = \langle KB_0, \Sigma, Goals, Strategy, TC \rangle$ at a time τ, the planning transition needs a *planning selection function* $SelP(S, \tau)$ to select a goal, subgoal or precondition G belonging to $Goals$ or $Strategy$, to be planned for. We define $SelP$ so that G satisfies the following properties:

- neither G nor any ancestor or sibling of G is timed out at τ;
- neither G nor an ancestor of G is achieved at τ; i.e. G is not obsolete and it does not hold at the current time;
- no plan for G belongs to S.

Definition 8. *Given a state* $S = \langle KB_0, \Sigma, Goals, Strategy, TC \rangle$ *at a time* τ, *the* planning selection function $SelP(S, \tau)$ *returns a goal, a subgoal or a precondition* $G = \langle holds\_at(L, T), \_ \rangle$ *such that:*

- $G \notin TimedOut(S, \tau)$;
- $G \notin Obsolete(S, \tau)$, *and it is not the case that*
  $P_{plan} \cup KB_0 \models_{LP(\Re)} holds\_at(L, T) \wedge T = \tau \wedge TC \wedge \Sigma$
- *there exists no* $G' \in Strategy$ *such that* $G = Parent(G')$;

Clearly it may be possible that a number of goals, subgoals and preconditions in a state satisfy the above properties and thus could be selected. We could further incorporate a number of heuristics to restrict the number of candidates G to be selected amongst.

6.2   Execution Selection Function

Given a state $S = \langle KB_0, \Sigma, Goals, Strategy, TC \rangle$ at a time τ, the execution transition needs an *execution selection function* $SelE(S, \tau)$ to select an action A in $Strategy$ to be executed at τ. We define $SelE$ so that A satisfies the following properties:

- neither A nor any ancestor or sibling of A is timed out at τ;
- all preconditions (children) of A are satisfied at τ;
- no (goal, subgoal or precondition) ancestor of A is satisfied at τ;
- A has not been executed yet.

Definition 9. *Given a state* $S = \langle KB_0, \Sigma, Goals, Strategy, TC \rangle$ *at a time* τ, *the execution selection function* $SelE(S, \tau)$ *returns an action* $A = \langle assume\_happens(O, T), \_ \rangle$ *such that:*

- $A \notin TimedOut(S, \tau)$;
- *for each* $P = \langle holds\_at(P, T'), A \rangle \in Strategy$, $P \in Obsolete(S', \tau)$
  where $S' = \langle KB_0, \Sigma, Goals, Strategy, TC \cup \{T = \tau\} \rangle$;
- $A \notin Obsolete(S, \tau)$;
- *there exists no* τ' *such that* $executed(O, \tau') \in KB_0$ *and* $T = \tau' \in \Sigma$.

Notice that in the second condition, we need to add $\{T = \tau\}$ to the temporal constraint of the state S because preconditions have to be checked in a state where the time of execution of the selected action is τ. Again, heuristics could be incorporated within the execution selection function to restrict the number of selectable actions.

7   An Example

In this section we show a simple example of life-cycle of an agent in the blocks-world domain of examples 1 and 2.

We assume to have three blocks, a, b, c, all on the table initially. The formalisation of the initial configuration, using a special location $table$, is as follows:

$initially(on(a, table))$, $initially(on(b, table))$, $initially(on(c, table))$,
$initially(clear(a))$, $initially(clear(b))$, $initially(clear(c))$

Our objective is to have a tower with c on b on a by time 20. We can formalise this via top-level goals:

$G_1 = \langle holds\_at(on(b, a), T_1), \bot \rangle$ $G_2 = \langle holds\_at(on(c, b), T_2), \bot \rangle$

where $TC^0 = \{T_1 = T_2, T_1 \leq 20\}$

The following is a possible life-cycle of the agent, achieving G_1 and G_2.

Initial State: $S_0 = \langle \{\}, \{\}, \{G_1, G_2\}, \{\}, TC^0 \rangle$

Time 1 - Sensing Transition: $\models_{Env}^1 \{\}$

Resulting state: $S_1 = S_0$

Time 2 - Revision Transition: There is nothing to be revised at this point.

Resulting state: $S_2 = S_1$

Time 3 - Planning Transition: Assume that $SelP(S_2, 3) = G_1$. Let (Δ, C) be the abductive answer wrt KB_{plan}, $\Delta_0 = \{assume\_holds(on(c, b), T_2)\}$ and $C_0 = TC^0$, where $\Delta = \{assume\_happens(mv(b, a), T_3)\}$ and $C = \{T_3 < T_1\}$. Let

$Strategy^3 = \{ \langle assume\_happens(mv(b, a), T_3), G_1 \rangle = A_1$
$\langle holds\_at(clear(a), T_4), A_1 \rangle$
$\langle holds\_at(clear(b), T_5), A_1 \rangle \}$
$TC^3 =$ $TC^0 \cup C \cup \{T_4 = T_3, T_5 = T_3\}$

Resulting state: $S_3 = \langle \{\}, \{\}, \{G_1, G_2\}, Strategy^3, TC^3 \rangle$

At this stage the tree structure is the one given earlier in the picture in Section 4.

Time 4 - Execution Transition: as the preconditions of action A_1 are both achieved at this time due to the $initially$ rules in KB_{plan}, then $A_1 = SelE(S_3, 4)$ (A_1 is the only action that can be selected at this time). Let

$KB_0^4 = \{executed(mv(b, a), 3)$
$\Sigma^4 =$ $\{T_3 = 4\}$

Resulting state: $S_4 = \langle KB_0^4, \Sigma^4, \{G_1, G_2\}, Strategy^3, TC^3 \rangle$

Time 5 - Sensing Transition: Assume that the sensing capability of the agent forces it to observe that b is actually on c at this time and that a is clear, namely $\models_{Env}^5 \{on(b, c), \neg on(b, a), \neg on(c, table), \neg clear(c), clear(a)\}$. Basically, there has been either a problem in the execution of A_1 or an interference by some other agent. Then,

$KB_0^5 = KB_0^4 \cup \{ observed(on(b, c), 5),$ $observed(\neg on(b, a), 5),$
$observed(\neg on(c, table), 5), observed(\neg clear(c), 5),$
$observed(clear(a), 5)\}$

Resulting state: $S_5 = \langle KB_0^5, \Sigma^4, \{G_1, G_2\}, Strategy^3, TC^3 \rangle$

Time 6 - Revision Transition: At this time the revision transition deletes from the strategy the action A_1 and its preconditions as A_1 has been executed.

Resulting state: $S_6 = \langle KB_0^5, \Sigma^4, \{G_1, G_2\}, \{\}, TC^3 \rangle$

Time 7 - Planning Transition: Assume that the selected goal is again G_1, $SelP(S_6, 7) = G_1$. (Note that G_1 is again selectable as it is not achieved at time 7.) Similarly as for the previous planning transition, let:

$Strategy^7 = \{ \langle assume\_happens(mv(b,a), T_3'), G_1 \rangle = A_1'$
$\qquad\qquad \langle holds\_at(clear(a), T_4'), A_1' \rangle$
$\qquad\qquad \langle holds\_at(clear(b), T_5'), A_1' \rangle \}$
$TC^7 = \qquad TC^3 \cup \{T_3' < T_1, T_4' = T_3', T_5' = T_3'\}$

Resulting state: $S_7 = \langle KB_0^5, \Sigma^4, \{G_1, G_2\}, Strategy^7, TC^7 \rangle$

Time 8 - Execution Transition: as the preconditions of action A_1 are both achieved at this time, due to the *initially* rules in KB_{plan} and to the observations in KB_0, then $A_1' = SelE(S_7, 8)$ (A_1' is the only action that can be selected at this time). Let

$KB_0^8 = \{executed(mv(b,a), 8)$
$\Sigma^8 = \quad \{T_3' = 8\}$

Resulting state: $S_8 = \langle KB_0^8, \Sigma^8, \{G_1, G_2\}, Strategy^7, TC^7 \rangle$

Time 9 - Sensing Transition: $\models_{Env}^9 \{\}$

Resulting state: $S_9 = S_8$

Time 10 - Revision Transition: At this time the revision transition deletes from the strategy the action A_1' and its preconditions as A_1' has been executed.

Resulting state: $S_{10} = \langle KB_0^8, \Sigma^8, \{G_1, G_2\}, \{\}, TC^7 \rangle$

Time 11 - Planning Transition: Assume that the selected goal is $SelP(S_{10}, 11) = G_2$. Note that at this time G_2 is the only goal that can be selected because goal G_1 is achieved. Similarly as for the previous planning transitions, let:

$Strategy^{11} = \{ \langle assume\_happens(mv(c,b), T_6), G_2 \rangle = A_2$
$\qquad\qquad \langle holds\_at(clear(a), T_7), A_2 \rangle$
$\qquad\qquad \langle holds\_at(clear(b), T_8), A_2 \rangle \}$
$TC^{11} = \qquad TC^7 \cup \{T_6 < T_2, T_7 = T_6, T_8 = T_6\}$

Resulting state: $S_{12} = \langle KB_0^8, \Sigma^8, \{G_1, G_2\}, Strategy^{11}, TC^{11} \rangle$

Time 12 - Execution Transition: action A_2 is selected. Let

$KB_0^{12} = KB_0^8 \cup \{executed(mv(c,b), 12)$
$\Sigma^{12} = \quad \{T_3 = 4, T_3' = 8, T_6 = 12\}$

Resulting state: $S_{13} = \langle KB_0^{12}, \Sigma^{12}, \{G_1, G_2\}, Strategy^{11}, TC^{11} \rangle$

Time 13 - Sensing Transition: $\models_{Env}^{13} \{\}$

Resulting state: $S_{13} = S_{12}$

Time 14 - Revision Transition: At this time the revision transition deletes from the strategy the action A_2 and its preconditions as A_2 has been executed. Moreover as both G_1 and G_2 are achieved, the revision transition deletes them from the goals leading to a successful final state.

Resulting state: $S_{14} = \langle KB_0^{12}, \Sigma^{12}, \{\}, \{\}, TC^{11} \rangle$.

8   Related Work and Conclusions

Planning has been a very active research and development area for some time. Systems have been developed for a range of applications such as medical, robotics and web services. Many approaches to planning have been proposed (e.g the

STRIPS language with its improvements and related state-of-the-art systems such as Graphplan [1]). Here we concentrate on those closer to our work.

Our approach to planning is based on the abductive *event calculus*. It is thus closely related to Shanahan's abduction and event calculus planning work [14, 15, 16, 17, 18] and to the approach based on the *situation calculus*. The latter forms the basis of GOLOG [11], an imperative language implemented in PROLOG incorporating macro-actions (as procedures) and non-determinism. GOLOG has been shown to be suitable for implementing robot programs as high-level instructions in dynamic domains.

The contribution of our paper is in describing a system that allows partial planning and the interleaving of planning with sensing and executing actions. This integration is particularly suitable for (possibly resource bounded) agents situated in dynamic environments. Our partial plans, to some extent, have the flavour of the *compound actions* of Shanahan [16]. If well defined, both approaches allow us to find executable actions quickly. However, our formalisation is simpler than [16] as we do not need to use compound actions in our theories in order to achieve partial planning.

Compound actions are also exploited in the situation calculus, in particular [12] gives formal characterisations of compound actions and their preconditions and postconditions. Investigating how to incorporate them in our framework is subject of future work.

An important feature of our approach is the revision of the plans obtained by the Revision transition. The tree structure in the *Strategy* part of each agent state allows an intelligent, selective way of revising the (partial) plan. This means that, if replanning becomes necessary, it is done only for unachieved goals and subgoals, thus avoiding the "replanning from scratch" method seen in [16].

There are issues that we have not addressed yet. These include ramification problems, which are addressed in [17] where it is pointed out that the *state-constraints* formalisation of ramifications can lead to inconsistencies. State-constraints are of the form

$$holds\_at(P, T) \leftarrow holds\_at(P_1, T), \ldots, holds\_at(P_n, T)$$

This rule can cause inconsistencies if, at a time t, $P_1, \ldots, P_n$ and thus P hold. But at an earlier time, say t_1, $\neg P$ may hold and it is not clipped before the time t. As rules of above form are needed to model subgoals, ramification is an important issue to be addressed. One way to avoid the problem of inconsistency could be to add, for each state constraint of the form above, another rule of the form

$$declipped(P, T) \leftarrow holds\_at(P_1, T), \ldots, holds\_at(P_n, T)$$

This approach is similar to the one that we have taken in the *bridge rules* of Section 3, but needs to be further investigated.

The *Sensing transition*, described in Section 5, is important for a situated agent, but is rather simplistic. It simply adds the observation to the agent's knowledge base and the *bridge rules* in the knowledge base perform some implicit conflict resolution. An alternative approach is presented in [16]. This proposal is that, once an observation is made, (possibly abductive) explanations of it are sought, thus avoiding some possible inconsistencies and giving a richer account of causes and effects. This approach has obvious disadvantages in cases where observations are such that the agent cannot be expected to find explanations for. E.g., in a communication scenario, an agent could observe that the network is down but has no way of knowing (or even guessing) why.

Another drawback of our Sensing transition is that it is random and passive. The agent collects information from the environment as a passive observer. An *active* form of sensing is described in [7, 2] where, as well as performing physical actions, the agent can perform active knowledge-producing (or sensing) actions. Such active sensing actions do not affect the external environment but they affect the agent's knowledge about the environment. Such an active sensing action can be performed, for example, to seek information from the environment about preconditions of actions before they are performed or to seek confirmation that an executed action has had its desired outcome. Active sensing actions are also addressed in [13] for imperative GOLOG programs where they allow conditional plans whose conditions are checked at "run-time".

An issue related to observations is that of *exogenous actions*. Our handling of observations combined with the Revision transition seem to be effective to capture both exogenous actions and their effects in the sense that, if our agent detects an action or a fact which invalidate a plan or a subplan already executed, the revision procedure will replan for that part (and only for that part). Another approach to exogenous (malicious) actions is that in [5] where, if exogenous actions change the external environment, a recovery procedure is performed with which the agent is able to restore the state to the one before the exogenous event occurred.

With respect to our framework, drawbacks of that approach are that a number of assumptions have been made, in particular that the agent knows what kind of exogenous actions can be done and what their effects are. Also, this approach does not take into account the possibility that an exogenous action can "help" the agent to achieve its goals making certain subgoals and action unnecessary.

Finally, we remark that to properly evaluate our techniques, we are studying formal results such as soundness and completeness and we are doing practical experimentation with the CIFF system [4, 3] as the underlying abductive reasoner.

Acknowledgments

This work was partially funded by the IST programme of the EC, FET under the IST-2001-32530 SOCS project, within the Global Computing proactive initiative. The last author was also supported by the Italian MIUR programme "Rientro dei cervelli".

References

1. A. Blum and M. Furst. Fast planning through planning graph analysis. *Artificial Intelligence*, 90:281–300, 1997.
2. A. Bracciali, N. Demetriou, U. Endriss, A. Kakas, W. Lu, P. Mancarella, F. Sadri, K. Stathis, G. Terreni, and F. Toni. The KGP model of agency for global computing: Computational model and prototype implementation. In C. Priami and P. Quaglia, (eds.): *Global Computing: IST/FET International Workshop, GC 2004 Rovereto, Italy, March 9-12, 2004 Revised Selected Papers*, LNAI 3267, pp. 340–367. Springer-Verlag, 2005.
3. U. Endriss, P. Mancarella, F. Sadri, G. Terreni, and F. Toni. Abductive logic programming with CIFF: system description. In J.J. Alferes and J. Leite (eds.): *Logics in Artificial Intelligence. European Conference, JELIA 2004, Lisbon, Portugal, September, 27-30, Proceedings*, LNAI 3229, pp. 680-684. Springer-Verlag, 2004.
4. U. Endriss, P. Mancarella, F. Sadri, G. Terreni, and F. Toni. The CIFF proof procedure for abductive logic programming with constraints. In J.J. Alferes and J. Leite (eds.): *Logics in Artificial Intelligence. European Conference, JELIA 2004, Lisbon, Portugal, September, 27-30, Proceedings*, LNAI 3229, pp. 31-43. Springer-Verlag, 2004.
5. G. De Giacomo, R. Reiter, and M. Soutchanski. Execution monitoring of high-level robot programs. In A. G. Cohn, L. K. Schubert, S. C. Shapiro (eds.): *Proceedings of the Sixth International Conference on Principles of Knowledge Representation and Reasoning (KR'98), Trento, Italy, June 2-5*, pp. 453–465. Morgan Kaufmann, 1998.
6. J. Jaffar and M.J. Maher. Constraint logic programming: a survey. *Journal of Logic Programming*, 19-20:503–582, 1994.
7. A. Kakas, P. Mancarella, F. Sadri, K. Stathis, and F. Toni. The KGP model of agency. In R. Lopez de Mantaras and L. Saitta (eds.): *Proceedings of the Sixteenth European Conference on Artificial Intelligence, Valencia, Spain*, pp. 33–37. IOS Press, August 2004.
8. A. C. Kakas, R. A. Kowalski, and F. Toni. The role of abduction in logic programming. In D. M. Gabbay, C. J. Hogger, and J. A. Robinson, (eds.):, *Handbook of Logic in Artificial Intelligence and Logic Programming*, vol. 5, pp. 235–324. Oxford University Press, 1998.
9. A. C. Kakas and R. Miller. A simple declarative language for describing narratives with ations. *Journal of Logic Programming*, 31(1-3):157–200, 1997.
10. R. A. Kowalski and M. Sergot. A logic-based calculus of events. *New Generation Computing*, 4(1):67–95, 1986.
11. H. J. Levesque, R. Reiter, Y. Lesperance, F. Lin, and R. B. Scherl. GOLOG: A logic programming language for dynamic domains. *Journal of Logic Programming*, 31(1-3):59–83, 1997.
12. S. McIlraith and R. Fadel. Planning with complex actions. In S. Benferhat, E. Giunchiglia (eds.): *9th International Workshop on Non-Monotonic Reasoning (NMR 2002), April 19-21, Toulouse, France, Proceedings*, pp. 356–364. 2002.
13. R. Scherl and H. J. Levesque. Knowledge, action, and the frame problem. *Artificial Intelligence*, 144:1–39, 2003.
14. M. Shanahan. Event calculus planning revisited. In *Proceedings of the 4th European Conference on Planning*, LNAI 1348, pp. 390–402. Springer Verlag, 1997.
15. M. Shanahan. *Solving the Frame Problem*. MIT Press, 1997.

16. M. Shanahan. Reinventing shakey. In *Working Notes of the 1998 AAAI Fall Symposium on Cognitive Robotics*, pages 125–135, 1998.

17. M. Shanahan. The ramification problem in the event calculus. In T. Dean (ed.): *Proceedings of the Sixteenth International Joint Conference on Artificial Intelligence, Stockholm, Sweden*, pages 140–146. Morgan Kaufmann Publishers, 1999.

18. M. Shanahan. Using reactive rules to guide a forward-chaining planner. In *Proc. of the Fourth European Conference on Planning*. Springer-Verlag, 2001.

19. K. Stathis, A. C. Kakas, W. Lu, N. Demetriou, U. Endriss, and A. Bracciali. PROSOCS: a platform for programming software agents in computational logic. In R. Trappl (ed.): *Proceedings of the 17th European Meeting on Cybernetics and Systems Research, Vol. II, Symposium "From Agent Theory to Agent Implementation" (AT2AI-4), Vienna, Austria*, pp. 523–528. Austrian Society for Cybernetic Studies, 2004.

Desire-Space Analysis and Action Selection for Multiple Dynamic Goals

David C. Han and K. Suzanne Barber

The Laboratory for Intelligent Processes and Systems,
Electrical and Computer Engineering,
The University of Texas at Austin,
Austin, TX 78712
{dhan, barber}@lips.utexas.edu

Abstract. Autonomous agents are given the authority to select which actions they will execute. If the agent behaves rationally, the actions it selects will be in its own best interests. When addressing multiple goals, the rational action may not be obvious. Equipping the agents with decision-theoretic methods allows the agent to mathematically evaluate the risks, uncertainty, and benefits of the various available courses of action. Using this evaluation, an agent can determine which goals are worth achieving, as well as the order in which to achieve those goals. When the goals of the agent changes, the agent must replan to maintain rational decision-making. This research uses macro actions to transform the state space for the agent's decision problem into the desire space of the agent. Reasoning in the desire space, the agent can efficiently maintain rationality in response to addition and removal of goals.

1   Introduction

Decision theory is the mathematical evaluation of risks, uncertainty, and benefits to calculate the value of alternative choices. Applied to agents, decision theory can form the basis for rational action selection. An agent acts rationally if it performs actions that are in its "best interests" [1]. The best interests of an agent correspond to the goals an agent holds. Armed with decision theory, an agent can weigh the rewards to be gained from achieving each of its goals against the costs of actions to determine which goals are worth achieving, as well as the order in which to achieve those goals.

Over time, the interests of an agent may change, changing the actions a rational agent should take in a given situation. As a simple example, after an agent achieves a goal, it may lose interest in pursuing that particular goal. Additionally, goals may be added, removed, or modified by the designer of that agent or through interactions with other agents. Agents, being autonomous entities, are given freedom to decide their own course of action for satisfying their goals.

Determining a course of action is a sequential decision problem, where the initial decision impacts future decisions (i.e., the agent must consider not only the effects of its actions in the current state, but also the future consequences of

J. Leite and P. Torroni (Eds.): CLIMA V, LNAI 3487, pp. 249–264, 2005.
© Springer-Verlag Berlin Heidelberg 2005

any actions it takes). Further complicating the matter, the agent must consider the consequences of each action in relation to each of the goals the agent holds.

Markov decision processes (MDPs) are often used to represent and reason about sequential decision problems. Already suffering from the "curse of dimensionality," application of MDPs to domain problems containing multiple goals further exacerbates the computational issues (by adding dimensions to the state representation). These additional dimensions, representing the achievement status of goals, do not reflect the behavior of the environment, but rather the internal state of the agent. The behavior of the environment (e.g., the domain physics) is conceptually different from the goals of an agent situated in that environment. It is due to limitations of the MDP reward structure that goal information must be represented as part of the state description.

When moving from theory to practice, priorities on the characteristics of the approach shift. Taking an engineering approach, the concept of optimality takes a back seat to the concept of satisficing. Abstraction and estimation are used in the pursuit of computational efficiency at the expense of optimality. Towards this end, this work addresses a restricted class of MDPs, using simple domains to explore complex goal related behaviors. Making the assumption that the set of goals assigned to an agent is much smaller than the total set of domain states, this research uses *macro actions* to abstract away the domain physics, reasoning about the desire space of the agent. As an added benefit, desire space reasoning enables efficient computation of rational behavior in the face of changing goals for this class of problems. In multi-agent systems, an agent cannot negotiate with other agents without knowing the value of its own goals and actions. Calculation of values based on desire analysis provide the agent with the knowledge with which to negotiate with other agents. For example, when following a conversation policy, as presented by Bentahar et. al. in this volume [2], an agent can decide, through desire analysis, whether it should accept a commitment or continue argumentation or persuasion.

This paper provides a formal presentation of the problem, a formulation of the domain using goal factoring and macro actions, and algorithms for maintaining an approximate solution under dynamic goals.

2   Action Selection

Though very different in approach, a number of approaches presented in this volume seek to address the same problem of agent operation in dynamic domains. Mancarella et. al. attack much the same problem through a qualitative approach [3], compared to the quantitative approach used in this paper. Alferes, Banti, and Brogi address action description updates through logic programming [4], accounting for changes in the physics of the domain, which includes goal modification.

Planning techniques [5] provide agents with methods for analyzing the effects of their capabilities on the environment. In planning, an agent's capabilities are represented as action descriptions and desires are represented as goals. Classical

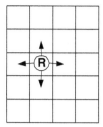

Fig. 1. Navigation Domain Example

planning finds a sequence of actions whose execution will transform the current state into a goal state. Although classical planning was not designed to handle dynamic environments (where exogenous events can occur), elaborations upon the same basic methods do. Continuous planning methods [6] allow an agent to adjust to unexpected situations by interleaving planning and execution. Decision-theoretic planning, as described by Boutilier, Dean, and Hanks [7][8], uses MDPs to perform this reasoning by allowing a range of reward values. As another benefit, MDPs naturally capture and handle the uncertainty inherent in the domain. Since the solution to an MDP consists of a policy describing the action to take in any given state, MDPs are suited for adaptation to continuous planning as well.

A Markov decision process M is a representation of this action selection problem, consisting of four components: the state space, $S = \{s_1, s_2, ..., s_N\}$; actions the agent can execute, $A = \{a_1, a_2, ..., a_L\}$; a transition function describing the probability that executing each action a in some state s will result in some state s', $T : S \times A \times S \mapsto [0, 1]$; and a reward function describing the value earned by the agent for reaching each state, $R : S \mapsto \mathbb{R}$. The product of an MDP planning algorithm is a policy $\pi : S \mapsto A$ describing what action the agent should execute for any state it may find itself in.

The class of problems addressed in this paper reflects "cost-to-move" frameworks. In cost-to-move problems, each action the agent executes incurs some cost $c < 0$ as part of the reward structure. This provides incentive for the agent to reach its goal states with the minimal amount of movement actions. An example cost-to-move domain problem is robot navigation. Figure 1 illustrates the basic setup of a robot navigation domain. The **R** in the figure shows the location of the agent in the physical environment, which is in this case modelled as a Cartesian grid. The actions available to the agent are the cardinal directions, *north*, *south*, *east*, and *west*. The cost can represent resource usage by the robot as it moves from one location to another. The desires of the robot in these domains are represented in the reward structure. For example, $R(s) \geq 0$ for those states, s, in which the robot achieves its goals.

Macro actions are used to combine the primitive actions available to the agent. Clever use of macro actions can improve computational efficiency for action selection. The remainder of this section discusses the representation of macro actions, the application of macro actions to goals or subgoals, and the concept of using macro actions to reason in the desire space of an agent.

2.1   Macro Actions

Computational efficiency for solving an MDP is greatly impacted by its size. Factoring has been used to reduce computation through abstracting the MDP into higher level states and actions. This research makes use of the concept of macro actions, specifically, the *option* model developed by Sutton, Precup, and Singh [9]. Macro actions generalize actions into courses of action. Consider, for example, a navigation problem where a robot has primitive actions allowing it to move in each of the cardinal directions. Macro actions are defined as policies using those primitive actions that describe higher level objectives such as moving from room to room. Figure 2 shows the difference between options and actions. The solid arrow represents the effects of executing a primitive action (*north, south, east, west*), while the dashed arrow represents the effects of executing a macro action (*leave-the-room*).

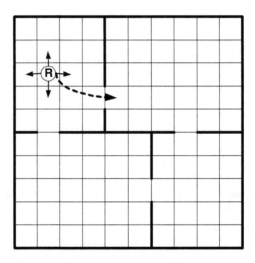

Fig. 2. Navigation task illustrating the difference between primitive actions and macro actions

According to Sutton, Precup, and Singh [9], *options* consist of three components: a policy $\pi : S \times A \mapsto [0, 1]$, a termination condition $\beta : S \mapsto [0, 1]$, and a set of initiation states $I \subseteq S$. A macro action can only be invoked from a state within the initiation states I. Although formulated slightly differently, policies as defined here satisfy the same requirements as those presented above, namely prescribing which actions to execute in each state. Requiring $\sum_{a_i \in A} \pi(s, a_i) = 1$, policies describe probabilistic selection of actions for each state. While executing, the agent will perform actions according to the policy π until termination according to the termination condition β.

It is obvious that if the agent were planning using macro actions, the agent can move farther for each decision it makes as compared to planning using only primitive actions. Macro actions constructed to group actions related to achieving goals or subgoals can be used to improve computational efficiency for decision-making.

2.2   Macros and Goals

The use of the basic reward structure for MDP models is limiting in that if the agent has multiple goals to achieve, those goals must be represented as part of the state definition. For example, consider if the domain states are defined as a product of state variables, $S_{domain} = V_1 \times V_2 \times ... \times V_L$. If an agent desires to sequentially visit multiple states in the domain, the actions that the agent selects will be different depending on which of the goal states the agent has already visited. Desire states of the agent can be defined as a product of the goal variables (boolean values indicating whether each goal has been achieved), $S_{desire} = G_1 \times G_2 \times ... \times G_K$. The states represented in MDP M must be able to differentiate between the same domain states when the agent has different desire states, hence $S = V_1 \times V_2 \times ... \times V_L \times G_1 \times G_2 \times ... \times G_K$.

Macro actions can be used to factor the desires of the agent from the state description. This yields the benefit of separating analysis of the domain characteristics from analysis of the desires. This allows reuse of the domain analysis when desires change. If a navigation problem is on a 10x10 square grid, the general solution for reaching any single location is a set of 100 policies, each of size 100, one for each possible goal location. If the agent has a goal to visit two locations, there are 10,000 policies, one policy corresponding to each set of two locations. Additionally, the size of each policy is 300, since for each location, the agents may still desire to visit either goal location or both (assuming termination after visiting both locations). In spite of this exponential increase in complexity, the basic problem domain remains navigation.

Recent work by Lane and Kaelbling has addressed complexity due to multiple goals in the domain of robot package delivery [10]. In their work, the agent is tasked with the goal of navigating to a number of locations. Each location is treated as a subgoal, but no reward is given until the agent has successfully visited all locations. Each subgoal (i.e. moving to a given location) is represented by a boolean goal variable, denoting an undelivered package. Initially all goal variables are set to 0. Upon reaching a subgoal location, the goal variable is set to 1, and can never be set to 0 again signifying that packages cannot be undelivered. Goal variables in this domain are independent of each other, given the location of the agent.

Using the concept of options presented above, Lane and Kaelbling create a macro action for each subgoal. An approximate policy is then generated for the overall goal of visiting all locations through application of a travelling salesman algorithm to determine the order in which the subgoals are visited.

For example, take the domain illustrated in Figure 3. Locations labelled **1** through **3** represent the subgoals the robot desires to visit. Unlike primitive actions, execution of a macro action will have variable cost depending on the distance from the state in which the macro action was initiated to the goal location. Assuming uniform cost per move, the cost for execution of a macro is

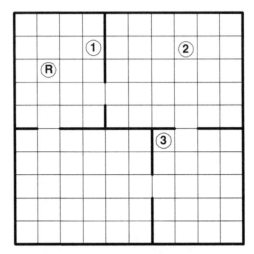

Fig. 3. Multiple goals in a navigation task

equal to the cost per move times the expected number of moves from the current state to the termination state (Equation 1).

$$C(macro_1, s) = cE(\text{\# of moves from } s \text{ to the termination state}) \quad (1)$$

The costs of macro actions are used to form a weighted graph among all the subgoals as shown in Figure 4. Many algorithms exist for finding the shortest path visiting all nodes in a graph [11]. The application of travelling salesman algorithms determines the order for a compound macro action which describes a sequential ordering of macro actions. While this is useful for goals that exist in an 'AND' (i.e., reward is not given unless all subgoals have been achieved) relationship, goals can be related in other ways yielding more complicated behavior by the agent. Of particular interest to this research is the ability of agents to choose whether or not to address a goal they have been tasked with.

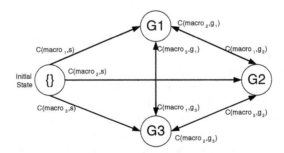

Fig. 4. Weighted graph relating costs to travel among the goal locations

2.3   Desire States and Goal Analysis

As a departure from the robot delivery domain used by Lane and Kaelbling [10], this work addresses cases where reward values are set for each goal, rather than for the completion of all goals. An important characteristic of an autonomous agent is the ability to decide which goals to pursue. Towards this end, the agent's desires may be combined in an 'OR' fashion, where the agent may receive rewards for goals independent of other goals . In this case, the agent must consider not only the order in which to achieve goals, but whether to try to achieve each particular goal at all - the cost to achieve a goal may outweigh the reward. Additionally, since execution of actions will change the agent's distance to the respective goals, pursuing one goal may make it more or less profitable (even unprofitable) to pursue other goals.

As a concrete example of a domain problem matching this description, imagine a tourist visiting a new city. The tourist has a limited amount of money for sightseeing, and must select from a set of recommended sights to visit. The sights are rated by the tourist based on interest, assigning a reward value to each. Additionally, transportation costs for travel in the city are based on distance, making it a cost-to-move framework in a navigation domain.

By creating macro actions to achieve each individual goal, the entire set of state variables can be abstracted away. Instead, reasoning can be performed purely in terms of desire states, referred to in this paper as the *desire space*. Figure 5 shows the desire space for the example robot navigation domain shown in Figure 3. Each state is labelled with the set of goal variables denoting which goals have been achieved in that state. Initially, the agent is in the state marked by the empty set and the current location. Application of each macro leads the agent to the desire state where the appropriate goal is marked as achieved, leading up to the state with all goals being achieved. Unfortunately, the complete domain space cannot be factored out because the cost function for the macro actions is dependent upon domain state. Luckily, if an agent executes actions according to this decision-making mechanism, the only relevant states are the current state and the termination states of the macro actions.

The motivations for reasoning in the desire space include: (1) the desire space is smaller than the complete state space, and (2) the structure of the desire space can be exploited algorithmically for efficient computation. The model for reasoning about the desire space is defined as follows. Given the state space of the problem S_{domain}, some subset of those states are marked as goals, $Goals \subseteq S_{domain} = \{g_1, g_2, ...g_K\}$. The states of the desire space are built from the goal variables and the agent's location in the domain space. Each macro action is constructed to move the agent to a given goal state. The terminal states are represented as a probability distribution over the domain states. However, due to the nature of macro actions, the probability is concentrated on the goal state. It is possible for a macro to have termination states that represent failure of that macro to achieve its goal but, for simplicity of explanation, this paper expects the macro actions to always terminate in its goal state without fail. The desire states are denoted by a tuple $\langle G_{ach}, s \rangle$. The first element of the

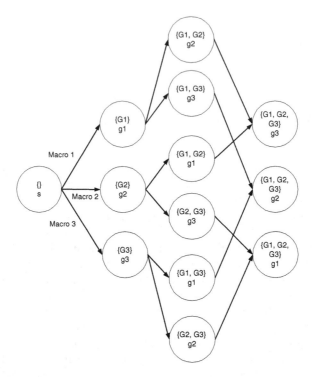

Fig. 5. Desire space for the three goal navigation domain

tuple,G_{ach} is the set of goals that have been achieved. This element could also be represented by the complement of the set of achieved goals (i.e., the set of unachieved goals), but will be labelled as the achieved goals for this discussion. The second element of the tuple is the location of the agent in the domain states, S_{domain}. The agent can only be located at the initial state $s_{initial}$, or as a result of executing a macro action, in an accomplished goal state g_i, hence, $S_{desire} = \{\langle\{\}, s_{initial}\rangle, \langle G_{ach}, g_i\rangle$ s.t. $G_{ach} \subseteq Goals$ and $g_i \in G_{ach}\}$. The action set $A_{desire} = \{macro_1, macro_2, \dots, macro_K\}$ is the set of macro actions, one for achieving each goal the agent hold. Finally, the reward function, $R : Goals \mapsto \mathbb{R}$, assigns a separate reward value to each goal.

Since the reward function is assigned slightly differently from that used in a MDP, the valuation of states and actions is changed to match. Global termination states are those states in which there are no profitable macro actions. States in which all goals have been achieved are global termination states since all rewards have already been collected. The global termination states (where all goals have been achieved) are assigned a value of 0, indicating that no further action will yield any reward. The expected value of desire states is defined as follows:

$$V(\langle Goals, s\rangle) = 0 \qquad (2)$$

$$V(\langle G_{ach}, s \rangle) = \max \left(0, \max_{macro_i \in A_{desire}} \left(\begin{array}{c} C(macro_i, s) \\ +R(g_i) \\ +V(\langle G_{ach} \cup \{g_i\}, g_i \rangle) \end{array} \right) \right) \quad (3)$$

The value of a state is simply the sum of the cost of executing the macro from that state (a negative number), the reward for achieving the immediate goal through macro execution, and any expected value for being in the resulting state, due to expected future goal achievement. Note that if no action is profitable (i.e., the cost of each action outweighs or equals its benefits), then the state is also a global termination state and is given a value of 0.

The specific structure of the graph offers many exploitable characteristics. Since the domain does not allow goals to become unachieved, loops cannot exist in the graph, forming a tree structure. This enables calculation of the expected values to proceed through simple accumulation of the values from a single graph traversal.

3   Model Modification for Dynamic Goals

Multi-agent systems operate in dynamic environments. Dynamism may come from many sources. The priorities of the agent designer may change, causing changes in the agent's reward structures. Additionally, agents are affected by the behavior of other agents in the system, either implicitly through competition for domain resources, or explicitly through argumentation or negotiation. Even the agent's own actions may change the decision model it follows if there is uncertainty in the environment. Regardless the cause, the agent's priority is to maintain rational action in the face of these changes. To the system designer, in addition to rationality, computational efficiency is also an issue. This can be addressed through the reuse of previous computations in the planning process. Satoh also attempts to reuse computation in his abductive planning system [12].

3.1   Maintaining Rationality

Although goals may change over time, the overall style of operation of the agent may remain constant (i.e., the agent will always try to maximize its rewards). Hauskrecht et. al. [13] built on the work of Sutton, Precup, and Singh to solve hierarchical MDPs using macro actions. In their work, they address local changes in reward structure or system dynamics by constructing a hybrid MDP using both macro actions and primitive actions. The area of the MDP most affected by goal changes is recalculated using the primitive actions. Their work assumes that the reward function and system dynamics remains the same in all but a few regions of the state space. In those regions where the state space is not changing, Hauskrecht advocates reuse of the macro actions. When dealing with multiple goals, the addition or removal of goals may cause large changes in the overall state space for an agent. However, due to the structure of the desire space, much of the previous computation can still be reused. It is from this reuse that computational efficiency is gained.

As a simple elaboration in the robot package delivery domain, suppose the robot can accept packages for delivery as well. Each package is represented as a goal, so accepting a package equates to goal addition. Also, upon delivery, the package is no longer the responsibility of the agent. This corresponds to a simple example of goal removal. For various reasons, packages may become more or less urgent, corresponding to changing reward values for the goals.

In a dynamic setting (i.e., one in which events exogenous to the agent may modify the world) achieving optimality is impossible except through happenstance. Optimality requires that the agent have a perfect predictor for future system behavior. Rationality requires only that the agent act in its believed best interests. In a domain with complete knowledge (past, present, and future), rationality would equate to the optimal solution though still computationally expensive. With incomplete knowledge, the agent should try to perform as well as it can, given its limited knowledge and resources. Lacking any information about the future, an agent can be considered rational if it executes actions which are considered optimal in the model the agent holds at the time it executes those actions. When faced with new information, the agent maintains rationality by revising its model and continuing execution with whatever action is then believed to be optimal. The following sections describe algorithms for maintaining rationality by modifying the decision model in response to changes in the desires of the agent.

3.2   Goal Removal

Goal removal allows the agent to reduce the size of the desire space that it models. There are two cases for goal removal: (1) the goal has already been achieved and (2) the goal has not already been achieved. Both cases are simple due to the structure of the desire space.

The first case is trivial due to the structure of the desire space. The agent needs only treat the current state as the new root of the model with no recalculation necessary. All desire states that are not reachable from the current desire state can be pruned from the model (e.g., those desire states in which the goal being removed has not been achieved). In fact, the goal variable itself can be removed from the representation used by all remaining desire states. Since the value assigned to that goal variable will be equivalent for all remaining states, it can be safely factored out of the desire state representation without affecting any of the remaining desire state values.

Algorithm 1. REMOVEGOAL(d,g)

$location = d.location$
$d =$CHILD(d, g)
$d.location = location$
UPDATE$(V(d))$

When the goal being removed has not already been achieved, recalculation is necessary to remove the value of the goal from the action-selection reasoning. Due to the structure of the desire space (Figure 5) , the value of any given node is dependent only on the unachieved goals and state of the agent at that node. Computation is saved by caching the values of each node. Algorithm 1 describes the removal of goal g. The function CHILD(d, g) returns the desire state that results from executing the macro to achieve g in the desire state d. The agent transitions in the desire space as if it had achieved goal g. The resulting state in the desire space is then updated with the agent's current location in the state space. Finally, the value of the current new state is recalculated based on the new location. The values of the children states had previously been calculated, but due to the new location, the costs to reach the children have changed. This may cause a new macro to be selected as the most profitable when calculating the new $V(d)$.

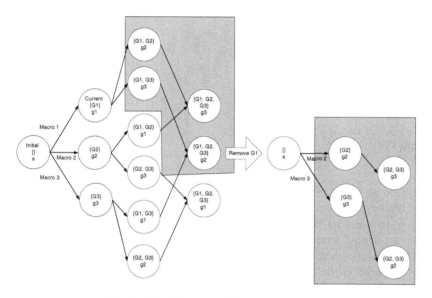

Fig. 6. Modification of desire space for goal removal

Figure 6 illustrates the effect of pruning goal g_1 from the desire space. Note that the desire states highlighted in gray show the reused state values after the removal of g_1. To highlight this reuse, note that by Equation 3, $V(\langle\{G1, G2\}, g2\rangle) = C(macro_{G3}, s) + R(G3) + V(\langle\{G1, G2, G3\}, g3\rangle)$. Since achievement of all goals, with $Goals = \{G1, G2, G3\}$, results in a terminal state, $V(\langle\{G1, G2, G3\}, g3\rangle) = 0$. After removal of $G1$, $Goals = \{G2, G3\}$, making $\langle\{G2, G3\}, g3\rangle$ a terminal state. The value of being in state $\langle\{G2\}, g2\rangle$ is $C(macro_{G3}, s) + R(G3) + V(\langle\{G2, G3\}, g3\rangle)$, equivalent to the pre-removal value of state $V(\langle\{G1, G2\}, g2\rangle)$.

3.3   Goal Addition

Goal addition can be handled in a single traversal of the graph. Algorithm 2 describes the process for adding goal g to desire state d. This algorithm describes the desire state in terms of the unachieved goals, $\overline{G_{ach}}$, rather than G_{ach} because upon addition of a goal, the reuse of desire state values is linked to the unachieved goals in that state. For desire state d, a new macro action is added for achieving goal g and the resulting desire state d' is created. The children of d are added to d'. After the addition of the children, the value of d' can be calculated, selecting the best macro to execute in that desire state. The new goal g is then added to each of the children of d, constructing a depth first traversal of the tree. Finally, the value of s is updated, possibly changing the best macro to execute.

Algorithm 2. AddGoal(d,g)

$d' = \text{new STATE}(\langle d.\overline{G_{ach}}, g \rangle)$
$d.\overline{G_{ach}} = d.\overline{G_{ach}} + g$
for all $i \in d.children$ **do**
    ADDCHILD(d', i)
end for
UPDATE($V(d')$)
for all $i \in d.children$ **do**
    ADDGOAL(i,g)
end for
$d.children = d.children + d'$
UPDATE($V(d)$)

Replication saves the computational cost of recalculating the values for states which will have equivalent values to preexisting states. Figure 7 shows the result of adding g_1 to a model that already includes g_2 and g_3. Desire states marked in gray are replicated from the original model into the resulting model through ADDCHILD in the algorithm described above. In the diagram, there are multiple paths to reach some of the later states in the model. Caching of desire state values further reduces computation as a node only needs to be computed once and can be reused for each other incoming edge.

3.4   Goal Modification

The rewards associated with goals may change. This may be due to the passage of time or acquisition of new information. States in which the goal has been achieved are not affected by any change in the value of that goal. Only those states leading up to achievement of that goal are affected. Similar to the addition of goals, desire state values can be updated by a single traversal of the graph. By intelligently caching the value calculation results large sections of the desire space are not touched.

The overall objective when handling dynamic goals is to reuse the calculations that stay static across changes. In each of the removal, addition, or modification

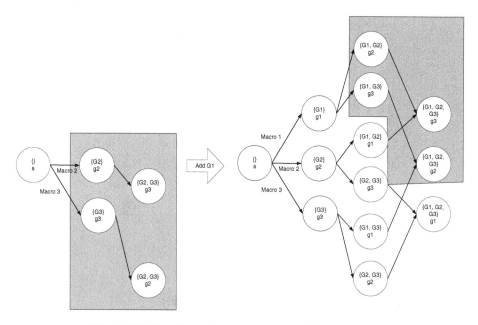

Fig. 7. Modification of desire space for addition of a goal

cases, the desire space is divided into sections by the appropriate macro action. On the originating side of the macro action, desire states require recalculation. On the resulting side of the macro action, previously calculated values can be reused.

4   Application to UAV Domain

Applying this research to build an operating system raises other interesting opportunities for approximation and estimation. The work presented in the previous sections has been implemented for experimentation and demonstration in the domain of unmanned aerial vehicle (UAV) control. Figure 8 shows the graphical user interface for the simulation. In the simulation, the environment has been abstracted into a Cartesian plane. Targets are placed at various points in this plane and the agents, controlling the UAVs, are tasked with visiting the various targets. Uncertainty is introduced into the domain by the movement of the targets, forcing the UAVs to operate with possibly stale information regarding the location of the targets. Three UAVs are shown by the dark circles. Lines extending out of the UAVs show the past and future planned movement.

At the most basic level, an agent has control over the heading and speed of a single UAV. A state in the state space is defined by the location, heading, and speed of the UAV in conjunction with the locations of the targets. Even in this simple domain, analysis of the state space directly is computationally intractable. Approximation and estimation methods are used to further reduce computation required for decision-making.

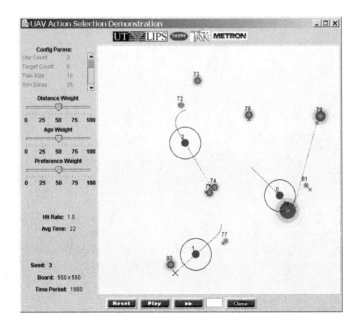

Fig. 8. UAV demonstration of decision-theoretic action selection

Macro actions are constructed to move to each target location, enabling reasoning in the desire space. Through domain analysis, macro actions can be created manually to control the operation of the UAVs. The macros consists of the actions required to turn the UAV towards the specified target and move until the destination is reached. If the target is not found, then a simple search pattern is executed. Though not necessarily optimal, good domain analysis may yield macros that reasonably approximate the optimal behavior for each goal.

Each target has an associated reward value, illustrated by the circles surrounding the targets. Calculating the exact expected cost is rather complex due to the movement of the targets. Probabilistic encounter models could be used. E.g., cost of each macro usage can be cheaply estimated as a function of the distance between the UAV and the target.

Targets are added to the system regularly. Additionally, with more than one UAV operating in the system, targets may be removed through the action of the other agents. These additional estimation methods, the manually constructed macro actions and cost estimation functions, aid in producing the quick decisions that are necessary for operating in highly dynamic domains that demand computational efficiency.

5   Conclusion

Autonomous agents are provided with independence in the selection of which actions they should perform. Although they are provided this independence, the agent's actions must also reflect its desires. Over time, desires may change. This research extends previous work on using MDPs to provide rational action selection in the face of changing desires.

MDPs provide the means for decision-theoretic reasoning but are afflicted by the "curse of dimensionality". Macro actions enable reasoning on a more abstract level than the primitive actions in the domain at the cost of possible suboptimality in the actions of the agents. For a restricted class of domain problems, such as the "cost-to-move" framework, structure in the desire space can be exploited to reduce computation needed to make approximately optimal moves. Macro actions encapsulate the domain characteristics, enabling the decision problem posed to the agent to be transformed into the desire space. Reasoning in the desire space of the agent allows the agent to approximately weigh the costs and benefits of each of its goals at an abstract level. In the desire space, the agent can simply add, remove, and modify goals. The drawback of this approach is that it ignores possible action or subgoal interactions among the goals.

Analysis presented in this paper addressed goals composed in an independent manner, as compared to the work of Lane and Kaelbling which addressed sets of goals where a single reward was given for completion of the whole set. Further analysis of the dependencies among goals will enable efficient reasoning over goals that are composed using other operators (i.e., 'NOT' or 'XOR') or composed hierarchically. Quantitative analysis of the exact computational savings is currently being pursued. Additionally, methods for integrating the goal valuations with negotiation and argumentation mechanisms are being pursued.

Acknowledgements

This research was funded in part by the Defense Advanced Research Projects Agency and Air Force Research Laboratory, Air Force Materiel Command, USAF, under agreement number F30602-00-2-0588. The U.S. Government is authorized to reproduce and distribute reprints for Governmental purposes notwithstanding any copyright annotation thereon. The views and conclusions herein are those of the authors and should not be interpreted as necessarily representing the official policies or endorsements, either expressed on implied, of the Defense Advanced Research Projects Agency (DARPA), the Air Force Research Laboratory, or the U.S. Government.

The research reported in this document was performed in connection with Contract number DAAD13-02-C-0079 with the U.S. Edgewood Biological Chemical Command.

References

1. Wooldridge, M.: Reasoning about Rational Agents. The MIT Press, Cambridge, Massachusetts (2000)
2. Bentahar, J., Moulin, B., Meyer, J.J.C., Chaib-Draa, B.: A computational model for conversation policies for agent communication. In this volume.

3. Mancarella, P., Sadri, F., Terreni, G., Toni, F.: Planning partially for situated agents. In this volume.
4. Alferes, J.J., Banti, F., Brogi, A.: From logic programs updates to action description updates. In this volume.
5. Georgeff, M.P.: Planning. In Allen, J., Hendler, J., Tate, A., eds.: Readings in Planning. Morgan Kaufmann Publishers, San Mateo, California (1990) 5–25
6. desJardines, M.E., Durfee, E.H., Ortiz Jr., C.L., Wolverton, M.J.: A survey of research in distributed, continual planning. AI Magazine **20** (1999) 13–22
7. Boutilier, C.: Planning, learning and coordination in multiagent decision processes. In: Theoretical Aspects of Rationality and Knowledge, Amsterdam, Netherlands (1996) 195–201
8. Boutilier, C., Dean, T., Hanks, S.: Decision-theoretic planning: Structural assumptions and computational leverage. Journal of Artificial Intelligence Research **11** (1999) 1–94
9. Sutton, R.S., Precup, D., Singh, S.P.: Between MDPs and semi-MDPs: A framework for temporal abstraction in reinforcement learning. Artificial Intelligence **112** (1999) 181–211
10. Lane, T., Kaelbling, L.P.: Nearly deterministic abstractions of markov decision processes. In: Eighteenth National Conference on Artificial Intelligence (AAAI2002), Edmonton, Alberta, Canada (2002) 260–266
11. Gutin, G., Punnen, A.P., eds.: The Traveling Salesman Problem and Its variations. Kluwer, Dordrecht, The Netherlands (2002)
12. Satoh, K.: An application of global abduction to an information agent which modifies a plan upon failure- preliminary report. In this volume.
13. Hauskrecht, M., Meuleau, N., Kaelbling, L.P., Dean, T., Boutilier, C.: Hierarchical solution of Markov decision processes using macro-actions. In: Uncertainty in Artificial Intelligence (UAI98). (1998) 220–229

Organising Software in Active Environments

Benjamin Hirsch[1], Michael Fisher[1], Chiara Ghidini[2,*],
and Paolo Busetta[2]

[1] Department of Computer Science,
University of Liverpool, United Kingdom
{M.Fisher, B.Hirsch}@csc.liv.ac.uk
[2] Automated Reasoning Systems Division,
ITC-IRST, Trento, Italy
{ghidini, busetta}@itc.it

Abstract. In this paper, we investigate the use of logic-based multi-agent systems for modelling active environments. Our case study is an intelligent support system for a so-called "active museum". We show the approach of structuring the "agent space", i.e., the social organisations acting within the environment, is well fitted to naturally represent not only the physical structure of the application, but also the virtual structure in which it operates. The adoption of a logic-based modelling system provides high-level programming concepts, and allows the designer to rapidly design and develop flexible software to be used in active environments.

1 Introduction

In recent years, computing devices have become extremely powerful while, at the same time, being small enough to integrate within portable devices. Together with the advent of wireless communication methods, the technological pre-requisites for ubiquitous computing are beginning to be in place. However, it is much less obvious how to actually make use of these devices in order to create an environment where the complexity of the surrounding computing environment is hidden from users, while still being available and able to adapt to movements/preferences of the users.

Within the agent research community, many paths to tackling the complexity of interactions, communication, co-ordination and organisation have been pursued [16]. Some of the theories developed have been quite deep, yet few have found their way into viable programming approaches for multi-agent systems. An exception is our earlier work [12, 15], which is based on a strong formal theory of agency combining modal, temporal and multi-context logics. By *directly executing* specifications provided in such a theory [9], the behaviour of individual agents can be implemented [11]. Overlayed on top of this is a multi-agent organisational model comprising the notion of *agent groups*, providing the flexibility and adaptability to program more complex multi-agent computations.

---

* Work supported by MIUR under FIRB-RBNE0195K5 contract.

J. Leite and P. Torroni (Eds.): CLIMA V, LNAI 3487, pp. 265–280, 2005.
© Springer-Verlag Berlin Heidelberg 2005

The firm foundation in formal logic also provides the possibility of carrying out *verification* of computation under varying environmental conditions [2].

Our aim in this paper is to utilise the approach above [12, 15], which is essentially based on the METATEM executable temporal logic [1], in order to show how computational logic in general, and temporal logic in particular, together with a structured agent space, allows us to quickly and naturally model complex real world computing environments.

To reinforce this claim, we will apply the above approach to a specific active environment, namely the so-called "active museum" [19]. We will show how such a logic-based multi-agent system, while being relatively straightforward to build, can be an effective and high-level tool for modelling computing environments that are inherently flexible, adapt to changes within their environment (and therefore to the users), and extensible. We will show how the approach of structuring the "agent space", i.e., the social organisations acting within the environment, is well fitted to naturally representing not only the physical structure of the application, but also the virtual environment within which the software artefacts reside.

The structure of this paper is as follows. To begin with, the concept of the active museum is explained in Section 2. Then, in Section 3, we introduce the key concepts of the particular logic-based programming language we aim to utilise. The resulting multi-agent system is explained in Section 4 and its implementation is described in Section 5. The application of this approach to the active museum scenario is presented in Section 6, and the advantages of this approach, particularly as mobile agents move through the organisational layers, are discussed in Section 7. Finally, in Section 8, we provide concluding remarks.

2   The Active Museum

In work on the PEACH project[1] [19] the concept of "active museum" is being investigated. This is a form of *active environment* [18], and can be seen as a large scale multi-user, multi-media, multi-modal system. In the case of PEACH, museum visitors are provided (either on demand or pro-actively, depending on the context) with information about exhibits they may see within the museum. This information may be drawn from a variety of information sources and media types (museum server, online remote servers, etc.), and presented to the visitors by a variety of clients (for example, hand-held devices such PDAs, kiosks, wall screens, and so on).

Generally speaking, active environments have some characteristics that make them substantially different from traditional computing and HCIs. For instance, multiple users may be in a single place, interacting with different applications simultaneously. The set of users changes dynamically over time. Users are unaware (and uninterested) that the environment is formed of many distributed components. Therefore, they interact with the environment as if it were a single,

---

[1] http://peach.itc.it

monolithic system. However, services are provided by a variable set of components that join and leave the environment on mobile devices or that may be running anywhere else. Services provided by these components can (partially) overlap; therefore, they need to coordinate in order to decide, for instance, who provides a specific service, and how it is provided, in a specific context.

In our reference scenario, the active museum, users' positions and resource availability may impose constraints on the generation and display of information; resources may rapidly change over time, while users move around. In the background, user modelling agents silently record histories of user interactions and build profiles by observing their behaviour; their goal is to customise presentations, avoiding repetitions or inappropriate content. Furthermore, one long-term objective of the PEACH project is supporting groups of visitors, such as families or classes of children, by providing tools that allow the sharing of experience and improve learning. All these requisites imply intensive communication among the software collaborating to provide services well beyond current communication architectures and service composition techniques. The objective here is to create a highly distributed and dynamic environment, where the number of components capable of providing services continuously varies.

The implementation of an active museum that has been provided in PEACH relies on the ability of sending messages to *roles*, rather than to individual components, and *overhearing* conversations happening among any set of components of the system. This enables the aggregation of service-providing agents into teams that have been called *implicit organisations* [5, 6]. In turn, this enables context-sensitive behaviour to be built into objects embedded in the environment, freeing high-level applications (concerned, for instance, with supporting knowledge sharing within a group) from issues concerning service composition and delivery in a specific environment. The implementation of this idea is based on a form of group communication called *channelled multicast* [4], which is supported by an experimental communication infrastructure, called *LoudVoice*. LoudVoice supports the creation of channels on-the-fly; messages sent on a channel are received by all agents tuned into it.

3   MetateM

Over the last few years many different theories and specification languages, together with implementations of individual agents [17] and organisational aspects, such as teamwork [20], have been developed. However, those areas of research seldom overlap. Many specification languages are too complex to directly translate into a (executable) program, and often ignore issues that arise with interaction and collaboration between agents. On the other hand, implementations of multi-agent systems often have only a fleeting connection with agent theories or theories about teamwork.

Many specification languages are based on logic, which allows for (potential) verification of the specification, and the ability to use high level concepts, while also often resulting in a concise representation. Agent theories are typically based on the so-called BDI logic [3], combining strands for *belief*, *desire*, and *intention*. By using those mentalistic notions, the agents' reasoning about their environment, their choice or creation of plans, as well as the pursuit of goals can easily be expressed in logical terms. However, this expressive power leads to a very high complexity involved in handling the resulting specifications.

The specification language we use here, based on METATEM [1], is an executable logic. That is to say, we can *directly* execute the logical specifications, thereby partially bridging the gap between theory and practice. The multi-agent environment natively supports the dynamic structuring of the agent space into groups (and teams). METATEM is based on propositional linear temporal logic [14], extended with modalities for (bounded) belief, confidence and abilities [12]. The resulting logic is still expressive, yet simple enough to be directly executed. Belief is modelled using a modal multi-context logic that is roughly equivalent to the standard KD45 modal logic, while confidence is modelled as "believing that eventually" something will happen. Ability is very simple, being little more than a modality that can be used to prefix formulae. While arbitrary temporal formulae can be used to specify the agent behaviour, agents are, in practice, programmed using a special normal form called SNF, which is particularly amenable to execution and verification [10]. As an example of a simple set of SNF[2] 'rules' which might form part of an agent description, consider the following

$$\textbf{start} \rightarrow in\_office$$
$$(in\_office \land \neg hungry) \rightarrow \bigcirc in\_office$$
$$(in\_office \land hungry \land A_{me}\, buy\_food) \rightarrow B_{me} \bigcirc (\neg in\_office \land buy\_food)$$
$$(buy\_food \land A_{me}\, eat) \rightarrow \Diamond \neg hungry$$

Here, '$\bigcirc$' means "in the next moment", while '$\Diamond$' means "at some future moment". Thus, the above describes a scenario where I am in the office at the beginning of execution, and will continue to stay in the office while I am not hungry. However, once I become hungry and I am able to buy food ($A_{me}\, buy\_food$), then I believe (B_{me}), that in the next moment in time, I will leave the office and buy food. Finally, if I buy food and am able to eat ($A_{me}\, eat$), then eventually I will not be hungry.

The execution essentially forward chains through a set of such rules, gradually constructing a model for the specification. If a contradiction is generated, backtracking occurs. Eventualities, such as '$\Diamond \neg hungry$' are satisfied as soon as possible; in the case of conflicting eventualities, the oldest outstanding ones are attempted first. The choice mechanism takes into account a combination of the outstanding eventualities, and the deliberation ordering functions [11].

As mentioned above, belief is modelled using bounded multi-context logic. Simply speaking, belief operators are computed by creating new time lines and checking them for consistency. As each B_i operator is expanded, a record of the

---

[2] For clarity the rules are presented in this way, even though they are not in *exactly* the SNF form.

depth of nesting of such operators is kept. Once the current bound for expanding the belief contexts is reached, exploration of the current belief context ceases. Because abilities and beliefs are not used in this paper, we refer the interested reader to [12] for an in-depth discussion on bounded belief.

4   Structuring the Agent Space

While the above approach is essentially concerned with single agents, the extension to Concurrent METATEM [8] was concerned with modelling and programming general multi-agent computation. This approach has been developed over a number of years, with an important aspect being the notion of *flexible agent grouping* [13]. Here, agents are organised in groups, and groups themselves appear, to the outside world, as agents. Conversely, agents can contain other agents (and thereby appear as groups for them), and groups can be contained in agents (that is, groups can contain other agent groups). Thus, agents can be members of several groups, and can contain many agents. It is vital to understand that while we use the words *agent*, *group*, and *group agent* at different times to refer to aspects of agents, we are always talking about one and the same entity.

During execution, each agent, a, has two main sets it uses for communication, its *Content* and its *Context*. The *Context* contains references to the groups (agents) that a is member of, while the *Content* contains references to agents that are members of a. Figure 1 shows three different ways of representing nested agents: as overlapping sets; as a membership tree; and as a membership table. In the latter, **CN** denotes the agent's *Content*, and **CX** its *Context*.

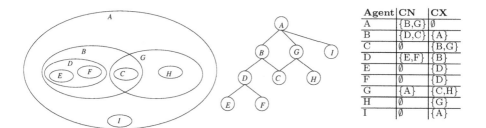

Agent	CN	CX
A	{B,G}	∅
B	{D,C}	{A}
C	∅	{B,G}
D	{E,F}	{B}
E	∅	{D}
F	∅	{D}
G	{A}	{C,H}
H	∅	{G}
I	∅	{A}

Fig. 1. Different views of nested agents

The key reasons we wish to identify agents and groups are:

- this is a natural way to represent complex problems and software;
- many types of meta-data can (concurrently) be represented (task structure, abilities, physical location, ownership, social relations, teams, etc) within the agent space topology; and
- groups can evolve from "dumb" containers into smart entities with refined policies, reactive/deliberate behaviour, etc.

Effectively, groups and agents are viewed as one and the same entity, avoiding the need to introduce separate mechanisms to deal with agent structuring and organisation.

4.1   Dynamic Grouping

While a multi-agent system generally starts out with some pre-defined structure, agents can dynamically adapt the structure to fit their needs. In particular, agents can *add* agents to, and *remove* agents from, their *Content* (resp. *Context*); i.e., they can *move* within and *change* the structure. In addition to being able to move through the hierarchy, agents can *cease* and *clone* themselves, and can *create* new agents (and hence new groups).

By creating new agents, they can harness the power of the structure. Agents can, for example, create group agents and instruct them to invite other agents with a certain ability φ to join. Now the creating agent has a group of agents able to do φ at its disposal. Because groups are in fact agents, their behaviour can range from pure "containers" of other agents, through to complex behaviours such as only allowing agents to join that agree to a certain set of rules [15]. For example, if all agents in a group were to have the rule

$$receive(M) \ \Rightarrow \ \bigcirc do(M)$$

meaning "whenever you receive a message, make it true in the next moment in time", as part of their behaviour, then the group agent would be able to utilise the abilities of all these agents simply by asking them to do something.

The structure of the agent space can be used to encode many different types of information, avoiding the need for individual agents to keep an extensive knowledge base and to keep that knowledge consistent with the (dynamic) environment. The types of information range from task and ability structures, to representations of some physical space to meta information such as owner information, trust relations, and so on. For example, if an agent is to accomplish some task, but does not have the corresponding abilities, it can create a group agent that contains agents that can accomplish (sub-) tasks, which in turn again can invite other agents to their respective content. Eventually, the structure becomes an accurate representation of the different sub-tasks involved in executing the main task. Similarly, by re-creating the physical structure within the agent space, agents can be modelled as being part of both physical and virtual structures.

4.2   Communication

In order to make effective use of different structures within the agent space, a flexible message passing system has been devised. Whilst the general idea is to broadcast messages to either *Content* or *Context*, agents are also allowed to send

1. messages to specific subsets of agents (e.g., `send(SE,Message)`),
2. nested messages (e.g., `send(SE1,send(SE2,Message))`), and
3. recursive messages (e.g., `sendAll(SE,Message)`)

In case (1), the agent can either specify a set of one or more agents by name, or it can specify a *set expression*. The sent message can in turn be a send message (case (2)), thus providing a form of *forwarding*. Finally, the `sendAll` directive instructs the receiving agent to re-send the message to the same set (adapted to its own local *Content/Context*).

A set expression (*SE*) may be a single agent, a set of agents, the variables *Content* or *Context*, or any of the operations *SE1* ∪ *SE2* (union), *SE1* ∩ *SE2* (intersection), or *SE1* \ *SE2* (subtraction) applied to set expressions. Note that the special variables *Content* and *Context* are always interpreted locally.

Using this language, we can easily express the `sendAll` directive using the following equivalence:

$$sendAll(Set, Message) \equiv send(Set, Message) \land$$
$$send(Set, send(Set \setminus Self, Message))$$

The special variable *Self* refers to the sending agent. It is necessary to ensure that no message is repeatedly sent through the agent space. Note that while this does guarantee that no message is sent forever, it does *not* guarantee that each agent receives the message exactly once.

5   Programming Agents

We have created a `Java` implementation, in which agents are represented by threads, and communicate via shared objects.

Agents are driven by a METATEM engine, which interprets a set of rules that describe the behaviour of the agent. At each cycle, the agent first checks its Inbox for new messages, and passes them to the METATEM engine, which then, based on those predicates that were made true from the last state, and eventualities that still need to be honoured, creates a new state. If the created state turns out to be consistent, the cycle is repeated with the newly created state, otherwise, backtracking occurs, firstly within the state (by making a different set of predicates true) and if that fails by rolling back states, again trying to resolve the contradiction by assigning different truth values to predicates within the state.

Note that while we internally use propositional temporal logic, we employ some syntactic sugar and allow predicates and variables in rules. However, only rules where all variables are substituted by a ground term "fire", and therefore only grounded predicates (essentially propositions) can be made true.

An agent is only allowed to backtrack to the point where it interacted with its environment, by sending messages or executing side effects connected with certain predicates[3]. This is due to the inability of agents to un-do effects on the environment.

---

[3] Reading messages is not direct interaction, as the agents keeps track of messages read during each cycle, and re-reads them in case of backtracking.

As mentioned above, certain predicates can have side-effects. We distinguish between *internal* side effects, which are provided by the system and include actions such as adding and removing agents to *Content* and *Context*, and *external* ones, that consist of Java objects and/or rules. External abilities can for example be used to connect to databases, or interact with sensors. Table 1 gives a short overview of predicates with side effects used in the reminder of this paper.

Table 1. Predicates and their side effects

send(S,M)	sends message M to agent-set S
doAddToContent(A)	adds Agent A to current agent *Content*
doAddToContext(A)	adds Agent A to current agent *Context*
prefer(P,Q)	re-orders eventualities P and Q, s.t. P is preferred over Q
wait(i,P)	sends P to itself after i milliseconds (external)

Agents are programmed using logical formulae in SNF form[4]. When programming an agent, rules themselves are clustered and tagged. The reason for this is twofold. First, it allows the programmer to structure her code. More importantly though, it allows for behaviours (which typically comprised of many formulae) to be exchanged within the agent.

We provide a (simple) implementation of several typical movements of agents, such as moving up and down the *Content/Context* hierarchy, in a file which agents can load. However, the programmer can write her own rules, which will (completely) overwrite (default) behaviours with the same tag.

Figure 2 gives a simple definition for addToContent/2 based on the internal predicates doAddToContent/1, doAddToContext/1, which indiscriminately connects agents (note that NEXT represents the "next moment in time" operator). In complex agents, this will most probably be adapted to, for example, only allow certain agents to join the agent.

```
addToContent: {
 addToContent($SELF,Sender)
       => NEXT doAddToContent(Sender).
 addToContent($SELF,Sender)
       => NEXT send(Sender, addedToContent($SELF,Sender)).
 addedToContent(Sender,$Self)
       => NEXT doAddToContext(Sender). }
```

Fig. 2. Tagged cluster of rules implementing addToContent

---

[4] It might be clear to the reader that while any temporal formula can be transformed into SNF, the transformation will result in a set of many small formulae.

6   MetateM in the Museum

Using the active museum as backdrop, we now show how the dynamic grouping structure and executable logic within the system can be exploited to represent different aspects of the scenario, and how we can design different layers and easily incorporate them into one system.

In our particular example, we chose to use two distinct layers. On the one hand, we use agents to represent the physical space, that is, the tangible structure of the museum, consisting of rooms, exhibits, and visitors moving between the different rooms; on the other hand we wish to represent an organisational structure of visitors, that will allow a visitor to receive preferences on the exhibits available in a room.

Using those two structures allows us to exploit the information they contain. The physical structure can be used to keep track of agent' positions, compute routes (on the fly), find nearby other agents, find the location of specific exhibits and so on. The organisational structure allows agents to receive appropriate suggestions or information, find and communicate with agents with the same interests, profile visitors and so forth.

The first grouping structure is depicted in Figure 3. It represents the physical layout of the museum. In our simplified example, museum M has two rooms (R1 and R2), with 3 exhibits in each room (Ex1...Ex6). Each room also contains a visitor (V1 in R1 and V2 in R2).

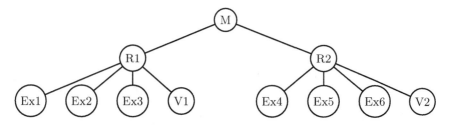

Fig. 3. Physical Structure of Museum Example

A separate organisational structure (Figure 4) shows three *interest groups*, the Artist Group (AG), ColourBlind Group (CB), and Time Group (TG). Visitor1 (V1) is member of both AG and CB while Visitor2 (V2) is only member of TG. The function of the interest groups is to provide visitors with an optimal path through the room, given the preferences of the visitor. In our example, V1 is interested in artists, so the system suggests a certain order to the exhibits. The group CB tags exhibits that primarily consist of hard to discern shades of red and green (for the sake of argument). It therefore recommends participants not to visit certain exhibits at all.

Given just the physical structure, the system should show the following behaviour. Upon entering a room (joining the content of R), a visitor sends a message to its context, informing it that it is looking around within R. R in turn asks its content what exhibits are available, and forwards the answers to the visitor.

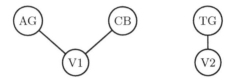

Fig. 4. Organisational Structure of Museum Example

The METATEM Rules needed to accomplish the above are rather straight-forward. Figure 5 shows the rules needed for V to "look around" and remember the exhibits it can see[5], as well as the rules R uses to send appropriate answers.

```
VISITOR
 exhibits: {
   addedToContent(Room,$Self) => NEXT lookAround(Room).
   addedToContent(Room,$Self), canSee($Self,Room1,Exhibit)
        => NEXT seen(Exhibit).
   lookAround(Room) => NEXT send(context, looking($Self,Room)).
   receive(canSee($Self,Room,Exhibit))
        => NEXT canSee($Self,Room,Exhibit).
   canSee($Self,Room,Exhibit), not(seen(Exhibit))
        => NEXT canSee($Self,Room,Exhibit). }

ROOM
 exhibits: {
   receive(looking(Visitor,$Self))
        => NEXT send(content,whatExhibit($Self,Visitor)).
   receive(exhibit(Exhibit,$Self,Visitor))
        => NEXT send(Visitor,canSee(Visitor,$Self,Exhibit)). }
```

Fig. 5. Physical space rules of both Visitor and Room Agents

The above rules are enough to allow our visitor agent to guide a visitor through a museum — given it has information about the different exhibits, or receives them from the room. However, each and every visitor would be directed towards the same sequence of exhibits.

We now add our organisational layer. As mentioned before, we wish to expand the system by allowing for interest-based guidance through exhibits, possibly excluding exhibits from the list. Figure 4 gives the (simple) structure of our organisational layer. Note that the visitor agents V1 and V2 are the only agents that appear in both structures.

Now, for the visitor agents to receive preferences about which exhibits to view, they each forward a canSee/2 message to their context. The interest groups

---

[5] Due to METATEM, predicates that need to be true in more than one moment in time have to be made true explicitly.

```
INTEREST GROUP AGENT
 preferences: {
    START => go().
    go() => NEXT prefer($room1,$exhibit1,$exhibit3).
    go() => NEXT prefer($room1,$exhibit3,$exhibit2).
    go() => NEXT prefer($room1,$exhibit1,$exhibit2).
    go() => NEXT prefer($room2,$exhibit6,$exhibit5).
    go() => NEXT prefer($room2,$exhibit6,$exhibit4).
    go() => NEXT prefer($room2,$exhibit5,$exhibit4).
    prefer(X,Y,Z) => NEXT prefer(X,Y,Z).}

 request: {
    receive(canSee(Visitor,Room,Exhibit))
       => NEXT canSee(Visitor,Room,Exhibit).
    canSee(Visitor,Room,Exhibit), prefer(Room, Exhibit1, Exhibit2)
       => NEXT send(Visitor,prefer(Room, Exhibit1,Exhibit2)). }
```

Fig. 6. Organisational space rules of Interest Group Agent

then reply by sending a preference relation over the exhibits, or alternatively exhibits that should be excluded (Fig. 6). Exclusion is accomplished simply by sending a discard/1 message. The agent receiving an exclusion message will go from not having seen the exhibit to seen, without ever making true the predicate goLooking/1 that represents the agent's action of looking at the exhibit (see Fig. 7). Note the message prefer/3 is followed by making prefer/2 true in the next moment of time. prefer/2 is an internal predicate which re-orders eventualities such that the agent tries to satisfy the first argument before the second (where it has a choice). The visitor agent will try to honour the eventuality goLooking/1 in the order given by the (set of) preferences. Eventualities are generally attempted in the order they were created. The primitive prefer/2 can change that order. Given a set of prefer/2 predicates, the agent tries to satisfy the constraints they represent. If not successful, it will try to satisfy a subset of the preferences. Also note that the order of eventualities is the same across moments in time, so it generally is sufficient to call prefer/2 only once. Note that several interest groups can send their preference relations, the visitor agent will internally try to make the order as consistent as possible.

In our scenario, the rules that accomplish this modification of eventuality order can be found in Figures 6 and 7. The visitor invokes interest groups by forwarding to them any information about exhibits it can see. Interest groups simply answer by sending preference relations on visible exhibits. (Executing send(V,prefer($room1,X,Y)) will send all preference predicates that match $room1). The rules of the visitor look complicated because the visitor, after learning which exhibits there are, has to remember those for some time while requesting preferences from the interest groups. During that wait, we must ensure that the eventualities are *not* honoured.

Also note that while (in this simplified setting) the agent takes only one moment in time to actually look at the exhibits, it still needs to "remember" which

```
VISITOR AGENT
 preference: {
    receive(prefer(Room,Exhibit1,Exhibit2))
       => NEXT prefer(Exhibit1,Exhibit2).
    canSee($Self,Room,Exhibit) => SOMETIME goLooking(Exhibit).
    canSee($Self,Room,Exhibit) => NEXT not(goLooking(Exhibit)).
    send(context,canSee($Self,Room,Exhibit))
       => NEXT wait(2000,waitforPref(Room)).
    waitforPref(Room) => NEXT startLooking(Room).
    send(context,canSee($Self,Room,Exhibit))
       => NEXT not(goLooking(Exhibit)).

    not(goLooking(Exhibit)), not(startLooking(Room))
       => NEXT not(goLooking(Exhibit)).
    goLooking(Exhibit),not(discard(Exhibit))
       => NEXT lookAt(Exhibit).
    lookAt(Exhibit) => NEXT seen(Exhibit).
    goLooking(Exhibit), discard(Exhibit) => NEXT seen(Exhibit). }

exclude: {
    receive(discard(X)) => NEXT discard(X).
    discard(X),not(seen(X)) => NEXT discard(X). }

exhibits: {
    receive(canSee($Self,Room,Exhibit))
       => NEXT send(context,canSee($Self,Room,Exhibit)). }
```

Fig. 7. Organisational space rules of Visitor Agent

exhibits it should exclude. The **exclude** rules ensure that discarded predicates are remembered as long as is necessary.

7   Discussion of the System

In the above example, while being rather simple, still highlights several aspects of both elements, the structure of the agent space and the use of temporal logic.

For one, the graph-like structure of the agent space can be exploited to contain information about the system. In the above example, the room agents do not know which exhibits they contain until they send a request. The agent space can be very dynamic, and agents do not need to have complicated mechanisms to ensure their internal representation of the world is accurate.

Secondly, not only can we use the structure in such a way, but we can represent different aspects of a system within the graph, design them independently, and combine them at run time. Given the rules in Figures 6 and 7, we can easily add more rooms, exhibits, visitors, and interest groups, without having to re-write or re-design the system.

The use of logic allows us to extend the system without having to change anything. For example, we can define just the physical structure, which would make the agent to randomly visit the different exhibits.

By adding a simple rule that sends requests for preferences when a `canSee` predicate is received, this can be adapted.

In Section 6 we described the basic scenario. In the following subsections, we will examine in more detail the dynamics between the agents.

7.1 Dynamic Aspects: Mobile Agents

In order to keep the example simple, we assume that some tracking agent tracks the visitors (in the real world) and sends `moveTo(Visitor,Room)` messages to the visitor agents. While we omit this in the current example, visitors can easily also be members of this tracking agent.

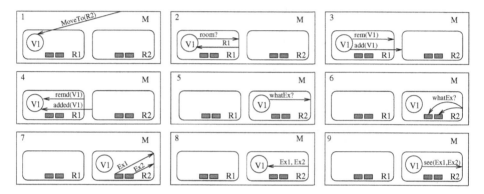

Fig. 8. Messages sent when moving to a room

Figure 8 shows the flow of messages that occur when an agent moves from one room to another[6] Upon receiving `moveTo/2`, agent V1 sends appropriate `addToContent` and `removeFromContent` messages to the new and old room, respectively. The `addToContent` message exchange (see Figure 2) ends with `addedToContent`, which, in turn, gives rise to the above described interchange between room and visitor which results in the visitor learning about the exhibits available in the (new) room. Note the second rule for the visitor in Figure 5, which basically ensures that the agent "forgets" exhibits it might not have looked at in the room it just left. Also note that we can add and remove exhibits on the fly, because the room agents always checks what exhibits are available.

The movement of agents is independent of other agents being in the rooms, because even though messages are often broadcast to *Content* or *Context*, they generally contain the name of the receiving agent, so that only that agent's rule will fire. While we could have made sure that messages are only sent to particular

---

[6] We omit "**send**" and abbreviate some of the messages for readability. Also, note that "movement" refers to virtual, rather than actual movement.

agents, this would not have allowed us to (at a later stage) take advantage of the ability to overhear messages within certain groups.

7.2   Dynamic Aspects: Modifying Interests

We get more interesting interactions when looking at the organisational structure. Visitor agents can "subscribe" to interest groups, which in our example determines the order in which the exhibits should be shown. In more complex settings, interest groups also determine or influence the type of information that the visitor will receive during her stay in the museum.

While our example is simple, we can already distinguish several situations. In the first, the visitor is not subscribed to any group; next, a visitor can subscribe to one or more interest groups that give (possibly conflicting) preference relations; she can subscribe to interest groups that suggest to not look at exhibits at all; and finally a combination of the latter two.

The interaction between visitor agents and interest groups works as follows (see Figure 9). After having received different exhibits that are available (canSee/3), the visitor re-broadcasts them to its context, and waits a specified time for answers (canSee/3 => NEXT wait/2). The rule in Figure 7,

```
not( goLooking(Exhibit)), not(startLooking(Room)) => NEXT
not(goLooking(Exhibit)
```

ensures that the eventualities containing goLooking/1 will not be made true until the predicate startLooking/0 is true.

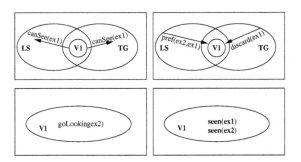

Fig. 9. Message exchange with interest groups

If the visitor agent is not subscribed to any interest groups (that is to say, there are no interest groups in the visitor agent's context), it will still wait for preferences. If none are sent, it will just work through its eventualities in a random order.

However, if the agent received one or more **prefer/3** messages, it re-orders the outstanding eventualities using the internal predicate **prefer/2**. If they are not consistent (due to different interest groups having conflicting preferences), it will try to honour as many of the preferences as possible, and choose randomly between the inconsistent preferences remaining.

In the case of receiving `discard/1` messages, our visitor just disregards the exhibit, even if it has a high preference. It should be clear though that we could easily add some rules to, for example, give discarded exhibits a very low preference.

8   Conclusions

In this paper, we have utilised a structured multi-agent programming language, and have shown how the structure can be exploited to create complex systems that are (a) relatively easy to specify, due to the possibility of designing different layers independently of each other, (b) dynamic, and therefore suitable for systems where many different agents interact in unforeseeable ways, and (c) potentially verifiable, due to the logical basis of the system. The key behaviours of individual agents are provided through varieties of executable temporal logic, while the over-arching group structure allows us to represent a range of physical and virtual organisations. This approach provides a powerful, flexible, yet logic-based, route to the design, modelling and development of software for ubiquitous computing applications.

Future work involves developing more complex scenarios, and comparing with other approaches to the theory of team building [20] and other (non logic-based) multi-agent programming systems [7, 17].

References

1. H. Barringer, M. Fisher, D. Gabbay, G. Gough, and R. Owens. METATEM: An Introduction. *Formal Aspects of Computing*, 7(5):533–549, 1995.
2. R. Bordini, W. Visser, M. Fisher, C. Pardavila, and M. Wooldridge. Model checking multi-agent programs with CASP. In *Proceedings of the Fifteenth Conference on Computer-Aided Verification (CAV-2003), Boulder, CO, 8–12 July*, 2003.
3. M. E. Bratman. *Intentions, Plans, and Practical Reason*. Havard University Press, Cambridge, MA, 1987.
4. P. Busetta, A. Doná, and M. Nori. Channeled multicast for group communications. In *Proceedings of the First International Joint Conference on Autonomous Agents and Multiagent Systems*, pages 1280–1287. ACM Press, 2002.
5. P. Busetta, T. Kuflik, M. Merzi, and S. Rossi. Service delivery in smart environments by implicit organizations. In *Proceedings of the First Annual International Conference on Mobile and Ubiquitous Systems (MobiQuitous 2004)*, pages 356–363, Boston, MA, USA, 22-26 August 2004. IEEE Computer Society Press.
6. P. Busetta, M. Merzi, S. Rossi, and F. Legras. Intra-Role Coordination Using Group Communication: A Preliminary Report. In *Proceedings of International Workshop on Agent Communication Languages, ACL2003 (in conjunction with AAMAS 2003)*, volume LNAI 2922, pages 231–253. Springer, July 2003.
7. J. Ferber and O. Gutknecht. Aalaadin: a meta-model for the analysis and design of organisations in multi-agent systems. Research Report R.R.LIRMM 97189, LIRM, Université Montpelier, France, December 1997.

8. M. Fisher. Concurrent METATEM — A Language for Modeling Reactive Systems. In *Parallel Architectures and Languages, Europe (PARLE)*, Munich, Germany, June 1993. (Published in *Lecture Notes in Computer Science*, volume 694, Springer-Verlag).

9. M. Fisher. An Introduction to Executable Temporal Logics. *Knowledge Engineering Review*, 11(1):43–56, March 1996.

10. M. Fisher. A normal form for temporal logic and its application in theorem-proving and execution. *Journal of Logic and Computation*, 7(4):429 – 456, August 1997.

11. M. Fisher and C. Ghidini. Programming Resource-Bounded Deliberative Agents. In *Proceedings of International Joint Conference on Artificial Intelligence (IJCAI)*. Morgan Kaufmann, 1999.

12. M. Fisher and C. Ghidini. The ABC of rational agent modelling. In *Proceedings of the first international joint conference on autonomous agents and multiagent systems (AAMAS'02)*, Bologna, Italy, July 2002.

13. M. Fisher and T. Kakoudakis. Flexible agent grouping in executable temporal logic. In *Proceedings of the 12th International Symposium of Intensional Programming Languages*, 1999.

14. R. Goldblatt. *Logics of Time and Computation*, volume 7 of *CLSI Lecture Notes*. CLSI, Stanford, CA, 2nd edition, 1992.

15. B. Hirsch, M. Fisher, and C. Ghidini. Organising logic-based agents. In M.G. Hinchey, J.L. Rash, W.F. Truszkowski, C. Rouff, and D. Gordon-Spears, editors, *Formal Approaches to Agent-Based Systems. Second International Workshop, FAABS 2002*, volume 2699 of *LNAI*, pages 15–27. Springer, 2003.

16. N. R. Jennings, K. Sycara, and M. Wooldridge. A roadmap of agent research and development. *Autonomous Agents and Multi-Agent Systems*, 1:275–306, 1998.

17. Agent Oriented Software Ltd. The JACK programming language, 2000. http://agent-software.com.au.

18. J. McCarthy. Active environments: Sensing and responding to groups of people. *Personal and Ubiquitous Computing*, 5(1), 2001.

19. O. Stock and M. Zancanaro. Intelligent Interactive Information Presentation for Cultural Tourism. In *Proceedings of the International CLASS Workshop on Natural Intelligent and Effective Interaction in Multimodal Dialogue Systems*, Copenhagen, Denmark, 28-29 June 2002.

20. D. Pynadath and M. Tambe. An automated teamwork infrastructure for heterogeneous software agents and humans. *Journal of Autonomous Agents and Multiagent Systems*, 2002.

Author Index

Lecture Notes in Artificial Intelligence (LNAI)

Vol. 3396: R.M. van Eijk, M.-P. Huget, F. Dignum (Eds.), Agent Communication. X, 261 pages. 2005.

Vol. 3394: D. Kudenko, D. Kazakov, E. Alonso (Eds.), Adaptive Agents and Multi-Agent Systems II. VIII, 313 pages. 2005.

Vol. 3392: D. Seipel, M. Hanus, U. Geske, O. Bartenstein (Eds.), Applications of Declarative Programming and Knowledge Management. X, 309 pages. 2005.

Vol. 3374: D. Weyns, H. V.D. Parunak, F. Michel (Eds.), Environments for Multi-Agent Systems. X, 279 pages. 2005.

Vol. 3371: M.W. Barley, N. Kasabov (Eds.), Intelligent Agents and Multi-Agent Systems. X, 329 pages. 2005.

Vol. 3369: V. R. Benjamins, P. Casanovas, J. Breuker, A. Gangemi (Eds.), Law and the Semantic Web. XII, 249 pages. 2005.

Vol. 3366: I. Rahwan, P. Moraitis, C. Reed (Eds.), Argumentation in Multi-Agent Systems. XII, 263 pages. 2005.

Vol. 3359: G. Grieser, Y. Tanaka (Eds.), Intuitive Human Interfaces for Organizing and Accessing Intellectual Assets. XIV, 257 pages. 2005.

Vol. 3346: R.H. Bordini, M. Dastani, J. Dix, A.E.F. Seghrouchni (Eds.), Programming Multi-Agent Systems. XIV, 249 pages. 2005.

Vol. 3345: Y. Cai (Ed.), Ambient Intelligence for Scientific Discovery. XII, 311 pages. 2005.

Vol. 3343: C. Freksa, M. Knauff, B. Krieg-Brückner, B. Nebel, T. Barkowsky (Eds.), Spatial Cognition IV. XIII, 519 pages. 2005.

Vol. 3339: G.I. Webb, X. Yu (Eds.), AI 2004: Advances in Artificial Intelligence. XXII, 1272 pages. 2004.

Vol. 3336: D. Karagiannis, U. Reimer (Eds.), Practical Aspects of Knowledge Management. X, 523 pages. 2004.

Vol. 3327: Y. Shi, W. Xu, Z. Chen (Eds.), Data Mining and Knowledge Management. XIII, 263 pages. 2005.

Vol. 3315: C. Lemaître, C.A. Reyes, J.A. González (Eds.), Advances in Artificial Intelligence – IBERAMIA 2004. XX, 987 pages. 2004.

Vol. 3303: J.A. López, E. Benfenati, W. Dubitzky (Eds.), Knowledge Exploration in Life Science Informatics. X, 249 pages. 2004.

Vol. 3301: G. Kern-Isberner, W. Rödder, F. Kulmann (Eds.), Conditionals, Information, and Inference. XII, 219 pages. 2005.

Vol. 3276: D. Nardi, M. Riedmiller, C. Sammut, J. Santos-Victor (Eds.), RoboCup 2004: Robot Soccer World Cup VIII. XVIII, 678 pages. 2005.

Vol. 3275: P. Perner (Ed.), Advances in Data Mining. VIII, 173 pages. 2004.

Vol. 3265: R.E. Frederking, K.B. Taylor (Eds.), Machine Translation: From Real Users to Research. XI, 392 pages. 2004.

Vol. 3264: G. Paliouras, Y. Sakakibara (Eds.), Grammatical Inference: Algorithms and Applications. XI, 291 pages. 2004.

Vol. 3259: J. Dix, J. Leite (Eds.), Computational Logic in Multi-Agent Systems. XII, 251 pages. 2004.

Vol. 3257: E. Motta, N.R. Shadbolt, A. Stutt, N. Gibbins (Eds.), Engineering Knowledge in the Age of the Semantic Web. XVII, 517 pages. 2004.

Vol. 3249: B. Buchberger, J.A. Campbell (Eds.), Artificial Intelligence and Symbolic Computation. X, 285 pages. 2004.

Vol. 3248: K.-Y. Su, J. Tsujii, J.-H. Lee, O.Y. Kwong (Eds.), Natural Language Processing – IJCNLP 2004. XVIII, 817 pages. 2005.

Vol. 3245: E. Suzuki, S. Arikawa (Eds.), Discovery Science. XIV, 430 pages. 2004.

Vol. 3244: S. Ben-David, J. Case, A. Maruoka (Eds.), Algorithmic Learning Theory. XIV, 505 pages. 2004.

Vol. 3238: S. Biundo, T. Frühwirth, G. Palm (Eds.), KI 2004: Advances in Artificial Intelligence. XI, 467 pages. 2004.

Vol. 3230: J.L. Vicedo, P. Martínez-Barco, R. Muñoz, M. Saiz Noeda (Eds.), Advances in Natural Language Processing. XII, 488 pages. 2004.

Vol. 3229: J.J. Alferes, J. Leite (Eds.), Logics in Artificial Intelligence. XIV, 744 pages. 2004.

Vol. 3228: M.G. Hinchey, J.L. Rash, W.F. Truszkowski, C.A. Rouff (Eds.), Formal Approaches to Agent-Based Systems. VIII, 290 pages. 2004.

Vol. 3215: M.G.. Negoita, R.J. Howlett, L.C. Jain (Eds.), Knowledge-Based Intelligent Information and Engineering Systems, Part III. LVII, 906 pages. 2004.

Vol. 3214: M.G.. Negoita, R.J. Howlett, L.C. Jain (Eds.), Knowledge-Based Intelligent Information and Engineering Systems, Part II. LVIII, 1302 pages. 2004.

Vol. 3213: M.G.. Negoita, R.J. Howlett, L.C. Jain (Eds.), Knowledge-Based Intelligent Information and Engineering Systems, Part I. LVIII, 1280 pages. 2004.

Vol. 3209: B. Berendt, A. Hotho, D. Mladenic, M. van Someren, M. Spiliopoulou, G. Stumme (Eds.), Web Mining: From Web to Semantic Web. IX, 201 pages. 2004.

Vol. 3206: P. Sojka, I. Kopecek, K. Pala (Eds.), Text, Speech and Dialogue. XIII, 667 pages. 2004.

Vol. 3202: J.-F. Boulicaut, F. Esposito, F. Giannotti, D. Pedreschi (Eds.), Knowledge Discovery in Databases: PKDD 2004. XIX, 560 pages. 2004.

Vol. 3201: J.-F. Boulicaut, F. Esposito, F. Giannotti, D. Pedreschi (Eds.), Machine Learning: ECML 2004. XVIII, 580 pages. 2004.

Vol. 3194: R. Camacho, R. King, A. Srinivasan (Eds.), Inductive Logic Programming. XI, 361 pages. 2004.

Vol. 3192: C. Bussler, D. Fensel (Eds.), Artificial Intelligence: Methodology, Systems, and Applications. XIII, 522 pages. 2004.

Vol. 3191: M. Klusch, S. Ossowski, V. Kashyap, R. Unland (Eds.), Cooperative Information Agents VIII. XI, 303 pages. 2004.

Vol. 3187: G. Lindemann, J. Denzinger, I.J. Timm, R. Unland (Eds.), Multiagent System Technologies. XIII, 341 pages. 2004.

Vol. 3176: O. Bousquet, U. von Luxburg, G. Rätsch (Eds.), Advanced Lectures on Machine Learning. IX, 241 pages. 2004.